T0305463

HIV, GENDER AND THE POLITICS OF MEDICINE

Embodied Democracy in the Global South

Elizabeth Mills

BRISTOL
UNIVERSITY
PRESS

First published in Great Britain in 2024 by

Bristol University Press
University of Bristol
1–9 Old Park Hill
Bristol
BS2 8BB
UK
t: +44 (0)117 374 6645
e: bup-info@bristol.ac.uk

Details of international sales and distribution partners are available at bristoluniversitypress.co.uk

British Library Cataloguing in Publication Data
A catalogue record for this book is available from the British Library

ISBN 978-1-5292-2191-6 hardcover
ISBN 978-1-5292-2195-4 ePub
ISBN 978-1-5292-2196-1 ePdf

Cover design: Qube Design
Front cover image: Getty/Vithun Khamsong
Bristol University Press use environmentally responsible print partners.
Printed and bound in Great Britain by CPI Group (UK) Ltd, Croydon, CR0 4YY

FSC
www.fsc.org
MIX
Paper | Supporting
responsible forestry
FSC® C013604

This book includes descriptions and discussions of sensitive material, including instances of sexual and gender-based violence and death. This material is included with ongoing consent from participants and with an awareness of the potential impact on those who might read it.

For Nondumiso Hlwele and Pumla Dladla

Contents

List of Abbreviations

ABIA	*Associação Brasileira Interdisciplinar de AIDS*
ACTA	Anti-Counterfeiting Trade Agreement
ANC	African National Congress
ANT	Actor Network Theory
APIs	active pharmaceutical ingredients
ART	antiretroviral therapy
ARV	antiretroviral
ASRU	AIDS and Society Research Unit
AZT	azidothymidine
BCM	Black Consciousness Movement
BRICS	Brazil, Russia, India, China and South Africa
BWG	Bambanani Women's Group
CAB-LA	cabotegravir
CCT	conditional cash transfer
CD4	cluster of differentiation
d4T	stavudine
DTG	dolutegravir
ET	*Equal Treatment*
FTA	free trade agreement
GPV	*Grupo Pela Vidda*
HAART	highly active antiretroviral therapy
IG	income-generation
IP	intellectual property
IPRs	intellectual property rights
LMICs	low- and middle-income countries
MSF	Médecins Sans Frontières
MTCT	mother-to-child transmission
NACOSA	National AIDS Coordinating Committee of South Africa
NVP	nevirapine
PMA	Pharmaceutical Manufacturers' Association
PMTCT	prevention of mother-to-child transmission
PrEP	pre-exposure prophylaxis

RCT	randomized control trial
RDP	Reconstruction and Development Programme
SGBV	sexual and gender-based violence
SJC	Social Justice Coalition
SPT	*Saúde Para Todos*
SUS	Sistema Único de Saúde
TAC	Treatment Action Campaign
TB	tuberculosis
TDF	tenofovir
TRIPS	Trade-Related Aspects of Intellectual Property Rights
UCT	University of Cape Town
UFPE	Universidade Federal de Pernambuco
WHO	World Health Organization
WTO	World Trade Organization

Acknowledgements

This monograph has been made possible by a wide network of people and organizations to whom I am deeply grateful.

Thank you to the people who form the heart of this book: Miriam, Brenda, Sibongile, Thandiswa, Zolani, Yandisa, Zama, Yvonne, Lilian and Sindiswa. Thank you for letting me into your lives, for coming into mine and for trusting me with your stories. I am indebted to all of you. I am also enormously grateful to the Bambanani Women's Group and the Treatment Action Campaign for letting me work with you and learn from you in South Africa. Numerous other organizations and people have also played a role in shaping this book, including: Médecins Sans Frontières, SOS Corpo, GTP+ and members of the Department for Social Development at the Federal University of Pernambuco. Thank you, Solange Rocha and Ana Vieira, for your invaluable guidance and support during my time in Brazil. My hope is that this book bears witness to the agile and resilient activism of these phenomenal people and organizations across continents and time.

Many academics have shown me how to bring kindness and care into dialogue with incisive scholarship. I am grateful for the learning – and unlearning – I have been able to do at the Institute of Development Studies and the Universities of Cape Town, Cambridge and Sussex. Thank you, in particular, to: Elaine Salo, Fiona Ross, Susan Levine, Nicoli Nattrass, Rebecca Hodes, Hayley MacGregor, Melissa Leach, Rebecca Marsland and Andrea Cornwall.

I have a wonderful network of friends – too many to name here. Some of the people I'd like to acknowledge for their care and insight include: Aditya Bahadur, Poppy Riddle, Alia Aghajanian, Eric Kasper, David Godleman, Marjoke Oosterom, Dacia Viejo-Rose, Frances Trahar, Dina Townsend, Jenni Kruger, Kate Muller, Peter Schaupp, Pumla Dladla, Semane Parsons, Nondumiso Hlwele, Matthew Wilhelm-Solomon, Alex Halligey, Marie Whitbread, Lucinda van den Heever, Katherine Hagerman, Paul Gilbert, Suda Perera, Demet Dinler, Anna Laing and Debra DeLaet.

I have received scholarships and research funding from several funding bodies including the British Chevening Scholarship Commission, the

Commonwealth Scholarship Commission, the Canon Collins Trust, the Oppenheimer Memorial Trust, the Momentum Trust, the British Fund for Women Graduates and the British Academy and Leverhulme Trust.

Thank you to the reviewers of this book and of related published work. The insights from this book's reviewers have been invaluable. I am also grateful to the Junior Research Associates who worked with me at the University of Sussex in preparation for this book, including Lily Kovacs, Nishant Bhakta, Caitlin MacClancy and Fernanda Pratz. Thank you to the editorial team, and Zoe Forbes in particular, at Bristol University Press for your careful work – you have been a wonderful team to work with.

My wife, Jenny Diggins, and our child, Anya, are my favourite and most inspiring people to explore the world and live life with, every day. Thank you for being exactly who you are, always unfolding. Thank you, too, to our broader Mills and Diggins families for your love. A special thank you to my sister, Caroline Mills, for her brilliant humour, insight and kindness.

Nondumiso Hlwele and Pumla Dladla: this book would not have been possible without you. I hope that beyond these words, you know my love and appreciation through the stories and years we've shared together. This book is dedicated to you.

1

Introduction

The shebeen's corrugated-iron walls were the same blue as the brutal skies that arch over Khayelitsha in winter.[1] In this part of Khayelitsha, called Nkanini, homes were built on top of the sand. Like the shebeen, their windowless walls were made from cardboard posters and sheets of corrugated iron. One of the shebeen's three co-workers had painted larger-than-life bottles of beer along the rippled wall with painstaking precision, each bottle a bright rendition of the real thing that, along with the pumping bass beating in my body, brought Nkanini's residents in to drink. We walked on, under snaking electricity wires, around Nkanini's single tap and over the muddy veins that leaked down the dusty road.

"This way sana, remember?" said Miriam as she looped her arm through mine.[2] We turned left after the tap and shuffled along a short alley, our bodies bumping into each other and the shack walls and wire fences that lined our route; against our sturdy bodies, these markers of home felt fragile. We turned right, left and finally right into her garden, where Masiphiwe, Miriam's 23-year-old brother, was washing clothes over a large metal tub. We had last seen each other a few days before when the three of us had become lost searching for paraffin heaters. Miriam did not have electricity and refused to use the stolen supplies that snaked around her home: the risk of electrocution rendered the benefit of warmth too precarious. The seasons were changing, and it was getting too cold to rely on the sun to dry the bowls, her principal source of income, that she made from paper and glue; too cold to keep her chronic backache at bay. I first met Masiphiwe through a series of photographs in which he was wrapped in a ceremonial blanket, wearing formal trousers and toe-capped shoes, a cap shielding his eyes. His body and all he wore signified Masiphiwe's transition to manhood; he had just returned from a traditional circumcision ceremony in the Eastern Cape, Miriam's family's rural home. On his return, he had stopped sharing the household chores, and Miriam had berated the ceremony, saying, "He is practising his manhood on me." On this day, Miriam was pleased with her brother.

We left Masiphiwe and walked through the door where Miriam had written 'Please do not vandalize my home! I'm begging you.' This was a message to Miriam's 25-year-old brother, Lwandle, who worked in the shebeen. In a fit of anger at Miriam's refusal to give him money, he had attacked her home with his fists and a metal rod. The violence imprinted in the battered door spoke to a broader web of precarity in Miriam's life and echoed a series of photographs that Lwandle had taken on her camera, which he later stole; in these photos, he posed with the shebeen's owner and artist, their shirts unbuttoned, thick jewellery across their chests, a gun in each hand.

I sat down in Miriam's sitting room, facing the open door, my shoes resting on the linoleum floor that kept out the fine beach sand that covers the Cape Flats: an impoverished peri-urban area that stretches across the barren land between the Cape Peninsula's two oceans. A translucent line had been walked into the linoleum; like a thin membrane, it linked the kitchen to the bedroom and broadened out around the single-seat couch that Miriam sat on when she made her bowls – bowls then sold to a local organization that, in Miriam's words, "exploited my HIV". This sentiment was confirmed by the programme manager's description of the fivefold profit margin derived from international sales to boutiques wanting to 'do good' for the 'poor women' whose names were cynically scrawled underneath their bowls and whose stories were told in a glossy brochure attached to the price-tag. The mantelpiece across from the couch displayed photographs of her two children and a single photograph of Miriam, at 17, as she stood in front of her high school. She had excelled at the top of her class but was forced to leave three months before her final examinations to take care of her mother who had been poisoned through witchcraft. Over a few months of spending time with Miriam, I came to understand the force of this photograph and the significance of its placement on the mantelpiece opposite the couch where Miriam made her bowls: the photograph bears witness to Miriam beyond labels like HIV-positive, poor, woman. It speaks to the possibility of another life.

In the adjacent bedroom, next to the handheld mirror on her dressing table, was a cluster of white tubs. Each tub held one third of a triple combination of antiretroviral therapy: 3TC, tenofovir and aluvia. Despite fighting as an activist to access the life-giving capacity held in the large, hard-to-swallow tablets, Miriam's relationship with antiretrovirals (ARVs) is also one of deep frustration. At times, she has said, "My treatment is killing me", referring to aluvia's side effects. When I first met Miriam, she was on her third ARV combination and on the second line of treatment along with her 12-year-old daughter, Nena. Nena started life on the brink of death, compelling Miriam to move to Cape Town in search of health care that could decipher and heal her dying child's body. Through this move, and in the face of the government's obdurate AIDS denialism, Miriam entered the Médecins Sans Frontières (MSF) trial in 2001. She is one of the first people to start ARVs in South Africa's public sector.

Months later, after spending the morning in a clinic with the women I worked with (who handcrafted bowls with Miriam) as they waited for their monthly supply of ARVs, I went to a workshop with MSF on South Africa's patent laws. The meeting was held in a high-security complex in Obs, a former 'Whites-only' area with houses built from bricks, resting on foundations sunk into fertile earth. Obs is spatially buffered by the M5 highway from the violent poverty in the former 'non-White' areas of the Cape Flats. My phone rang as I left MSF's offices. It was Miriam. She wanted to know if I had taken her question to MSF in asking whether there were options for more advanced ARVs when she developed resistance to her current treatment regimen. Looking out from Table Mountain towards Miriam's home, I told her that as far as I understood, newer medicines were available to manage more complex strains of HIV. But these more advanced medicines were not yet available in South Africa's public sector. We both knew what lay beneath my words: that for Miriam – when labels like HIV-positive, poor, woman become salient – her life would end when her HI virus had mutated sufficiently to outwit the medicines provided by the state; medicines held in tubs on her dressing table, provided by the state through her clinic, embodied as she moved through Nkanini's maze of homes into her own. Just as the photograph opposite Miriam's couch spoke to a dissonance in her lived and dreamt reality, the unspoken words between us spoke to the dream of a longer life and the contingent reality of the global governance of the medicines that Miriam embodied.

This book centres on the lives of women, like Miriam, who live with HIV and who have fought, through transnational activist networks spanning South Africa, Brazil and India, to access essential HIV medicines through their country's public health system. With these women at the centre, the chapters that follow first trace their everyday lives in detail and then move out to locate their lives and activism within a global assemblage of activists and policy actors that challenged and then transformed national, regional and international policies governing the creation, production and distribution of essential HIV medicines. Tiered over five ethnographic and analytical chapters, this book calls for a recognition of the fundamentally political nature of essential medicines, and it draws attention to the dynamics of democratic governance as it functions through the policy and practice of producing and providing essential medicines to people like Miriam, where the capacity to live is contingent on the state's provision of essential medicines through its public health system.

The chapters that follow integrate long-term multi-sited ethnographic and policy research to foreground the value of understanding the embodied and political dimensions of health policy, revealing the networked threads that weave women's embodied precarity into the governance of technologies and the technologies of governance. This study of women's activism to access HIV medicine is therefore not simply a study of global, regional and national health policy evolution but one that reveals the extent to which policy impacts the vitality and vulnerability of bodies, recognizing that bodies too are never the same and experience intersecting inequalities in profoundly unique ways. Specifically, I argue that the struggle to access essential medicines is a form of biopolitical precarity that is networked into the permeable body. This argument seeks to challenge the discursive construction of distance that divorces women's lives and bodies from the governance of life-giving medical technologies. Further, as a challenge to the hegemonic positioning of women as victims, particularly within development discourse, this book explores women's agency as they navigate complex assemblages of affective relationships, government institutions and global coalitions to secure their vitality. In sum, this book traces the networked threads linking funders in boardrooms in New York to EU–India trade negotiations and protests in Delhi to activists in Recife and Khayelitsha, along Nkanini's dusty streets, through the battered doors of corrugated-iron homes into plastic tubs holding medical technologies that enable life and, ultimately, into women's bodies and activisms that transform these technologies just as they are transformed by them.

Background

In 1997, just as highly active antiretroviral therapy (HAART) became internationally available, Brazil was the first country in the Global South to commit to providing HIV medicines to its citizens (Biehl, 2004; Galvao, 2005; Montenegro et al, 2020; Socal et al, 2020). At the same time, India's well-honed pharmaceutical industry started preparing to reverse engineer these prohibitively expensive medicines, and in just a few years it would become the leading provider of ARV medicines in the Global South, earning it the title of 'pharmacy of the Global South' (Löfgren, 2017; Plahe and McArthur, 2021). Seeking to provide these essential medicines to its citizens, Brazil instead used the threat of compulsory licensing and mandated the production of these medicines within its own pharmaceutical industry, citing the right of its citizens to access life-saving treatment (Le, 2022a). As ethnographers like João Biehl have shown, however, access to these medicines in practice is often harder for those who remain socially, politically and economically marginalized, thus challenging the notion of Brazil as an 'activist state' (Biehl, 2004, 2005, 2007; Biehl et al, 2012).

In the late 1990s, Brazil had the second highest number of reported HIV cases in the world (after the United States), whereas South Africa had a

HIV prevalence of just under 1 per cent (Nunn et al, 2012). Now, Brazil's prevalence remains below 1 per cent, and South Africa is home to the largest number of people living with HIV in any one country in the world (UNAIDS, 2022a). The reasons for these very different epidemiological profiles are well documented and reference Brazil's proactive stance on HIV prevention and its – often uneven – provision of HIV medicines to its citizens, which corresponded to the pace at which they were developed and released internationally (Teixeira, 2003; Biehl, 2004; Okie, 2006; Biehl et al, 2012; Valle, 2015; Benzaken et al, 2019; Montenegro et al, 2020; Socal et al, 2020; Le, 2022a). Transnational activist coalitions between countries like Brazil, India and South Africa placed further pressure on global governing bodies, like the World Trade Organization (WTO), to amend its patent legislation; and specialist techniques, like reverse engineering, enabled India to produce large quantities of affordable HIV medicines for up to 90 per cent of donor-funded countries in the Global South (Cassier and Correa, 2008; Malhotra, 2008; Plahe and McArthur, 2021).

In 2004, Brazil's AIDS response had averted more than half the 1.2 million projected AIDS cases (from 1990); by contrast, death notification data in South Africa over this same period show that the rate of death among women aged 25–54 more than quadrupled and that it more than doubled among men aged 30–39 (Nattrass, 2004; Chigwedere and Essex, 2010). Moreover, numerous studies have found that a third of a million people died as a result of the South African government's failure to provide essential HIV medicines at the turn of the century (Nattrass, 2007; Chigwedere et al, 2008). When South Africa did start rolling out HIV medicines through its public health sector, it relied heavily on India's ability to produce affordable generic versions of these medicines through its well-established pharmaceutical industry (Iqbal, 2009; Plahe and McArthur, 2021). Set against this history and building on two decades of research, this book traces the evolution of the HIV epidemic in South Africa and Brazil and considers the role played by transnational alliances in ensuring access to sustainable and affordable HIV medicines produced, primarily, in India. In the sections that follow, I outline my own journey and situate it within South Africa's political history.

From the inside out: a personal history

This book builds on my personal and professional history as a South African, as a researcher and as an activist. I first conducted ethnographic research in 2003 with a home-based care organization on the ramifications of the post-apartheid government's decentralization of health care for people living with HIV and on women who provided home-based care to them. The implications of poverty, gender inequality and crumbling public health systems were borne as young men and women died in their homes, frequently under the care of mothers and grandmothers, without access to ARVs and often without any food. Just as I was completing my fieldwork that year, cabinet instructed the government to initiate a 'universal' ARV rollout following years of high-level political equivocation on the efficacy of HIV medicines (Simelela et al, 2015; Hodes, 2018). The government commenced the universal rollout in 2004, but leaders like Health Minister Manto Tshabalala-Msimang continued to dispute the efficacy of ARVs compared to alternative approaches, including traditional medicine and nutritional supplements (Ashforth and Nattrass, 2006; Nattrass, 2007). During this period of contestation over the efficacy or toxicity of HIV medicines, South African activists and researchers turned to other middle-income countries with high levels of inequality, like Brazil, to highlight the positive potential that ARVs held for transforming HIV into a chronic and manageable illness.

In 2007, as the Deputy Director of the University of Cape Town's AIDS and Society Research Unit, I worked with the country's leading HIV activist organization, the Treatment Action Campaign (TAC), to support Nozizwe Madlala-Routledge, the former Deputy Minister of Health, in developing the 2007–11 HIV/AIDS and STI National Strategic Plan (2007–11 NSP). President Thabo Mbeki had appointed Madlala-Routledge, a long-standing activist and member of the South African Communist Party, to the role of Deputy Health Minister in 2004, and it was in this capacity that she began to engage constructively with the leaders of TAC from 2005 (Powers, 2013). Although she was swiftly barred from further meetings with TAC by the Health Minister, she was able to resume a collaborative relationship with activists and academics during a small window in 2007 when the Health Minister was incapacitated in hospital.

A period of unprecedented collaboration between HIV activists, policy makers and civil society blossomed under Madlala-Routledge's leadership (Baleta, 2007). Although quite limited, the timing of this collaboration was vital in South Africa's political history as it propelled the activists' demand for 'universal' access to ARVs forward at an institutional level (through the reconfiguration of the South African National Aids Council [SANAC], the council responsible for HIV policy development and implementation) and at a policy level (through the creation of the 2007–11 NSP) (Kapp, 2006). With the support of the then Deputy President Phumzile Mlambo-Ngcuka, an internal review was conducted into the composition of SANAC. This led to a restructuring of SANAC's membership to include a greater number of scientific researchers and HIV activists, with AIDS Law Project activist Mark Heywood serving as Deputy Secretary (Bateman, 2007). Although highly contested by many government officials, this hard-won state–activist collaboration resulted in the creation of a joint civil society–government institution that could (and would) compel the government to speed up the implementation of the ambitious goals laid out in the 2007–11 NSP (Makino and Shigetomi, 2009). It was therefore an enormous setback to the country and the HIV movement when, six months after initiating these institutional and policy changes, Madlala-Routledge was fired and Tshabalala-Msimang returned to her position as Health Minister (Madlala-Routledge and the Treatment Action Campaign, 2007; Nattrass, 2008).

Confounded by the government's actions, I, like many activists and academics in South Africa at the time, looked to Brazil to understand how the democratically-elected government had addressed HIV. Over time, however, I came to see the grey – the uncertainty, hope and risk linked to illness and to treatment – that lay between the black of 'AIDS denial' and white of 'AIDS science'. I also came to see how South African academics and activists, like myself, had constructed a narrative of Brazil as the 'activist state' in contrast to South Africa as the 'denialist state'; in both contexts, access to HIV medicines was framed by activists as access to life and linked into assumptions of the democratic state's responsibility to ensure the lives of its citizens through public provision of these medicines. It became clear, too, that countries could take specific actions to challenge global institutions (like the WTO) and international regulations (like Trade-Related Aspects of Intellectual Property Rights [TRIPS]) that together functioned to govern access to highly expensive HIV medicines. Brazil threatened to issue compulsory licences to enable domestic production of ARVs, and India used its very robust national legislation to enable its pharmaceutical industry to reverse engineer these vital medicines at a fraction of the cost (Eimer and Lütz, 2010). South Africa, at that time, seemed to be standing stubbornly still and refusing to take action to access or produce these vital medicines.

From 2008, I joined a collaboration with eminent scholars Solange Rocha and Ana Vieira along with other researchers at the Universidade Federal de Pernambuco (UFPE) in Recife, Brazil. Through this collaboration, my colleagues in Brazil highlighted some of the shortfalls of their country's HIV response, particularly in light of the increased rates of infection among poor women in the north-east of Brazil. In conjunction with my research in South Africa, and in collaboration with HIV activists and researchers in Brazil, I came to view the 'activist state' narrative more critically. I could see that this narrative was useful for particular political and activist purposes, but that it was also fraught with complexity that eludes easy categorization and discursive polarization.

The complexity intrigued me. Not only did I start to understand Brazil's history of HIV activism more critically, but through my research I came to appreciate that South Africa's struggle for ARVs was far more nuanced than the black and white debate around AIDS 'science' and 'denialism' (Mills, 2005, 2006, 2008, 2016, 2017, 2018; De Paoli et al, 2012). I saw this complexity as my friends struggled with serious side effects on ARVs. Rather than talking to people in their treatment support group or to their doctors – because they were afraid of being 'outed' as denialists – some of them decided to stop taking their treatment altogether. I saw how government officials, like Deputy Health Minister Madlala-Routledge, worked to transform South Africa's HIV treatment policies (among other HIV-related policies) at the risk of their political career. People who found themselves in these grey spaces seemed to be 'disciplined' on both sides of the 'activist/state' continuum. Over this first decade of research and policy engagement, then, Brazil's 'activist state' mythology was debunked, for me, through my collaboration with UFPE, and I began to question the way the 'activist/state' dichotomy was used (and useful) in South Africa.

In the second decade of my research, I sought to deepen my understanding of this 'grey space' between HIV activism and denialism. This book is based predominantly on research that I have conducted in this second decade (plus a few years) from 2010 to 2023, but I do refer back to my earlier work between 2003 and 2010 to contextualize some of the shifts I have witnessed across time through my lived experience and my research in South Africa. In this second decade, I became far more interested in how people themselves thought about the science of medicine as they experienced ARVs in their body; and I was intrigued to understand more about the relationship between people's embodied experiences of illness (with HIV) and health (on ARVs) and their perception of the post-apartheid government.

By working in activist, academic and policy spaces in South Africa (where I grew up) and the United Kingdom (where I currently live), and by conducting policy research around the world, and ethnographic research in Brazil and South Africa, my thinking was challenged, once again. As I go on to discuss in the following chapters, I found that illness is held in memories, bodies and relationships, and that it is not simply about the presence of a virus. I learnt that health is not only enabled through ARVs but that these technologies can also engender other kinds of embodied struggles, and that the virus, too, can enable different kinds of wellbeing. Finally, I saw how politics permeates every facet of our being, and that we too often do not – or cannot – hold actors in this global assemblage to account for the way they intimately affect our lives from a distance, at the most molecular level.

From the outside in: a political history

Because my own journey is rooted in South Africa, and because this book is anchored in the accounts of South African women, this section offers a brief political history of South Africa's response to HIV. The following chapter brings Brazil and India into focus. This structure mirrors the book, as it starts with the ethnographic accounts of the women I worked with in South Africa and develops this analysis over the first three substantive chapters, before moving out to situate their lives and activism in relation to the work of activists and networks spanning Brazil and India in the final two substantive chapters.

The journey of HIV and ARVs over South Africa's borders and into people's lives and bodies is told through many kinds of stories. This book speaks to South Africa's history through ethnography and policy research, including a mix of participatory and visual methods to reflect memories of this history that is held in people's bodies and borne through their relationships. While this book draws on stories told through photographs, body maps and women's accounts of their lives, this section quantifies South Africa's history of HIV with statistics as a foundation to the accounts that populate the rest of the book.

HIV was first recorded in South Africa in 1982, when two men were diagnosed with the virus. This discovery was followed by a study among men who have sex with men in Johannesburg, South Africa's largest city, where 12.8 per cent were HIV-positive (Sher, 1989). By 1991, cases of heterosexual and homosexual HIV transmission were equal, and since then, heterosexual transmission has become the main route through which HIV has moved into the general population (Mabaso et al, 2019).

In 2023, South Africa had the world's largest HIV epidemic, with an estimated 7.8 million people living with HIV (Johnson and Dorrington, 2023). While South Africa's national HIV prevalence stood at 12.7 per cent in 2022 (HSRC, 2023), prevalence varies substantially across different parts of the country and among different population groups. For example, the province of KwaZulu-Natal has the highest HIV prevalence (24.9 per cent) among 15–49 year olds, whereas the province in which I conducted my fieldwork, the Western Cape, has one of the lowest prevalence levels (11.2 per cent) among this same population group (Johnson and Dorrington, 2023). I discuss these data in detail in the methodology chapter but wish to note here that the majority of the people with whom I worked travelled from the adjacent Eastern Cape Province to access health care, education and employment in the Western Cape. Prevalence in the Eastern Cape stands at 25.2 per cent and is significantly higher than in the Western Cape (Johnson and Dorrington, 2023). HIV prevalence in South Africa also varies significantly across age and sex. Peak prevalence occurs in adults aged 35–39 years, with a significantly higher prevalence among females (39.4 per cent) compared to males (23.7 per cent). This disparity widens further with the younger population: HIV prevalence among 20–24 year olds is three times higher among females (15.6 per cent) than males (4.8 per cent) (Mabaso et al, 2019; Simbayi et al, 2019; Palanee-Phillips et al, 2022).

There have been numerous positive shifts in treatment coverage and viral load suppression at a national level, but there has also been a consistent increase in HIV prevalence recorded in each of the five National HIV Prevalence, Incidence, Behaviour and Communication Surveys, moving from a national prevalence of 12.2 per cent in 2012 to 14 per cent in 2017 (Shisana et al, 2014; Simbayi et al, 2019; Roomaney et al, 2022). A briefing by the Human Sciences Research Council on the sixth and most recent national survey was released in November 2023 noting a national prevalence of 12.7 per cent in 2022 (HSRC, 2023). The shifts in the HIV epidemic and in the vitality of South Africans tessellate with policy shifts in the provision of ARVs. It is predominantly in this space – where life expectancy and ARV provision intersect – that comparisons between South Africa's delayed rollout and Brazil's advanced rollout are made (TAC, 2010; Nunn et al, 2012; Rosevear, 2018). Nunn and colleagues, whose work traces the evolution of Brazil's treatment policies, encapsulate the comparison here, saying: 'Brazil's story contrasts starkly with that of South Africa, which had similar HIV prevalence in 1990 but only began providing treatment on a large scale in recent years and now has the most HIV/AIDS cases of any country' (Nunn et al, 2009b: 1104).

Brazil has been hailed as the first country in the Global South to commit to providing HIV treatment to its citizens in 1997 (Teixeira, 2003; Biehl, 2004, 2005; Okie, 2006; Cataldo, 2008; Mauchline, 2008). As noted earlier, South Africa's HIV prevalence at that time was less than 1 per cent, whereas Brazil had the second highest number of reported HIV cases in the world (after the United States) (Nunn et al, 2012). However, this epidemiological profile shifted radically following Brazil's proactive provision of HIV medicines, and by 2004 the World Bank reported that Brazil's HIV response had averted more than half the 1.2 million projected AIDS cases (from 1990) (Biehl, 2007). By contrast, it was only in 2004 that ARVs first started to trickle into South Africa's public sector. These figures become more textured when held up next to South Africa's political leadership, as ideological battles around the science of medicine, mortality rates and life expectancy shaped the stuttered start of what has eventually become the world's largest ARV programme.

During President Mbeki's tenure, South Africa witnessed a sharp decline in life expectancy as people died of AIDS when they could have lived with HIV on treatment (Dorrington et al, 2006; Johnson et al, 2013). In 2008, researchers found that a third of a million people died because of the Mbeki-administration's HIV policies between 2000 and 2005 (Chigwedere et al, 2008). The Actuarial Society of South Africa's (ASSA) model calculated that, with the ARV rollout from 2004, there had been a significant decline in the number of AIDS-related deaths, from 257,000 in 2005 to 194,000 in 2010 (Johnson, 2012).

Under the new leadership of President Jacob Zuma and Health Minister Aaron Motsoaledi, treatment services were scaled up by 75 per cent between 2009 and 2011. By October 2012, 80 per cent of all people in need of ARVs – around 2 million people – received ARVs through the public health system (UNAIDS, 2012). In 2023, under the leadership of President Cyril Ramaphosa and Health Minister Mathume Phaahla, South Africa had the largest ARV programme in the world (Babatunde et al, 2023). Numerous actors, spanning local, national and transnational activist networks, national leaders, evolving intellectual property agreements and international biomedical research developments have all played a role in moving ARVs into South Africa's public health system and into people's bodies and lives. I discuss the role of these actors in the following section.

Shifting landscapes

In a talk on sociotechnical imaginaries, Sheila Jasanoff (2019) explored how lines of sovereignty and territoriality have become blurred as new technologies prompt a reconfiguration of politics and therefore a recalibration of contemporary understandings of citizenship, voice and expression. Introducing some of these debates in her earlier writing, Jasanoff (2005) outlined two primary and destabilizing changes in the ways that we understand and view the world. First, a cognitive shift from a realist to constructivist understanding of science and knowledge opened up space for scepticism around absolutist claims and an awareness of risks, uncertainty and safety. Second, the fragmented authority of the state has prompted a political shift and has generated a rethinking of democratic governance and the state's ability to discern and meet citizens' needs.

This book is built on research that broadly aligns with a curiosity about the implications of these two shifts, but instead of focusing on Europe and the United States, as Jasanoff did in her earlier writing, I was concerned with understanding how technological changes linked to the creation of HIV medicines prompted shifts in the claims that citizens made on their governments in the Global South. Further, I was interested to see how these citizens worked transnationally to precipitate changes in policies that regulated the creation, production and distribution of these life-saving medicines. In order to do this, the second decade of my research (from 2010 to 2023) has explored two main facets of enquiry. The first centred on the embodied ramifications of accessing HIV medicines for people living with HIV, and the second traced the activist work of these individuals and transnational alliances to reconfigure national and international policy governing access to these medicines in the Global South.

The rationale underpinning the embodied facet of my research connects with the first shift away from absolute claims to certainty, and towards a recognition of complexity as I sought to understand how women embody and experience HIV medicines beyond the black and white discourse of 'the politics of life' that unambiguously positions biomedical technologies as a 'fix' to the problem of HIV. I do not dispute the capacity of ARVs to extend lives. Rather, I was interested to understand how women embody medicine in their lives and how these medicines may hold hope alongside uncertainty beyond activist discourses that cast these technologies as unequivocally 'life-giving'. The first component of the rationale, therefore, connects to the first dimension of my research focus. Similarly, it informed my methodology and connects with the final part of my conceptual framework, discussed in the next chapter, in which I explore theoretical approaches to biosociality, embodiment and precarity.

The second part of my rationale connects to and builds on the political shift identified by Jasanoff (2005), as it relates to the second dimension of my research focus. Through this facet of my research, I sought to understand how the South African state was imagined by citizens in relation to the set of needs they identified when 'seeing' and 'speaking' to the state. I also aimed to explore how HIV-positive citizens act on the state (and are not simply acted on) within a broader network of actors that spans local, national, regional and global sites of engagement around HIV medicines. Like the first component of my rationale, it also informed my research methodology (as I go on to discuss) and connects with the conceptual framework in which I explore theories of biopolitics, imaginaries of the state and everyday forms of citizenship. In the sections that follow, I trace the shifts that took place in the biomedical and political landscape over the second decade of my research, from 2010 to 2023. The subsequent chapters unpack these shifts in more detail, and I articulate ways that we can understand these biomedical and political shifts as functions of one another, rather than separate and isolated from each other.

A shifting biomedical landscape

The rationale underpinning the first facet – the embodied dimension of HIV medicine – centres on the construction of medicine as a solution to HIV, or as medicine has more recently been described, as a 'technofix' to illness: a magic bullet that catalyses a linear transition from 'near death' to 'full life' (Lock and Nguyen, 2018). Jasanoff's (2005) account of the cognitive shift in approaches to scientific knowledge away from assertions of certainty and towards a recognition of ambiguity relates to my interest in understanding how HIV and HIV medicines were thought about, talked about and embodied in people's everyday lives.

Lock and Nguyen (2018) suggest that two assumptions underpin the certainty that guided historical assertions – by HIV activists, for example – that HIV medicines were a magic bullet for restoring health and sustaining life. First, the assumption that biomedical technologies are autonomous entities reinforces the construction of health-related matters as objective, quantifiable and technically manageable. However, as Lock and Nguyen point out, and as I discuss in the chapters that follow, 'biomedical technologies are not autonomous entities: their development and implementation are enmeshed with medical, social, and political interests that have practical and moral consequences' (2018: 1).

Drawing on Appadurai's (1988) concept of the 'social lives of things', medicines can perhaps more accurately be understood as 'things', or material medica, that have social lives (Whyte et al, 2002; Tocco, 2014; Rhodes et al, 2019). These two distinct but related approaches to 'things' and to 'materia medica' bear relevance in slightly different ways to this strand of the rationale. Appadurai (1988) suggests that in following the circulation of commodities, we not only look at the function they perform in exchange (see Mauss, 2002) but at the value they embody. Simmel (1978), he writes, proposed that value is not inherent to objects but rather something that we ascribe to them through exchanges of sacrifice. However, Appadurai (1988) uses Simmel's (1978) observation to think about the way that 'economic objects circulate in different regimes of value in space and time', reflecting on the edited collection of essays that offer 'glimpses of the ways in which desire and demand, reciprocal sacrifice and power interact to create economic value in specific social situations' (1988: 4).

When ARVs first became available to the international market, in 1996, only a very small minority of wealthy people were able to afford these medicines (Epstein, 1996). With this in mind, Appadurai (1988) prompts us to think that the value of these 'things' not only lies in the prices that countries and people pay pharmaceutical companies in exchange for them but also in the way their value is conceptualized and negotiated. The idea of the social lives of things is useful to trace the biographies of medicines. These biographies draw attention to the global political and economic negotiations that enable medicines to be developed in countries like India and Brazil, then accessed by countries like South Africa and, finally, distributed through the public health system to enter the lives and bodies of people living with HIV.

However, the significance of medicines extends beyond their economic value established through systems of exchange: it includes the value that medicines take on in people's bodies and lives, and draws into focus the range of actors and actants that move into relation with, or assemble around, medicines as 'things'. With respect to the first point on value, medical anthropologists working in the field of HIV have consistently widened the aperture to integrate a finely calibrated understanding of the meanings that medicines hold for people's bodies and lives. For instance, Whyte and colleagues' (2002) approach to the social uses and consequences of medicines, as the material 'things' of therapy, and Rhodes and colleagues' (2019) approach to the materiality of clinical HIV care, offer a more honed set of tools for anthropologists to work with when thinking about medicine beyond Appadurai's (1988) original framing. While recognizing that medicines take many different forms, these scholars focused – as I do – on commercially manufactured synthetic medicines produced by the pharmaceutical industry. They recognize that medicines are commodities with a social life. 'They have vigorous commodity careers; their dissemination to every part of the globe has far-reaching implications for local medical systems' (Whyte et al, 2002: 3). But beyond their commodity value and the notion that these 'things' have histories that shape their current form, Whyte et al also emphasize the extent to which medicines 'are the most personal of material objects' (2002: 3), woven into the fabric of social relationships.

It is the latter – the fabric of relationships – that speaks to the second point, made earlier, on the value of understanding how medicines assemble around and through other actants and actors. Actor Network Theory (ANT), discussed in detail in the following chapter, advances an understanding of medicines as 'things' – or nonhuman actants – that not only support life but also come 'alive' through a complex interplay of social, economic and political relationships, policies and institutions. As I demonstrate in this book, these relationships move across scale from the most intimate spaces under the skin, between parents and children, across partners and into activist coalitions right out to global trade agreements unfolding in Delhi and New York.

Scale is vital, because although economic and political relationships are widely theorized, it is far harder – and therefore critical – to reveal their embodied ramifications at a molecular, individual and social level. And yet, these large-scale economic and political relationships must be critically analysed and held accountable because, as I argue in this book, they influence the very materiality of life: they regulate whether and how medicines move through pharmaceutical factories in India, into ships and airplanes, over borders, along national highways, into the rooms of public health clinics and clinicians, across pharmacy counters from one set of hands to another. To make these relationships visible, I have structured this book to offer an analysis that moves across scale, from the intimate to the global, and I operationalize ANT through assemblage theory to reveal how heterogenous actors and actants – medicines, HIV, activists, policy makers – become animate in a global assemblage. By situating medicines within a global assemblage and by exploring how they become animate with and through other political, social and economic actors and actants, I challenge the assumption, also critiqued by Lock and Nguyen (2018), that biomedical technologies are autonomous objects, dislocated from social, economic and political relationships.

The second assumption that Lock and Nguyen (2018) critique, and that informs the second strand of this rationale for my research, relates to the positivist construction of bodies as being essentially the same. Not only were medicines left largely unexamined, a 'gold standard against which other theories of bodily affliction could be measured' (Brotherton and Nguyen, 2013: 287), but bodies were 'black-boxed', left by anthropologists to be probed by biologists. This was, for important reasons, due to the scientific racism of the 19th and 20th centuries that equated race with biological difference and discursively located this difference in the body (Lock, 2012; Bharadwaj, 2013; Lock and Nguyen, 2018). The cost is that 'we are now blind to how social and political processes produce biological difference, and by extension, how biomedical interventions may unwittingly perpetuate or enact further inequalities' (Brotherton and Nguyen, 2013: 288). Thus, not only are medical technologies dynamic, as explored earlier, but they interact differently with different kinds of bodies.

Assertions of bodily sameness, among HIV activists in South Africa (Robins and Von Lieres, 2004) and Burkina Faso (Nguyen, 2008) for example, may account for successful collective action that cohered around HIV as a shared illness predicament. However, while assertions by these collectives, also described as therapeutic citizens (Nguyen, 2008), have certainly been powerful in the history of HIV activism (as I discuss in the following section), they have not accounted for the dynamic pathways that connect mutating viruses with ARVs in unique bodies that are located in shifting social, economic and political environments. For, we see that combinations of HIV medicine and regulations for the commencement of treatment are regularly revised by the World Health Organization and by national governments. Acknowledging uncertainty linked to the non-uniform effects of HIV medicines and recognizing bodily difference pose challenges to activist discourse that mobilizes around certain benefits of HIV medicines in addressing the shared vulnerability of HIV-positive people as a collective group.

With this in mind, I sought to understand the dynamic interactions between individual bodies and complex biomedical technologies beyond the assumption that ARVs precipitate a transition from bare life to full health. As such, the first dimension of my research sought to explore these embodied dimensions and asked: how are HIV medicines perceived and embodied by women?

A shifting political landscape

This section relates to the second dimension of my research rationale and situates the emergence of HIV and the provision of ARVs in South Africa's political landscape. In line with the second shift that Jasanoff (2005) identifies, it draws in a set of local, national and transnational actors and illustrates the porosity of South Africa's government and the constraints and failures entailed in its ability to respond to its citizens' needs for life-saving HIV medicines. This relates to the second overarching research question, which asked: how do women engage with the state and practise citizenship around HIV medicine?

HIV started to move into South Africa's general population just as the country was moving towards democracy. During this final decade of apartheid, the government declared two states of emergency – in 1985 and 1988 – that amplified violence across South Africa: by the time Nelson Mandela was released in 1990, the focus was necessarily on enabling a peaceful transition. Still, 1990 marks the country's first coherent response to the HIV epidemic: the African National Congress (ANC), along with other anti-apartheid activists and regional government officials, attended the Fourth International Conference on Health in South Africa and released the Maputo Statement on HIV and AIDS calling on leaders to address the HIV epidemic and to focus on prevention and the rights of HIV-positive people (Heywood and Cornell, 1998). It was at this meeting that Chris Hani, the head of uMkhonto we Sizwe (the ANC's armed wing), said: "We cannot afford to allow the AIDS epidemic to ruin the realization of our dreams" (Itano, 2007: 144). In 1992, a broad coalition of actors from civic groups, trade unions, business organizations, political parties and academics formed the National AIDS Coordinating Committee of South Africa (NACOSA); it is largely due to NACOSA's AIDS strategy that the ANC government was able to adopt a National AIDS Plan within months of the first democratic election in 1994 (Heywood and Cornell, 1998).

However, one of the first signs that HIV was not a priority for the Mandela-administration was the appointment of the AIDS Programme Director to the Department of Health and not to the President's Office, as originally stipulated in the National AIDS Plan. Other factors accounting for the delayed response to HIV during President Mandela's tenure include bureaucratic restructuring, the devolution of authority to provincial governments and the absence of a coherent strategy for addressing HIV as a multi-faceted human rights issue rather than a specific health concern (Crewe, 2000). These factors were later disputed by critics who argued that '[t]here is a limit to how long a government can blame its own bureaucracy without being held to account for that failure' (Nattrass, 2004: 44).

While the first term of democratic governance (1994–99) under the Mandela-administration can be described as one of political inaction with respect to HIV, the subsequent two terms (1999–2008) under the Mbeki-administration are more aptly described as periods of political negligence.

For almost a decade, the South African government under the leadership of President Mbeki and his health ministers prevaricated on the public provision of ARVs. Initially, the government claimed that it was simply too expensive to provide these essential medicines. This economic logic was quickly dismantled, as the government was shown that it would be substantially more expensive not to provide ARVs (Nattrass, 2004). When President Mbeki, elected in 1999, convened an AIDS Advisory Panel and consulted with AIDS denialists like Peter Duesberg, it became apparent that his objection was not on economic grounds but on ideological ones (Geffen, 2005).[3] For, even in 2001, when the government, along with TAC, challenged international TRIPS conditions to allow for the domestic production of generic brand medicines, it still did not start to provide ARVs to the hundreds of thousands of people who were dying prematurely of AIDS (TAC, 2010).

South Africa's particular history challenges the view that scientific knowledge is a straightforward matter of 'rationality' and a condition of 'democratic emancipation' as Geffen (2010) and Nattrass (2008, 2012) assert. Instead, I suggest that equivocation around the science of HIV and of HIV medicines may also relate to a complex political history that calls into focus epistemological questions around the deficit model of science (Leach, 2005; Pienaar, 2016a). For instance, some medicines, like Depo–Provera (an injection contraceptive), were used by the apartheid government to control Black men's and women's bodies and their sexual reproduction (Brown, 1987).[4] Looking from medicines to viruses, we see, too, that beliefs that White people introduced HIV as a means to control the Black population echo the documented actions of apartheid's Defence Force and employees like Wouter Basson who researched the use of HIV in biological warfare (Fassin and Schneider, 2003; Mills, 2005; Youde, 2005).

Mbeki's pseudoscientific approach to the science of HIV perhaps emerges, in part, from this complex history as he sought to destabilize the epidemiological link between unprotected sex and HIV transmission by foregrounding poverty as the primary structural determinant of HIV infection (Nattrass, 2008). By tethering HIV prevalence to structural inequality, Mbeki aimed to challenge racist assumptions that Black people were more likely to be HIV-positive because they were more sexually voracious than other race groups (Gevisser, 2008). (These were the same kinds of racist and pseudoscientific assumptions that medical anthropologists backed away from when researching the body in the 18th and 19th century.) In this way, Mbeki focused on holding South Africa's colonial and apartheid history accountable for its HIV crisis. In a cruel twist of irony, this meant that his administration did not develop the vital policies that would ensure, in this postcolonial era, that the lives of South African citizens were secured through the timely provision of HIV treatment.

Mbeki's epistemological equivocation had material implications for the vitality and mortality of HIV-positive South Africans who were unable to access life-saving HIV medicines through the public health sector because of his administration's political negligence. Over 340,000 lives were lost under President Mbeki's term in office as a result of his government's failure to scale up the provision of ARVs (Chigwedere et al, 2008; Nattrass, 2008).

The emergence and large-scale political mobilization of TAC in the period of the Mbeki-administration perhaps best illustrates the relationship between the local and the global in South Africa's shifting political landscape. I trace this account here as my fieldwork in the decade following 2010 took place with a group of people who had worked with TAC at the height of the struggle for HIV medicines. It is important to note, too, that while I worked with TAC and with many people who had been HIV activists, my fieldwork found that these political landscapes continued shifting and new kinds of biopolitical struggles were emerging in people's everyday lives, relationships and citizenships.

There were five main strategies through which TAC worked across transnational geographies and political ideologies to advocate around the legitimacy of HIV science and align this science with the constitutional entitlement of citizens to health and health care. First, TAC built a cadre of activists. This was done in part by harnessing the science of HIV and AIDS treatment through their Treatment Literacy Programme. Through this programme, 'scientifically literate' activists were – irrespective of their formal education levels – able to use the language and logic of biomedical science to highlight the importance of making ARVs available to South Africans (Robins, 2006). The large numbers of people who cohered in biosocial groups (Rabinow, 1996) around the struggle for ARVs, through marches for example, made this particular kind of biopolitics visible to the government and the world, as they brought their bodies into public spaces to bear witness to their embodied vulnerability without access to ARVs. TAC's first public event set the stage for foregrounding the relationship between citizens' vitality and access to medicines: it held a Fast to Save Lives on 21 March 1999 at the Chris Hani Baragwanath Hospital in Soweto, Johannesburg (TAC, 2010). The images from this event flew across South Africa's television screens, as the country witnessed images reminiscent of the anti-apartheid struggle in post-apartheid South Africa: activists lay on the ground in a 'die in' to symbolize their death and to make the connection between AIDS treatment and life visible to a government that was refusing to bear witness to the escalation of AIDS-related mortality (Geffen, 2010). I first worked with TAC in 2006, when developing the HIV/AIDS and STI NSP with the then-Deputy Minister of Health. During this time in the late 2000s, at the height of their activism, TAC had over 10,000 members and was active in community-level branches across the country. These community-level branches cohered around six district offices and cascaded into one national office in Cape Town.

Second, TAC used the law. TAC worked most closely with the AIDS Law Project in Johannesburg (now called Section 27). Jonathan Berger, one of the key actors in this organization, describes how TAC used the constitution 'as a tool':

> TAC's work is deeply grounded in the Constitution – in the rights it recognises, in the obligations it imposes on the state and the private sector, and in its recognition of the importance of the rule of law to good governance, accountability and service delivery. This understanding of the Constitution has helped TAC to frame its demands in human rights language and use the law as a tool for progressive social change. (TAC, 2010: 29)

Third, TAC worked with international partners to show the government that HIV medicines are effective. This was primarily accomplished through TAC's partnership with MSF. In 2000, MSF set up three clinics in Khayelitsha to provide ARVs to people who were most urgently in need of treatment to survive. In 2003, TAC and MSF set up a second trial in rural Lusikisiki, in the adjacent Eastern Cape Province. A number of the people I worked with, like Miriam, joined TAC when they started ARVs through the MSF trial in Khayelitsha. The data from MSF's ARV trial in Khayelitsha offered sufficient evidence for cabinet to order the government to initiate a public sector ARV rollout in August 2003 (Nattrass, 2012).

Fourth, TAC took to the streets in protest against the government. In 2002, TAC voted to initiate a countrywide civil disobedience campaign and to increase the use of marches. TAC's civil disobedience campaign, called 'Dying for Treatment', aimed to alert the government and the international community to the mortal implications of the government's failure to deliver a treatment plan. 'Die ins' were one of multiple forms of protest actions – including marches, disruptions to parliament, lawsuits – and they were used across the world to show the precarious nature of life in South Africa.

Finally, TAC challenged pharmaceutical companies to make HIV medicines more affordable to low- and middle-income countries. Initially, as I discuss in Chapters 3 and 7, TAC joined the South African government in a case that had been brought against it by the Pharmaceutical Manufacturers Association (PMA) and 40 multinational drug companies. The PMA sought to stop the enactment of the Medicines and Related Control Amendment Act (1997) that allowed for the substitution of brand-name drugs once the patent had expired; the Act also allowed for the importation of generic medicines. The PMA were publicly denounced by TAC's members, who stood outside the court in garish masks that caricatured the PMA as 'fat cat corporates' complicit in the death of South Africans who could not afford their drugs. Shamed by these public actions, and by TAC's activist network that denounced pharmaceutical profiteering in countries like Brazil and Thailand, the PMA dropped the court action in 2001. TAC also challenged specific pharmaceutical companies to make their medicines more affordable by threatening to use this law to import generics (Robins, 2005; TAC, 2010).

The transition to a new South African government in 2009, under President Zuma, marked a further shift in the politics of science linked to HIV and HIV medicine with the appointment of Health Minister Aaron Motsoaledi. Working for a decade in this capacity (2009–19), Motsoaledi brought an end to government-led equivocation around the efficacy of HIV medicines and fundamentally transformed the rollout of HIV medicines. This political shift generated momentum in the provision of HIV medicines through the public health system, and it has had significant material implications for the lives of HIV-positive South Africans. By 2017, South Africa had scaled up treatment services to reach 64 per cent of the HIV-positive population, increasing this target in line with UNAIDS' 90–90–90 targets to 73.2 per cent in 2023 (Simbayi et al, 2019; Johnson and Dorrington, 2023). UNAIDS' 90-90-90 fast-track targets called for 90 per cent of people living with HIV to know their status, 90 per cent of people living with HIV who know their status to be on antiretroviral therapy, and 90 per cent of people living with HIV on antiretroviral therapy to achieve viral suppression. These targets have since been updated by UNAIDS to call for 95 per cent coverage for testing, treatment and viral suppression by 2025.

South Africa's broad-based ARV scale up was what TAC activists had been lobbying for: essentially, they looked to get medicines into the country rapidly, at affordable prices, and to ensure they were then made available to the large number of HIV-positive South Africans in need of this treatment through the public health sector. However, even when the state heeded the activist call to scale up ARVs across the country, there remained (and emerged) a set of challenges that point to the constraints preventing the government from fully meeting the needs of its citizens. These challenges fan out from the historical urgency to make HIV medicines available to draw in a more complex set of challenges around living with HIV and ARVs in one of the most socio-economically unequal countries in the world. These factors point to the role of the state in sustaining life by providing ARVs, but they also illustrate some of the practical limits of the state's capacity to discern and meet the needs of its citizens. This is particularly salient as powerful new HIV therapies emerge not only to treat HIV but also to prevent transmission (through pre- and post-exposure prophylaxis). For instance, as I discuss in Chapter 7, one of the most ground-breaking therapies to emerge in the last five years – lenacapavir – has just been introduced to the international market as a long-acting injectable treatment that only needs to be administered twice a year (Dvory-Sobol et al, 2022). Although this medicine is now available to people and countries that can afford to pay for it, at the time of writing it was not available in South Africa, or indeed to the populations – including those in South Africa and six other Southern African countries – that were involved in the clinical trials of its safety and efficacy (Phillips et al, 2021).

In this book, I refer to the new set of challenges that surface more visibly in the wake of the decade-long struggle for ARVs as new generation struggles, and I explore them as they draw attention to the constraints not only placed on the lives of individuals but also on the governments that are biopolitically implicated in their vitality. These struggles point to the intersection of the shifting biomedical and political landscapes and together offer scope for considering the biopolitical dimensions in which people's embodied lives are networked into an assemblage around the politics of life linked to but extending beyond access to HIV medicine.

Book outline

This book is tiered across five ethnographic and analytical chapters to draw HIV-positive women's accounts into dialogue with activist coalitions in South Africa and Brazil, unique medical technologies in India and patent negotiations with the WTO. It is important to note here that this book does not seek to offer a comparative analysis of South Africa's, Brazil's and India's response to HIV, nor is it structured to give equal weight to each of these countries. The book is grounded in the lives of the people with whom I conducted most of my fieldwork in South Africa, predominantly in the second decade of my own research engagement (from 2010 to 2023), and as such, the first three substantive chapters (Chapters 3, 4 and 5) speak to this research. The subsequent two chapters move out to bring Brazil into focus (Chapter 6) before exploring how countries like South Africa, Brazil and India are networked into a global assemblage that governs the production and distribution of essential medicines (Chapter 7). These five chapters are structured to move the analysis across scale, from the individual to the national, transnational and global, to show the political and embodied ramifications of policies governing HIV medicines on individual lives.

In addition to using ethnographic research to trace the politics of HIV medicines in people's lives and bodies in South Africa and Brazil, this book draws on secondary research, including international and national policy analysis, to document the political power of transnational coalitions between countries like South Africa, Brazil and India. Further, and in a challenge to much research on gender and HIV, this book not only looks at the impact of global policy on national policy and local lives but considers the dynamic interplay of these spheres and traces the ways in which HIV-positive women have challenged and shaped national and global policies. In doing so, this book issues a challenge to the trope, present in much development literature, of HIV-positive women as subject to the actions of others, lacking in agency themselves. It concretely demonstrates how HIV-positive women have participated in local, national and transnational activist coalitions to bring about changes in global and national health policy and practice. I outline each of the chapters in the paragraphs that follow to indicate how they are structured to build this overarching picture.

The following chapter introduces the book's conceptual framework, followed by a short summary of each of the three main countries discussed in the book and the methods that were used in conducting primary and secondary research across these countries. The first section, on concepts, traces the theoretical trajectory from biopower to the politics of life linked to recent technological advances and their implications for governance. Thereafter, the chapter critiques this trajectory in light of two sets of literature that engage specifically with the two dimensions of the research focus – the embodiment and politics of HIV medicine. It proposes that feminist new materialism, science studies and anthropological theory around actor networks and assemblages might enable an integration of these sets of literature. Following the introduction of key concepts pertinent to the book, the second section locates the relevance of these concepts by providing contextual background to South Africa, Brazil and India. Thereafter, the chapter outlines the primary and secondary research methods that were used in each country. The methods include participant observation, ethnography, participatory photography and film, key informant interviews and policy analysis.

Chapter 3 is the first of the five substantive chapters in this book. This chapter zooms into the intimate worlds of women living in Khayelitsha, South Africa. Each of the following chapters then move out in scale, to draw in a wider focus on regional and global dynamics linked to the politics of HIV medicines. This chapter is based on fine-grained ethnographic research, and it brings to light the nuanced, intersectional struggles that women encounter in their sexual, social and economic worlds. These struggles are articulated, too, in relation to the history of South Africa's failure to provide HIV medicines and the subsequent increase in vertical transmission of HIV from parents to their children through birth and breastfeeding. This has had lasting implications for the women in this study, and for their children, and these implications are detailed in the first section of this chapter. The second section, on 'horizontal pathways', looks at the evolution of sexual and reproductive rights and women's experiences of gender-based violence in South Africa. The final section of this chapter explores women's tactical negotiation of these forms of harm and underlines the value of thinking more critically around the ways in which women act strategically to navigate their lives in highly complex and often violent contexts.

Chapter 4 traces a set of new generation struggles that have emerged following the large-scale provision of HIV medicines through South Africa's public health system. Just as HIV precipitated forms of embodied vulnerability when medicines were not readily available, so too have HIV medicines generated new forms of embodied vulnerability, including side effects, treatment fatigue and viral resistance. These struggles are less frequently discussed or considered when looking at the history of the struggle for HIV medicines, but they are increasingly important as they often lead to poor treatment adherence and sometimes death. The economic context in which people navigate their treatment regimens has also been shown to impact whether or not they are able to adhere to their medicines: some medicines need to be kept refrigerated, and without money for electricity (or access to electricity), this renders medicines ineffective (Kalofonos, 2008; Squire, 2010; Persson et al, 2016; Young et al, 2019). These linked struggles, around the embodiment of HIV medicines and the socio-economic context in which these medicines are taken, are foregrounded through ethnographic accounts drawn from my own research in South Africa and also from current research elsewhere in Africa, Latin America and South East Asia.

Chapter 5 traces changing citizenship practices as they are embodied by HIV-positive women in South Africa, and as they coalesce around emergent political concerns that fan out from the historic assertion of the right to life linked to HIV medicine. The chapter explores multiple dimensions of South African citizens' imaginaries as they 'saw' and 'spoke' to the state; these imaginaries reflect on and develop the set of new generation struggles that are detailed in the previous chapter and that, I argue, reflect South Africa's shifting medical and political landscapes in the wake of the ARV rollout.

With the provision of HIV medicine in South Africa, emergent concerns around access to newer medical technologies that have fewer side effects call a set of global actors into focus. These actors include Brazilian activists who have a long history of mobilizing the government for access to emerging medical technologies, national governments and countries that produce affordable ARVs (like Brazil and India), regional coalitions (like BRICS comprising Brazil, Russia, India, China and South Africa) and international actors (like the European Union and WTO). Chapter 6 draws South Africa's and Brazil's history of activism into dialogue, debunking the notion that Brazil can be solely understood as an 'activist state' and exploring some of the current challenges facing people living with HIV in both countries.

Chapter 7 moves further out in scale to articulate some of the regional axes of power, linking Brazil, India and South Africa, that have challenged global forms of governance that limit access to essential HIV medicines. The first section of this chapter extends the discussion on patent regulations introduced in Chapters 1 and 2, with a detailed focus on the politics surrounding the WTO's early role in governing access to essential HIV medicine through the TRIPS Agreement. It then turns to consider some of the 'patent wars' that were waged by countries like South Africa, Brazil and India. And it explores the crucial role played by India in reverse engineering HIV medicines that would otherwise have been inaccessible to most governments in the Global South due to their pricing (protected by patents) in the Global North.

The final chapter draws the findings of the five substantive chapters together and considers the implications of the shifting biopolitical landscape in which this multi-sited ethnography was located. In doing so, it explores the limits of agency of both governments and individuals to exert autonomy over their vitality within a global assemblage that draws actors that shape life under the skin (like HIV and ARVs) into a network with actors (like South

Africa, India, Brazil, the EU and WTO) that govern the development and distribution of essential HIV medicines.

In considering these implications, the conclusion reflects on the value of two overarching contributions of the book in researching the intersection between women's embodied experience of medicine and their political engagement with the state. First, the concept of diffracted biosocialities reflects emergent biopolitical struggles that fan out from a narrow focus on illness to include and integrate struggles that happen 'inside' the body (linked to HIV and ARVs) with the context 'outside' the body (linked to violence, unemployment, sanitation). Because these emergent struggles are experienced within the body, it is also through the body that they are articulated in people's political dialogues with the state, as activists and as everyday citizens. Second, the related concept of biopolitical precarity shows the entwined relationship between the state of the body and the body of the state and highlights the value of locating this historic biopolitical relationship in a global terrain to hold these multiple actors to account for the extent to which their actions continue to be embodied in women's lives.

Conclusion

I write this introduction cognizant that starting places matter:

> If you start from the 'negative minimalisms' (Thin 2008: 149) of sheer survival and bare life, of violence, suffering, deprivation, and destitution, then you provide a very different description of lives than if you begin from people's situated concerns … [O]ur tendency to focus on the dystopic has been at the price of forgetting to think about 'other ways of thinking' – supposedly this is what anthropologists do best. (Marsland, 2012: 464)

This book is distinct from the trajectory of the shifting biomedical and political landscapes discussed earlier, and from ethnographies of ARV programmes that were situated in the time lag between the international development of HIV medicines and their provision through national health systems. My research looks at what happens afterwards, when the light turns and the acute and visible struggle for ARVs becomes a chronic and quieter navigation of precarious life.

Situated in a dynamic biopolitical landscape after ARVs were first introduced, this book explores what happens when people's chronic struggle to survive without ARVs sifts back under the surface and these medicines become embedded in their everyday lives, when the possibility of hope attached to these medicines becomes embodied and then unfolds as a new generation of struggles of risks and side effects. It looks at what happens when the tide of AIDS funding turns, and global actors articulate a new set of priorities, when national governments start working with, and not against, activist organizations, and when life becomes much more about the struggle against brutal winters as they ease into the bones of people's bodies in the 'ephemeral constructions' (Fassin, 2007) of fragile corrugated-iron homes.

While I do not start from a point of 'negative minimalisms' that foregrounds the extent to which oppressive structures bear down on people's ability to navigate their life, this ethnography is also not reflective of the anthropology of hope, where 'the fundamental condition of politics is ... plural [and] goes on among plural human beings each of whom can act and start something new' (Marsland and Prince, 2012: 464). This ethnography lies somewhere in the middle: people are its starting place, and because it is situated in their lives, it is a far more complex story. It offers hope in the quieter everyday ways that the people with whom I worked resisted oppressive structures. But it also asks us to bear witness to the violent politics of their precarious lives and to consider how, through our own engagement in development practice, policy and pedagogy, we might work to engender a more equitable future.

2

Concepts, Contexts and Methods

> One could argue that no single disease has been so widely
> studied by anthropology, as both a starting point and a case study
> for developing and testing anthropological theory on meaning
> making, political economy, biopolitical governance, kinship,
> social movements, identity, gender, agency, care, sexuality,
> intimacy medicalization, and stigma. (Moyer, 2015: 260)

This chapter introduces the key concepts, contexts and methods that have
informed the ethnographic accounts I share in the chapters that follow.
While these concepts, contexts and methods are discussed in turn, they
are imbricated in one another. Moving across Brazil and South Africa
required an understanding of how concepts, like citizenship and activism,
translate between these unique, shifting and heterogenous contexts,
and therefore different methods were necessary for understanding the
practices of citizenship and activism that I observed and participated in.
Anthropological methods like participant observation also come up against
their own limitations when shifting beyond an ethnographically informed
understanding of how policy is perceived, embodied and resisted by citizens,
to tracing how policies governing access to affordable medicines in India,
for instance, are themselves built through global assemblages of actors that
function at an often inaccessible distance. As I go on to argue later in the
chapter, and throughout this book, there is too frequently a powerful political
and economic incentive to study these actors at a distance, away from
immediate accountability. And so, I suggest, there is also an imperative for
anthropology not only to develop and test anthropological theory through
empirical case studies, as Moyer (2015) suggests in the opening quote, but
also to actively disrupt the architecture that is built around global and national
policies that render some bodies more vulnerable, and more invisible, than
others. This chapter sets out the conceptual, contextual and methodological
foundation of the book and articulates avenues through which concepts and

methods might be utilized, together, to disrupt powerful policy dynamics across scale and in different contexts.

Concepts

> The smallest AIDS virus takes you from sex to the unconscious, then to Africa, tissue cultures, DNA and San Francisco, but the analysts, thinkers, journalists and decision-makers will slice the delicate network traced by the virus for you into tidy compartments where you will find only science, only economy, only social phenomena, only local news, only sentiment, only sex … By all means, they seem to say, let us not mix up knowledge, interest, justice and power. Let us not mix up heaven and earth, the global stage and the local scene, the human and the nonhuman. 'But these imbroglios do the mixing,' you'll say, 'they weave our world together!' 'Act as if they didn't exist,' the analysts reply. They have cut the Gordian knot with a well-honed sword. The shaft is broken: on the left, they have put knowledge of things; on the right, power and human politics. (Latour, 1993: 2–3)

The people I have met in my research have taken the feminist adage that the personal is political and mixed it up, thoroughly. Women's embodied accounts of the pathways that brought HIV and later antiretrovirals (ARVs) as actants into their bodies implicate a network of actors, including scientists capable of reverse engineering essential HIV medicines in India's laboratories, South Africa's and Brazil's capacity to negotiate international trade law to access these medicines, health systems and their professionals who dispense medicines through small 'ARV-only' pharmaceutical counters in Khayelitsha's clinics, activist coalitions with international organizations like Médecins Sans Frontières (MSF), and fraught relationships that women navigate as individuals, professionals, partners and parents. In this book, I trace the 'social lives' of HIV and ARVs as actants and explore this set of actors across the five main chapters, each moving out in scale from the molecular to the global. I use these scales to organize what is necessarily a structured argument across a linear book that moves from one page to another, from one chapter to the next. However, the line of argument is not linear, nor does it fit neatly within a set of theories around structure and agency (Giddens, 1990; Stones, 2017) or even practice (Bourdieu, 2001; Harker et al, 2016), with governance structures acting down on people's bodies or with people acting up on these structures. Just as my ethnography traced a delicate network that mixed up sex, social phenomena and science, justice and power, the global and local, so too does the conceptual framework outlined in this chapter.

The conceptual framework draws together insights from and critical engagements with several literatures to underpin the theoretical and ethical imperative of understanding the embodied ramifications of the governance of medicines as they are networked through and under the skin of the body – of the individual and of the population. The first section outlines how the research draws on the evolution of theory from biopower to the 'politics of life' linked to biomedical technology. The second section uses these approaches to engage with medical anthropological theories of the body and embodiment, broadly in relation to the embodied dimension of the research focus. The third section engages with literature on governance and citizenship, broadly in relation to the political dimension of the research focus. The fourth section maps out theory around assemblages and actor networks as the core concepts that bridge the two dimensions of the research focus and concludes by outlining the conceptual approach of biopolitical precarity.

Medicine and the politics of life

Foucault's concept of biopower concerns the biological existence of human beings and the mechanisms through which humans become an object of political intervention and strategy (Foucault, 1978). Biopower refers to the 'techniques of power' that manage and control the bodies of individuals (anatomopolitics) and the life of the population (biopolitics) (Foucault, 1978, 2008; Nadesan, 2010; Erlenbusch-Anderson, 2020). The first pole of biopower, anatomopolitics, centres on the discursive construction of the body as a machine, disciplined through strategies that optimized its capabilities, extorted its forces, increased its usefulness alongside its docility and ensured its integration into systems of economic and political control (Foucault, 1978). The second pole of biopolitics moves out in scale from the individual body to the body of the population and focuses on the 'species body – the body imbued with the mechanics of life and serving as the basis of the biological processes: propagation, births and mortality, the level of health, life expectancy and longevity, with all the conditions that can cause those to vary' (Foucault, 1978: 139). The emergence of biopower was marked by the proliferation of techniques, inculcated in schools, universities and military institutions, to subjugate bodies and control populations. The techniques also included the emergence of political practices and economic quantification linked to birth rates, mortality and public health (Foucault, 1978). Without detailing how, Foucault suggests that the two poles are not antithetical but are instead 'linked together by a whole intermediary cluster of relations' (Foucault, 1978: 139). This book unpacks the 'intermediary cluster of relations' that Foucault notes as an assemblage of networked actors in order to emphasize intersections across the poles.

Biopower, fundamentally, asserts a relationship between the vitality of the state and the body of the individual and the population. Specifically, Foucault's conception of governmentality considers linkages between the health of the population and the economic and political security of the state, and how these two, together, generate distinct biopolitical strategies for representing and acting upon populations (Foucault, 1978, 1998; Nadesan, 2010; Edwards and Fernández, 2017). Medicine forms one strategy through which states extend power into the bodies of the population: '[A]lthough medical technologies of government change across time, they tend to cohere around security problematics posed to, and by, the vitality, fecundity, and productivity of the population. Liberal regimes of medical government claim to optimize freedom by securitizing/regulating the conditions of life' (Nadesan, 2010: 103).

According to Rose (2019), technological developments have generated new 'economies of vitality' as power can be more intimately inserted into bodies through medical technology at a molecular level. I argue in the following chapters that vitality is increasingly entangled with the governance of medical technologies and therefore requires a closer appraisal of the networked relationship that draws politics, people and medicine together. The term 'politics of life' was developed by Rose (2009, 2019) to extend Foucault's (1978) theorization of medicine and the role of the state in governing life (and death) through medical policies and practices. Technological developments, particularly linked to engineering vitality through biomedical developments, correspond with changing technologies of governance. According to Rose, biomedical technologies are 'hybrid assemblages oriented toward the goal of optimization ... These are not merely medical technologies or the technologies of health, they are technologies of life' (Rose, 2009: 17).

This book proposes that biomedical technologies like ARVs are more than their material form and reflect a broader politics of life: they assemble potent economic coalitions, political alliances, particular ways of thinking about disease and about health, modes of clinical care and practices of interaction between health care practitioners and patients. Foucault's (1978) theory of biopower is productive here as it traces the relationship between the vitality of individual bodies and populations and the state; further, the 'politics of life' literature prompts us to explore how 'life itself' is conditioned through a complex array of forces that draw the state into the body through various technologies of governance that include biomedical technologies, as Rose and others have proposed (Rabinow, 1996; Rose 2009, 2019; Raman and Tutton, 2010; Brown et al, 2012; Edwards and Fernández, 2017).

However, reflecting Foucault's (1978, 1991) and Rose's (2009, 2019) call for theoretical agility that keeps pace with emerging technologies and shifting 'politics of life', this book engages with these foundational theories but also moves slightly away from a blanket application of theories of biopower and 'contemporary biopolitics'. This move is significant for a range of reasons, not least because the 'politics of life' literature is largely generated through studies conducted in the Global North and too often does not look at the nature of embodied inequality in shaping experiences of different technologies. This book, situated in the Global South, tackles this challenge both conceptually and empirically. Conceptually, the book advances the notion of biopolitical precarity to demonstrate the complex nature of intersectional inequality that moves across scale from the global stage to the most intimate space of the body. Empirically, this book operationalizes the concept of biopolitical precarity through my own ethnographic research, and in dialogue with a set of contemporary ethnographic studies, that advances a nascent trajectory of thought on the 'edges' of biopolitics in health research from the Global South.

The state of the body: embodiment

These literatures on biopower and the politics of life imply a particular way of thinking about embodiment: Foucault (1978) describes the state as 'vitalized' by governmentality, as animated through governmentality; the corollary, importantly, is the state's management of vitality, as embodied by populations and individuals. Historically, then, following Foucault (1978), the state of the body and the body of the state were tied together in a biopolitical contract of vitality. In this conceptualization, states and bodies were positioned in relation to each other, fundamentally connected to and shaped through each other, but also distinct. Karen Barad articulates the limits to this distinction in writing that 'for all Foucault's emphasis on the political anatomy of disciplinary power, he too fails to offer an account of the body's historicity in which its very materiality plays an active role in the workings of power' (2003: 809).

My research sought not only to look at how the body of the state and the state of the body are co-constructed but to see how their boundaries are porous as they are networked into each other. Specifically, by looking across the two dimensions – embodied and political – my research sought to understand how access to HIV medicines might offer a productive way to think about the world inside the body (the embodied dimension) and the world outside the body (the political dimension), and where these distinctions of 'inside' and 'outside' might be usefully disrupted. The structure of the following five chapters draws these two worlds together with a view to show their porosity. Chapters 3 and 4 start by exploring the world inside the body through the accounts of women's activism and everyday life in post-apartheid South Africa; the thread of political engagement around access to health is drawn out more explicitly in Chapter 5 with a focus on the different ways women saw and engaged with the state as citizens.

Chapter 6 then moves out in scale, across the ocean to Brazil, as it explores some of the limitations to the conception of Brazil as the 'activist state' in comparison to earlier constructions of South Africa as the 'denialist state'. The final chapter considers the role of international organizations and blocs, like the World Trade Organization (WTO) and EU respectively, in shaping trade agreements that govern whether or not countries like India can produce affordable medicines for people living with life-threatening illnesses in the Global South.

As outlined in the previous chapter, this focus on the porosity of boundaries between technologies, states and bodies emerged from a history in which the South African state was implicated in the precarious lives of HIV-positive people as they died or became very ill without access to essential HIV medicines; and it emerged from an interest in understanding how people made sense of the state in their bodies through their experience of illness and resumed health as the biopolitical landscape of ARV access shifted with time. In this respect, my book follows a trajectory in medical anthropology (Lambert and McDonald, 2009; Strathern, 2009; Vilaca, 2009; Yates-Doerr, 2017; Chapman, 2021) that calls for a shift away from dualities in which the body is viewed as substrate for cultural symbols (Douglas, 2003). For, research in the fields of medical anthropology and feminist new materialism have shown how technologies that are constituted from human biological material disrupt distinctions between human and nonhuman, nature and culture, self and other and generate new forms of life and biosocialities (Van der Tuin, 2011; Haraway, 2013; Hinton, 2014; Lupton, 2019; Barad and Gandorfer, 2021; Fullagar and Pavlidis, 2021). Further, conceptualizations of governmentality that incorporate technological developments in pharmacology, genomics and neuroscience have shifted away from notions of bounded bodies and towards a conception of co-constructed entanglement (Rose, 2018, 2019; Carvalho et al, 2020).

In addition to foregrounding the entanglements between things – like bodies, medicines and viruses – medical anthropological ethnographies on ARV programmes in the 'age of treatment' have emphasized the importance of bringing inequality into focus (Moyer, 2015: 260). Reviewing anthropological research across two decades (1995–2015), Moyer identifies epistemological continuities in research that took place before ARVs were developed ('the age of AIDS') and, later, during and after ARVs became widely available ('the age of treatment'). With the provision of ARVs, anthropological research shifted from a prevailing focus on the challenges of managing HIV as an acute illness towards a greater recognition of the social and material conditions that impact whether and how people are able to live a long life with ARVs. While ethnographies reflect continuities in experiences of HIV-related stigma and discrimination, anthropologists have also started to reveal the consequences of inequality on treatment access, efficacy and adherence for people living in under-resourced settings (Merten et al, 2010; Decoteau, 2013; Kavanagh et al, 2015; Cancelliere, 2020).

In their reflections on inequality and the genealogy of biopolitical theory, Fassin (2009), Marsland (2012), Prince (2012) and Biehl and Locke (2017) ask whether the politics of life literature relies on assumptions generated in the Global North, where biomedical technologies, in particular, are more freely available than they are in the Global South and therefore have different outcomes on whether people live or are, without access, 'left to die'. They suggest that this literature may also place an unfair emphasis on the neoliberal discourse of choice that locates responsibility for vitality on the individual and shifts attention and resources away from addressing the underlying inequalities that affect the kinds of lives people live even when they are able to access ARVs as 'technologies of life'. Or put slightly differently, perhaps we can understand ethnographic research and theoretical interventions in the 'age of treatment' as never quite finished. As Biehl and Locke (2017: x) write, '[e]thnographic creations are about the plasticity and unfinishedness of human subjects and lifeworlds ... Unfinishedness is a feature as generative to art and knowledge production as it is to living.' And so, while the ethnography in this book challenges the framing of HIV medicine as sufficient for sustaining life, it also reveals some of the implications of inequality as it moves across scale – from under the skin out to a global assemblage that governs access to medicines – and it opens up questions about the imbrication of policy and bodies with a recognition that this terrain, in the 'age of treatment', is constantly unfolding.

As I discuss later in the chapter, I use the term 'precarity' to denote multiple axes of inequality in which the state and a set of global actors are implicated in people's embodied lives. In doing so, I suggest that the politics of life is not only a question of technologies through which governmentality operates but that it is also a process through which inequalities are (re)produced and embodied. Further, I argue that to move beyond binaries that separate the state of the body from the body of the state, we need to see how bodies (historically viewed as nature) are permeable and co-constructed with politics and technologies (historically viewed as culture). In using the notion of precarity, we move away, too, from privileging biomedicines and viruses, and the world within the body, as the only legitimate 'local biologies' (Bharadwaj, 2013; Brotherton and Nguyen, 2013). This in turn enables an understanding that the embodied efficacy of HIV medicines is mediated, at times, by chronic unemployment and food insecurity where taking these potent medicines with food is simply not possible. Or it becomes more possible to see that susceptibility to HIV infection may be mediated by the biopolitical dynamics of structural violence, like poor sanitation and the increased risk of sexual assault. To this end, in line with feminist new materialist approaches to embodiment (Van der Tuin, 2011; Fullagar and Pavlidis, 2021), I propose a reading of the body as permeable. This approach, which recognizes embodied entanglement, complicates a reading of agency that locates responsibility on the individual to navigate large-scale oppressive structures. Instead, as I discuss subsequently, a reading of the body as permeable draws attention to the role that individuals, groups and networks of activists play in each other's vitality as they see and speak to the state through everyday forms of citizenship.

The body of the state: governance and citizenship

The third area of literature unpacks the dynamics of governance and citizenship with a focus on imaginaries of the state and embodied dimensions of subjectivity that surface through multiple and intersecting citizen practices.

The 'modern state', according to Weber (1984), was developed in Western Europe in the 19th century with a dual institutional structure that managed processes of decision (politics, policy and state organization for deliberation) and structures of bureaucracy (state mechanisms for policy implementation). This conception of the state connects to the empirical trajectory informing Foucault's (1978) theory of biopower in which the 'modern state' works through policy processes and bureaucratic mechanisms to subjugate bodies and control processes of life. More recently, however, transitions in development and technology have prompted reappraisals of such conceptions of the bounded state that 'acts down'. In particular, the economic reform agendas of the 1990s to roll back the state and privatize public services (see Naseemullah, 2023) came under vociferous criticism and prompted a new emphasis on democratic state–citizen relations and NGO–government partnerships (Stiglitz, 2003). Consequently, theoretical approaches to governance emerged where multiple actors were recognized that were understood to transect and move beyond monolithic bounded entities of state, corporation or civil society, and where interactions within and across actors and entities pointed to blurred boundaries and the value of understanding networks of governance (Leach et al, 2007; Blanco et al, 2011; Sørensen and Torfing, 2018).

I use the concept of networked governance because it recognizes the porosity of state boundaries and opens up space for complicating interactions across a network of actors linking multiple and intersecting sites of engagement that move across scale from the global to the molecular. This conceptualization is developed across the book as it traces networks spanning South Africa, Brazil and India around the politics of life and the governance of HIV medicine and reflects an emerging dialogue between political science and the anthropology of policy (see Tate, 2020) that recognizes: the shift from government institutions to governance networks and policy assemblages (Shore, 2012); the importance of moving away from universalist descriptions of governance to understanding regional variations through empirical research (Parker, 2007; Yi et al, 2018); the necessity of engaging citizens to understand, through their eyes, how they perceive the state (Scott, 1999; Wilson, 2019; Leeds, 2020; Levenson, 2021); the multiple levels of governance as it is networked across scales and spaces into people's lives (Biehl, 2007; Sum, 2008); and the porosity of governance structures and the networks through which governmentality operates (Ferguson, 2002; Nadesan, 2010; Ferlie et al, 2012).

Moving beyond conceptualizing governmentality as disciplining techniques that act on the bodies of individuals (anatomopolitics) and populations (biopolitics), as described earlier, shifts in science and technology have also engendered new forms of citizenship as people 'act up'. This book considers citizenship in its most quotidian sense as it is embodied in everyday life. As such, it explores the multiple and mutable subjectivities that women strategically bring forward in different spaces (see Nyamjoh, 2007; Cornwall et al, 2011; Dziuban and Sekuler, 2021) as they 'act up' and on the global assemblage into which their vitality is woven. These dynamics are articulated through the ethnographic accounts presented in Chapters 3 and 4, with a particular focus on different forms of citizenship that centre on everyday life in South Africa (Chapter 5) and Brazil (Chapter 6). This focus moves out in scale in Chapter 7 to trace some of the international economic and political relationships and institutions that give shape to this global assemblage and govern whether or not countries in the Global South can produce, distribute and procure affordable medicines for their citizens.

Medical anthropologists have introduced a slew of theoretical approaches to citizenship, initially articulated by Adriana Petryna (2013) in their conceptualization of biological citizenship. Biological notions of citizenship draw on and extend Foucault's theorization of biopolitics and the networks that link governments and citizens around biological identifications (Young et al, 2019), technology (Dumbrava, 2017) and responses to risk (Petryna, 2004, 2010). Importantly, theories of biological citizenship extend the scope and space of engagement from the nation-state to transnational practices and networks of governance. However, in line with the poststructuralist approach to citizenship as a reflection of multiple and overlapping subjectivities, biological citizenship has been criticized for focusing on a narrow conception of identity linked to a single biological condition. Based on their own research around HIV and access to medical treatment in Burkina Faso, Vinh-Kim Nguyen (2008) developed a theory of therapeutic citizenship which expands on biological citizenship by considering the range of identities and coalitions that form around particular illnesses and treatments. This concept points to the growing transnational influence of biomedical knowledge and practice across transnational networks connecting human and nonhuman actors. Theories of biological and therapeutic citizenship, however, do not fully engage with the multiple identities that individuals may hold beyond 'biological' predicaments and corresponding therapeutic interventions. Further, neither set of theories considers the embodied dimensions of subjectivity that may inform multiple and intersecting citizen practices beyond shared predicaments and therapeutic interventions.

Although I engage with these medical anthropological conceptions of citizenship, my fieldwork emphasized the importance of understanding 'everyday citizenship' as it is lived and embodied in the most quotidian sense (Robins et al, 2008; Cornwall et al, 2011; Puumala and Maïche, 2021). The notion of 'everyday citizenship' speaks to Cornwall et al's (2011) call for a more nuanced understanding of particular contexts, or states, of citizenship as they unfold across time and in very different spaces: 'Rather than seeking a unified definition of citizenship that covers all dimensions of human action, entitlement and belonging, we are interested in the everyday, and often highly contingent and improvisational, negotiations and performances through which people define and pursue their desires and aspirations' (2011: 8). Two pertinent imaginaries – how citizens see the state (Corbridge, 2005) and how states see citizens (Scott, 1999) – generate the 'mutually constitutive nature of the citizen–state relationship, and the extent to which different kinds of states make different kinds of citizenship possible' (Cornwall et al, 2011: 7).

The book builds on these sets of theories in conjunction with the notion of biopolitical precarity to foster a deeper understanding of citizenship and governance as it is embodied by women living with HIV. Throughout my fieldwork, I have integrated visual methodologies to build a fuller understanding of how people 'see' and 'hear' the state in their everyday life. Building on this research, this book proposes, specifically in Chapter 5, that by moving away from a governmentality approach that considers how the state exerts control in and through the bodies of people and the broader population, it can become possible to explore how people themselves conceptualize and strategically navigate their relationship with a dynamic state.

The importance of understanding the state through the embodied experiences of people reflects a broader theoretical shift in research around gender and governance, an approach advocated by scholars advancing Southern Theory. The move to decentre theory from the academy and from the Global North reflects the work of decolonial scholars, and particularly scholars like Robert Morrell (2016), Pallavi Banerjee (2018), Rebecca Hodes (2018) and Raewyn Connell (2020), who have collectively advanced theory – specifically as it relates to gender – from the Global South. As Debbie Epstein and Raewyn Connell suggest:

> Southern theory does not exist simply to be picked up and adopted or showcased. It is a challenge, something that needs to be developed; and it is something that has been, is being and will be developed by scholars who are mindful not only of existing gender and geopolitical

inequalities but also of the skewed shape of academic publishing. It is a project that is an integral part of campaigns for democracy and social justice though it invites fresh, and possibly iconoclastic, approaches to old problems. (2012: 472)

Bearing in mind the call to generate fresh approaches to old problems and to understand geopolitical inequalities – like unequal access to essential HIV medicines – through theory that centres people's experiences and decentres expertise from the Global North, and particularly academies in the Global North, the chapters that follow engage with a range of methods that bring people's voices and experiences into the foreground. This necessitates a re-thinking of historical, and predominantly Northern, approaches to understanding citizenship and governance. To this end, this book refers to the state with an understanding that shifting governments animate state institutions – like the health care infrastructure – through policies that, in turn, have embodied ramifications in very specific contexts that, in the case of South Africa, Brazil and India, are postcolonial.

This approach to thinking about governance and citizenship in postcolonial contexts requires a recognition of temporality and the spectres of oppressive histories and actors – like the apartheid state, in the case of South Africa, or the authoritarian state in Brazil – as they play a role in how people conceptualize and advocate for health as a democratic right. This recognition is threaded through each chapter in this book and engages with scholarship by political anthropologists who call for decolonial approaches to understanding governance and citizenship. For example, in their ethnographic and theoretical contributions, scholars like Artwell Nhemachena (2016), Cris Shore (2012), Andrea Cornwall (2020), Winnifred Tate (2020), Jairo Fúnez-Flores (2022) and César Abadía-Barrero (2022), call for closer attention to be paid to the trajectories of citizenship experience across time and place in the Global South. Building on Southern Theory and the work of these scholars, broadly in the field of the anthropology of policy, the chapters that follow consider how people engage with different subject positions over time to pursue particular (and shifting) socio-economic and political ends. Further, as discussed in the following section, not only is the state affected by its history, as held in people's embodied memory and its institutions, but it is also networked into a regional and global set of actors, and this speaks to Southern Theory's concern to foreground geopolitical inequalities from the perspective of the Global South.

Global assemblages and actor networks

As discussed previously, this book builds an argument that precarity is networked into the permeable body. In doing so, it calls attention to the porosity of boundaries and the extent to which we need to work against binaries that reify and separate states from citizens, technologies from bodies, nature from culture, the past from the present. In making this argument, I engage with two principal concepts – assemblages and actor networks – across each chapter of the book. This section therefore presents this core set of theories, as they are central to the overarching argument and enable me to trace the networked threads that draw the global actors into an assemblage that is networked into the permeable body.

As discussed, globalization and technological developments have prompted a re-thinking of governance in which we recognize that the contemporary 'body of the state' is far less 'sovereign' and far more porous than it was – ontologically and epistemologically – in the time of Arendt's (1958), Weber's (1984) and Foucault's (1998) theorizing. Scholarship from around the world, and particularly the Global South (Grugel and Uhlin, 2012; Purkayastha, 2021), has since revealed that not only are the state and citizen porously implicated in each other's vitality but their own lives form part of a much larger assemblage. The term 'global assemblage' was coined by Ong and Collier (2008) to capture this dynamic and has been used to reflect on the conflicts and controversies of globalization, as changes in technologies, bodies and governments precipitated and were precipitated by global–local transformations. This conceptualization of assemblages has been drawn on across numerous fields, including medical anthropology, as I discuss in the following section. It has also been applied by scholars working in the field of climate change, which resonates with the approach taken in this book, where intimate lives are framed as strongly shaped by transnational and global politics and processes around environmental degradation. Nathalie Seddon, Nick Fox and Pam Alldred, for example, have integrated Southern Theory with the concept of global assemblages to show how individual lives are enmeshed with national and global policies and processes that, as we see with the current COP27 negotiations on climate disaster funds, fail to adequately address the climate crisis and place the burden of responding to the crisis on those states and people who are least resourced and most directly impacted (Fox and Alldred, 2020a, 2020b; Seddon et al, 2021).

As a concept, 'global assemblages' is a particularly useful tool for challenging narrow approaches of citizenship that centre on a particular identity (or biological condition) and protected set of entitlements based on membership of a nation-state. Instead, global assemblages reflect how 'practice, entitlement and benefits are realized through specific mobilizations and claims in milieus of globalized contingencies. The movements of global markets, technologies and populations interact to shape novel spaces of political mobilization and claims' (Ong, 2005: 697). In this book, and particularly in Chapters 5, 6 and 7 on the political dimension of my research, I explore how the state's capacity to provide life-giving biomedicine is contingent on an assemblage of actors spanning global coalitions, regional alliances, financial markets, national and provincial health institutions, health care practitioners, pharmaceutical dispensaries, transport networks and so on. I propose that when biomedicine moves through these channels from the global sphere to the national repertoire of public health policy and resources, then individual lives are not only a function of sovereign will but also part of a global assemblage. I therefore use the term 'global assemblage' to denote this heterogeneous collection of actors that assemble around HIV medicine and its technological possibilities for life in an era where the vitality of individual bodies reflects and implicates a network of global, national, local and molecular actors.

While the concept of 'global assemblages' is helpful, it is also limited. As Peck et al (2010) argue, it is not enough to simply look at the nature of assemblages. We also need to understand the factors that generate assemblages and, in turn, how these assemblages affect people's lives. In their work on the Sowa Rigpa (also known as Tibetan Medicine) industry, Stephan Kloos (2020) offers the concept of the 'pharmaceutical assemblage' to address the historically narrow focus on biomedicine in research on the connections that link health and subjectivity to contemporary forms of medical markets, governance and science. Increasingly, and often with reference to ethnographic studies of precarity during the height of the COVID-19 pandemic, anthropologists like Kloos have worked with Actor Network Theory (ANT) to understand but also 'interfere in' the nature of global assemblages (Ashman et al, 2022).

Actor networks reflect a complex cosmology that includes human and nonhuman actants that: according to the principle of irreduction, cannot be reduced to any other; according to the principle of translation, are linked to each other through the work of mediation; and finally, according to the principle of alliance, do not have an inherent strength but which gain strength through their alliances within more or less durable networks (Latour, 1988). Although ANT is often discussed in abstract terms, even referred to as a theory, it is in fact grounded in the materiality of our everyday lives. As Law writes: 'Theories usually try to explain why something happens, but actor network theory is descriptive rather than foundational in explanatory terms, which means that it is a disappointment for those seeking strong accounts. Instead it tells stories about "how" relations assemble or don't' (2009: 141). I find ANT useful as a way of thinking through the kinds of people, institutions, viruses and technologies (among others) that came together and affected each other's vitality in my fieldwork.

This approach follows scholars also working across medical anthropology and science and technology studies, who have, for instance, used ANT to explore the implications of approaching the virus (McAlister, 2021) as well as phylogenetic HIV tests (Sandset, 2020) and pre-exposure prophylaxis (PrEP) (Michael and Rosengarten, 2012) as actants traversing social, political and biological networks. Michael and Rosengarten, for example, consider two case studies – of the AIDS Clock and accounts of randomized control trials (RCTs) – and explore how their 'global reach weaves into various local contingencies, particularly localizing critiques that emphasize the conditions of infection and death, and local political protest against the clinical trials' (2012: 95). In the same way that I hope to show the linkages between actors that assemble under the skin, out into the national, regional and global policy arena, and then back under the skin, these authors argue that 'there are topological interconnections among these globalizing and localizing enactments … [W]e see how the globalizing of both the AIDS Clock and RCTs/ethics is localized in various ways, but also how such localization draws on ostensibly globalizing resources' (2012: 95, 102).

In the following chapters, I similarly trace the threads weaving HIV and ARVs, as nonhuman actants, between the local and the global and argue that, as nonhuman actants, they cannot be separated from the institutions, bodies, ethics, economics and politics that coalesce around the hope for life and the threat of death.

I draw the two facets of my research focus – the political and the embodied – together by tracing the routes that actants (HIV and ARVs) travel into women's bodies, and by tracing the threads linking these actants into an assemblage of social relationships, health care systems and practices, national governments, regional economic coalitions and global trade agreements. Assemblages and actor networks are not only conceptually useful; they are also politically important: in using them together, they work against isolating politics from the body and offer a set of tools to think usefully about the ways that actants and actors across scale, from the global to the molecular, are networked into an assemblage around the biopolitics of life. In doing so, I seek to trace the threads that draw these actors into a network, and to show how they are woven into women's vitality. Ultimately, these theories speak of connection and against the discursive construction of distance that relies on reified entities held separate through their pairing in dichotomies. If we think about bodies, governments and technologies as related and porous, then it is harder not to face each other and hold actors accountable for actions that ricochet across this assemblage and permeate people's bodies and their lives.

Biopolitical precarity in the permeable body

If global assemblages show that entwined threads weave life from the global arena into and out of the permeable body, and actor networks describe how these threads come to be connected, we are still left with the issue of women's embodied precarity, as their vitality is, in varying degrees, contingent on this assemblage. In this sense, the argument in this book moves from Foucault's

(2008) assertion that the vitality of the state and the vitality of the body are tied together in a biopolitical contract to suggest that the body of the state and the state of the body are part of a transcendent assemblage that they are only partially able to negotiate. I explore this tension through the concept of biopolitical precarity.

Biopolitical precarity denotes the intersection of the embodied and the political facets of the research I discuss in the following chapters and foregrounds the book's overarching argument that biopolitics – with a focus on HIV medicine – is shaped through an assemblage of actors networked into the permeable body in ways that implicate precarious life. Precarity designates

> that politically induced condition in which certain populations suffer from failing social and economic networks of support and become differentially exposed to injury, violence, and death. Such populations are at heightened risk of disease, poverty, starvation, displacement, and of exposure to violence without protection. Precarity also characterizes that politically induced condition of maximized vulnerability and exposure for populations exposed to arbitrary state violence and to other forms of aggression that are not enacted by states and against which states do not offer adequate protection. (Butler, 2009: 2)

Ethnographies in the 'age of treatment' from South Africa (Le Marcis, 2012; Pienaar, 2016b), Mozambique (Chapman, 2021; Kalofonos, 2021) and Kenya (Bosire et al, 2018; Copeland, 2018; Musyoki et al, 2021) similarly reflect the importance of integrating an understanding of inequality when looking at access to essential HIV medicines and the broader politics of life in which this access is enabled or constrained. Reflecting on these ethnographies in the earlier discussion on embodiment, I indicated that when I use the term precarity, I am referring to the extent to which people embody multiple and intersecting inequalities as they manage precarious employment, as they navigate live electricity lines underfoot, as they use unlit toilets in the middle of the night. Further, by integrating biopolitics with precarity, I suggest that we draw political actors into view and understand how their actions, within this assemblage, affect people's ability to access newer biomedical technologies for themselves, affordable education for their children and safe water and electricity for their households. In doing so, I argue that the context in which people live their lives on ARVs – as they take their medicines with or without food, as they remember to step over live electricity lines or are forced to use unlit toilets and risk rape – becomes embodied as forms of biopolitical precarity.

Therefore, I argue that HIV-positive women's lives are woven into a biopolitical assemblage that makes it more or less possible for them to be able to secure their own vitality. The dynamics of this assemblage generate particular sources of vulnerability for women that are embodied and experienced, for example, through side effects from old generation medicines or through the limits placed on life by limiting treatment possibilities in the public sector to older, less effective medicines that are unable to outwit HIV's resistant strains. However, and in line with recent reflections (including my own) on the usefulness of the notion of 'vulnerability' in anthropology and in the field of global health (Han, 2018; Mills, 2018, 2019; Marino and Faas, 2020), I suggest this term is conceptually limited and politically dangerous: there is a risk that using it emphasizes an individual's relative lack of agency, and in doing so it fails to bring attention to potent geopolitical inequalities that intervene in people's capacity to live their life with greater degrees of agency. With this critique in mind, I use the term 'biopolitical precarity' with reference to Judith Butler's 'precarious life' (2012) to denote the intra-action of actants that shape and are shaped by women's embodied experience of precarity in a biopolitical network that is threaded into the permeable body.

Further, in recognition of the limitations of binary thinking in development discourse that positions women as either having agency or being vulnerable, I draw on the notion of performativity to explore how individuals embody, reproduce and subvert discourse through particular sets of strategies and tactics, with reference, too, to de Certeau (1984). In particular, I use the concept of posthumanist performativity as

> one that incorporates important material and discursive, social and scientific, human and nonhuman, and natural and cultural factors. A posthumanist account calls into question the givenness of the differential categories of 'human' and 'nonhuman,' examining the practices through which these differential boundaries are stabilized and destabilized. (Barad, 2003: 808)

Further, this book integrates performativity, and posthumanist performativity in particular, with ANT through the concept of intra-action (Barad, 2008: 174). Through this concept, I explore how bodies become the meeting place for HIV and HIV medicines, or nonhuman actants in Latour's terms (2005): HIV medicines, for example, disrupt distinctions or causal connections between the body they animate and the life they take on through this animation. As such, '[d]iscursive practices and material phenomena do not stand in a relationship of externality to one another; rather the material and the discursive are mutually implicated in the dynamics of intra-activity' (Barad, 2008: 174). I use 'intra-action' in place of 'interaction' as the latter reflects the Newtonian legacy in which 'things', or actants, are constructed as determinant, stable, prior-existing and bounded (Barad, 2003). Intra-action, instead, reflects Donna Haraway's (2006, 2013) call for a material-semiotics that transcends (by connecting) the materiality of things – like medicines, bodies, viruses – and the discourses that shape them – like beliefs around health or practices of self-care, for example.

Contexts

It is important to state upfront that this book is not a comparative study of the politics of HIV medicine in India, Brazil and South Africa. It is an unusual hybrid of ethnographic research and policy analysis that is grounded in long-term research in South Africa, shorter-term research in Brazil and policy analysis that includes a critique of international intellectual property law and India's legislative approaches to navigating this law through its own national legislation around patents and its pharmaceutical industry. Further, I cannot and do not seek to offer a comparative perspective on South Africa's and Brazil's relative approaches to accessing HIV medicines across almost three decades since ARVs first became available. Instead, I bring these three countries into dialogue with one another in a very specific way to foreground the scale through which policy functions and activism operates to impact who can and cannot access affordable HIV treatment.

In this section, I provide a synopsis of each of the country's profiles around HIV policy and current and historical trends in HIV transmission and treatment. The contextual summaries that follow provide a foundation to the discussion that unfolds in the following five chapters, but they should not be read as indicative of the relative weight of the analysis across the book. These summaries are necessarily brief, given that the first chapter introduces South Africa's and Brazil's history in more detail, and these histories are picked up, brought into the present and threaded into the following substantive chapters with a focus on South Africa in Chapters 3, 4 and 5 and a focus on Brazil and South Africa in Chapter 6. Chapter 7 moves out in scale to look at global policy on intellectual property rights (IPRs) and situates the struggles around access to affordable medicines in light of India's own legislation and role in providing almost 90 per cent of HIV treatment in the Global South.

South Africa

South Africa's response to HIV is currently guided by the fifth National Strategic Plan (2023–28 NSP), an ambitious five-year plan that is articulated around four strategic goals: breaking down barriers to achieving outcomes for HIV, tuberculosis (TB) and STIs; maximizing equitable and equal access to services and solutions for HIV, TB and STIs; building resilient systems for HIV, TB and STIs that are integrated into systems for health, social protection and pandemic response; and fully resourcing and sustaining an efficient NSP led by revitalized, inclusive and accountable institutions (SANAC, 2023).

In contrast with the first two NSPs (Wouters et al, 2010), the current and previous NSP have had the backing of significant resources and, importantly, political will (Simbayi et al, 2019; Myburgh et al, 2023). In the short section that follows, I articulate the current nature of South Africa's HIV epidemic with a focus on HIV prevalence, transmission and treatment. These statistics paint a limited picture but offer important context to situate the long-term ethnographic accounts of living with HIV and accessing HIV treatment in the chapters that follow.

In 2022, 7.6 million people lived with HIV in South Africa, representing a prevalence of 12.7 per cent in a country with a population of around 62 million people (HSRC, 2023; Johnson and Dorrington, 2023). Of those living with HIV, the prevalence among women (aged 15–49) is significantly higher (23.5 per cent) than among men (12.1 per cent) (UNAIDS, 2022a). Women aged 35 to 39 years have a significantly higher prevalence (39.4 per cent) compared to men of the same age (23.7 per cent) (Mabaso et al, 2019; Simbayi et al, 2019; Palanee-Phillips et al, 2022). As I discuss in the following chapter, the higher prevalence among women is often linked to the high rates of sexual violence, with around one third of all women likely to experience intimate partner violence in South Africa (Simbayi et al, 2019). Younger women and girls are especially vulnerable to HIV infection, in part because of the prevalence of cross-generational relationships with older men and the consequent discrepancies in agency around negotiating safer sex (Harrison et al, 2015). There is a plethora of research on the interlinked 'epidemics' of HIV infection and sexual and gender-based violence, often speaking to women's interlocking social, biological and economic vulnerabilities to HIV infection (Madiba and Ngwenya, 2017; Mabaso et al, 2019). While addressing gender inequality should be a central component in any measure to address HIV infection in South Africa, the chapter that follows speaks to the importance of an approach that holds institutions and individuals more fully accountable for their role in perpetuating structural and sexual violence.

In addition to cisgender women, transgender individuals also carry a disproportionately high burden of HIV. The factors underpinning higher prevalence are varied, often linked to fear of discrimination, and speak to the pervasive stigma faced by transgender individuals within South Africa generally, and within the public health system specifically (Brown et al, 2023; Cloete et al, 2023; Van der Merwe et al, 2023). Sexual practices that are highly stigmatized, including sex between cisgender men, also account for higher rates of HIV transmission; this is also a consequence of the social stigma and fear of discrimination that deter men who have sex with men from accessing health care resources (Duby et al, 2018). In addition to variance between genders, HIV infection rates vary significantly across different geographic regions, with high prevalence rates in eastern regions. These higher rates have been attributed to a number of factors, including significantly fewer health care providers compared to the western and northern parts of the country (Mabaso et al, 2019).

In addition to the distinction of having the highest number of people living with HIV in the world, South Africa also has the world's largest HIV treatment programme (UNAIDS, 2022c). Stretching back in time, to 2010, the successful HIV treatment programme would have been hard to envision as the country emerged from a decade of high-level government denialism of HIV science and a stringent refusal to scale up essential HIV treatment (Simelela et al, 2015; Pillay-van Wyk et al, 2019). South Africa has signed up to work towards the latest UNAID's 95–95–95 global targets in which 95 per cent of people with HIV will know their status, 95 per cent of people with HIV who know their status will be on treatment and 95 per cent of people with HIV on treatment will be virally suppressed (UNAIDS, 2022c). In 2022, 94.5 per cent of people with HIV know their status in South Africa. Of this cohort, 90 per cent are accessing HIV treatment (representing 77.4 per cent of all people living with HIV), and of this cohort, 91.5 per cent have suppressed viral loads (representing 66 per cent of all people living with HIV) (Johnson and Dorrington, 2023). Currently, people are encouraged to start taking HIV treatment as soon as they test positive, with over 5.7 million adults (over the age of 15) receiving treatment in 2022 (UNAIDS, 2022a). This current treatment regimen (dolutegravir-containing fixed dose combination) was changed in 2017 and has been shown to have fewer side effects and higher rates of adherence (Vagiri et al, 2018; Vreeman et al, 2019).

Brazil

Like South Africa, Brazil is classified as a middle-income country. Both countries fall under the World Bank's categorisation of low- and middle-income countries (LMIC). However, unlike South Africa and many other LMICs, Brazil has an unusual track record of proactively managing HIV from the 1990s. The country's policy response over this time has included setting up a universal and free public health system (Sistema Único de Saúde [SUS]), investing in the development of generic HIV medicines through the country's pharmaceutical industry and working with the powerful mechanism of compulsory licensing to keep these medicines affordable (Benzaken et al, 2019). In line with the previous section on South Africa, I articulate the current nature of Brazil's HIV epidemic with a focus on HIV prevalence, transmission and treatment. This contextual overview is extended in detail in Chapter 6, where I introduce a series of actors who have played a role in reconfiguring global and national HIV treatment policies, including Brazilian activists who have a long history of mobilizing the government for access to emerging medical technologies.

Covering almost half of Latin America, Brazil is the fifth largest country in the world and has a population of 217 million people. Following the identification of the first HIV case in 1982, over 900,000 cases had been identified by 2018, with significantly higher rates of infection among cisgender men (559,000) compared to women (307,000) (Brasil, 2018). Like South Africa, stigma plays a significant role in shaping whether or not marginalized individuals are able to access critical health services and resources, including condoms, PrEP and ARVs. Research on HIV transmission in Brazil finds that cisgender men who have sex with men, sex workers and transgender individuals experience the greatest degree of discrimination and also have significantly higher rates of HIV prevalence compared to the general population. For example, a national survey conducted in 2016 with men who have sex with men found HIV prevalence to be significantly higher (18.4 per cent) than the prevalence in the general population at the time (0.5 per cent) (Kerr et al, 2018). Fear of discrimination has been found to deter people from testing for HIV and accessing HIV treatment, and it accounts for higher levels of transmission among a range of population groups. For instance, research has found that fear of discrimination from health workers has deterred sex workers (Murray et al, 2019), male soldiers (Figueiredo Catelan et al, 2022), transgender and gender diverse people (Costa et al, 2018) and men who have sex with men (Kerr et al, 2018) from accessing HIV treatments.

The role of discrimination in deterring access to vital HIV resources, and therefore driving HIV transmission among marginalized groups, comes into focus when looking at national prevalence. Across Brazil, HIV prevalence has been consistently low (0.6 per cent or below) since HIV was first recorded in 1982 (Brasil, 2018). One of the key reasons for maintaining a low prevalence across the general population has been the country's historic commitment to providing free ARVs through its public health system (SUS). SUS is an outcome of powerful civil society mobilization that followed two decades of dictatorship and was formalized in Brazil's 1988 constitution (Paiva and Teixeira, 2014). A number of shifts took place in Brazil, both ideologically and institutionally, at the end of the country's dictatorship: for many activists, creating an efficient and effective health system was one of the most powerful ways of overthrowing the dictatorship, and this approach was taken up in the constitutional affirmation of health as an individual right for all (Nunn et al, 2012; Montenegro et al, 2020).

Looking further back in Brazil's history, the shift to preventative medicine in the 1950s and the establishment of various influential health centres in the 1970s (like the Brazilian Centre for Health Studies/Centro Brasileiro de Estudos de Saúde [Cebes]) prompted a recognition by left-leaning health professionals and activists that provision of preventative health care was critical for improving health overall, and for reducing expenditure on preventable illnesses (Paiva and Teixeira, 2014). In the late 1980s, as the country entered democracy, the shortage of staff with the requisite scientific and technical skills in SUS created an opportunity to bring in medical professionals that had the skills required and also the visionary and often left-leaning thinking to drive progressive change from within the health system and government itself (Montenegro et al, 2020; Biehl, 2021; Waisbich et al, 2022).

Together, these factors may account for Brazil's pioneering decision, in 1996, to provide ARVs to all citizens who needed them. This programme has been lauded for bringing Brazil's HIV epidemic to a halt: at the start of the 1990s, South Africa's and Brazil's epidemics had a similar profile, with less than 1 per cent of the population (15 – 49) living with HIV (Nunn et al, 2012). By 1995, South Africa's HIV prevalence had reached 10 per cent, whereas the infection rate in Brazil had halved (Iqbal, 2009). The visionary work of Brazil's SUS, including the provision of ARVs and the expansion of prevention programmes, occurred in parallel with cross-continental neoliberal shifts towards a minimalist state (Biehl, 2004, 2021). As I discuss in more detail in Chapter 6, the implementation of a radical and visionary health system that could traverse an enormous country with high levels of socio-economic inequality was fundamentally constrained by a powerful trend towards neoliberalism. In 2022, prior to the November elections, this was potently represented by the country's former President Jair Bolsonaro, who worked, at every turn, to strip back the state. His actions, described by scholars as 'neoliberalism unchained' (Stewart et al, 2021), have led to rocketing inequality and have profoundly undermined or legally reversed hard-won rights for the environment, for women and for LGBTQIA+ people (Iamamoto et al, 2021; Gomes and Tanscheit, 2022).

India

India shares a complex history with South Africa and Brazil around securing access to essential medicines, including HIV medicines. While Brazil outpaced South Africa and India with its proactive provision of ARVs to HIV-positive citizens in 1996, India and South Africa both played important and distinctive roles in ensuring that HIV medicines could be accessed by those who needed them, including those living in the Global South (Iqbal, 2009; Eimer and Lütz, 2010). South Africa, along with Brazil and other countries like Thailand, worked at a legal level to challenge patent legislation that governed the production and distribution of HIV medicines. And India, with its powerful pharmaceutical industry, worked to ensure that generic medicines could be produced and distributed to the Global South at an affordable price (Plahe and McArthur, 2021). These three countries, and the different tools they used to challenge restrictive IPRs and international trade law, form the focus of Chapter 7. This section briefly outlines India's own history of HIV prevalence, transmission and treatment and concludes with a focus on the country's political and economic evolution, leading to the creation of its unique pharmaceutical industry.

The latest available data, drawn from India's National AIDS Control Organization, suggest that 2.3 million people live with HIV in India. The number of new infections has decreased by 46.3 per cent between 2010 and 2021, with a prevalence (15–49 years) of 0.21 per cent in 2021 (India, 2021). India's legal landscape has shifted dramatically with the Indian Supreme Court recognizing transgender people as a distinct gender (in 2014) and decriminalizing homosexuality (in 2018). The framing of these rights-based advances has come under strong critique (Boyce and Dasgupta, 2019), and high levels of stigma and marginalization of transgender people, gay men and men who have sex with men are widespread and powerfully undermine any efforts to ensure universal access to HIV prevention and treatment (Bhattacharya, 2019). Despite some level of recognition of the rights of these marginalized groups, since 2014 the Modi government has fostered populism, increasingly stifled opposition and constrained the work of civil society organizations (Joshi, 2021). The Modi government has come under significant scrutiny for its human rights violations against activists, religious minorities and other groups (Werleman, 2021). In addition, political support for HIV prevention programmes has been significantly reduced by the Modi government. In 2015, the government reduced central AIDs funding by 22 per cent and told individual states to provide additional contributions. This led to funding gaps at the state level, as a result of which many states resorted to laying off staff and withholding pay (Kalra and Siddiqui, 2015). So, while India has maintained a low HIV prevalence rate and seen a decrease in the number of new HIV infections, a number of challenges have emerged in the last decade to counter these successes at a national level.

At a global level, India's ability to reverse engineer active ingredients has earned it the title of 'pharmacy of the Global South': India is the largest supplier of ARV medicines in the world, providing almost 90 per cent of all donor-funded ARVs to LMICs (Löfgren, 2017; Plahe and McArthur, 2021). The technological capacity to identify and reverse engineer active ingredients relates to the Indian government's legislative infrastructure, which has historically protected its domestic pharmaceutical market (Löfgren, 2017). India's government actively encouraged the growth of the domestic pharmaceutical industry from the 1960s, as legislated with the Patents Act in 1970 (which removed composition, but not process, patents from food and drugs). The absence of patent protection in India deterred international companies from entering its market and enabled Indian companies to carve a niche in the national and international market through its expertise in reverse engineering. Significantly, through competition, India's production of generic HIV medicines has driven down the price of brand name medicines (Bor, 2007; Waning et al, 2010; Jayaraman, 2013; Wouters et al, 2013; Horner, 2014; Plahe and McArthur, 2021). It is through competition stemming from Indian generics that the cost of first-line HIV medicines has dropped from more than US\$10,000 per person per year in 2000 to around US\$95 per person per year in 2022 (Mattur and Habiyambere, 2022).

Methods

In Chapter 1, I described how the shifting biomedical and political landscapes informed the rationale underpinning the political and embodied dimensions of my activism and research over the last 20 years. Together, these shifting landscapes not only prompted me to look into South Africa with 'fresh eyes' but also prompted me to 'look out' from South Africa to countries like Brazil and India as it became apparent that the lives of the people I worked with were networked into a global landscape where bodies and governments are porous, and where essential HIV medicines move, or are blocked from moving, across their borders. The concepts discussed earlier explored, in turn, the sets of literature that reflect on the interface between the state of the body and the body of the state as they are drawn, porously, in each other's vitality while also being precariously networked into a global assemblage that they were only partially able to navigate. My ethnography builds on this rationale and conceptual framework and was an active search first to identify and then to find ways to get to know the key actors that were networked into this global assemblage. In this section, I trace the ethnographic journey I undertook in this search to find and form relationships with actors in this assemblage.

Research design

This book is based on multi-sited ethnographic research and encompasses a range of visual and participatory methods developed in conjunction with the people with whom I have worked across time and in different places. My engagement in policy, activism and research in South Africa traverses two decades: the research on which most of this book is based (and which I discuss in detail subsequently) took place in the second decade, from 2010 to 2023, although I do refer back to earlier ethnographic research that I conducted from 2003 to 2009. In this first decade of research, I held different roles, as discussed in Chapter 1, and my research built on both qualitative and quantitative methods. As an undergraduate student at the University of Cape Town (UCT), I conducted ethnographic research with a home-based care organization in Nyanga, Cape Town, and I built on this research – and continued to work with this organization – over two years in my capacity as a researcher at the UCT's AIDS and Society Research Unit (ASRU).

During this time at ASRU (2004–5), I also worked on the first panel survey of its kind to track the relationship between income status, employment and access to HIV medicines among people living with HIV in Khayelitsha (Coetzee and Nattrass, 2004; de Paoli et al, 2010). From 2006, as Deputy Director of ASRU, I conducted further qualitative research around gender, stigma and HIV while also overseeing the survey and convening a policy advisory panel for the Deputy Minister of Health in conjunction with the Treatment Action Campaign (TAC). From 2009, I have conducted research in different capacities – as a doctoral student, Research Fellow and Senior Lecturer – based in the Institute of Development Studies (2009–16) and the University of Sussex (2016 to the present). It is this period of research, from 2010 when I commenced my doctoral fieldwork up to 2023 when I completed the first stage of fieldwork as part of a two-year project looking at the intersections of HIV and COVID-19, that forms the basis of this book and that I discuss in detail in the paragraphs that follow.

The research methodology that guided my fieldwork from 2010 was informed by the first decade of my work in South Africa and built on my doctoral research: the methodology was, and continues to be, designed around the two research dimensions outlined in Chapter 1 that seek to understand the connection between embodied experiences of illness and health and how this influences people's perception of and engagement with the state. Through my fieldwork in South Africa after 2010, in what Moyer (2015) describes as the 'age of treatment', I researched women's embodied experience of HIV medicine and their political engagement with the state, and through my fieldwork in Brazil, I located my findings on women's embodied experiences of precarity in South Africa within a matrix of networks that moved between the molecular and the global. Therefore, in this book, 'multi-sited' refers to the approach I took in my fieldwork to work across scale, from the local to the global, with women living in Khayelitsha, the activist organization they had worked with, the actors and activists in Brazil to whom South Africa had looked during the struggle for ARVs, and the national and international policy actors who made decisions about these women's ability to access medicines that would enable them to live a long life.

I describe this approach to ethnography as 'connective' because it sought to identify how and which actors and actants were connected in women's embodied vitality linked to HIV medicine. While I have worked with a wide range of different participants over the course of my research career, I have identified five primary sets of actors who have informed the shape of this book. I have delineated these actors into five groups for the purpose of clarity; however, these groups are interconnected, as reflected in the ethnographic and analytical chapters and overarching argument.

The first dimension of my research focus, namely the embodied ramifications of HIV medicine, was explored through ethnographic research located primarily in Khayelitsha, South Africa. From 2010 and into the present, my research has spanned all five groups of actors. I introduce them here briefly and in more detail later on. First, I conducted ethnographic research with a core group of ten women who had been HIV activists, were on ARVs and who were living in Khayelitsha. I worked most closely with this group, and their lives are the foundation of this book. Second, I conducted narrative interviews with members of the Bambanani Women's Group (BWG); this group of men and women were on ARVs, had also been HIV activists and had developed body maps tracing the effects of HIV and ARVs in their bodies. My fieldwork with these groups of people, and with their families and friends, strongly informed the findings that connect to the first dimension of my research. As such, the first three ethnographic chapters centre primarily on their lives as I trace the pathways through which HIV came to enter their bodies, their evolving relationship with the government as citizens calling for the public provision of ARVs, and more recently, for a broader set of conditions to support life beyond access to these medicines.

The second dimension of my research focus, namely women's political engagement with the state around HIV medicine, was explored through participant observation with all five groups of actors. In addition to working with the two related groups of men and women who were on ARVs and who had been activists with TAC, I have conducted research with a further three groups who provided insight into the political dimension of my research focus; I discuss the specific details on sampling, access and methods in the following section. The third research group comprised 40 men and women who were on ARVs but who had not necessarily engaged as activists around HIV medicine. By conducting narrative interviews with this group, I sought to work also with both men and women and with activists and non-activists in order to understand whether the struggle to access HIV medicine may or may not have shaped the way people perceived and engaged with the state. The fourth set of actors were networked around TAC, the organization through which all those in the core group and in the BWG had engaged as activists. I conducted participant observation with TAC, principally as a researcher and writer for their *Equal Treatment* (ET) magazine. Over time, I observed how TAC was networked into a set of local, national and international activist organizations. I therefore also conducted fieldwork with the primary activist organizations that were linked to TAC in South Africa, including MSF, Section 27 and the Community Media Trust, along with numerous new activist organizations that have spun out of TAC to address the conditions of life for all people, and not only the essential biomedical requirements to support life. Finally, I conducted 20 key informant interviews with activists, academics and policy makers in South Africa and Brazil in order to trace some of the policy dialogues taking place across the two countries, and more broadly in relation to the global governance of HIV medicines.

Multi-sited ethnographic research

[E]thnographic engagement can help us chart some of the complex and often contradictory ways in which neoliberalizing health structures, moral economy, and biology are forged in local worlds where biotechnology and structural violence now exist side-by-side. (Biehl, 2004: 125)

The focus of my research centred on women's experiences of HIV medicine, but it also explored how their lives were influenced by actors across a network that moves between the global and the molecular. This focus, therefore, underlined the value of engaging in research that looks at interconnections, rather than discrete actors or sites, through multi-sited ethnographic research.

The value of multi-sited ethnographic research for tracing the global–local, and even molecular, routes that medicines travel into people's bodies and lives has been well established by anthropologists whose methodological and conceptual approaches have guided my work over the years (Nguyen, 2011; Le Marcis, 2012; Marsland and Prince, 2012; Brotherton and Nguyen, 2013; Persson et al, 2016; Yates-Doerr, 2017; Chapman, 2021). These ethnographies largely reflect one of two prevailing approaches to the formation of identity and subjectivity in relation to health. The first approach relates to a concern with biopower and subjectivity and emerges from the work of ethnographers like Petryna, Nguyen and Biehl that places health identities in 'the context of national history and global connections' (Whyte, 2009: 12). The second approach, that of the politics of identity, reflects a paradigm in which health and development are closely coupled, and individuals and groups emphasize rights linked to a particular identity – HIV, disability, leprosy – in order to secure national and international resources.

In conducting an ethnography to explore people's shifting (embodied and political) subjectivities and experiences of health through the lens of biopower, I was aware that, as anthropologists like Constance Mackworth-Young and colleagues (2020) and Bridget Bradley (2021) caution, I would run the risk of masking the complexities of lives lived beyond a single identity – as 'HIV-positive', 'woman', 'on ARVs'. Further, I was conscious that I needed not only to look at how people made claims and secured resources by mobilizing particular identities but that their embodied subjectivities may also speak to deeply rooted forms of structural violence. As eminent medical anthropologist Susan Whyte argues, '[t]here is a danger that we lose sight of the political and economic bases of health in our concern with identity, recognition, and the formative effects of biomedical and social technology' (2009: 15).

More recently, following Whyte's call to engage with the political and economic dimensions of health, anthropologists working across multiple sites like Sierra Leone and Tanzania (Lees and Enria, 2020), or Sierra Leone, the United States and Mozambique (Benton et al, 2017), have highlighted the value of comparative ethnography. Each of these ethnographic accounts reflects the value of moving out from a narrow focus on health in order to anchor people's lives in their social, economic and political relations.

With these ethnographic approaches and reflections on their relative limitations in mind, I conducted a multi-sited ethnography that focused on connections between, rather than comparisons of, related sites. This ethnography is comparative to the extent that comparative ethnographies prompt us to really engage with the contexts of particular sites and their relationship with each other; but it was not comparative in the strict sense of identifying two or more sites with enough important similarities to warrant reasonable research on where these sites may also differ. I could not and did not wish to conduct a comparative ethnography, despite the many salient similarities in Brazil's and South Africa's social, economic and political profiles and their very different national AIDS responses. I did, however, want to move away from an exceptionalist paradigm in which, as I described in the introduction, the biopolitics of HIV medicine in South Africa was regarded as entirely unique. In the introduction, I described, too, why I perceived this paradigm as problematic because it does not consider the porosity of borders and the nature of networked governance.

National exceptionalism, like nationalism, discursively isolates and simplifies what is happening within a nation's borders from the intricate global assemblage into which states are and always have been woven. It also speaks to the legacy of imperialism that persists into the present, most visibly in the inscription of many states' borders (Woo, 2011; Snelgrove et al, 2014; Steinman, 2016; Subramaniam et al, 2016; Ibrahim, 2022). If epidemics reveal anything, it is that national borders are both flimsy constructions and insidious consequences of colonial power. In this book, and through the methodological approach I have taken, I argue that national exceptionalism is not only ontologically incorrect but is empirically dangerous for two reasons. First, it serves to dislocate regional and global actors (like India, the EU and WTO) from the implications their policies have on a national government's capacity to discern and meet the vital needs of its citizens. Second, it fails to account for the hard-won agency of individuals and activist networks that 'act up' and through this global assemblage in ways that challenge discrete readings of singular sites, or states. For these reasons, the methodological approach underpinning this book speaks against this dislocation of global, transnational and national actors from individual lives and instead traces the entanglement of bodies and politics across scale. Although 'multi-sited ethnography' broadly captures the nature of the fieldwork that I have done, it is also a thoroughly contested term that speaks to postcolonial critiques of anthropology's complex history.

Postcolonial critiques around sited and multi-sited ethnographic research bear a great deal of similarity to the critiques around nationalism and national exceptionalism outlined earlier. There is an intimate and long-standing relationship between anthropology and colonialism: both have learnt from and supported each other, and both have emphasized their right to knowledge and their claim to sites that were not theirs to claim. Early scholars like Bronislaw Malinowski 'pioneered' a field that reified boundaries around 'a field site' and rewarded claims of 'capturing' site-specific knowledge (Lewis, 1973; Herzfeld, 2010; Issar, 2021; Ibrahim, 2022). Postcolonial critiques of this approach to research have centred on the problematic nature of generating and then claiming knowledge through extractive relationships in sites where the power differential is strongly weighted away from the research participants and towards the researcher (Clifford, 1997; Foks, 2018; von Vacano, 2019; Jobson, 2020). These critiques do and should permeate discussions around the viability and usefulness of anthropology in the present, with some scholars suggesting that perhaps we just need to 'let anthropology burn' (Jobson, 2020). In addition to long-standing postcolonial critiques of the foundations of anthropology, and the dangers of inscribing boundaries around field sites (Hawari et al, 2019), scholars have critiqued site-specific fieldwork for failing to capture connections across sites that are constantly under negotiation and in flux, including those that are inhabited online (Hjorth et al, 2017; Walker, 2010; Marino, 2020).

Multi-sited ethnography can and does address some of the limitations of site-specific fieldwork. In fact, anthropologists – including Marcus (2012, 2021) – have long debated the value of thinking about research as located in a 'site', or even in multiple sites (Falzon, 2016). On the other hand, some have argued that there is value in thinking about how space and sociality function together in particular sites (Candea, 2016), while others have called for a recognition of depth (built through social, political and economic relationships in particular sites) in addition to the breadth that is signified by a multi-sited approach (Horst, 2016, 2018). Scholars working in fields that call attention to connections rather than locations, like those studying transnational migration (Marino, 2020; Riccio, 2021) or the movement of technologies using ANT (Schäfer, 2017; Ourabah, 2020), tend to foreground relationality over geography.

Building on the critiques articulated in the previous paragraphs, and with specific reference to his fieldwork in South Africa, Didier Fassin (2013, 2020) advances a form of critical multi-sited fieldwork in which anthropologists move beyond thinking about 'horizontal' sites that fit together into a single ethnography towards thinking about 'vertical' sites in which multiple scales and locations intersect with each other. He describes this kind of ethnography as multi-layered (Fassin, 2013). This book also works across multiple scales and locations, and it creates an argument around the conceptual and methodological value of this approach. By tracing the entanglements of bodies, technologies and politics across scale, it not only transects multiple sites and geographic borders, but more fundamentally, it reveals the fallacy – and risk – of attempting to construct boundaries around any one of these things.

Perhaps there is a need for a new language around fieldwork and field sites. I suggest that we consider fieldwork as a site of relationships, a multi-layered place where meaning is built over time, in different spaces, alongside the people we come to know and who come to know us. To this end, I use the term 'connective' multi-sited fieldwork in recognition of the value and critiques noted earlier around multi-sited fieldwork, and because it best captures the approach I have taken in my work. As a 'connective' multi-sited ethnography, I researched how multiple sites (global, national, local, molecular) are connected through a network of actors (bodies, viruses, medicines, families, homes, clinics, governments, trade agreements, pharmaceutical laboratories) in a global assemblage that has implications for women's embodied precarity. The following section articulates the specific methods that comprised the ethnography on which this book is based.

Research methods

As I followed the lives of the people I came to work most closely with, my field site in South Africa became less about the space of Khayelitsha (where they lived), the Cape Town metropole (where they worked) or even the Eastern Cape (where they grew up). Instead, my field site became more about a site of relationships in a network of fields where technologies, institutions, people, space, photographs, drawings, words and silences co-existed, crashed into and missed each other.

This is not to say that space did not matter; it was critical, as discussed throughout each of the following chapters. But in relaying 'where' this fieldwork was conducted, I also hope to show, here and in the following chapters, how the spaces of my ethnography reflect time and the presence of history in these sites and how these 'space-times' (Massey, 2005) are generative of and produced through social relationships (Lefebvre, 1991). I discuss the relationships that were the site of my research in the following section. Thereafter, I move out from South Africa and across to Brazil, where I conducted fieldwork in Recife, in Brazil's north-eastern province of Pernambuco.

Ethnographic research with women in Khayelitsha

I did not know my fieldwork would become more about relationships and less about the space in which they took place, but perhaps I should have anticipated this when I sought Nondumiso Hlwele's advice about what she thought would be good to explore together. I have worked with Nondumiso for almost 20 years, initially at UCT in 2004 and later as a co-researcher through numerous projects with the Institute of Development Studies and the University of Sussex; I am currently working with Nondumiso on a two-year project to look at the intersections between HIV, COVID-19 and gender. I met with Nondumiso when I returned to South Africa from the United Kingdom in 2010 to commence some of the research on which this book is based, and to explore how we might work together again, although in a different capacity from how we had previously worked together at UCT.

Nondumiso listened as I talked through my ideas and then told me her thoughts about the relative risks and benefits of working with a group of people who had historically fought for ARVs but whose lives now were much more of a daily struggle to feed, clothe and school their children. Nondumiso, too, had experienced this economic precarity and wondered if the era of collaboration between former activist organizations and the government had precipitated a fall in AIDS-specific funding to those same activist organizations and their employees and beneficiaries. The shift in HIV funding that Nondumiso raised with me in these early conversations speaks to the shifts in the biomedical and political landscapes outlined in the rationale for this research: structural inequalities that were eclipsed by the vital politics of access to HIV medicines in the first decade of this century remain in place and are even more visible in the wake of the rapid scaling up of the ARV rollout. Nondumiso's observation reflects ethnographic research from elsewhere in Africa. For example, Ruth Prince's ethnography in Kisumu, Kenya, substantiates 'the argument that the focus on keeping bodies alive with medicines may leave persons more vulnerable when humanitarianism or human rights discourses fill in for a politics that can address socioeconomic inequalities and pursue a political program of change' (2012: 555).

In our conversations in 2010, we agreed that it would be worth exploring how people are living in this 'post-ARV-struggle' world because, as Nondumiso said, "Now, it's not just about people dying." It was only after this meeting that I felt slightly more sure-footed about the research focus and the route I would follow in the subsequent years as I conducted this ethnography. Nondumiso agreed to assist by introducing me to a group of women who had similarly worked as activists, who lived in Khayelitsha and who were on ARVs but whose lives were, quite evidently, so much more than these characteristics. I trusted Nondumiso to be frank about me to her network of colleagues and friends and, because there was no financial incentive to work with me, that the people she eventually introduced to me would have a clear enough picture of who I was.

It was therefore through Nondumiso that I met the women whose lives would come to form the core of the ethnography on which this book is based. The ethnographic research I conducted with this group of women, from 2010, enabled me to develop an understanding of the intimate intricacies of their lives, and from this knowledge, to explore how they were networked into an assemblage of actors that moved from the molecular to the global. The networks I traced in my fieldwork with this group of women were, in some respects, quite visible, but in other cases, they were less tangible and more elusive. In this instance, though, I formed relationships with a group of women who all knew Nondumiso and each other. This allowed for a more textured ethnography where our relationships were multi-faceted, moving into each other's, but the visibility of this web of relationships also presented a set of ethical dilemmas that I discuss in more detail in a later section. Further, the specific characteristics of this group of women, particularly as former HIV activists, delineate the boundaries of this book in a number of ways that I reflect on subsequently.

All ten women had worked as activists with TAC, were on ARVs and lived in Khayelitsha. These basic criteria were important for me to be able to trace the connections between the two facets of my research – namely women's embodied experience of ARVs and their political relationship with the state as citizens. These initial criteria were also practically useful as a way for Nondumiso to identify, from a very large group of colleagues and friends, a group of women who might be prepared to work with me. Although I had planned to work with a group of women with these predefined characteristics, they quickly slipped away from the surface of our interactions when we were hanging out. It was their embodied life, and not any single (often externally imposed) identity, that mattered. Therefore, although this group of women share a number of characteristics that I had identified in order to focus my research, the way we worked to co-construct this ethnography rendered labels like 'HIV-positive person' and 'research participant' redundant. As far as possible in this book, I avoid descriptions like 'people living with HIV' or 'HIV-positive man' or 'HIV-positive woman': it was everyday life, and not any single identity, that I was most concerned with. This is not a matter of semantics, but a matter of ethics. Just as this research traced the routes through which actors are networked into each other's vitality and into women's bodies, my fieldwork became a site of mutual accountability.

I met Miriam first. Her text message pinged on to my phone on a warm November morning. It said, 'Call me.' I did, and we met two days later. In the following chapter, I introduce her and all of the women in this core group in detail, so here I will relay the way we came to know each other and how we worked together in my fieldwork.

In this first meeting, we had talked about the ethical parameters of working together, and the kinds of things I hoped to work on with her, like using photographs and film as a way of sharing important parts of her life with me, drawing social maps of her close family and friendship networks, and just hanging out together (I discuss these methods subsequently). It was after this initial exploratory meeting, sitting quietly in the car and listening to the station she had found for us on the radio, when she said, "Ya, ok. Let's do this. But you should know that there are some dark things I don't like talking about." I was concerned about drawing out sadness in my desire to understand the women's lives and their histories, and Miriam prompted me to address this from the outset. I committed the following three things to her, as I subsequently did with all the people I came to work closely with. I said that I would be careful not to ask too many questions. Miriam then suggested that we could also write to each other in a diary in the times between hanging out, and this, along with the photo-stories, came to be an important thread of our fieldwork conversations. Second, I proposed that, if she wanted, I would tell her about my life, that we could hang out in my home as well as hers, and that I would introduce her to my family and friends and not only ask to be taken into her world. Finally, I said that I did not view this as a time-bound 'research relationship' and committed to staying in touch with her, if she wanted this, when I returned to the UK. We had reached the taxi station at this stage, and I had double-parked as cars sped past us, hooting. Miriam sat next to me, in no apparent rush to get out of the car, laughing. "Yoh! Nondumiso said that you're an odd one. Now I understand." Miriam turned the radio up for my journey home and opened the car door, bemused by my confusion. As she climbed out of the car, she said, "I'll see you soon. Call me."

Over the next few weeks, I met each of the other nine women I came to work most closely with. Miriam worked with five other women in the core group in an NGO called *uYaphi*, located in one of Cape Town's wealthier suburbs called Obs. Through a combination of Nondumiso's initial contact followed by Miriam's affirmation, I was contacted by Brenda, Sigbongile, Thandiswa, Zolani and Yandisa. We each met to talk about whether and how we might work together. In this slightly more formal meeting, before we started 'hanging out', we both signed a consent form. In it, I agreed to the specific terms they had stipulated for our relationship – such as the ones I described in Miriam's case. The form also included a set of ethics criteria that I agreed to follow, such as my commitment to confidentiality and anonymity in all the forms that their work – in photographs, films, maps – might be represented in publications like this book.

Despite entering my fieldwork with an idea of the people I hoped to work with, and the methods I planned to use, as I worked with this group of women my ethnography took on a life of its own. It was only possible to really get to know the women I worked with by hanging out with the people who mattered to them, in the places they were prepared to take me into and show me. This entailed 'deep hanging out' (Geertz, 2001) in anthropological terms. In practical terms, it meant that I walked alongside their lives: learning about paper mâché bowl making, travelling the routes they travelled and getting to know the people they spent time with as they moved between their home, work and clinic; taking care of their children while they worked or while they waited in the long monthly line to withdraw their grant money; attending court cases, media briefings, parliamentary pickets, marches, health check-ups; witnessing birthdays and births, funerals and deaths.

In addition to participant observation, informal conversations and life-history interviews, I used a set of visual research methods including participatory photography and film (Gubrium and Harper, 2016; Shankar, 2019) and actor network mapping (MacLeod et al, 2019; Vokes, 2021). For my research, the participatory photography (Poletti, 2011; Allen, 2012) and film (Gubrium and Harper, 2016; Shankar, 2019) methods entailed providing digital cameras to each of the ten women and working with them to document, for example, where they felt the absence or presence of the state in their lives. The photographs took me into parts of the women's lives that would have otherwise been extremely difficult to access, including, for example, stick fighting ceremonies that marked the transition of one woman's family member as he re-entered the family village from the mountains where he had been circumcised in the Eastern Cape. Together, we collected over 3,000 photographs and about 100 gigabytes of digital data including film.

Actor network mapping entailed working with a set of visual methods in conjunction, at times, with life-history and narrative interviews in order to develop a fuller sense of the women's lives, kinship networks, affective relationships and organizational associations. To this end, I worked with the core group to develop a set of journey maps (tracing the woman's life from her birth to the present moment), social maps (showing family relationships and the spaces of homes, for example) and digital maps (using Google Earth and layering stories and photographs on to space). These methods, together, enabled me to conduct ethnographic research beyond what was said, to understand how meaning is made in and through practices (Grimshaw et al, 2021), senses (Schneider and Wright, 2021) and space (Galvao, 2005; Marcus, 2021).

Narrative life-history interviews and body maps with the BWG

Second, I engaged with a group of seven people (one man and six women) with whom I have worked in various capacities since 2004 and with whom I continue to work, now looking at the intersections of gender, HIV and COVID-19. In this book, I reflect on the narrative life-history interviews

(Portelli, 2019) with this group in conjunction with a series of body maps they created in 2003 and 2011 (see Cornwall, 2002; MacGregor, 2009). I was invited by the group to participate in the series of workshops in which the second set of body maps were developed by the artists with the support of Jane Solomon, who had developed this method and worked with this group in 2003. The second set of body mapping workshops included several 'visual enquiries' that I proposed to the group (including creating an 'ARV timeline' and showing where they 'felt' medicine in the body) which I then explored in greater detail through narrative and life-history interviews with the artists.

These body maps represent a trajectory of activism through art in which the embodied ramifications of ARVs and HIV are made explicitly visible. In 2003, the positive effects of ARVs were made visible as a means to compel the government to provide HIV medicine (MacGregor, 2009). The second set of body maps, created after the ARV rollout had begun in earnest, bear witness to the longer-term implications of medicine, and of a longer life. These body maps therefore enabled me to explore continuity and changes for this group across time. Like the women in the core group, all the members of the BWG had engaged with TAC in the struggle for HIV medicine, and many of the people in this group were friends, or colleagues, of the women in the core group.

Narrative life-history interviews

Third, I conducted 40 narrative life-history interviews (Cole and Knowles, 2001; Bernard, 2011; Portelli, 2019) with people who were receiving ARVs but who had not necessarily been involved as activists in the struggle for ARVs. While I sought to understand women's embodied accounts of HIV medicine and their perception of and engagement with the state as citizens, over time I extended my research to incorporate both men and women, and both activists and people who had not been activists. The focus of my ethnography remained with the core group and the BWG, but I also recognized that I was working with a very particular set of people and that for my research to have broader validity beyond the narrow focus on women (who were activists and on ARVs), I would also need to engage with men and with people who were not activists. I therefore, again with Nondumiso's help, identified a group of people who lived in the Cape Town metropole (and were not necessarily living in Khayelitsha), who were on ARVs through the public health sector and who had not been involved in HIV activism.

Participant observation with TAC

Fourth, I conducted participant observation with TAC throughout my fieldwork in South Africa as a writer and researcher for the ET magazine.

ET is distributed to over 55,000 people in South Africa, and this publication is the principal method that TAC uses to convey information on HIV science, HIV medicines and prominent national and international policy developments to its members. Working on ET therefore enabled me to understand the critical policy debates taking place between activist coalitions (within and beyond South Africa), and between the South African government and global actors (including the Global Fund). It was also a critical opportunity to feed the emergent findings of my fieldwork back into these policy and advocacy processes. Findings from my fieldwork were used to provide empirical evidence to support TAC in their policy advocacy around addressing side effects of older medicines, for example, or on Brazil's SUS health system and the lessons South Africa could learn from Brazil in developing its own national health insurance policy. My work with TAC was a central aspect of my fieldwork, as it enabled me to understand contemporary policy dialogues between activist organizations and the government, and because it offered a platform for myself and my colleagues to feed our research and experiences back into TAC's activism through the articles we wrote for ET.

Key informant interviews with policy actors in Brazil and South Africa

Finally, I conducted 20 key informant interviews with policy makers, activists and academics in South Africa and Brazil in order to develop a deeper understanding of both policy processes and outcomes in each country tied to the political dimension of the research focus. For this aspect of my fieldwork, I used a snowball sampling method (Flint et al, 2023) where I worked with an initial and small group of respondents and asked them to advise me of other people whom I should also interview. In South Africa, I had a reasonable understanding of the policy terrain and identified ten key respondents who were engaged as activists or academics in South Africa. These respondents were based in TAC, in TAC's affiliate organizations (including MSF and Section 27), uYaphi and a media organization. These interviews followed a structured format as I aimed to understand, in particular, the current policy challenges that were emerging in South Africa in the wake of the struggle for ARVs. I conducted these interviews in English, in the offices of each of the respondents. I obtained written consent prior to conducting these interviews, and in addition to recording the interview, I also took notes. The notes and the interview were transcribed and later analysed in NVivo.

As discussed in the previous sections and in Chapter 1, the research I conducted in South Africa emerges from a long-standing research history that started in 2003 at UCT. During this time, I worked with TAC, developed research relationships with NGOs (including TAC's partners in the Community Media Trust and Section 27) and government officials (including the former Deputy Minister of Health). In contrast to South Africa, I was far less familiar with the geographic and political landscape of Brazil, and I was far more reliant on my colleagues in Recife not only to gauge the important policy debates currently taking place in the country but also to navigate the space of Recife itself. The research I conducted in Brazil emerged from an academic collaboration with the Department of Social Development at the Universidade Federal de Pernambuco (UFPE). Starting in 2009, I conducted research on gender and HIV in South Africa and shared this research through collaborative workshops and joint publications with a group of academics and activists in Brazil over a period of five years.

My interviews in Brazil were with key informants from the network of activist and academic organizations with whom I had worked in this research partnership; they include academics at UFPE and activists in feminist and HIV organizations in São Paulo and in Recife. Unless otherwise agreed, these accounts have been anonymized. I cannot speak Portuguese. While this was part of the reason I did not opt to do a full-length ethnographic study in Recife, I also wanted to find a way around this barrier, as I had found through my previous collaboration with UFPE that there was much to learn from the network of activists and academics whom I had started to know, albeit tentatively and with much translation assistance from my colleagues. I therefore prepared interview questions in English, had them translated into Portuguese and sent the written documents (including the translated consent form) to the respondents who had agreed to be interviewed. This applied to seven of the ten key informants; I conducted three interviews in English. In all interviews in South Africa and Brazil, I asked the respondents to reflect on their role in each country's policy landscape, to discuss where they saw each country's socio-economic historical transformation and contemporary challenges and to share their perceptions of each country's respective policy response to the provision of HIV medicines in the public sector. My research in Brazil also moved over the edges of formal interviews and into what could also be described as 'hanging out'; I do not use the term 'ethnography', however, as this would give disproportionate weight to my fieldwork in Brazil compared to my fieldwork in South Africa. It was, however, these more subtle conversations, as I discuss in Chapter 6, that really enabled me to understand the texture of the policy and embodied dynamics around HIV medicine in Brazil.

Reflexive analysis

My fieldnotes were a central component to my 'sense-making' during fieldwork and, in essence, functioned as a way to reflexively analyse my research as I moved through my ethnography. As I discuss in the previous section, it was through reflecting on the potential limitations of focusing solely on a group of women who had been HIV activists that I introduced a further dimension to my research and conducted interviews with 40 men and women who were similarly on ARVs but who had not been activists. My ethnography also spanned out to include participant observation by hanging out and spending time with the families of the people with whom I worked and engaging in the activist politics taking place in my field site by joining the marches, pickets, press conferences and protests that were taking place across Khayelitsha and in the Cape Town metropole more broadly. In reflecting on my ethnography, and on the analysis in the chapters that follow, I acknowledge that although my research was multi-faceted, and multi-sited, it was still ultimately grounded in the lives of the core group of women I worked most closely with.

The two research dimensions – the political and the embodied facets of HIV medicine – intersected during my fieldwork with each of the groups I worked with. Further, the conceptual framework outlined in the previous chapter calls for an understanding of the connections that draw these actors and actants into relationship with each other. Therefore, the findings I present in the following chapters locate this core group of women within a much larger assemblage that incorporates all of these research groups and methods but ultimately anchors them in the lives of the women in this core group. For the women with whom I worked, principally in the core group but also in the BWG, had engaged as powerful political actors and through these activist histories had been able to shape and navigate their lives in the ways that I detail in the following chapters. I do not, and could not, consider the political and embodied dynamics of access to HIV medicines for the general population of HIV-positive people in South Africa as this was not the aim of my research.

I recognize, then, that the findings of this book apply to this particular network of research actors, and I do not claim that the argument I develop over the book pertains generally to all HIV-positive people living in South Africa, or even all HIV-positive people living in Khayelitsha. I do, however, suggest in Chapter 8 that the main argument I develop across this book, that biopolitical precarity is networked into the permeable body, may hold theoretical and political relevance beyond this book: this argument calls attention to the embodied ramifications of the global governance of medicine on countries in the Global South – and individuals in these countries – as they navigate access to affordable medicines within this assemblage.

Ethics

As stated earlier, I secured ethical approval from the University of Sussex prior to commencing my fieldwork. In this section, I reflect on my positionality and the practical measures entailed in the ethical conduct of this research.

I was aware that, even with all the ethical permissions and procedures in place, my research could also be a process through which an ethnographic impression is taken – taken as photographs, videos and fieldnotes, taken away from these women, taken back to England's Brighton. This dynamic is, as I note earlier, a facet of anthropology's colonial history and indeed, in many ways, continues to cloud anthropology's present. Postcolonial scholarship challenges researchers to become aware of the power asymmetries that frequently underpin research relationships, with some scholars writing that even with awareness, these asymmetries can never fully be addressed (Weber-Sinn and Ivanov, 2020). Writing about their research on the Truth and Reconcilliation Commission in Burundi, for instance, Astrid Jamar (2022) explores the long-term durabilities of colonialism that surface in the present through epistemic violence and the reification of Western legalism in transitional justice (TJ) practices. While calling attention to these colonial durabilities in TJ arenas, Jamar also calls for an awareness of epistemic violence in which certain forms of knowledge are concealed or the people who generate this knowledge are occluded.

Epistemic violence is not only something that can be seen, researched and written about; it emerges in the way researchers 'see', 'do' and 'write' research. The dangers of generating forms of epistemic violence through research has been raised by postcolonial scholars and researchers working around the world, and specifically in postcolonial contexts like South Africa, where legacies of colonialism and apartheid permeate the present (Devisch and Nyamnjoh, 2011; Mignolo, 2011; Cesarino, 2012; Mushonga and Dzingirai, 2022). Ethics approval is never enough in any context, but particularly not in contexts that have 'colonial durabilities' of violence (Jamar, 2022). And while reflexivity is necessary, it is also not enough because rather than effectively dismantling power asymmetries, it can circle back into a form of academic narcissism that is propelled by 'a White saviour' complex. As a White cisgender South African, I have made many mistakes in my research that speak to the ways that my intersectional privilege – linked to my race, gender, class, education – is itself a form of colonial durability. Rather than write about how I 'got it right' in my research, I also share where I got it very wrong in this book. Given the overlapping ways that my privilege manifests in my body and in the spaces and resources I can access, the risk of creating forms of epistemic violence through my research was far from theoretical. I grappled with it privately and in open conversations with the people I worked with. In fact, the women I worked with were very clear that having experienced extractive research in the past, they would stop returning my calls or text messages if they felt this was happening in our relationship. I was told in no uncertain terms that they had given up on White people. They explained that it was only because they trusted Nondumiso, who trusted me, that they were prepared to give me a chance. My relationship with

Nondumiso was also at stake: because I relied on her trust so fundamentally, I knew that I needed to make sure I did not alienate the very people who were giving me this rare chance and who all knew each other in the network of HIV activists that I so strongly wished to know better.

In addition to the ways that my intersecting privilege – as a cisgender, formally educated, White South African – might result in unethical and asymmetrical relationships with the people I worked with, I was also working in a highly complex and contested field of research. The industry that has been built around HIV research is riddled with subtle and, perhaps less often, overt ethical contraventions. Having worked as a researcher in South Africa since 2003, and as the Deputy Director of a HIV research centre at UCT since 2006, I had become increasingly uncomfortable with 'HIV research' and my role in it. I had observed how quickly even the most 'human-centred and participatory' research could slip into obscuring the messiness of people's complex lives. This slippage happened, perhaps, in a quest to make research 'relevant' for policy by applying labels like 'HIV-positive', 'woman', 'Black', 'poor' in order to support development interventions aimed at precisely those people who – for all their complexity – struggled to live because these labels intersect so powerfully to generate precarity in South Africa. But the danger with this dislocation of people's stories from their everyday lives lies in the perpetuation of a construction of the HIV-positive other. I attempted to address this risk of 'ethical slippage' in two ways.

First, I was rigorous in following the ethics procedures of consent and of ensuring confidentiality and anonymity in my research relationships, as outlined earlier. This meant a constant discussion with the people with whom I worked about how and whether to use the accounts they shared with me during my fieldwork, and also afterwards when writing this book. For instance, the core group of women with whom I worked as well as the women in the BWG had been publicly 'known' and visible as activists in court hearings, photographs and documentary films; our ethnographic work also drew very intimate details of their life into focus, and even though they had said that it was fine (for some it was preferable) that I name them in my book, I needed to check that this still applied for some of the stories they had shared with me. In most cases, we decided to use pseudonyms after all. I have therefore assigned pseudonyms to all of the people with whom I worked, unless explicitly asked to do otherwise, and I have removed identifying characteristics from my ethnographic accounts in the chapters that follow. The members of the BWG specifically requested to be named in my book, and it was with this understanding that they gave me specific information that they were comfortable with me sharing (and where I was in doubt, as occurred twice in my interviews with this group, I did not include the account in this book).

Second, I integrated a series of visual methods into my research in part to understand people's lives and thoughts in a slightly different way from those afforded through participant observation. It was also important that the tools of these methods – the art materials used in creating the journey maps and the cameras used to take photographs and films – belonged to the people I worked with and not to me. This was also clearly stated in the signed consent form, in which I stated that I would provide these materials, and that if the women, at any point, did not want to continue working with me, that this would be fine, and they would still own all these materials. I purchased cameras, SD cards, camera cases and batteries at the start of my relationship with each of the women; in doing this at the beginning, and not as a subsequent outcome, of our relationship, I trusted that if the women only wanted the tools and not a relationship with me, that they would not contact me again. When we discussed the films and photographs, I wrote detailed notes 'or photo-stories' about each image and built up a composite understanding not only of the worlds of the women I worked with but of the ways they saw their world: the kinds of skies they found beautiful, the people they treasured, the rituals they knew I would never be able to see with my 'own eyes' and wanted to share with me. I have used none of this visual material in the book. This decision is an ethical one: although the research process entailed participatory art, photography and film, this material is not mine to share. Working visually offered a different kind of dialogue, one that enabled rich conversations and deeper relationships that I did not want to compromise. I have also not used images of the body maps or journey maps because they are artworks that – although very accessible online – hold a complex history around ownership; I have written elsewhere about the dangers of appropriating activists' art (Mills, 2019), and I have worked as carefully as possible in this book to avoid this form of appropriation.

With respect to my own positionality and the nature of this fieldwork, I acknowledge, in line with Whyte's (2009), Mackworth-Young's (2020) and Bradley's (2021) caution about research on health and politics discussed earlier, that working with a particular group of people based narrowly on a health condition like HIV is also problematic, not least given that I am cisgender, White, middle-class, educated at a tertiary level and a HIV-negative woman. Not only was I all these labels – but I am a queer South African. My positionality contrasted starkly with those women with whom I sought to work, namely women who were HIV-positive, heterosexual and on ARVs. South Africa's history remains, as we see in this book, very present in all South Africans' lives, from the socio-spatial organization of race and class in Cape Town, to the chronic levels of unemployment among South Africans who are the same age as me but who have not grown up with the historical (and contemporary) privileges conferred on White South Africans. I could understand why, in our first meetings, I was treated with a great deal of caution.

Instead of pretending that these labels did not exist and pretending that I knew what I was doing in working with them, I tried another approach, which may or may not have been wise. I 'outed' some of the labels. In the initial meetings with the women in the core group, I said that I was not quite sure how best to secure their trust, or even sure how I was going to do this ethnography, and I asked for their advice in figuring this out. I also spoke of my own experiences of precarity, and where appropriate, I shared my personal history of physical and sexual violence. For instance, I had been attacked and stabbed during my fieldwork in Nyanga, in 2004, and nearly died from a pneumothorax; it was the rapid care I received in Nyanga's day clinic, a clinic that had formed part of my fieldwork on HIV and palliative care, that saved my life. In my later fieldwork, in Khayelitsha, there were many days when I got very lost in its maze of streets and could hear my voice reaching a hysterical pitch. Because the women I worked with knew that I had been attacked during this earlier fieldwork, they knew to point out that, at that moment, we were safe. This fear placed me very much in their hands: I was dependent on the women I worked with not only for engaging with me during my fieldwork but also for caring for me when I was (often) lost or anxious. This was embarrassing, too, because I could not pretend I was not very afraid in the places that we hung out every day, in areas where they were forced (by apartheid and by its legacies) to build their homes and nurture their families with fierce love and profound fear. Over time, as our relationships deepened, I could sense that I was trusted because I became the source of much teasing. I was teased for the way I danced, the way I made tea, my poor attempts at speaking isiXhosa, the way I drank too much coffee, even the way my voice shook when we got lost in Khayelitsha.

This approach to 'outing' labels did not always work, and there were also many times when I was deeply uncomfortable with the disparities that marked such embodied differences in our lives. I did not, for instance, acknowledge that my partner was a woman, when so many of our conversations were about men, love and sex. This felt deeply disingenuous, but I did not know how to 'out' this particular label. I did finally come out to Miriam, in 2018, when I told her about my wife and our brand-new baby; she was completely unfazed and simply said, "That explains the hair, sana." When we were chatting in Cape Town in June 2023, Miriam asked me to "get better" at WhatsApp. When I asked her what she meant, she said that she wanted me to send her more photographs of my wife and child, asking, "Sana, why do you hide them?" Much of my journey with Miriam, and the women I have come to know for over a decade now, has entailed a process of making myself more visible: more vulnerable to their potential judgement but also more open to shared care, and therefore much more vulnerable to the loss of relationships that have come to mean a great deal to me.

Beyond some of my closer relationships with the core group of women where we established a fuller understanding of each other over the years we came to know each other, I also heard a number of accounts of homophobia from people with whom I worked. I was concerned, for instance, when a photograph was published in a local newspaper of me at a march against lesbian hate crimes; I was afraid that my colleagues with whom I had been working would refuse to work with me (they did in fact come up to me with the newspaper, shocked, and I did not know how to respond). I was concerned, too, that in outing myself – even peripherally through the circulation of these public photographs – that I might place myself at risk in Khayelitsha, where the rape of lesbians was an extremely worrying feature during my fieldwork (Gaitho, 2021).

The ethics of my research continue to unfold, but the central challenges remain. Not only have I needed to grapple with my own subjectivities in relation to the people and organizations with whom I have worked but, in recognizing the presence of colonial durabilities in my own life, I am also aware that these subjectivities will always inhere a privilege that no amount of 'ethical research' can erase.

Conclusion

Although this book emerges from long-term fieldwork that traced connections linking actants and actors across multiple sites, it is not a comparative ethnography. Instead, I have attempted to illustrate some of the conceptual and empirical dialogues I observed between and beyond South Africa, Brazil and India in order to create a differentiated picture that shows

> not only the uneven seepage of science and medicine into social life, but also the uneven effects of different social conditions on the possibilities for the formation of health identities and subjectivities. With such ethnography in hand, we can begin to make comparisons over time and across social settings – still a major task for anthropology, medical and otherwise. (Whyte, 2009: np)

As I articulate in the earlier discussion on multi-sited ethnography, there is value in Fassin's (2013) approach to 'layered ethnography' that seeks to look at sites through a slightly more critical lens, where multiple actors and spaces are considered as 'sites' in addition to locations historically viewed as a 'field site'. With this approach in mind, my aim for this book is that in addition to developing a textured understanding of health and politics in a particular site, like Khayelitsha, the chapters build iteratively on each other to make a political argument about the value of understanding the extent to which life in places like Khayelitsha is contingent on a wide range of actors that operate across scale from the molecular to the global. This recognition then necessitates – as Southern Theory scholars make clear (Connell, 2020) – more robust and creative approaches that advance and connect theory, policy and methodologies for and with those living in the Global South. In the chapters that follow, I seek to both show these connections and reveal the embodied political consequences that flow from them.

3

Gender, Health and Embodiment

'It's like when the skies fight, when the clouds are angry and dark.
They crash into each other and lightning flies across the sky. You never
know where the lightning is going to hit. That's what it's like with
HIV.' (Conversation with Zama)

The rain splattered across the windscreen as Zama and I drove along the
highway leading out from Cape Town over to her office in Muizenberg
where she worked as an administrator and HIV treatment literacy facilitator.[1]
In 2023, Zama lived with her partner and with her two sons (four and
18 years old), in a brick home in Khayelitsha; she also frequently shares her
home with her sister and her two nieces and in late 2023 her mother hurt
her hip and also started to live with them. She acquired her home through
the Reconstruction and Development Programme (RDP) and views the
stability of her home, its solid brick walls and robust gates, as a significant
personal accomplishment. She also views her home, as indicated in a series of
photographs she took in which she spoke to the state's presence and absence
in her life, as an indication of the government's capacity to fulfil some of its
constitutional obligations to her as a citizen in post-apartheid South Africa.
When chatting in July 2022, Zama said that she was looking to move into
a bigger home, but that without a more stable income it was unlikely she
would be able to make this dream a reality for her family. A year later, in
2023, Zama told me that her home was feeling increasingly too small to
hold her family, but that without a better income, she could not see a viable
way to move into an area that was both safer and more affordable. On this
particular day, a few years earlier, as we travelled to Zama's office, she told me
more about her diagnosis in 2001 and the journey she took to start treatment
through the Medicines Sans Frontiere's (MSF) trial in Khayelitsha in 2002.

By the time we arrived at Zama's office, the temperature had dropped
and neither of us wanted to stop our conversation. I turned the heating on,
and we sat together, twisted in our seats, talking as the rain collected and
dropped down the windscreen. As Zama spoke about her younger self and

the men she had had sex with without feeling that she could say no, without knowing how to say no, without believing she had the right to enjoy sex, I was struck by the clanging dissonance between what I thought I knew and how little I really understood. In 2022, when we met outside her work on another rainy day, Zama and I had known each other for almost 20 years. But it took over a decade before Zama was willing to tell me how she had come to live with HIV; I first needed to see what Zama showed me before she would tell me what she actually meant.

One evening, a few months after our conversation about the skies that fight, Zama invited me to join her at a hip-hop poetry performance at the City Hall entitled 'Age is a Beautiful Phase' in honour of an anti-apartheid poet, James Matthews. Hanging out at the reception before the performance, we started chatting to Matthews' grandson. The conversation turned to the meeting place of dreams and memories, of South Africa's history of dreamt possibility and our thoughts of its present. He asked us what we dreamt of becoming one day. Zama looked at him and said, "I am an artist. I am my dream." That evening was symbolic of continuities across age and across generations of struggles that span apartheid and post-apartheid South Africa. Matthews, frail with old age, spoke of his experience of forced detention and abuse, of the hands of the apartheid government that reached through the bodies of policemen in an attempt to quell his dissent. A young jazz singer put Matthews' poetry to music as break dancers contorted their bodies over and under each other across the floor to the rhythm of the poetry's beat. Matthews' poetry of South Africa's apartheid history was spliced with hip-hop artists rapping about South Africa's post-apartheid struggles like gang violence, poverty and drug abuse. In the course of the evening, and precipitated by the conversation with Zama and Matthews' grandson, the title of the performance started to make sense: age can be a beautiful phase because it offers the possibility of actualization. Zama's description of living her dream spoke to the realization of hope: Zama was an artist. She was not first and foremost a woman living with HIV on antiretrovirals (ARVs). I had to see this before she would show me herself as a younger woman negotiating multiple and intersecting pathways of precarity.

This chapter explores the skies that fight, the proverbial lightning strikes that bring HIV into women's lives and bodies, through the theoretical lens of precarity and along three interlinked pathways. Since first starting fieldwork in 2003 and continuing through to my most recent fieldwork in 2023, the prevailing source of precarity for the women I have worked with centres on women's and girls' bodies as corporeal sites of state and interpersonal violence. In this chapter, I explore the various routes that HIV came to enter women's lives, and bodies, and I aim to collapse a distinction between state and interpersonal forms of violence by working with the linked concepts of biopolitics and precarity.

The term 'precarity' has a complex history in the field of anthropology that transects economic and political theory (Han, 2018). In this book, as discussed in the previous chapter, I work with the concept of precarity (Butler, 2009). I use precarity in place of concepts like 'vulnerability' in order to foreground the political dimensions of inequality as women experienced them within their bodies, and in their lives, as they managed precarious employment, or navigated live electricity lines underfoot, or had to use unlit toilets in the middle of the night. As discussed in the previous chapter, I extend existing conceptions of precarity by integrating it with the concept of biopolitics. Through the concept of biopolitical precarity, I seek to draw political actors into view and understand how their actions affect people's ability to access newer biomedical technologies for themselves, affordable education for their children and safe water and electricity for their households. In doing so, I argue that the context in which people live their lives on ARVs – as they take their medicines with or without food, as they remember to step over live electricity lines or are forced to use unlit toilets and risk rape – becomes embodied as forms of biopolitical precarity.

In contrast with the other empirical chapters, this chapter centres on the core group of ten women with whom I conducted ethnographic fieldwork in Khayelitsha, South Africa. I argue in this chapter that epidemiological terminology, like 'vulnerability' or 'routes of transmission', belies the complex actors and networks that make it possible for HIV to move into and become animate in people's bodies and lives; further, the narrative framing of HIV transmission along epidemiological 'routes' limits discursive expansion and locks policy responses for HIV prevention, treatment and care. Therefore, for practical and analytical purposes, I use the term 'pathways' in dialogue with 'routes' and the concept of 'precarity' in dialogue with 'transmission'. This chapter delineates three 'pathways of precarity' that intersect and reinforce each other in order to highlight the interplay between HIV as epidemiology and HIV as a nonhuman actant (Latour, 2005), a 'thing with a social life' (Appadurai, 1988) that moves along social, economic, political and biological fissures, into and between people's bodies and lives. I argue in this chapter that precarity is borne through the body with HIV, as an actant, entering women's and girls' lives through relational networks that travel vertical pathways across generations, horizontal pathways between partners and diagonal pathways among kin.

"So my baby gets HIV too": vertical pathways of precarity

Pregnancy followed by the birth, illness and potential death of a child were the metaphorical lightning strikes heralding HIV for most of the women with whom I conducted my fieldwork. This section details vertical pathways of precarity and centres on babies' vulnerability to HIV through vertical transmission and the state's historical failure to provide treatment for the prevention of mother-to-child transmission (PMTCT). This section also points to the pressures placed on women as carers for generations that come before and after them.

By 2022, South Africa had become a global leader in preventing vertical transmission from pregnant people to their children (Maingi et al, 2022). In a study analysing the provision and uptake of HIV testing and treatment to prevent mother-to-child-transmission (MTCT) in 41 countries in Sub-Saharan Africa, South Africa was only one of three countries to have successfully achieved a rate of less than 5 per cent MTCT in 2019 (Astawesegn et al, 2022). This rate is stark when held in contrast to countries like Somalia, Sudan and Madagascar, which have rates of MTCT greater than 30 per cent (Astawesegn et al, 2022). Now, more than 90 per cent of people in South Africa who have tested positive for HIV during their pregnancy are moved on to ARV treatment compared to only 57 per cent in 2007 (Tait et al, 2020).

The history of the provision of treatment to prevent MTCT is pertinent in this chapter, as most of the women I have worked with had children in South Africa at a time when treatment was not available to prevent vertical transmission. The absence of this treatment, in the early 2000s, is a direct result of the then President Mbeki's and Health Minister Tshabalala-Msimang's strident AIDS denialism. Despite studies showing the efficacy of single-dose nevirapine (NVP) and short-course azidothymidine (AZT) for preventing HIV transmission from mothers to children, President Mbeki claimed that AZT was toxic (Heywood, 2003). This stance was corroborated by the former Health Minister, who similarly claimed that NVP was toxic (Geffen, 2005). The obstructive impact of these leaders' equivocal stance on the provision of PMTCT treatment is evinced, for example, in the government's decision to deny an offer of a free five-year supply of NVP by the pharmaceutical manufacturer, Boehringer Ingelheim, in 2000 (Heywood, 2003: 285). In 2001, the Treatment Action Campaign (TAC) took the Health Minister to court to compel her to authorize all public health facilities to provide NVP. TAC won the court case, which was then appealed, and on 5 July 2002 the Constitutional Court found that the South African constitution 'required the government to devise and implement within its available resources a comprehensive and co-ordinated programme to realise progressively the rights of pregnant women and their newborn children to have access to health services to combat mother-to-child transmission of HIV' (SAFLI, 2002: 5). A second appeal by the state was denied, and a national PMTCT treatment programme was finally initiated in 2003 (Simelela et al, 2015). In 2015, antenatal services were further improved by ensuring that all pregnant people were able to access lifelong

ARV treatment if they were HIV-positive (Burton et al, 2015; Peltzer et al, 2017). With these interventions, the HIV-infection rate at birth is around 1 per cent (Woldesenbet et al, 2021). Stretching back in time, however, many of the women I worked with had children when the government refused to provide treatment to prevent vertical transmission. As this section illustrates, the legacy of the government's AIDS denialism and failure to provide PMTCT treatment is a vertical pathway of precarity that women and their children continue to navigate in the present.

Lineages of loss

Brenda was born in 1979 in the Eastern Cape and moved between this province and its adjacent neighbour, the Western Cape, throughout her life until she settled in 1997 to complete her high school education in the Eastern Cape. In 1999, in her penultimate year at school, Brenda became pregnant. Her partner had told her that he was HIV-positive, but this disclosure held little meaning for Brenda because she did not know about HIV: "He was the first boyfriend. So we had sex without a condom. At that time I didn't understand HIV. That was 1999. So my boyfriend [told] me he was HIV-positive, but like a joke." Brenda's geographic location in a rural village in the Eastern Cape placed her on the periphery of available HIV information and health services: "So I don't understand what he was talking about because I don't understand even HIV. I was in the Eastern Cape, not here." The spatial correlation between Brenda's rural home and the absence of public health resources generated a further correlation: living on the periphery of public health services and information engendered Brenda's embodied precarity through her exposure to HIV. As noted in Chapter 2, HIV prevalence is higher in rural parts of South Africa, and in the Eastern Cape in particular, compared to urban areas (Johnson and Dorrington, 2023); research has found that this is partly because there are fewer health care resources including education about safe sex and access to resources like condoms and HIV tests (Mojola et al, 2020; Gittings et al, 2022). In 1999, when the public health infrastructure was particularly under-resourced (Madiba and Ngwenya, 2017), and without information about safe sex or any resources to prevent HIV transmission or pregnancy, Brenda contracted HIV, became pregnant and terminated high school prematurely. When recounting this period in her life, Brenda emphasized the layering of personal shocks: "It's the first time I sleep with a boyfriend, and then I get HIV and at the same time I get a baby." The spatial absence of the state in rural peripheries generated conditions of precarity through Brenda's inability to access public health resources like HIV-related information, condoms and treatment.

Without information about the routes that HIV travels, in this case through sex (without condoms) and through pregnancy, labour and delivery (without treatment), Brenda was unable to stop the virus from entering her or her child's body. Brenda's first child died because "[i]t was 1999 [and there was] no treatment. So my baby gets HIV too." In 2001, Brenda became pregnant with her second child. During this time, she also became very seriously ill. Hoping to access life-saving health care for her daughter and her daughter's unborn child, Brenda's mother brought her to Cape Town. In the absence of PMTCT treatment, Brenda's second child, a girl, was born with HIV in 2001. She recalls spending the first few months of her child's life in and out of hospital until she died a year later.

In the same year that Brenda's second child died, the South African government introduced single-dose nevirapine (NVP) to pregnant women. Brenda's mother's rationale for bringing her daughter to Cape Town reflects an overarching theme in my fieldwork, namely the spatial distribution of public health resources in South Africa and its ramifications on the politics of life for people contracting and living with HIV. When compared to the rural peripheries, urban centres held a greater density of public health resources and therefore offered a greater possibility of life in terms of preventing horizontal and vertical transmission and sustaining life across generations through the provision of essential HIV medicine. Historically, two factors differentiated the Western Cape from the Eastern Cape. First, MSF set up an ARV trial in Cape Town in 2001, three years before the government started to roll out ARVs through the public health sector. It was only in 2003 that MSF set up an ARV trial in Lusikisiki, a rural region in the Eastern Cape (Bedelu et al, 2007). Second, the Western Cape contravened the national policy for mono-therapy by introducing dual-therapy treatment to pregnant women in 2004 (Youngleson et al, 2010). This provincial policy was informed by a Thai study that had confirmed that dual-therapy NVP and AZT was significantly more effective in preventing vertical transmission (Lallemant et al, 2004). Outraged by the failure of the national government to provide PMTCT treatment across all provinces in South Africa, TAC launched a series of court cases and civil disobedience campaigns in the early 2000s. Women, like Brenda, who had lost children because they had been unable to access PMTCT treatment, joined TAC as activists and became central in TAC's bid to compel the government to roll out PMTCT and ARV programmes through the public sector.

Lilian, born in Johannesburg in 1972, spearheaded TAC's campaign to compel the government to provide PMTCT treatment; she testified on behalf of TAC, and her affidavit was used as evidence in the court case. During our work together, over a decade after joining TAC in 2002, Lilian created a journey map where she documented the journey of her life. Starting 40 years earlier, in 1972, Lilian notes her birth on the top left-hand side of the map. Next to this date, she writes of the abuse she endured throughout her childhood because she did not have the protection of her parents. This aspect of Lilian's life, described in the following section, generated conditions of embodied precarity that reinforced each other: to combat apartheid's structural economic violence, her parents left her with strangers as they went to find work. Without any protection, Lilian was abused and raped by these strangers, and then later, after running away from them, she was raped by relatives. She ran away again, and because she did not have any social or economic resources to draw on, she lived on the streets, where she entered an abusive relationship and became pregnant in 1999. Like Brenda, her baby was extremely ill, and she spent the first year of her child's life moving in and out of hospital with her until, in June 2000, her baby died. She learnt that she was HIV-positive after her child tested positive, and shortly before her child died.

Like Brenda, Lilian also joined TAC after testing positive and as a result of losing her child. This story is documented on the right-hand side of her journey map, in contrast to and in dialogue with the narrative on the left of the map documenting her embodied vulnerability to rape and abuse in the years leading up to her daughter's birth. On the top right-hand side of Lilian's journey map is a photograph of a pregnancy scan, a foetus in profile, pictured in black and white, and underneath is the phrase 'Keeping tabs of baby's health by keeping tabs on mom's health.' Next to the image, she writes, 'Preg with my daughter.' The three photographs below this top image are tiered and mirror the progression of her life into activism.

The first photograph is of a waiting room in a clinic in Khayelitsha with a woman holding her child. The second photograph is of a grave strewn with flowers. Next to this photograph, she has written 'Death of my child made me an activist.' She has drawn an arrow connecting this photograph with a third photograph of people lining up in a queue. Next to it, she has written '1999. Queuing in cold, to cast my vote, hoping for a "better life"', and along the arrow to the photograph of the grave representing her dead daughter, she has written 'only to be disappointed'. Lilian's experience of losing her daughter 'marked a turn in my life': it prompted her to join TAC and start ARV therapy. In bright yellow paint, she has written 'Light at the end of the tunnel'; the words circle around a small piece of paper with the MSF logo promoting the Campaign for Access to Essential Medicines. This visual account of Lilian's life conveys the journey she travelled from losing her daughter into becoming an activist; as Lilian writes, 'the death of my child made me an activist'.

This points to Lilian's belief that the democratic state is intimately entwined with her and her child's capacity to live; these politics of life are reflected in Lilian's conviction that the state should ameliorate precarity by creating conditions for a 'better life' by providing essential HIV medicines through the public health system. Her rationale for becoming an activist, therefore, was to challenge the way the democratic state was creating conditions of vulnerability through its failure to provide treatment to prevent vertical transmission. Lilian now has an adult son, who, she says, is 'living proof' of her work as an activist to compel the government to provide PMTCT treatment.

The pathways that enabled HIV to move into Brenda's and Lilian's bodies, and into their children's bodies, illustrate the biopolitical nature of precarity in two ways. First, in Brenda's case, she was placed at 'heightened risk ... of exposure to violence without protection' (Butler, 2009: 2). This violence was layered into Brenda's embodied experiences of poor education, and unequal sexual relationships, culminating in contracting HIV through unsafe sex. This was a consequence of the failure of the public health system to reach rural areas with essential public health resources (like HIV information, condoms and biomedicine). Second, the state generated 'politically induced conditions of precarity' (Butler, 2009: 2) through its failure to provide treatment to prevent vertical transmission from Brenda and Lillian to their children, and through its failure to provide essential AIDS treatment through the public health system when they became ill.

Generations of life

When I first met Brenda, she was pregnant with her fourth child. I follow the narrative of her pregnancy and her child's birth in this and the following sections to illustrate the ways in which the pathways of precarity intersect with and shape each other.

In Brenda's maternity hospital, the long queue of pregnant women was apparently best served by solid lines of hardwood benches that stretched down a corridor which doubled-up as a waiting area. The individual blue chairs were reserved for the smaller number of women seeking specialist care in doctors' offices just off the main corridor. I was Brenda's birth-partner, and we were at the hospital for her final check-up before her due date in May. I waited on the bench as Brenda moved in and out of rooms along the corridor for various check-ups. Sitting next to the only man in the waiting area, he told me that his partner was having a boy; he first referred to her as his wife and then looked me in the eye and said, "Actually, she's not my wife yet but I hope she will be." His partner came out of her appointment a few minutes later, and he left with her, not a word spoken between them, but his hand touched hers briefly as they moved towards the exit. Brenda came and sat down on the bench in the spot that had just been vacated by the man when he left with his partner. Her feet were swollen, and her turquoise dress was stretched across her stomach. When I met Brenda a few months earlier, this dress had hung loosely on her body. We sat on the bench as I read through the paperwork Brenda had given me about my responsibilities as her birth partner. I read and signed two sets of documents and handed them back to her. "No, this one is for you Beth", she said in her soft deep voice as she handed back one set of forms. I took the forms thankfully and kept them in my bag to buttress my flailing confidence until her son, Mpilo, was born six weeks later. I return to Brenda's pregnancy and Mpilo's birth in the following section.

Miriam, like Brenda, was born in 1979 in the Eastern Cape. Like Brenda, Miriam too moved to the Western Cape to access medical treatment. In Miriam's case, however, her move to the Western Cape was prompted by her daughter's failing health and not by her own ill-health. Miriam was compelled to stop high school three months before her final examinations to take care of her mother. When she returned to her mother's home, she entered her first sexual relationship and, like Brenda, became pregnant through her first sexual relationship in 1997. Unaware of how HIV is transmitted and unable to access PMTCT treatment, Miriam was unable to protect herself or prevent her daughter, Nena, from contracting HIV.

Nena was born as Miriam's mother died. Miriam wrote rather than spoke the stories of her younger self in the pages of a diary that moved like an unspoken conversation between her bag into mine. Sometimes she would refer to statements from her diary but never to the stories in their entirety. I understood not to refer to them but to know them intimately so that I could 'get' Miriam's oblique references to them as mutual affirmations of trust. In her diary, Miriam wrote about shutting down her mother's home after she gave birth so that she could live in the hospital between the wards that held her mother and her daughter – holding them in beds but not restoring their ill bodies to health. She wrote of her heartbreak at choosing between her mother's death and her daughter's life and her discomfort with her decision to leave her mother, knowing she would never see her again, so that she could take her daughter out of the frail failing clinic in the heart of the Eastern Cape to the medical hub of urban Cape Town. Miriam's partner encouraged her to bring their daughter to his city because it held promise of medicine that would decipher her child's illness and potentially save her life. Miriam left her mother and moved to Cape Town, where her daughter was given excellent, albeit belated, medical care. Nena's illness was deciphered in 1998; like Lilian and Brenda, Miriam learnt of her own HIV status when she learnt that her daughter was HIV-positive. She and her partner then both tested HIV-positive, but her partner refused to believe his status and therefore refused to join support groups and access the same MSF trial that enabled Miriam to commence ARVs when she became eligible in June 2001. Nena's father died in 2006.

One day, when leaving the clinic after Miriam's monthly ARV check-up, Miriam pointed back at the clinic and said, "Cape Town's my home because it gave life to my child … I don't even want to tell you how small she was when we got here. But I want to die in the Eastern Cape because it is the home of my ancestors." When I met Miriam in 2010, Nena had lived with

HIV for 12 years and [was] on second-line ARV treatment. Thirteen years later, in December 2023, as we had lunch under the trees near parliament in Cape Town, Miriam told me that Nena had decided to stop her treatment altogether; Miriam said that now that Nena is an adult, there is very little she can do to persuade her to "care for her life". As a result of her delayed treatment at the onset of her life, Nena has severe cognitive disabilities. Like Nena, Zama's nephew was born in the Eastern Cape. He, too, was born on the cusp of death, abandoned by his father because the actual cost of his care outweighed, in his father's mind, the potential of his son's life. Unlike Nena, he did not survive by being moved to an urban 'medical hub' like Cape Town; he survived because a doctor in the Eastern Cape paid privately for him to access HIV medicine. His delayed treatment, however, resulted in both physical and cognitive impairments. The ill-health that characterized the beginning of these children's lives fundamentally constrains their current and future health and wellbeing. In line with Fassin's (2007, 2009) ethnographic work on embodied memory and HIV, and as I discuss in more detail in the next chapter, these children bear witness to the persistence of embodied precarity as a result of delayed treatment and the legacy of poor health care in rural South Africa.

In this section, vertical pathways span epidemiological routes, as HIV moves from mothers to babies, and social pathways, as seen in the shifting biopolitical relationship between women and the state around access to health resources, and particularly PMTCT treatment. The generation of children born in the 'window period' between escalating rates of HIV transmission and the provision of ARVs and PMTCT treatment serve as a visceral memory of the government's absence and of the political and profoundly personal struggles that ensued for HIV-positive women as they negotiated the precarity of their own and their children's lives. Further, they illustrate the vertical transmission of precarity as their mothers were unable to access health resources to enable them to prevent HIV from entering their own or their children's bodies.

"It's hard to be a girl in this country": horizontal pathways of precarity

Like a Polaroid image that becomes defined with time and light, the proliferation of rape and abuse of the women I worked with and of the generations of girls that stretched before and after them moved into sharp relief over the course of my fieldwork. This reflects a broader context in which HIV has become discursively welded to gender-based violence. The words go hand in hand with statistics that shock and numb; that are so real they become unreal, and people become numbers. As discussed in the previous chapter, and in the previous section, women bear a disproportionate burden of the epidemic both in terms of caring for household and family members, and in terms of the substantially higher rates of HIV prevalence among women (23.5 per cent) compared to men (12.1 per cent) (UNAIDS, 2022a, 2022d). HIV prevalence among young women (20–24 years) is four times higher than HIV prevalence among men of the same age in the most recent national HIV prevalence and incidence survey (Lewis et al, 2022; SANAC, 2023).

Several factors may account for these stark figures, including the very high rates of sexual and gender-based violence (SGBV) among young girls and women. One of the most comprehensive research studies on SGBV in South Africa found that 27.6 per cent of all men had raped a woman or girl; rape of a current or ex-partner was reported by 14.3 per cent of the men; 11.7 per cent had raped an acquaintance or stranger (but not a partner); and 9.7 per cent had raped both strangers and partners (Jewkes et al, 2009). Of all the men who were interviewed in this study, almost half (42.4 per cent) had been physically violent to an intimate partner (Jewkes et al, 2009). In a population-based national household survey, Mabaso and colleagues (2019) find that despite almost 30 years of democracy, racial and gender disparities continue to strongly shape the country's HIV epidemic. The authors suggest that the low socio-economic status of women reinforce unequal gender power dynamics, with women holding minimal negotiating power relative to men around condom use, or frequency or type of sex. These findings are corroborated by a recent cross-sectional study with people accessing HIV testing and counselling, where the authors found that 12 per cent of women in the cohort had been forced to have sex the last time they had sexual intercourse (Klazinga et al, 2020). The study also found a high lifetime prevalence of sexual violence (14 per cent) and physical violence (16 per cent) among women (Klazinga et al, 2020).

Building on Kimberlé Crenshaw's (1993, 1997, 2017) ground-breaking critique of (initially legal) approaches that tended to centre on single-axis notions of identity, like gender, without considering the interactions between gender subordination, race and class, postcolonial scholars have called for a greater awareness of the structures that reinforce intersectional inequality (Hankivsky et al, 2014; Ross, 2017; Sidanius et al, 2018; Campbell, 2021; Akobirshoev et al, 2022; Patterson et al, 2022). This means that while the figures cited earlier centre on the prevalence of sexual and physical violence among women, it is almost impossible to start to understand – or even address – these statistics without looking at and unpacking the structures that create conditions of oppression for people in South Africa who are marginalized through a complex interplay of their race, nationality, ethnicity, class, sexuality, age and disability. As I go on to discuss in this chapter, these structures are rooted in the country's history of colonialism and apartheid, and they persist in the present through profoundly under-resourced education, health and social welfare systems. In this chapter, these structures are explored through women's embodied experiences of intersecting forms of inequality, and they are located within broader systemic forms of inequality that connect to South Africa's colonial and apartheid histories.

In addition to tracing the embodied ramifications of intersectional inequality, this chapter reflects on women's accounts of navigating their sexual and bodily autonomy within post-apartheid South Africa's complex social, political and economic terrain. The horizontal pathways articulated in this section therefore span epidemiological routes of transmission between individuals through unsafe or coercive sex and rape, and social pathways of precarity, like gender and racial inequality, that contribute to horizontal transmission. As discussed earlier, the intersection of these epidemiological and social pathways is widely theorized in South Africa, both reflecting and fuelling national and international categorizations of Black, poor women as 'vulnerable populations' susceptible to HIV infection (Kim and Watts, 2005; Ahooja-Patel, 2007; Chong and Kvasny, 2007; Montgomery, 2015).

These intersections did emerge in my ethnography and are discussed subsequently. However, in line with de Certeau's (1984) notion of 'making do', women simultaneously embodied, resisted and performed precarity in complex configurations that reflect decolonial approaches to the gender and development paradigm that challenges linear assumptions of women as either 'deserving subjects' or as 'autonomous agents' (Coetzee and du Toit, 2018; Rutazibwa, 2018). In their article on decolonizing sexual violence in South Africa, for example, Azille Coetzee and Louise du Toit argue that 'both the phenomenon of ongoing rampant sexual violence mainly against women and children in the South African post-colony, and the large-scale social and institutional complicity which prevents it from being effectively contained, should be interpreted against this historical background, inclusive of slave history' (2018: np). The corollary in the representation of Black women living with HIV as 'deserving victims' is – too frequently – the colonial image of the Black male rapist that similarly draws on colonial racist tropes.

Writing about the intersections of race, culture and sexuality in South Africa, Shireen Hassim (2014) reflects on the predicament that feminists face where power has, particularly in the case of former President Zuma, been marked by a projection of virility and entitlement to women's bodies, but where that power is also operating in a postcolonial context. In line with the findings of Mabaso and colleagues (2019), and a plethora of studies on the interlinkages between race, class, gender and sexuality in driving the HIV epidemic in South Africa (Madiba and Ngwenya, 2017; McKinnon et al, 2017; Klazinga et al, 2020), any analysis of gender inequality must necessarily be intersectional. Further, in line with the decolonial approach advocated by

Coetzee and du Toit (2018), this intersectional approach must also actively work to decolonize analyses of sexual violence by recognizing 'the large-scale and institutional complicity' of a range of actors and interpreting this form of violence against South Africa's historical background. Cognizant of the responsibility inherent in sharing accounts of the intimate lives of the women with whom I have worked, particularly given my own positionality as a White South African, the following section works to foreground these women's own narratives and sense-making of the ways that they experienced sex and sexual relationships. While there is robust evidence that speaks to higher HIV prevalence among women compared to men, and to almost unspeakably high rates of sexual violence against women, the accounts in this section of the chapter reflect the complex ways that women actively and strategically navigated their sexual lives and relationships.

It's hard to be a girl in this country

Having completed her general check-ups in the various rooms that led off the maternity hospital's main corridor, Brenda's last stop was the HIV-specialist doctor. We moved across to sit on the blue chairs closer to the doctor's office in a smaller waiting area on the other side of the corridor. A piece of pink paper hung like a speech bubble from the ceiling outside the doctor's office; a cheerful backdrop to the 'HIV' that was handwritten in large black letters. The connection between the HIV speech bubble, the consulting room and the people sitting in the smaller waiting room was tacit but present. The architects or hospital planners had perhaps considered stigma when they created an even smaller waiting area – effectively a line of chairs sandwiched between two walls – where people could wait without being seen by those passing through or sitting in the main corridor. Brenda was open about her HIV status: having sufficient legroom was the main consideration in choosing where to sit.

Brenda's body ached, and she moved around in her chair trying to get comfortable as she waited to see the 'HIV doctor'. She brought her camera out of her bag, and we slunk down in our chairs, our legs stretched out into the more private space of this waiting area. We sat for about ten minutes watching a film she had made with her friend in her partner's home in Kuyasa. Brenda chopped vegetables and washed dishes as she spoke about her life to her friend, how she had come to contract HIV and the impact that HIV had had on her life since 1999. After watching the film, Brenda took me through the photographs she had taken since we had last seen each other. She stopped at a photograph and adjusted her body to look at me looking at the photograph. It was a picture of her grandmother, her face lined with age, sitting on a bench in the sun outside her home. She looked sternly at the camera with each arm stretched around the small shoulders of her two great-granddaughters. The girls looked blankly at the camera, both in frayed dresses with grazed knees, unsmiling, seeing but not seeing Brenda behind the camera.

Brenda touched the camera's screen, tracing the faces of her relatives. "Beth, do you remember that school teacher?" She spoke with a tone of urgency, a tone that asked me to hear the underlying implications of what she was saying. I moved up in my chair and looked at her. "You know, the one who's been in *Vukani* [a weekly local newspaper distributed in Khayelitsha]? The one who raped 30 children in Khayelitsha", she said. "He raped these two girls." I put my hand on her hand on the screen still showing her grandmother and nieces, generations that came before and after her; we sat in silence, shoulders touching. Later, Brenda was called into the doctor's office. It was a quick consultation, and she came out saying "It's a boy, Beth." Travelling back to Khayelitsha, she said, "I'm glad it's a boy. It's hard to be a girl in this country … But Beth! I really wanted a girl."

As a young girl the same age as Brenda's nieces, Lilian's parents left her to live with strangers. As described earlier, the precarious decades of life leading up to her daughter's death are documented along the left-hand side of Lilian's journey map. In the top left-hand corner, next to a photograph of a piece of coal in the shape of a light bulb, she writes that she was born in Johannesburg, a coal mining hub, in 1972. Above a photograph of a group of young girls in school uniforms, she writes '1979 – Started School' and under this '1979 – 1980 – Endured abuse.' Next to the dual commencement of school and abuse, she has pasted an excerpt from a magazine article which says, 'I've been through hell and survived. You can too!' In blue paint, and in large letters, she writes, 'Tired of abuse, left and all alone in the streets.' Under this statement are two photographs, one that she has taken herself and one cut from a magazine. The magazine photograph is of a hunched woman walking alone on a wet dirt road under a bleak bleached white sky. Lilian's own photograph sits alongside this image and is of a homeless person in a sleeping bag lying on top of folded cardboard boxes next to a dustbin. She explained to me that she took this photograph because it reminded her of her life as a young woman before she joined TAC. A third photograph in the quadrant of the map that displays her childhood depicts three men, of different generations, with their arms around each other. Under this, in red pen, she writes, 'Raped by a family friend – 1982.' Lilian's experience of abuse, the topographies of precarity recounted through her journey map, wound along a pathway that took her into an abusive relationship where she became pregnant. Without access to PMTCT treatment, these horizontal pathways of precarity shifted into a vertical route of HIV transmission, and she gave birth to a HIV-positive child, who, like Brenda's and Miriam's children, started life on the cusp of death.

Eschewing shweshwe: *navigating risk and pleasure*

In my living room, I had a bright red *shweshwe*-patterned bowl made by Miriam. It held condoms, femidoms and lubricant received from an LGBTQIA+ organization for free, and so they were covered with rainbows and statements like 'celebrating sexual diversity' or 'homophobia is un-African'. Knowing about femidoms and condoms, the women in the core group were most interested in the lubricant. They did not want to 'encourage' their partners with intimations of desire, but they said that they often experienced a great deal of pain through sex. The women oscillated between wanting the lubricant and not wanting the messages on the packaging. I left it at that but later realized that all the sachets had been removed from the bowl. An unspoken agreement ensued: I kept the bowl stocked with lubricant, and the women kept taking the sachets. Weeks later, Miriam told me that she thought lubricant was an excellent invention.

A few months after we had first met, Lilian told me that she had found out that her partner was having sex with other women. She laughed, saying that he was "a catch" and that his infidelity was not sufficient reason for her to end their relationship. However, Lilian struggled to reconcile her love for her partner with his infidelity. A year later, Lilian had become angry. Unwilling to negotiate her partner's infidelity any longer, she ended their relationship.

Miriam's partner, too, had multiple sexual relationships. She had learnt that her partner, Samkelo, was having sex with multiple other partners by reading the text messages on his phone. When Miriam confronted him the first time, he said that she was his only partner and that the last time he tested (five years previously) he was negative; he repeated this to her each time she challenged him about his infidelity until Miriam decided to stop asking and simply work on the understanding that he was lying, and that he was having sex with other people. Samkelo did not believe that he needed to test again and felt that he, and not Miriam, was at risk when having unprotected sex because Miriam had been open about her HIV-positive status. With this rationale, he refused to wear condoms. This generated great concern for Miriam because she felt compelled to have sex with him in order to keep him in her and her children's lives but was concerned about contracting other viral strains and developing resistance to her ARVs.

Her concern for her health extended to her commitment to parent her daughter, Nena: "I have my daughter to look after Beth. At least my son has his father. But my daughter only has me. I have to take care of myself for her." Her son, Khanyo, stayed with Samkelo – his father – in Kuyasa because he attended the school across the road from Samkelo's home. Miriam chose to keep Khanyo in this school as a strategic measure to compel Samkelo to take parental responsibility for their son. These measures also distributed the financial responsibility of Miriam's children across two households and enabled Miriam to maintain her economic independence and to negotiate the frequency of her contact with Samkelo.

I first learnt about Samkelo on Miriam's birthday: we had gone up Table Mountain where we could look out over the peninsula. Standing on the mountain, Miriam traced the vein of the N2 highway out of the city to Khayelitsha and said, "It's hard to see beauty when you're down there. Sometimes you can't even see the sky." Later, Miriam took me through the photographs that she had recently taken. She showed me a photograph of a friend's skirt and pointed out the fabric. It was a fine pattern of white lines on a blue background. This pattern, called *shweshwe*, indicates that the wearer is married. A long conversation ensued as Miriam told me that she would never get married because "[m]en are macho when they get married. If I got married the xhosa tradition would kill me." I asked Miriam if she believed that traditions could change, and she said yes, "[a]s women we can live our own lives better now compared to our mothers. But marriage will never change. That's why you'll never see me wearing *shweshwe*. I will never get married." By opting out of marriage, Miriam was able to insist on living in her own home with Nena, and by remaining in a sexual relationship with Samkelo, she ensured that her son's father stayed in his child's life and shared responsibility for her children as a co-parent.

Miriam's beliefs around marriage and 'macho men' were also expressed by Yvonne, who refused to marry her partner because it would entail "submitting to his family", to his mother, and to isiXhosa traditions and expectations of women. Yvonne was born in 1982 in Johannesburg and moved to Cape Town with her mother and stepfather, both of whom were strongly involved in the anti-apartheid movement. Their involvement would later shape her decision to become an activist with TAC, as discussed in the following chapter. Yvonne worked with Zama as a HIV treatment literacy trainer and lives with her young son and mother in a peri-urban area neighbouring Khayelitsha. She eschewed marriage, saying that isiXhosa traditions would "trap her". According to Yvonne, isiXhosa marriage traditions entail solely wearing skirts, wearing a headscarf, never wearing trousers, not talking back or up to her husband, only spending time with other married women and never saying no to sex. Over Christmas, Yvonne had travelled to her family's home in the Eastern Cape and spent time with her partner and his family as they celebrated his brother's circumcision. She said that she was treated as his wife, even though she was not married to him, and that she was glad to return to Cape Town where – in contrast to her time in the Eastern Cape – there was accessible water, functional electricity and women did not need to do all the work or take care of all the men. Yvonne maintained intimacy with her partner but established and exerted her physical, social and economic autonomy by refusing to get married, by living in her own home with her mother and her son and by sustaining her financial independence.

These narratives indicate a confluence of factors that engender vulnerability, particularly for young women, alongside strategies that women draw on to navigate intimacy and pleasure and complicate the picture painted by studies showing linear causality between gender inequality and HIV. Eight of the ten women in the core group lived in a separate home away from their partner. Earning their own income and living in their own home, or with their parents, were central strategies for the women to negotiate their desire for intimacy and partnership alongside their concerns about the risks that intimacy entailed for their bodies and their lives. Brenda, however, lived with her partner and therefore employed different strategies for negotiating the embodied implications of his insistence on unprotected sex. After her final hospital check-up, we navigated our way back to the home where Brenda lived. As we drove past the 'three thousands', the metal shacks the size of a small room that cost R3,000 (around £150), Brenda said that this would be her last child. Her partner was HIV-positive and did not want to use condoms when having sex; she felt unable to insist on using condoms because she was living in his home and not in her own recently purchased 'three thousand'. She had not finished paying it off and needed to rent it out to her cousins to pay the final instalments. Her tactical response to the difficulties entailed in owing money, in negotiating sex and in preventing pregnancy was tubal ligation.

Brenda checked into hospital at the end of May with contractions; she was ready to give birth. We waited over two days, chatting and napping on gurneys in the corridor, for the long line of emergency caesareans to abate. Brenda was taken into the operating theatre, and once she was prepared for surgery, I was brought in and positioned on a chair next to her head. She lay with her arms stretched out and held down, drips going in and clips sending measurements out to the blinking board monitoring heart rates and blood pressures. Just as the doctors told her that they were starting the caesarean, she said, "Tie". The doctor checked with her that she meant that she wanted her "tubes tied", and she said, "Yes". A clipboard with the consent form was brought to her right hand, still tied to the table, to sign. She signed, and the doctors proceeded with the caesarean. Brenda lay still behind a blue sheet constructed a few centimetres away from her chin. The doctors, sensitive to her possible sense of disconnection, spoke sparingly but considerately to her through the surgery. Finally, they said that her son was ready to come out, and that she would feel some pressure up against her ribs. Brenda's eyes filled with tears. Her son was born, immediately bundled up and taken to a scale by one of the doctors to be weighed. Brenda looked at me and, echoing the statement she made the previous month, whispered, "It's so hard to be a woman." Mpilo was brought around the operating table so that Brenda could see him. I held him while Brenda, still crying, spoke to him; on the other side of the blue sheet, the doctors tied her tubes and stitched her womb closed. Brenda's decision to have her tubes tied was one way for her to navigate the pressures placed on her by her partner's insistence on unsafe sex; she was not, however, able to protect herself from contracting other strains of HIV, and this placed her at higher risk of developing resistance to her ARVs.

This section illustrates the dynamic interplay of gender and HIV based on the lives of the women who formed the core of my ethnographic fieldwork. Deviating from structuralist approaches that permeate analyses of South Africa's 'gender and HIV' nexus, I suggest that women's lives are not dialectically shaped by structures that enable, enact and sustain violence *or* by women's agency as they 'act up', also described as 'globalisation from below' (Robins, 2005). Instead, a more complex picture emerges from these situated accounts as the women expressed a desire to have sex and sexual relationships and worked to navigate their sexual autonomy within a highly complex landscape characterized by high levels of racial, gender and sexual inequality. As these accounts reveal, at times this navigation required resisting assumptions of vulnerability while also carefully working to ensure some degree of financial and bodily autonomy.

"I am the household": diagonal pathways of precarity

The third pathway transects vertical and horizontal modes of transmission and explores diagonal pathways of precarity that include structural inequalities as they are manifested in high rates of unemployment, substance abuse and implicit economic pressures placed on women as primary care-workers in households. These structural inequalities, specifically linked to poverty and unemployment, speak to the complexity of intersectional inequality discussed earlier in this chapter, and they bear witness to the legacy of South Africa's history of colonialism and apartheid. Poverty and unemployment emerged throughout my fieldwork as the main sources of discontent for the women I worked with; many of the women's accounts, often shared through their photo-stories, spoke of substance abuse linked to unemployment. When we spoke about these photographs, they directed their frustration to the state rather than to the individual who was struggling with substance abuse. The findings from the photo-stories, films and interviews in which people 'spoke to the state' are discussed in detail in Chapter 5. This section seeks to foreground women's affective relationships with kin. It departs from the epidemiological framing of 'vertical' or 'horizontal' transmission routes by placing emphasis on the relational and intersectional dynamics of precarity that people of all genders navigate in households and kinship networks. I consider, in particular, a series of structural factors that put strain on these relationships.

The intersectional dynamics of poverty and unemployment were the most significant factors that impinged on women's relationships with their kin. Financial insecurity, in particular, was a persistent form of precarity that all people, regardless of gender, struggled to negotiate in the context of high levels of unemployment and poor levels of education (Mahadea and Kaseeram, 2018; Nonyana and Njuho, 2018; Kwenda et al, 2020; Wakefield et al, 2022). In the fourth quarter of 2019, 6.73 million people were unemployed, representing 29.1 per cent of the country's labour force (StatsSA, 2020). Postcolonial scholars in the field of economics argue that structural unemployment is the most serious form of unemployment in South Africa (Van Aardt, 2012; Plagerson et al, 2019). Structural unemployment refers to a mismatch between the skills that are supplied through education and the skills that are demanded by the labour market (Wakefield et al, 2022). The country's history of racial segregation continues to be structurally enforced through under-funded state schools that are ill-equipped to enable historically and currently disadvantaged people – particularly Black South Africans – from reaching their full potential and entering the labour market with the requisite skills (Tshishonga, 2019; Webster and Francis, 2019). For this reason, the transition between unemployment and employment for many South Africans remains 'neither a smooth nor an immediately successful one' (Ingle and Mlatsheni, 2017: 1).

The challenges of negotiating intersecting inequalities, including their manifestation as structural unemployment, surfaced throughout my fieldwork as partners, brothers and sons of the women in the core group moved back and forth between unemployment and informal employment. This economic volatility prompted some men to rely on women for material support. In turn, this placed pressure on women to stretch their meagre earnings to accommodate their kin and sometimes also placed women at risk when they refused to share their earnings or other material resources. Economic volatility also prompted some of the women's kin to resort to crime as an economic survival mechanism; this placed men in positions of vulnerability, with heightened risks of exposure to violence, alongside the vulnerability their acts entailed for those who experienced the crime.

Negotiating affect and harm

Sibongile was born in 1986 and lives with her uncle and her two sons in Gugulethu. Gugulethu is an informal settlement next to Nyanga where I had conducted fieldwork in 2004, almost a decade prior to meeting Sibongile. "I am the household", she told me as she explained her uncle's alcoholism and the relentless demands – "Boys eat so much!" – of being a mother to two boys and like a mother to her uncle. Sibongile was 13 when she had her first son. She shared this story with me as we walked down the road together, both of us looking ahead, trying to pick our way through the traffic:

'My family were really disappointed in me at first. I was to blame after all [for getting pregnant]. But then they supported me; my grandmother especially supported me. My mother is schizophrenic, so I've never been able to rely on her. My grandmother was there for my boys. But she died last year, and then I got into a very dark place. I'm trying to come out of it now.'

Sibongile lived with her children in the home that her grandmother had secured as part of the post-apartheid reparations process. This home, however, is owned by her uncle, her grandmother's son, and she feels unable to negotiate "household matters" with him because "[h]e has the power. I must just do everything. Buy the food, cook, clean. He just drinks his money." Sibongile was deeply frustrated by her uncle's alcoholism and his financial dependence; the income she derived from her work with uYaphi's income-generation programme was difficult to predict, and this further entrenched her dependence on living with her uncle and catering to his financial demands, because she was unable to afford her own home.

Thandiswa, like Sibongile, earned a meagre income through her work with uYaphi. Unlike Sibongile, she lived in her own home. It was awarded to her after many years of negotiating the complex RDP housing process. Thandiswa was born in 1969, and she has two children, Lindisizwe and Babalwa, who were 27 and 14 years old respectively when we first met. She lives in her home with her two children, her sister and her sister's two children, and her brother. All of the members of her household are financially dependent on Thandiswa. Therefore, in order to supplement her meagre income from uYaphi, Thandiswa buys frozen chickens wholesale in Bellville, a suburb north-east of her home in Khayelitsha; she then cuts the chickens into their constitutive parts, breasts, thighs and so on, and bundles different parts together in 'chicken packs' and sells them to people in her neighbourhood. Thandiswa is an artist like Zama, and like her son Lindisizwe.

When I asked her about her family, she picked up a sheet of paper and a brown pen, put them on her lap and drew each of her family members as she told me about them. Thandiswa drew herself in the middle of the sheet, with her son and daughter drawn on either side of her, their profiles facing Thandiswa. Babalwa is drawn wearing a skirt, with raised eyebrows and round eyes that look like question marks. Babalwa, in fact, looks very similar to this painted image. Her face and her demeanour are inquisitive. She excels at school, and when I asked her what she wanted to do when she was older, she said, "I want to be a doctor. I want to help people." Thandiswa's principal objective in earning money through selling chicken pieces and sometimes repairing clothes is to make sure that Babalwa can finish high school with all the resources she needs to be able to attend university. Her ambition for her daughter is foiled, frequently, by the cost of her son's heroin addiction.

In order to pay for heroin, Lindisizwe had stolen everything of value in Thandiswa's home aside from the items of furniture that were too heavy to remove. He had done this on multiple occasions over the period of his addiction – five years – and Thandiswa lived in anticipation of returning from work to a barren home. Thandiswa often sat with me, crying with despair at her son's drug addiction. She spoke of her son and of his addiction separately; she was extremely loving towards her son but very angry with his addiction. One day, we decided to go up to Signal Hill with her daughter for a walk. Thandiswa showed us various medicinal plants and told us about their healing properties. We sat together on the grass looking out over towards Robben Island and, as I rubbed the leaves of an *imphepho* plant between my fingers, she told me too about her son's recent decision to enter a rehabilitation centre.[2] Her sense of relief was palpable. Later, Thandiswa pulled out a plastic envelope that held about ten A4 sheets with different drawings on them. Her son, she said, wanted to be a designer. Using coloured felt tip pens, Lindisizwe had crafted funky shoes, long elegant dresses, waist-high pencil skirts and business shirts. Those drawings were an indication of the possibility of another life for Thandiswa's son as a designer and not a drug addict. Months later, she told me that her son was taking heroin again. He had left the rehabilitation programme and engineered a way to redeem the deposit that she had put down with an adult education programme for a course he agreed to take in computer literacy.

Drug use and alcoholism impacted the lives of the women in the core group directly and indirectly. In Sibongile's case, her uncle's alcoholism undermined his capacity to seek employment; or perhaps employment had not been possible, and this struggle in a country with such high levels of structural unemployment had manifested through alcoholism. Sibongile's uncle's alcoholism, and his unemployment, in turn placed financial pressure on Sibongile to 'be the household' and wash, cook, clean and pay for all the household costs. The impact of substance abuse was directly felt by Thandiswa as she lost all the items of value in her house to her son's addiction.

In Miriam's case, both she and her home were physically threatened as a result of her younger brother's drug addiction. As an older sister, Miriam had cared for her two younger brothers, Khumbuzile and Lwandle, following their mother's death. This care was not always reciprocated, although in 2023 Miriam explained that her brothers had been bringing meat over to her house to braai (barbeque) on Sundays, which she was pleased about. When I first visited Miriam's home in 2010, she showed me the dents in the front door. These dents were a reminder of her brother's attacks on her home and his latent capacity to hurt Miriam if she challenged his dependence on her.

It was therefore in her best interest, on multiple levels, for her brother to be earning an income even if it was through illegal activities, like running the shebeen over the road from her home.

In the middle of a night, I woke up to the sound of a text message. Miriam wrote saying that Khumbuzile was drunk and threatening to burn down her house. Khumbuzile had asked Miriam for money and had insisted on staying in her home because he could no longer stay in the shebeen. His aggression alerted Miriam to the possibility of a repeated attack on her home, but she felt unable to negotiate rationally with him because he was high on a drug called Tik (crystal methamphetamine). He had been addicted to Tik for months, and Miriam had slowly withdrawn from having any contact with him as she watched him lose weight and become more deeply entwined in his work, and possible criminal activity, with his friends in the shebeen. He had asked Miriam for money because he had been arrested by the police a week earlier for selling alcohol illegally in the shebeen. Miriam was angry with the police for arresting her brother, saying, "It's not fair. He is trying to earn money so that he doesn't need to rely on me so much, and now the police are even taking that away." She was angry, too, because she would be placed in a position of capitulating to her brother's financial dependence or resisting his requests and facing the threat of his violence.

I called her that night, but she did not answer the phone. When I reached her the next morning, I learnt that she had taken her daughter and moved across to stay in Samkelo's home. In seeking shelter from her brother, she had to concede to Samkelo's insistence on sex. Miriam was extremely angry with her brother for placing her home at risk and for forcing her to move in with Samkelo. A few days later, however, Miriam had worked out a plan. A distant relative had died in the Eastern Cape, and she offered to buy her brothers a bus ticket to travel back to his funeral. They agreed, but she only bought one-way tickets for each of them. Two weeks later, we stood in the long queue outside the Checkers money market counter where Miriam only transferred money to her younger brother, Alungile, for his return ticket. In this way, Miriam managed to resolve this issue by effectively consigning Khumbuzile to the Eastern Cape without money to return to Cape Town.

The accounts in this section reveal the ripple effects of addiction for the women I worked with, as they navigated the social, physical and economic costs of caring for – and protecting themselves from – their kin. As I discuss earlier in this chapter, an intersectional approach to understanding inequality reveals the multiple axes of marginalization that accrue to create embodied forms of precarity. In these accounts, the precarity shifts across genders and is strongly linked to historical forms of structural violence enacted through, for instance, colonial and apartheid forms of segregated education that powerfully disadvantaged Black people of all genders. Postcolonial scholars like Fomunyam and Teferra (2017), Msila (2020), Oyedemi (2021) and many others (Epstein and Morrell, 2012; Donohue and Bornman, 2014; Adeyemo et al, 2020; Drerup, 2020) working to decolonize the education system in South Africa argue that the country's high rates of unemployment and corresponding poverty need to be understood as a product of this history. Further, the relationship between substance abuse, unemployment and poverty also requires a sensitive recognition of the intersecting forms of structural violence that manifest in quite different ways for different genders. In my research, I found that women worked hard to manage the consequences of substance abuse within their homes and relationships, as men experienced the pernicious and long-term impact of poverty and unemployment, and lack of state support, in their bodies through their substance abuse. Despite their different manifestations in people's lives, these accounts suggest that intersectional inequality linked to race, unemployment and poverty is profoundly embodied across genders, both through the actual substance abuse and through the felt impact of that abuse at a household and interpersonal level.

Conclusion

The accounts in this chapter reveal the complex pathways through which HIV moves into people's bodies and relationships. By paying attention to the socio-economic contexts that give form to certain kinds of material embodiments, they reveal the value of understanding precarity through an intersectional lens. This chapter centred on HIV as the primary nonhuman agent: it zoomed in on this actant in order to uncover the wide network of interpersonal, socio-economic and political relationships that assemble around HIV. In doing so, I sought to extend epidemiological frameworks that frame the movement of HIV along horizontal routes into women's bodies, or along vertical routes into babies' bodies. Across each section in this chapter, we see how HIV came to enter women's bodies and lives along these pathways, and we see too, at each junction, how women navigated the intersectional inequalities that generated these precarious dynamics: by moving across the country to access life-saving medical care for their children, by joining TAC and working as activists to compel the government to provide ARVs through the health system and by maintaining financial independence and separate households in order to be in a position to negotiate sexual relationships. My ethnography, therefore, challenges the discursive construction of HIV-positive women as passive victims; however, I recognize that I worked with a particular group of HIV-positive women who accessed socio-economic resources and were also strongly politicized through their anti-apartheid and HIV activism. Although these findings cannot be generalized, they point to a more nuanced set of gender dynamics that I introduced in this chapter and reflect on in the following chapters, namely women's constrained agency to act on and through a network of actors that are implicated in their embodied precarity. This chapter and the next focus on two primary actants within this network, namely HIV and HIV medicine, as they draw attention not only to their intra-action with(in) women's bodies but also to a broader set of socio-economic dynamics that enables these actants to enter and become animate in women's lives.

The proliferation of sexual violence in the accounts that emerged during my fieldwork reflected a larger backdrop in which HIV transmission is linked to intersectional racial and gender inequality in South Africa. HIV was able to move into women's bodies through unprotected sex because, as Brenda explained, she was not aware that she needed to protect herself from the virus; or as Zama told me, she did not feel that she was able to negotiate the frequency or kind of sex that she had as a young woman. While the presence of gender inequality, and its brutal manifestation as sexual violence in girls' and women's lives, was a strong feature of my fieldwork, I was still confronted by the explanatory limitations of epidemiological assertions that stipulated a correlation between gender inequality and higher rates of HIV infection among women compared to men. I do not dispute this correlation; in fact, part of the rationale underpinning my research lay in the multiple and intersecting inequalities that seemed to drive HIV, in epidemiological terms, into women's lives and bodies.

There is a plethora of research that suggests that sexual violence and its relationship to HIV occurs against an inflected backdrop of pervasive and entangled inequalities in South Africa, where gender, sexuality, race and class powerfully intersect to reinforce poor Black women's vulnerability (Mabaso et al, 2018; Mampane, 2018; Jacques-Aviñó et al, 2019; Mabaso et al, 2019; Akobirshoev et al, 2022). The trope of 'transactional sex' perhaps best characterizes the accounts of HIV and intersectional inequality. These studies suggest that (particularly young) poor Black women are less able to negotiate sex, or in some cases, that women actively engage in sex with wealthier men in exchange for material goods. This has been observed in South Africa (Leclerc-Madlala, 2003; Dunkle et al, 2007; Mampane, 2018) but also further up the continent, in inland fisheries for example (Béné and Merten, 2008; Howard-Merrill et al, 2022), where life and livelihoods are, like most places in the world, relational and navigated materially through affect and intimacy.

Although these studies give texture to the correlation between gender inequality and high rates of HIV incidence among women compared to men, they also seem to support a paradigm that has fuelled development interventions to 'empower' women by foregrounding women's relative lack of power compared to men. This critique has emerged strongly in recent work by postcolonial and decolonial feminist scholars who challenge development interventions that frame Black women as 'victims' in heterosexual relationships (Makama et al, 2019; Mushonga and Dzingirai, 2022; Okyere-Manu et al, 2022). For instance, looking at Zimbabwean women's relationships with Nigerian migrants in Harare, Mushonga and Dzingirai (2022) explore social mobility among women and foreground the principle of patronage as a way to recognize their agency in exchanges of sex, money and emotional favours.

The recognition of women's agency in relationships that might have otherwise been considered 'transactional' has surfaced most keenly in research around migration, with some studies suggesting that rather than becoming subordinate to men through economic and sexual transactions, women may in fact be exploiting migrant men for particular ends (Dzingirai et al, 2014; Groes-Green, 2014). Cornwall (1997, 2004, 2007) has similarly argued that by analytically positioning women as victims and men as perpetrators, we not only fail to see how men too navigate fraught social and economic landscapes alongside women but also fail to see the strategies women draw as they actively navigate their everyday lives. More recently, ethnographic research in Sierra Leone has shown how relationships are formed around the flows of fish and love in a tightly stretched maritime economy: fishermen and bandawomen – women who dry and sell the fish harvested by fishermen – both resent and rely on the affective ties of obligation and care that draw them into a relationship with each other (Diggins, 2013, 2018).

In my fieldwork, it was Zama's account of the skies that fight, of the pathways she travelled in her life, that brought the complex realities of women's lives 'to life' and prompted a shift in my sense-making of the HIV–gender dyad in South Africa. As we see in this chapter, although HIV entered women's bodies and lives along horizontal, vertical and diagonal pathways, women also worked strategically to manage their precarity. Yvonne, for example, insisted on living in her own home, away from her partner, in order to be in a position to negotiate sex. Miriam, too, stayed in her own home as a way to manage her sexual relationship with her child's father. We see, too, how women negotiated their material wellbeing strategically through their sexual relationships, as Miriam placed her son in his father's care by keeping him registered at the school just over the road from his father's home.

Further, if HIV generated precarity as it entered and became animate in the body, then it is also analytically important to understand how it came to take on this life in women's bodies. In this respect, my research connected with and also challenged prevailing accounts of the gender–HIV dyad. Simply ascribing HIV transmission, in epidemiological terms, to entrenched gender inequality does not, in itself, engage with the complex pathways that women navigate between desire and risk in their sexual relationships and in extremely difficult socio-economic contexts. In this respect, my ethnography found that women are subtly, and sometimes with great difficulty, negotiating their intimate relationships with men by forming separate households and by working and establishing their financial independence. This was not a straightforward matter of asserting agency or submitting to intersecting structures of inequality; here, my research challenges structural theories that position agency in relation to structure (see Giddens, 1990) without looking at the 'grey space' in between.

For, we see that although Brenda enjoyed her sexual relationship with her partner, she felt unable to insist on using a condom when having sex because she was reliant on her partner for her home. If we consider her decision to have her 'tubes tied' in light of this picture, it seems that Brenda's life fits the 'gender–HIV' narrative of the economically dependent woman struggling to negotiate sex in an unequal relationship. We could also interpret her relationship as transactional: providing sex in exchange for a home. But we might be wrong. By looking at the multiple pathways that HIV travelled into women's bodies, we not only see the socio-economic structures that "make it hard to be a girl in this country"; we also see the myriad tactics that women employ along these pathways to seek medical care for their children, to secure their financial independence and negotiate the risks and desires that surface in sexual relationships. Brenda's decision to have her 'tubes tied' was a tactical one, just as her decision to stay in her partner's home was a conscious, if not difficult, choice; she was not financially dependent on her partner, and she made these difficult decisions on the basis that she had recently bought her own shack and was financially navigating the repayment of her home by renting it to her cousin while she stayed in the home of her boyfriend. Therefore, as we see with Brenda, although it was not always possible to fully negotiate sexual relationships, this dynamic cannot simply be ascribed to gender inequality or explanations held in transactional sex analyses; it requires a more fine-grained understanding of biopolitics and precarity.

Where precarity surfaces in sexual relationships, it has embodied implications for women's and men's wellbeing: through unprotected sex, HIV, as an actant, becomes more adept at mutating and resisting ARVs when moving, through horizontal pathways of blood and semen, between partners' bodies. The ability of HIV to mutate and become resistant to ARVs underlines the importance of developing and distributing new HIV medicines, like the recently developed long-acting injection, lenacapavir, that can continue to block the life cycle of this particular actant. Women, as I discuss in the following chapters, not only exert their constrained agency in their social and sexual relationships but also very much in their political relationship with the state through various shifting citizen practices around HIV medicine. Lilian, for example, describes how her child's death marked her decision to join TAC and fight for her own and other HIV-positive people's lives. These nuanced dynamics connect to but also problematize the 'gender–HIV' dyad in which gender inequality is one of the main 'drivers' of the HIV epidemic in South Africa (Madiba and Ngwenya, 2017; Mabaso et al, 2019; Klazinga et al, 2020). I suggest that the gender–HIV dyad is problematic not only because it positions women as passive victims of men who are, conversely, held to be active perpetrators or 'vectors of transmission'. More fundamentally, it is problematic because these discourses direct our attention towards individuals or 'cultures of inequality' and away from the biopolitics of structural violence in which the state is implicated.

The ethnographic accounts in this chapter suggest that not only does the state enter the body of individuals or populations through disciplining techniques (Foucault, 2008) but we also see how its absence, too, exerts an effect on the body. For Miriam, the state was absent in the Eastern Cape, as it was in many of the women's lives, in so much as it did not provide essential AIDS therapies that would have blocked HIV from moving into her daughter's body and stopped her daughter from starting life on the cusp of death. The absence of the state was visible too in the responsibility that was conferred on women, implicitly, to provide unpaid care for kin who could not access health care in rural parts of the country, or who could not access essential medicines that would sustain their lives even when health centres were accessible and functional. Bearing Arendt (1958) and Agamben (1998) and in mind, it is not simply that the state is absent but rather that the state – through its absence – refuses to engage with citizens. Butler (2003) describes this 'refusal to engage' in light of Levinas's (1979) philosophy of the face in which the other's precarity becomes visible only when we look; if the state does not look, then it does not see the precarity that it induces. In refusing to acknowledge the emergence of HIV in South Africa and the vital importance of providing PMTCT treatment, the state refused to acknowledge the biopolitical population of HIV-positive pregnant women. I suggest, therefore, that the expectations of care placed on women and the limited life of their children born in this 'window period' bear witness to Agamben's figure of *homo sacer*: 'Bare life is thus paradoxically made part of the political by the very fact of its exclusion' (1998: 206).

I conclude this chapter by proposing that the state's failure to address the conditions that enabled HIV to move along these three intersecting pathways is illustrative of two strands of biopolitical precarity; each strand speaks to the relative presence and absence of the state as it is embodied as precarity in people's lives. First, the absence of the state was visible in the failure of the education and employment sectors to address the intersecting social and economic inequalities of apartheid's racist education system, which continues to have ramifications for generations of Black South Africans who are disproportionately affected by unemployment and intransigent poverty. This is evident, in particular, in the diagonal pathways of precarity in which structural violence is felt in the struggle with unemployment experienced by most of the men who were related to the women with whom I worked; it is not clear whether Sibongile's uncle's alcoholism was a result or a cause of his inability to work. Nor is it clear that Lindisizwe, Thandiswa's son, was more prone to drug addiction because he could not find work. But these interrelated dependencies speak to a despondency I observed among the men I came to know, albeit more peripherally, a despondency that, in turn, translated into Khumbuzile's decision to work in a shebeen and on the shadowy edges of criminality to earn a living. Without access to a fair and equal education as they were growing up during apartheid, these men struggled to earn a living as adults; the women I worked with, on the other hand, were placed under enormous strain to care for these members of their financially stretched households. The absence of the state in these systems in turn placed women at 'heightened risk of disease, poverty, starvation, displacement, and of exposure to violence without protection' (Butler, 2009: 2). Miriam, for example, was threatened with physical violence by her brother, Khumbuzile, when she attempted to assert her independence – and drew his attention to his own relatively limited capacity to earn money.

The second biopolitical strand of precarity relates less to the absence of the state evinced in failing social and economic systems and more about the active presence of the state in creating politically induced conditions of vulnerability 'for populations exposed to arbitrary state violence and to other forms of aggression that are not enacted by states and against which states do not offer adequate protection' (Butler, 2009 2). This strand connects to vertical and horizontal pathways of precarity. Women's ability to stop HIV from entering their own bodies was very much connected to their constrained and fluctuating agency in their sexual relationships. This, as discussed earlier in the chapter, is connected to intersectional inequalities, like the gendered expectations around care that forced Miriam to terminate her education and start caring for her brothers and her mother; this is evinced, too, as Zama entered her first sexual relationships, like Miriam and Brenda, without knowing how to insist on using condoms and, at times, without feeling it was possible to say no. The historic failure of the state to provide treatment to stop HIV from travelling along vertical pathways from mothers into their children's bodies generated further sources of precarity. Lilian describes how, like Miriam, her child's illness was indecipherable, and that her child's death was directly attributable to the state's refusal to provide PMTCT treatment to HIV-positive pregnant women. Further, as I explore in the following chapter, once ARVs were introduced, the state's biopolitical presence came to be felt in the embodied memory of pre-ARV illness, the persistent ill-health of HIV-positive children, side effects of treatments and the state's failure to introduce newer and more effective treatments to those who were failing the existing treatment regimens available through the public health system.

I suggest that the three interlinked pathways traced in this chapter are, one, a function of the first biopolitical strand of precarity, namely the failure of social and economic systems to mitigate against women's and girls' corporeal exposure to violence. Two, the pathways speak to Black men's and women's embodied memory of historical and contemporary structural violence, exacted by the government, in line with the second biopolitical strand of precarity. Finally, women's tactical negotiation of structural violence within each pathway opens a discursive space for resisting epidemiological and social constructions of vulnerability as they navigated their affective and interpersonal relationships. These actions take place in the space between the current conceptualizations of structural violence as 'top-down' or resistance as 'globalization from below'.

4

New Generation Struggles

The previous chapter focused on HIV and three epidemiological and social 'pathways of precarity' that enabled the virus to move into women's bodies and become animated through their lives.[1] In doing so, it highlighted the biopolitical dynamics of precarity linked to vertical transmission, horizontal transmission and diagonal networks of kinship and affect. Mirroring the previous chapter's conception of HIV as an actant that replicates and engenders vulnerability in the body, this chapter introduces HIV medicine as an actant that halts, for a time, the progression of HIV to AIDS.

Across this chapter, I explore iterations of biopolitical precarity and performativity in relation to the struggles encountered by the people with whom I worked, at different stages and in different spaces of their lives. In the previous chapter, I approached HIV from an oblique angle: instead of looking at HIV incidence solely as an indicator of women's socio-economic and biological susceptibility to infection, I discussed how – in each pathway – women worked to secure their vitality as they, too, struggled with their own and their children's embodied precarity linked to and extending beyond the manifestation of HIV in their bodies. In this chapter, I move from exploring the biopolitical pathways along which HIV travels into women's bodies to understanding how HIV medicines are differently embodied and experienced in their lives.

The importance of thinking about biomedicine through a social lens, as it is held and embodied differentially, follows a long history of medical anthropological research. Rayna Rapp's ethnographic research on diagnostic technologies and amniocentesis (Rapp, 2014a, 2014b), for example, emphasizes the importance of looking beyond narrow framings of biomedicine as a 'programme', located in a clinical space and decentred from people's everyday lives. She describes a 'bio-techno-sociality' that emerges between knowledge formed within the families she worked with and biomedical and technicist discourses:

[O]ur understandings of new biomedical technologies are significantly enhanced when we examine them in a wide social framework and do not confine our investigation to the clinic. This broader perspective enables us to see technologies in play, as they are understood, appropriated and occasionally resisted by the parties who deploy them. (2000: 205)

In line with Rapp's call to understand new biomedical technologies in their social contexts, I found that, in the 'era of treatment' (Moyer, 2015) under Presidents Zuma and Ramaphosa, HIV medicines can no longer be framed as a 'technology of life' (Rose, 2009) or as the 'technofix' to the problem of HIV and potential death (Lock and Nguyen, 2018). These dynamics with and in the body prompt a rethinking of sociality as subjectivities shift across time and in different spaces. Across this chapter, I explore the intra-action of HIV and antiretrovirals (ARVs) with(in) the body and describe how these actants generate different forms of risks and opportunities as they are embodied over time. I propose that, in understanding HIV and ARVs as nonhuman actants that travel complex pathways into and within women's bodies, we can also start to view some of the more nuanced dynamics that women negotiate in their everyday lives, through their relationships, and beyond categorizations that frame HIV infection as a problem, a proxy for women's vulnerability, with ARVs cast as the solution.

Two linked sets of narratives around the embodiment of these actants emerged in my fieldwork, and they draw the focus out from the body to situate the body in relation to South Africa's shifting biopolitical landscape. The first set of narratives articulates how people perceive the intra-action of HIV and ARVs in their sustained vitality.[2] What I mean by this is that predominantly in the first decade of my fieldwork, the women I worked with fought for access to ARVs because they viewed them as central to their ability to live a long life with HIV as a chronic condition. In this way, the first set of narratives I discuss in this chapter speaks to the evolution of the struggle to access ARVs in South Africa and reflects a long-standing history of medical anthropological research on embodiment. Arthur Young, for instance, called for a 'situated discourse' that views 'the cultural production of the body as an unstable contested object, the result of ongoing encounters and exchanges between local and global knowledges' (1982: 145). Over time, scholars like Emily Martin (1991, 1992, 1995), Nancy Scheper Hughes (2001, 2002), Margaret Lock (1993, 2012) and Vinh-Kim Nguyen (2008, 2019) have foregrounded the interplay of corporeality with politics, emphasizing the value of understanding people's experience of this interplay rather than offering any singular framing of 'the body' as an ontological given. Anthropologists like Kwasi Konadu (2008) and Nolwazi Mkhwanazi (2016) have critiqued these historical anthropological approaches to thinking about the body in postcolonial contexts like Ghana and South Africa respectively where their research reveals how legacies of domination and extraction persist in the ways people embody nuanced forms of precarity in the present. Building on this scholarship, the second set of narratives articulates the complex embodiment of vitality alongside precarity in ways that reflect South Africa's apartheid and colonial history. Over time, ARVs came to be experienced as generative of vulnerability and not only as a symbol of vitality. These embodied experiences of vulnerability were linked to living in Khayelitsha, without access to safe water, electricity or toilets in their homes while navigating precarious working conditions or inadequate state grants.

These two sets of narratives flow into each other and do not represent a totalizing view of the effects of HIV and ARVs in the lives of the people with whom I worked; the positive effects of ARVs – as unequivocally essential for sustaining life – were implicit, and the precarious vitality of the people with whom I worked was fundamental. However, I discuss this set of narratives here because in my fieldwork I found that a related and emergent set of struggles was becoming salient: speaking to the narratives of embodiment described earlier, they complicated the view that ARVs are a 'technofix' and present a challenge to the idea that only 'local biologies' like HIV and ARVs are embodied. These emergent struggles were biopolitical, and they related first to the intra-action of HIV and ARVs 'within' the body, and second, to the 'outside' socio-economic context in which people's bodies were situated. I describe these emergent concerns as new generation struggles. The first part of this chapter explores these struggles 'within' the body, and the second section situates these embodied struggles within the social, economic and political terrain in which women navigated their lives.

"*Amandla! Awethu!*": the struggle for ARVs and embodied vitality

On a crisp autumn morning in June, Khayelitsha resonated with vuvuzelas, drum majorettes and song as hundreds of people, many wearing HIV-positive T-shirts, marched through the streets linking the Ubuntu Clinic in Site B with the OR Tambo Stadium. A few weeks earlier, Miriam and I had sat in the sun on the pavement outside the Treatment Action Campaign (TAC) and Médecins Sans Frontières (MSF) offices in Khayelitsha as a photographer took photographs of ten people against a brick wall in the crowded parking lot. There was a great deal of hilarity as we stumbled down the staircase trying to get chairs out into the parking lot, as people pulled faces at the camera, sang, tried on and swopped HIV-positive T-shirts and spoke of "how far we've come since those dark days". The photographs were collated and printed as a banner that was carried by the marchers through Khayelitsha and placed in the front of the OR Tambo stadium to celebrate the start of the MSF trial over a decade earlier, in 2001. The photographs were of people who, like Miriam, had been part of the first cohort of people to start ARVs through this trail-blazing trial. Walking from the march into the OR Tambo Stadium, we were met by large banners saying 'Early treatment for HIV-positive infants saves lives. Treat the children!', 'Take control. Take an HIV Test!' and 'STOP TB.' The posters called for ongoing activism and indicated a shift from accessing essential medicines to a focus on introducing new medical technologies, saying 'Save Lives. Transform TB prevention, diagnostics and treatment.' Body maps made by the Bambanani Women's Group (BWG) hung from the first floor of the auditorium over the heads of people as they entered the ground floor. School children were seated in stalls that circumscribed the first floor, each school singing songs in competition with the others. It was a festival for ARVs, a celebration of life and an affirmation of collaboration between activist coalitions and local and provincial government.

The spatial configuration of political alliances and of biosocial groupings was visible in the organization of chairs – who sat where and next to whom – in the auditorium. White chairs for 'VIPS' – those on ARVs – lined the periphery of the stage on the ground floor. The chairs on the left-hand side were for the first cohort of HIV-positive people who started ARVs, and the chairs on the right were for the speakers and representatives from local and provincial government, MSF and TAC. Miriam, Thandiswa and Brenda went to sit on the left of the stage; Miriam was later called out, and I saw her then processing down the aisle of the auditorium with the other ten people who had been photographed and a larger group of activists, ululating, singing and dancing. They moved down to the open area in front of the stage and formed a circle, still dancing and singing. The MC for the opening ceremony came into the centre of the group shouting, "Amandla!" (Power!). Everyone in the stadium stood up, and we shouted: "Awethu!" (To us/the people!). Acknowledging the legacy of the struggle for HIV medicines, the MC recited a series of names of people who had died. At one point, she shouted, "Long live the spirit of Christopher Moraka, Long Live!" Moraka had died of treatable oral thrush because he could not afford to pay for the cost of fluconazole under Pfizer's patent, and the government refused to provide this treatment through the public health system. People bearing witness to the legacy of activists like Moraka, those who had been able to access essential medicines, fanned out from the central circle to sit on the white chairs to the left of the stage, followed by the keynote speakers who moved to the chairs on the right of the stage. One of the keynote speakers was Thobani, a veteran TAC activist who had worked with Miriam in the early years of the struggle for HIV medicine; their images were on the banner – the backdrop to the day's events and a reminder of the legacy of MSF's trial in the face of South Africa's failure to provide HIV treatment at the turn of the century.

When Thobani started ARVs through the MSF trial in June 2001, he weighed 30 kilograms, and his CD4 (cluster of differentiation) count was 174. A CD4 count has historically been used as a marker of illness and health: a high CD4 count indicates good health, whereas a low CD4 count indicates illness or susceptibility to illness. ACD4 cell is a white blood cell that forms the frontline defence cell in the body's immune system; the higher the CD4 'count', the greater the body's capacity to defend against illness. Thobani reflected the skeleton of his story, and the weakness of his immune system, in a body map that he created, but did not complete, in 2003. Almost a decade later, he participated in an initiative with the Departments of Public Works and Health to create a new body map. The second set of body maps track the journey of each artist's life since starting ARVs and have been placed in the waiting areas of Khayelitsha's recently built hospital as mosaics; like the activists described earlier, the artists' mosaics bear witness to the legacy of the struggle for HIV medicine and the efficacy of prevention of mother-to-child transmission (PMTCT) treatment and ARVs in sustaining their lives over the course of the last decade. I discuss the body maps that were created across these two periods, first at the height of activism and then a decade after the introduction of ARVs in Khayelitsha through MSF's trial.

In his second body map, and in his speech at the MSF ten-year celebration, Thobani notes the change in his health over the last decade: in 2011, his CD4 count was 622 and his viral load is undetectable. These biomedical indicators connect to the life cycles of HIV and ARVs as actants, with ARVs having successfully prevented HIV from co-opting CD4 cells and replicating, thus supporting the CD4 cells in sustaining his immune system. In the contours of his body, he has drawn his source of strength: a spear, represented by a red sheath and a white handle. This spear, he said when describing the symbols on his map, represented his isiXhosa heritage and the way that he was encouraged (particularly through traditional male circumcision) to be strong. This is reflected in the message he wrote for other people living with HIV: 'Life is a challenge – face it.' He attributes his emotional strength to his heritage and his physical strength to HIV medicine. The white markings drawn inside the contours of his body symbolize his ARV tablets. He said, when discussing his body map, that he had been on ARVs for so long that they had become part of who he is: that they were not simply pills that he put into his body but that they were his body. HIV medicine had intra-acted so intimately with his body that he no longer distinguished between the boundaries of the medicine and the boundaries of his body – they had become each other. As an activist, Thobani had called on the state to intervene in the space of his body by providing medicines; with these medicines, he had not only resumed full health but had also come to embody ARVs so fully that he no longer separated the boundaries of the pill from the state of his body. His account draws into focus the biopolitical dynamic that linked the state of his body with the body of the state.

Further, Thobani draws his cultural heritage, that of strength represented by a spear, within his body and alongside the ARVs that gave his body strength, disrupting dichotomies that separate the social from the science, discourse from materiality, human from nonhuman. Drawing on the definition of posthumanist performativity as 'one that incorporates important material and discursive, social and scientific, human and nonhuman, and natural and cultural factors' (Barad, 2003: 808), Thobani's account illustrates how a nonhuman actant, HIV medicine, moved into and became a part of Thobani's materiality, his body, and in turn played a role in the discursive performance of his wellbeing. Thobani's discursive practices, his body map, his photograph on the MSF banner, his speeches in TAC marches and at MSF's ten-year celebration, are aspects of Thobani's performance of activism and of health, precipitated by the presence of HIV in his life and his awareness of the value of HIV medicine for sustaining his life.

The visual depiction of his body filled with HIV medicine illustrates the posthumanist dimension described by Barad (2020, 2021, 2022) as iterative intra-activity. Barad introduced the term 'intra-action' to reflect a long-standing recognition – at least in the field of quantum physics – that entities are not only interacting but also mutually re-constituted through their being/doing. Feminist writers on embodiment have taken up this term to make sense of the ways that matter *matters* (Van der Tuin, 2011), that it is not simply a 'passive substance onto which culture and language etch meaning. Matter here is agentic, surpassing the discursive–material relation, as it "intra-acts" in and with its world(s)' (Fischer and Dolezal, 2018: 90). Applying this approach to medicine as matter that *matters*, it becomes possible to see how – for Thobani – his ARVs were not only pills that he put into his body to sustain his life; they *were* his body, they were his life. HIV medicine had intra-acted so intimately with his body that he no longer distinguished between the boundaries of the medicine and the boundaries of his body – they had become each other.

Bongiwe, too, spoke of the impact of HIV medicine on her body and in her life through two sets of body maps. Bongiwe was born in 1975 in Gugulethu, in Cape Town. She tested HIV-positive in August 2001 and started ARVs in 2002. When discussing her body map, she said:

> 'It's nine years down the line and I'm still going strong. I'm not afraid to say that I'm HIV [positive]. This is my body map … Here I show what HIV looks like now. Before I said, in the previous body map, I said HIV looks like fire, you know it burns. I used to have a lot of pains at first, but now I feel like the fire has cooled down. That's why I show some coals here. It's coming down to ashes and it's thanks to ARVs.'

As a way to describe how ARVs 'cooled' the fire of HIV, Bongiwe echoed the other body map artists by referring to a set of biomedical indicators of relative illness and health that had changed between 2003 and 2011: "My CD4 count was 18 at the time, and I was weighing 48 kg. This is me now: my CD4 count is 1045, my viral load is undetectable and I weigh 76 kilograms." Bongiwe's account suggests, as does Thobani's, that the self-care practices entailed in adhering to ARVs were embodied by resumed health, indicated through these biomedical markers. These markers suggest an 'internalization' of scientific knowledge generated through TAC's treatment literacy programme: as ARVs prevent HIV from changing its genetic material and entering the CD4 cell, they enable healthy cells to support the body's immune response and quell the effect of HIV as a 'fire' that burns.

During this conversation, Bongiwe and I sat together with prints of the body maps on our laps and a pot of tea at our feet talking about the changes that had taken place in South Africa since she had created her first body map in 2003. In this body map, Bongiwe had drawn a very much smaller body within the larger outline of her body map to describe how small and frail she was when she started ARVs. I asked her about the white marks she had drawn in her second body map. She said, "These are the ARVs." Tracing her hand over the red contour of her body, moving in and out of the white circles representing the ARVs, she echoed Thobani, saying, "They're all over the body." Bongiwe's description suggests that the ARVs had, as with Thobani, become her body; by intra-acting with HIV, her ARVs were embodied in the fuller fleshier body she contrasts with her frail 'pre-ARV' self. However, at the time that Bongiwe started ARVs, she was conscious of accounts, fuelled by former President Mbeki and Health Minister Tshabalala-Msimang, that ARVs were toxic and even deadly.

The following excerpt from our conversation illustrates Bongiwe's initial concern about taking ARVs and her unfolding relationship with these medicines. She was wary of the medicines as she did not know what they were going to do to her, but over time, they intra-acted with HIV to make "pains go" and in doing this and showing her "the way out" of illness, ARVs became her friend:

Me: How are you feeling in your body now?

Bongiwe: Yeah, great!

Me: And when you did your last body map?

Bongiwe: I did not have hope, but things are different now. Because at first I was taking ARVs and I did not know what they were going to do to me, where they would take me to. Now I can see the way out. Now they are my friend.

Me: And the new message in your body map?

Bongiwe: It says shine where you are. You mustn't be afraid. Like they say: stomach in, chest out! … The pains are gone, I'm healthy now. I'm fresh. It's like a Bongiwe that's risen up from the dead.

We looked up from the body maps and I said, "Like a Phoenix?" Bongiwe laughed and then we were quiet for a moment. "Like an Eagle", she said, waving her arms next to her as if she was flying.

Across the body maps, ARVs were depicted as powerful nonhuman actants that had challenged the power of HIV within the arena of the body. Noloyiso, for example, spoke about her sense of ARVs "calming" the storm of HIV within her body through her second body map. In her 2003 body map, she writes that she was born in Tsolo, Eastern Cape, and tested HIV-positive in 2001. She started ARVs in the same year. Like Bongiwe, she describes how her health changed as a result of ARVs, between 2003 and 2011, with reference to biomarkers:

'I started to take ARVs in 2001 my CD4 count was 1. My viral load was 76,000. My weight was 47 kgs. Before, in my other body map, I drew HIV: it looks like a storm. When a storm comes, it brings a lot of things: heavy rains; thunderstorms; lightning; wind. When your body aches, it's like falling of hairs, thrush, everything like that.'

In Noloyiso's second body map, she had drawn small footprints that move up her legs, her stomach, chest and across her shoulders down her arms; the footprints in the upper part of her body are drawn against a backdrop of small blue waves. I asked her about her depiction of HIV as a storm in her first body map and about the footprints and blue waves in her second body map. In her response, she described how ARVs have enabled her to "stand on" HIV, making it "like nothing" to her now:

'HIV is like nothing to me now. I'm not worried about it. Because I just see that it is calm. I show in this [second] map that I'm walking up on – on top of – it. It's like the sand, you know, when you walk on the sand there is that mark … [With] wet sand it leaves a mark and then when the water comes it just wipes that mark. It's like the treatment that I already am taking has wiped the HIV. So now I don't feel like I have HIV.'

Noloyiso's description of ARVs as radically transformative, an actant able to 'wipe HIV away', is a theme in many studies conducted just as ARVs became internationally available (Biehl, 2005, 2012; Rasmusen and Richey, 2012). Robins (2006), for example, refers to the 'treatment testimonies' of activists who give accounts of the 'lazarus effect' of HIV as they transitioned from bare life to full health. Their bare life was, as Robins argues, a result of the state refusing to provide ARVs and therefore withholding their citizens' ability to secure long-term vitality; he links the 'lazarus effect', however, both to the medicines themselves and the responsibilities entailed in taking them. Similarly, although activists like Thobani, Bongiwe and Noloyiso accorded agency to ARVs, as actants, in their embodied health, I found, too, that their resumed health was linked to a set of complex disciplining techniques in which the activity of HIV medicine with HIV within the body is played out or performed. As Marsland writes:

> From learning how to narrate their experiences to become 'therapeutic citizens' in Burkina Faso (Nguyen 2005), to the 'responsibilized' citizen–activists of the Treatment Action Campaign (TAC) in South Africa (Robins 2006), and the new social movements that worked with the Brazilian state to make ARV therapy available to all (Biehl 2004), these groups of people living with HIV have become known for their political radicalism, and docility in practicing new regimes of care that are oriented toward the requirements of the pharmaceutical (Biehl 2007). (2012: 471)

These 'regimes of care' speak to Foucault's conception of 'technologies of the self' (1998). He describes the 'techniques of self' prescribed by ancient Greek pagan morality in order to condition sexual ethics. His work has been taken up by anthropologists researching biomedical regimes of care to show a contradiction in the practices required of those receiving ARVs (Kalofonos, 2008; Hörbst and Wolf, 2014). For people on ARVs are told to follow a set of practices, a regime, that entail strict adherence to their medicines and healthy eating.

Unlike the ancient Greeks, Marsland (2012) describes the contradiction she observed in Tanzania as the people with whom she worked were not moving from a place of decadence and plenty into one of ascetic restrictions. Instead, they were required by biomedical regimes of care to – almost impossibly – secure scarce food and other material resources as techniques of 'positive living' on ARVs. In South Africa, Thomas Cousins (2016) articulates this tension vividly through ethnographic fieldwork in KwaZulu-Natal. Also writing in the aftermath of the struggle for ARVs, Cousins considers the new forms of hunger that arise with ARV rollout, and particularly in light of the pharmaceutical vision for controlling and eradicating the epidemic through 'treatment as prevention' interventions. Like Marsland (2012), Cousins describes how in his fieldwork he found a tension between a commitment to adhere to ARV treatment on the one hand and a struggle to meet this commitment in the context of profound food insecurity on the other. He describes how, after the struggle for ARVs has subsided, HIV can be understood as a chronic condition that reveals the underlying conditions of structural violence. This research resonates with Kalofonos's (2008, 2021) ethnographic work in Mozambique, where ARV programmes can have 'dehumanising effects' for those who cannot afford to eat but also cannot afford to take their ARVs without food because of the 'torture of increased hunger pains brought on by ARVs in undernourished bodies' (2008: 364).

New generation struggles and embodied precarity

Returning to my own ethnography, context mattered. I take context to matter both within and beyond the body, as I read the body itself as permeable. This approach builds on these existing studies around life in the aftermath of ARV provision, and it also calls attention to the interplay between the context in which people live their lives as well as the lives of medicines and viruses within people's bodies. In the sections that follow, I look into the body to see how, as actants, HIV and ARVs intra-act in complex ways with each other to generate risk and also opportunity. As we see in the following sections, a new set of struggles have surfaced that problematize both the context in which ARVs intra-act with HIV 'within' the body and the context in which people live that, too, is precariously embodied.

The context of the body: side effects, adherence and viral resistance
"My treatment is killing me": side effects

Accounts from the journey maps, body maps, interviews and ethnography point to the precarity not only generated by HIV but also by HIV medicines. Miriam, for example, frequently spoke about how "my treatment is killing me". One day, she brought me the information sheet that was included in the tub of her aluvia (lopinavir/ritonavir combination) tablets and showed me the section under side effects where it said that alluvia is associated with gastrointestinal side effects. Stabbing her finger at the sheet, she asked, "And they expect me to take this and just shut up?" Miriam struggled with her weight and attributed this struggle to the effects of her treatment. Her frustration was exacerbated by her sense that the health care workers dismissed her health concerns as a consequence of her weight. In addition to feeling that her general health concerns were not taken seriously, she also felt that her concerns around the side effects of her treatment were not taken seriously.

Years later, in 2023, Miriam's frustration with health care workers had taken on a different but related shape. Sitting together in Cape Town on a warm winter's day, along with her daughter Alizwa, she told me that her concerns about her heightened vulnerability to COVID-19 (due to her HIV status and a chronic lung condition) were not taken seriously enough by health workers during the pandemic; without access to a vaccine for the first two years of the pandemic, she confined herself to her home, asking her children to do anything that entailed her being outside and risking infection. She has managed not to contract COVID-19 since the start of the pandemic, but she felt very alone in her management of the risks linked to the disease. She believed this was because of her weight and a sense that health workers viewed her heightened vulnerability to be, in part, her fault and therefore her responsibility to manage.

Lilian also experienced the side effects of ARVs, and, like Miriam, she struggled to be taken seriously when raising her concerns with doctors. She said, "If you're a patient, they will take you as if you're mentally ill." Miriam and Zama, unlike Lilian, had first started taking ARVs through the MSF trial; they both recounted a shift as they moved from a relationship characterized by respect with their MSF doctor to one that was, largely, characterized by suspicion and mistrust with their clinic doctor. Although Lilian wanted to "work with" her ARVs and had been careful to adhere to practices of "positive living", she was frustrated that when her ARVs no longer worked for her, she was not taken seriously by her doctor. She went on to explain how she experienced health care practitioners as punitive and explained how this form of communication has ramifications on the knowledge that health practitioners withhold from patients:

> 'We make mistakes but we deserve to be treated in the right way. Like if I miss my dates, I will be shouted at by the nurses that if I miss my dates, I will die. And no one wants to be reminded that she will die. Sometimes if the doctor finds something wrong they won't tell you, they just write it down in the folder to the pharmacist without telling you … that you must change your medication. They will just send you to the pharmacy, without telling you why you must change the medication.'

Yvonne traced her treatment biography on a large piece of paper with me, telling me about the different effects of the "nukes" and "non-nukes". Nukes refer to nucleoside/nucleotide reverse-transcriptase inhibitors and non-nukes refer to non-nucleoside reverse-transcriptase inhibitors. This colloquial terminology points to a discursive construction of HIV medicine as a weapon in the war against HIV and reflects a broader discourse employed by HIV activists around 'the struggle for ARVs'. It also connects to Sontag's (1988) cautionary discussion of metaphors that perpetuate myths and reinforce stigmas by 'blaming the victim'. 'Nukes' and 'non-nukes' are not, as argued throughout this book, autonomous technologies: they have different effects on different bodies. This description belies variable effects of biomedical technologies and may enable a 'blaming', described earlier by Lilian, by placing responsibility on the individual for developing viral resistance or experiencing side effects and not on the interaction of pathologies with medical technologies, bodies and their social context. The non-linear pathways in which people do not simply resume health on ARVs but also experience a range of struggles with these medicines confound the earlier activist discourses, mobilized globally, in which ARVs were cast by biosocial groupings as a 'technofix' (Lock and Nguyen, 2018).

There was a disjuncture in how the groups of people I worked with navigated these new generation struggles as citizens, and I discuss this in detail in the following chapter around biosocial fragmentation and emergent citizenships. The women in the core group, who had been HIV activists, found strategic ways to manage difficult and distrustful relationships with their doctors, who were, ultimately, the gatekeepers to their ARVs. The people I worked with who had not been HIV activists, however, said that they preferred to "just keep quiet with my doctor". Lilian and Yvonne both experienced lipodystrophy (the redistribution of body fat) on their initial treatment regimens and were able to negotiate with their doctors to change their medicine. Their proactive engagement with medical practitioners was anomalous given the number of people I engaged with in activist organizations and across the course of my research who struggled to discuss and negotiate their concerns around the side effects of HIV medicines with medical practitioners. It was perhaps, as Lilian herself remarked, their history of activism with TAC that had "made us strong enough" to negotiate their "right to the right medicines".

The creation of the body maps traces a history of activism among this group of women, where they noted how organizations like MSF and TAC encouraged them to advocate for their right to 'the right medicines'. This institutional encouragement was visualized as a form of support and solidarity, often drawn along hands or arms, and it was echoed across the body maps that were created by this group of activists. What was striking, too, is that in addition to visualizing institutional support, the maps also reveal the care between the activists themselves: each map holds a faint outline of the person who supported them in creating the map. In the work of creating the early body maps in 2001, the women would also offer to attend clinic appointments with each other if this would be helpful or assist each other in disclosing their HIV status to their family members. The potency of these forms of care – at an institutional and individual level – lies in the confidence that it generated among this group of activists to prioritize their wellbeing and their right to health. In her ethnographic research with activists in Thailand (2020) and the gendered nature of infant feeding and food insecurity (1994, 2017), Penny van Esterik similarly finds that what might be referred to as actions of solidarity among activists could also be understood as practices of care between them. The height of HIV activism corresponded with a great deal of care among the activists I knew, and the unravelling of these networks, and the care that built them, is perhaps one of the most striking losses of the activist wins. I discuss this dynamic in more detail later in the book, and in what follows I focus on some of the specific challenges linked to side effects.

Yvonne has changed her treatment regimen twice because of side effects. First, she moved from azidothymidine (AZT) and nevirapine on to stavudine (d4T) and efavirenz because she experienced liver damage and anaemia. Lipodystrophy was a commonly experienced side effect on d4T among the people I met in my research before it was phased out of South Africa and replaced with abacavir, a medicine that had far fewer side effects. Yvonne had also experienced lipodystrophy, but because her biomedical 'health indicators', like her viral load, had remained the same, her request to change her medication was met with a threat to move her on to second-line treatment. She describes this process in relation to the new generation of struggles that are emerging with the ARV rollout:

'Sometimes people get bored because it's a life-long treatment ... Also side effects: I've experienced side effects. I tell myself that if the doctor doesn't want to change me, I'll stop taking ARVs. It's a reminder now, I've accepted my status and that's ok. But if every time I look at myself and I see I'm not the same person I was before, it's a reminder. So I tell my mother if they won't let me take a new treatment, I will stop. And if I can write it in my folder, I will say I stopped because they didn't change me ... Although my shape had changed, the viral load is suppressed, so he told me that I need to continue with ARVs or he will put me on second line. I think that they feel if you are impatient, it's because you don't have information. It's only them who have information. I knew that I must change to TDF [tenofovir]. So I challenged him. That's when he said I must go home and that he would discuss with other doctors. Then early in the morning, I was there, waiting in front of his door, and I was to find out he never consulted other doctors. He only consulted them when he saw me waiting in front of his door, and they said if I have a problem I must be changed, and he said, "Ok I will change you."'

Here, Yvonne described how the side effects make her aware of her HIV status by showing her that she was not the "same person I was before". Lilian also experienced lipodystrophy, or "lipo" as she referred to it, but she experienced it as a result of AZT and not d4T. In addition to feeling "outside" her body, a body that did not feel like it was her own, she also raised the issue of signification.

Like Yvonne, Lilian described her sense of alienation in her body and spoke of her compassion for people who experience a range of other side effects that 'mark' their HIV, inadvertently disclosing their status to people around them through markings on their skin, for example:

'Yes we need the medication. Yes medication is going to have side effects. But still, are we going to ignore the fact that these things [side effects] when they are showing we are fine with them? I'm not fine with the fact that I've lost my booty [bum], I'm not fine with the fact that I'm losing flesh on my legs. No! In my case I'm empowered: I'm an activist. When I noticed something was changing in my body I went to my doctor I spoke to my doctor … I told him, "You're taking me out of this!" Not everyone is empowered to notice and to go to the doctor … [I]t works on you psychologically … What does it say? It says everybody can see there's something wrong with you.'

Like the struggle for HIV medicines, these new generation struggles are also embodied as a form of biopolitical precarity and continue to require strategic negotiation between health care workers and citizens as they navigate their right to health care within the public health system. These struggles are, however, even more complex because they call attention to the myriad effects of HIV medicines beyond the earlier assertions of their 'lazarus effect' in bringing people 'back to life'. The struggle for ARVs was a clear one: without ARVs, people would die. Now, struggles around side effects, and as I go on to discuss, around viral resistance and treatment fatigue, are more difficult to mobilize around because they are embodied differently.

"You feel tired!": treatment fatigue and viral resistance

During my fieldwork with TAC in the wake of the ARV rollout after 2010, it became apparent that branch members across the country were raising concerns around adherence, side effects and viral resistance. In an effort to address these concerns, and to call on the government to introduce new biomedical technologies (for tuberculosis [TB] and HIV), we developed an *Equal Treatment* issue on these new generation struggles. Nathan Geffen wrote the editorial for this issue. Writing about the life cycle of HIV, he described how HIV medicines and viruses are constantly changing inside the body. These changes, wrought through the intra-action of older HIV medicines with an agile shape-shifting virus, underlined the political imperative to bring new generations of more effective medicines to South Africa to reduce the risk of side effects, to increase the likelihood of adherence and to provide advanced treatment to people who have developed resistance to second-line treatment. For many women that I worked with, they were first able to access single fixed-dose triple combination therapy in 2017, almost 15 years after starting ARVs. The current fixed dose tenofovir/lamivudine/dolutegravir (TLD) regimen has been shown to have fewer side effects and lead to improved adherence. In 2022, roughly 60 per cent of the 5.4 million people on ARVs were receiving this first-line treatment, but guidance from the Southern African HIV Clinicians Society has advocated for broader distribution (SAHCS, 2022; Nel et al, 2023). One of the key reasons for this recommendation cites the increased risk of drug resistance to the older treatment regimen of tenofovir/emtricitabine/efavirenz (TEE). The TLD fixed-dose regimen also has fewer side effects, is easier to take than the TEE formulation and has fewer negative interactions with other medicines, including those used to treat TB (Steegen et al, 2019).

Fixed-dose combinations, like TLD, have been found to significantly reduce treatment fatigue and increase adherence. This is, in part, because instead of taking three different medicines every day, all three medicines are administered in a single tablet (Maskew et al, 2018; Ramlagan et al, 2018; Kruger-Swanepoel et al, 2022). The importance of providing more effective treatments, including TLD, was repeated across my research as people were not only concerned about side effects or viral resistance but also about treatment fatigue, becoming too tired to keep on remembering to take their medicines every day. Several activists I engaged with through TAC referred to a prominent activist who had also become tired and who had 'given up' taking his medication; it was a shock to them because he was well informed, worked to raise awareness around the efficacy of HIV medicine and yet had reached a point where he was too 'tired' to continue taking his treatment. His treatment fatigue was also compounded by depression and alcoholism: he became very seriously ill with meningitis and asked to be placed back on ARVs, but by this stage his body had developed resistance to all available lines of treatment and he died.

Treatment fatigue and viral resistance are two interlinked new generation struggles that emerged in my fieldwork. These interlinked struggles have also been highlighted in research by scholars working in South Africa to understand barriers to HIV adherence in the 'era of treatment' (Adeniyi et al, 2018; Flämig et al, 2019; Van Wyk and Davids, 2019; Kruger-Swanepoel et al, 2022). In their work with 14 adolescents living in Cape Town, Van Wyk and Davids (2019) highlight the importance of understanding the influence of interrelated psychosocial factors like treatment fatigue, disclosure and household dynamics on individuals' ability or willingness to take HIV medication consistently each day. In research conducted further afield, in New Mexico's Española Valley, Angela Garcia worked with people undergoing treatment for heroin addiction. Garcia found that underneath expressions of fatigue around living everyday life – "I think I was just tired" (2010: 142) – and also around their treatment programme lay a profound sense of hopelessness. Garcia's rich ethnography speaks to tiredness as a kind of weight: the weight of years and a heaviness borne through cycles of interpersonal and socio-political neglect, abuse and dispossession. In my research, participants used the term 'tired' to describe their frustration with taking medicine every day at a particular time. This tiredness may well have spoken to a dual frustration with having worked so hard to access HIV treatments, and the subsequent work of adherence to ensure that the treatment remained effective. In my research, and in Garcia's work, tiredness seemed to surface as a frustration with repetition: the repetition of the forms of precarity that may have led to HIV infection, the repetition of the labour by activists to compel the government to provide ARVs and the repetition of taking the medicines in a context where, too often, it was not possible to have the food necessary for warding off side effects like nausea.

In the face of her tiredness, and the requirement of repetition that underpins adherence, Brenda decided to 'take a break'. During a conversation about the government under then President Zuma, she said:

> 'Tablets are not easy to take. It's not easy to take ARV tablets every morning. That's why they have a lot of defaulters. So I think Zuma must try again or try harder to get something to help us. Because ARVs, wow! They're good, but if you take tablets … Yoh! You feel tired! But if I'm getting injection for a month to protect my virus, I think it's good for me.'

As a result of interrupting her treatment, the virus had mutated sufficiently to outwit her first-line ARVs, and she was therefore placed on second-line treatment. The long-acting treatment that Brenda had hoped for – lenacapavir – has just recently been launched internationally. However, although one of the clinical trials was conducted in South Africa, this highly expensive and effective HIV treatment remains at the time of writing unavailable to people like Brenda who rely on the state and the medicines that are provided through its public health system. As I discuss in Chapter 7, there are several barriers to accessing more effective treatments like lenacapavir at an affordable price, including highly restrictive international patent legislation but also including South Africa's own failure to utilize safeguards that can circumvent some of this legislation, in part because the government has failed to amend its onerous patent legislation since 1978.

The accounts of treatment fatigue surfaced throughout my research after 2010, but I was most struck by accounts of treatment fatigue in the research I conducted prior to 2010 with people who were on treatment but often felt ambivalent about their treatment because of their own embodied experiences of side effects and their sense that perhaps the then President Mbeki was right to raise concerns about the toxicity of HIV treatment (see for example Mills, 2005, 2008). The discursive dissonance – between government leaders and activist organizations like TAC – about the efficacy of medicine led to a great deal of uncertainty among many of the people I worked with in the early years of the HIV epidemic. However, these narratives of uncertainty continued, although in quieter ways, even after government leaders aligned with TAC to unequivocally support the efficacy of HIV medicines.

Nomonde was one of the seven people commissioned to develop new body maps in 2011. Her map, unlike the others, is not complete because she died in the course of creating it on 13 May 2011. Her life started in

Cape Town in 1980, as represented by the outline of Table Mountain on the right-hand side of her body map. Her message to other people, placed below her feet against a gold background, is: 'We are all affected'; echoing this assertion of interconnection, her death rippled across the group of people she had known as an activist and as a friend. The importance of sociality, of shared care, is iterated in the process of developing the body map: each body map is created in dialogue with another person, as shown through the two outlines of bodies on each of the maps. Underlining the importance of sociality, each person wrote down their sources of support and inspiration in the outline of the person who assisted them in creating their body map. Nomonde writes that her sources of support were her boyfriend and TAC, and her source of inspiration was Nelson Mandela.

The accounts of her death varied according to each person I spoke to. On the evening of her death, I was told that she had been so tired after seeing her doctor at the clinic that she had lain down on a bench, fallen asleep and died. Another friend said she had died of depression and isolation: Nomonde had been in hospital for a year because of TB meningitis, and when she was creating her second body map, she had spoken of her loneliness in hospital, her despondence with HIV and her frustration with ARVs because they had not protected her from the effects of HIV. A third narrative account of her death related to Nomonde's increased interest in traditional medicine and her sense of the limitations of biomedicine, and ARVs in particular. She had started training to become a traditional healer, believing that her chronic illness was an indication from her ancestors that she should follow this route: that she should become a healer in order to become healed. Nomonde's 'tiredness', depression and frustration with both chronic illness and with HIV medicine permeate these accounts. Beneath the explicit narratives were implicit wonderings, unspoken thoughts linked to 'giving up'. Nomonde's death prompted reflections from her friends, also research participants, about their own corporeal vulnerability: that HIV medicine could ward off the effect of HIV for a time, but that ultimately the length of this time was finite.

In 2013, South Africa made third-line drugs such as ritonavir-boosted darunavir and raltegravir available through the public health system for people who had developed resistance to second-line regimens containing protease-inhibitors; and in 2016 the government introduced dolutegravir (Steegen et al, 2019). These more recent changes in treatment options have addressed some of the concerns raised by the women around drug resistance and side effects. However, the potential for developing resistance to first- and second-line treatment remains a concern at an individual and systemic level. In a recent AIDS Drug Resistance Surveillance Study, researchers found that, in South Africa, existing drug resistance among HIV-positive people increased the likelihood of virological failure after a period of five months on ARVs (Li et al, 2021). For individuals, concerns around side effects can lead to inconsistent adherence and, in turn, low levels of adherence can lead to HIV mutations and drug resistance. A number of studies show a conclusive link between lower levels of adherence and drug resistance, particularly among people for whom taking HIV medicines might risk disclosure in contexts and households where people may be concerned about HIV-related stigma or violence (Adeniyi et al, 2018; Psaros et al, 2020; Kalichman et al, 2021). And at a systemic level, low adherence and the possibility of ARVs failing to suppress a person's HIV viral load has epidemiological implications for managing drug-resistant HIV mutations across a broader population as well as clinical and economic implications for accessing more expensive second- and third-line treatments (Hamers et al, 2018; Jennings et al, 2022).

Emerging research on the linked struggles around adherence and drug resistance speaks to the importance of understanding the social contexts in which people manage HIV as a chronic illness. In research with pregnant women in the Eastern Cape, for example, depression and fear of stigma were found to be the biggest factors in their non-adherence to HIV medicines. Individuals experiencing depression or increased HIV-related stigma were far less likely to access social support and as a result were less likely to adhere to treatment to prevent mother-to-child HIV transmission (Psaros et al, 2020). Research from the Western Cape also found that stigma played an important role in undermining ARV adherence, challenging the assumption that increased access to HIV medicines – and a consequent reframing of HIV as a chronic and manageable condition – would lead to a reduction in stigma. In this study, one in four participants acknowledged they had not taken their HIV medicines in order to avoid stigmatization in their household (Kalichman and El-Krab, 2021). This research from the Eastern and Western Cape is consistent with broader research on barriers to adherence across the world. In a systematic review and meta-analysis of data from 125 studies around the world, researchers found that 10 per cent of adults and 22 per cent of children's caregivers kept medications secret in order to avoid stigma, leading to reduced levels of adherence (Shubber et al, 2016).

In addition to understanding the social contexts that shape how and whether people feel able to take HIV medicines, my own and others' research speaks to the importance of recognizing the role of economic precarity in people's ability to manage HIV as a chronic illness. In a systematic review of research on HIV-related mortality in South Africa, scholars found that low socio-economic status is closely mapped on to HIV mortality for a range of interlocking reasons. They write:

> In South Africa, being of low SES [socio-economic status] is associated with reduced food security, lower food diversity and an increased

likelihood of skipping meals and going hungry. Food insecurity is an important barrier to antiretroviral treatment adherence. Beyond that, generation of immune cells highly depends on various nutrients. Hence, malnutrition (e.g. deficiency of trace elements and vitamins) due to lack of food and compensating strategies can accelerate the progression of HIV/AIDS and increase mortality risk. Interactive effects between malnutrition and HIV (and antiretroviral treatment) increase the risk of other infectious diseases such as tuberculosis, which in turn increases mortality risk. (Probst et al, 2016: 847)

The South African government's management of the COVID-19 pandemic, in part through a series of lockdowns, has been shown to have increased economic inequality and moved substantial swathes of the population below the poverty line (Muchena and Kalenga, 2021; Campbell et al, 2022). In a cluster randomized control trial, researchers found that not only was there a conclusive link between HIV-infection and higher rates of mortality as a result of COVID, but that 'lockdown regulations had negatively impacted ART [antiretroviral therapy] adherence by creating and exacerbating inequalities in access to health care, as well as by impacting food supply chains and generating economic insecurity' (Campbell et al, 2022: 1906). It is indisputable that the socio-economic context in which people navigate chronic illness matters, and as I discuss in the section that follows, it matters not only because socio-economic inequality directly impacts health outcomes but because the state is directly implicated in measures to address structural inequality and in the management of epidemics that move into the fissures created by this structural inequality.

The body in context: unemployment and economic insecurity

The artists of each of the body maps represented HIV in different ways inside their bodies. Bongiwe, for example, drew HIV as the embers of a former conflagration, saying that ARVs had 'cooled' the fire down. Noloyiso described HIV as the soft indentations of footprints on the wet sand, saying that ARVs had 'calmed down' the storm of HIV. In contrast to all of the body maps developed in 2003 and 2011, Nondumiso drew HIV outside her body. She said that now HIV was not what defined her and that, instead, it was a source of opportunity for her. HIV was symbolized by white ribbons around her body. Inside the ribbons, she had drawn maple leaves; the leaves referred to the artistic collaborations that she had entered into with colleagues in Canada through her HIV activism and art. Her body map extends Thobani's description of ARVs as his body. Nondumiso, in an interview about her body map, said that ARVs had been so powerful that they had moved HIV outside her body. She pointed to the marks on her body, shown in the map as light brown markings along her legs and arms, saying, "Yes, the effect of HIV is still on my skin, but HIV is not who I am."

Through this representation of HIV outside her body, Nondumiso asserted that HIV was present in her life through the kinds of opportunities she was able to access while also making it clear that she did not want to be labelled as 'HIV-positive'. When telling the rest of the group of artists about her map, she explained that she wanted to be thought of as "[j]ust someone living with X. X is my child, or my art. I'm not my HIV." As noted in Chapter 2, ethnographers like Mackworth-Young and colleagues (2020) and Bradley (2021) have similarly found that single identities – like 'HIV-positive' – are increasingly shifting below the surface to make room for a wider array of subjectivities. This further reflects Whyte's (2009) call to understand how subjectivities shift as people's embodied experience of illness changes. In Nondumiso's case, her experience of illness changed markedly after she accessed HIV treatment in 2002. More than ten years later, I visited Nondumiso, Bongiwe and Thobani at an exhibition in London. They had worked with the British Council, in conjunction with the Paralympics, to develop a body of work with a British artist, Rachel Gadsden. As part of this exhibition, I watched a performance where HIV took the form of a dancer's body as she flew around the stage, wild and dangerous, before ARVs – another dancer – came to tame her. In the discussion following the dance, Nondumiso, Bongiwe and Thobani engaged with an audience of about 500 people. Nondumiso spoke about her vision as an artist and her dream of improving education for youth in South Africa. She did not discuss HIV, nor was she asked to. In contrast to the body map exhibitions in South Africa, New York and London during the struggle for ARVs, this exhibition was not linked to her and her colleagues' experience of HIV. Rather it was a testament to their artistic creativity and capacity to create beauty from their experience of life beyond their chronic illness.

As we see in Bongiwe's and Thobani's accounts, it is through the intra-action of ARVs with HIV that Nondumiso was able see HIV as 'beyond' her body. It is also through her discipline and self-care practices, particularly around adherence, that she was able to manage HIV to the extent that she could 'see' it outside herself in the opportunities she was able to access. This presents another layer to the earlier discussion around Thobani's body map and posthumanist performativity as ARVs intra-act with HIV: it is through taking ARVs, every day, that Nondumiso 'saw' the presence of HIV in the form of her ARVs even as it was felt to be absent from her body. A tension therefore surfaced for Nondumiso between wanting to move away from being defined by HIV, and the struggle for ARVs, and recognizing that ARVs also enabled her to move 'beyond HIV'. She spoke of this tension at length in the course of our work together and spoke too of her frustration with her sense that people also patronized her and overlooked her skills because she was HIV-positive and a woman.

This tension was a strong finding in my ethnographic research with the women in the core group, and I discuss the economic dimensions of this tension in the paragraphs that follow. In contrast to the notion of 'bare life' described by Robins (2005) and generated through the state's historical failure to provide essential HIV medicine, the way in which precarity was strategically performed by the people I came to know in the wake of the struggle for ARVs points to a different narrative. In connection with the previous chapter's discussion of pathways of precarity, I suggest that instead of being either reduced to bare life or 'acted on' by national and international development programmes, women 'acted up' by strategically placing themselves within the 'development subjectivities' that had been discursively narrated through development interventions and policies that framed women as economically, socially and biologically 'vulnerable' to and as a result of HIV-infection.

In 2022, a few weeks after the South African government rescinded its 'mandatory mask' policy – a tentative sign that the country was moving into a new phase of the COVID-19 pandemic – I met with a number of health activists who reflected on the new challenges facing people living with HIV in South Africa. These conversations followed the Defend our Democracy Conference, held in July 2022, that articulated the importance of understanding rising fuel and food prices as fundamentally linked to food insecurity and ill health. At this conference, activist organizations like TAC had called on the government to fulfil the 'political freedom and bread' development agenda set out in the country's constitution (Defend our Democracy, 2022). The socio-economic costs of the COVID-19 pandemic were very present in the conversations that I had with health activists and policy makers in South Africa over this time in 2022, and they echoed conversations of an earlier time in South Africa's history when the government agreed to the ARV rollout. The decade-long health crisis, linked to the government's initial failure to provide ARVs and subsequent failure to scale up the rollout of these essential medicines, shifted as the government under President Zuma agreed to take responsibility for providing essential medicines. With this shift, around 2011/12, came a larger-scale shift in global funding away from supporting non-governmental agencies – like activist organizations – and towards ensuring the government was equipped to scale up its ARV programme across the country. In 2022, I was having very similar conversations to the ones I had over a decade earlier, where activists expressed a deep frustration at the fickle nature of global funding for managing both HIV and COVID-19: that funding can come in a rush, at a time of crisis, and then 'dry up' almost as quickly, leaving people who are the most socio-economically vulnerable – and the organizations representing them – to find their own ways to cushion the rapid decline in health funding when the health crisis is deemed 'under control'.

For instance, in the early months of 2011, my conversations with TAC's staff in Khayelitsha and Cape Town rippled with the news that the Global Fund had stalled on the final payment (R15 million) to the National Department of Health (R7 million was finally paid in March 2012). Along with shifting donor priorities, this had very real and negative ramifications for those working in TAC and other recipient organizations: Lilian, Yvonne, Zama and another friend and TAC activist I came to know called Judith, all worked in recipient HIV organizations, and they were all retrenched by the end of 2011. These women had all been instrumental in the activist work around access to ARVs in South Africa, just as activist organizations like TAC had been instrumental in their lives and career trajectories.

As described earlier and in the previous chapter, Lilian spearheaded TAC's campaign to compel the government to provide PMTCT treatment. Both Lilian and Thandiswa testified on behalf of TAC, and their affidavits were used as evidence in the court case. Lilian, like Zama, worked with a HIV treatment literacy organization and had been extensively filmed on the *Siyanqoba* (Beat it!) television series (Hodes, 2007).[3] A year later, I had sat with Lilian in Cape Town's summer sunshine, catching up on the months since I had last seen her. In the intervening months, Lilian had lost her job along with the other three women working in the HIV activist field. I understood that Lilian had challenged the poor working conditions of her employment, with long working hours at a low wage. She was told she was being unreasonable given the demand for employment in South Africa's context of high unemployment and poverty; an impasse ensued, and her contract was terminated. As a result of losing her job, Lilian had to cancel her lease agreement on her home and move back to live with her sister in Khayelitsha. Not wanting to lose her son's place in his school and risk having to send him to a school in Khayelitsha with fewer resources, Lilian wakes up at 4 am to get her son dressed and ready by 5 am in time to make the long trip on public transport to his school. "I don't breathe until he gets home in the afternoon. You know what the townships are like for children."

Women like Lilian, Judith, Thandiswa and Zama who were employed through the HIV activist machinery were the first people to feel the consequences of the turning tide in funding restrictions and donor priorities. Despite extensive work experience in the field of HIV activism, prevention and treatment literacy, formal education surfaced as a key factor informing their employability. These women were told that they did not have sufficient formal education to warrant ongoing employment in these shrinking organizations. This circles back to the complex feelings that Nondumiso expressed earlier: she saw HIV 'outside' her body in the professional opportunities she accessed, like travelling to Canada and to the UK as an artist and consultant in body-mapping methods. While not wanting to be defined as 'living with HIV', it was through being HIV-positive that she was able to express her passion for art and her desire to connect with other artists globally. Lilian and Judith also resisted the way they were typecast: not only did they resist the 'HIV-positive' label but they resented their employers' racist and sexist assumptions that they believed were attached to the composite term 'Black, uneducated women.' With one employer, whom they shared in the work they did on a HIV research project, they resented his assumption that they were not in a position to negotiate the terms of their employment. They were even angrier that this assumption was partly accurate because they were not in a financial position to challenge the unfair terms of their employment or the unfair assumptions that, they said, underwrote these terms.

The sources of precarity described in the previous chapter resurfaced in Lilian's, Judith's, Thandiswa's and Zama's redundancy. Technical phrases like 'formal education' conceal the complex histories of these women's struggles in rural schools where they had access to only very poor education as part of the apartheid government's 1953 Bantu Education Act (Msila, 2020), and who, as young girls, too often experienced sexual violence and struggled without the support of their carers or parents. Phrases like 'insufficient formal education' work to render women as faceless, unreal, against whom structural violence can be legitimated, in this case through retrenchment. This connects to Farmer's description of suffering that 'is "structured" by historically given (and often economically-driven) processes and forces that conspire – whether through routine, ritual, or, as is more commonly the case, the hard surfaces of life – to constrain agency' (2005: 40).

Structural violence was also legitimated by explicitly and strategically drawing on women's vulnerability to propel company profits by exploiting HIV-positive women's labour. This emerged during my fieldwork with the other six women who worked with uYaphi, a so-called 'HIV empowerment organization'. In the late 1990s uYaphi set out to provide employment opportunities to HIV-positive Black women on the understanding that this group was most vulnerable to the impact of HIV in South Africa. Miriam, Thandiswa, Yandisa, Zolani, Sibongile and Brenda all derived their main income through the paper mâché bowls they made for uYaphi each week. Each woman had been funnelled into uYaphi through support groups they had joined when they started ARVs. At first, in the late 1990s and early 2000s, the women acknowledged that the organization had worked respectfully with them, paying them a decent wage for their work.

With the shift in management in the late 2000s, the income-generation programme became focused on selling products internationally to increase their profit margin. When I first met him a few years after this shift in focus, the IG manager explained that although the women were not given an increase in payment per product, they would benefit from increased sales by receiving larger orders. The women I worked with told me they had not received an increase in pay for five years. According to Miriam, every time they raised this issue, their programme manager "uses words and drawings and treats us like children but doesn't actually explain anything or listen to what we say". Miriam became increasingly angry with *uYaphi* and eventually challenged the manager directly, telling him that he was "exploiting my HIV". Miriam claimed she was punished the following week when she received an inordinately low order for bowls. Yandisa, one of the oldest women working at *uYaphi* and a close friend and neighbour of Miriam's, also challenged the manager during a period of heightened contestation around wages. She asked him why a White man was running an IG programme for Black HIV-positive women: his response was that there were no suitably educated Black women to take his position. When I saw the women after this exchange, they were both outraged by and resigned to his power: they recognized there was no space for engagement or negotiation and were concerned about the financial implications of continuing the struggle with *uYaphi*'s management. They did, however, irk him as often as possible by speaking about their frustrations with him in isiXhosa when he was in the same room; this frustrated him and gave an indirect power to the women, because although he heard his name, he did not speak this language and was powerless to directly challenge them as he had no basis on which to claim they were being disparaging.

In an interview with me, the income generation manager boasted about an R24 million turnover and said, repeatedly, "The women must just get with capitalism." As he was explaining the women's short-sighted business acumen, he answered his smartphone and discussed the fencing he was erecting around his pool at home. He then went on to explain the model of the IG programme: the women who made the paper mâché products were classified as 'self-employed' and not as employees of the organization. This way, he explained, the women were not entitled to any legal employment benefits, and any negotiations that I did take place were at the discrepancy of *uYaphi* and a good-natured sign of their "willingness to help where they could". The little brochures that are glued on to all the products speak about the women's lives, their poverty, their experience of gender inequality, and places the imperative on the buyer to 'do the right thing by the women by buying the bowl'.

Seeing the absence of state machinery in their lives beyond their ability to access ARVs and grants, the women shifted their precarity through performance into a resource that facilitated access to the HIV activist and employment sector. The way these women actively engaged with these structures could be understood as an example of performativity because they tactically navigated a set of restrictive, even oppressive, structures by subverting them. This performance was based on a strategic recognition of the development sector's construction of the HIV-positive other: the at-risk population group of poor, Black women in South Africa. A set of struggles, resonant with Hacking's (1990) notion of a 'looping effect', proceeds from this apparently strategic mobilization of precarity as women resisted the labels of poor, Black and HIV-positive and came to resent the way that organizations benefitted from their participation by using these labels, by exploiting their HIV.

In thinking about the absence or presence of the state – I discuss this in detail in Chapter 5 – these women's strategies connect with de Certeau's (1984) conception of 'making do' as people employ a set of tactics to navigate precarity wrought through repressive or absent state structures. He looks, for example, at the hidden struggle of indigenous people in South America as they resisted Spanish colonizers, suggesting that

> [s]ubmissive, and even consenting to their subjection, the Indians nevertheless often made of the rituals, representations, and laws imposed on them something quite different from what their conquerors had in mind; they subverted them not by rejecting or altering them, but by using them with respect to ends and references foreign to the system they had no choice but to accept. (1984: xiii)

This account also connects to the women's use of language to exclude the IG manager from their discussions, and to – albeit indirectly – challenge his authority. The struggles around performing and resisting precarity linked to HIV indicate that, on the one hand, it is possible to use the power of categorization to secure resources, in this case economic capital. All the women I worked with in the core ethnographic group were able to secure a degree of financial autonomy through their work in HIV activist organizations or NGOs. On the other hand, these findings also reflect the danger of operationalizing responses to the 'gender and HIV' dyad, particularly within NGOs that may "exploit our HIV", without critical reflection about institutional capacity to reinforce rather than challenge structural inequality.

Conclusion

The celebration of MSF's first ARV trial in Khayelitsha was a poignant and powerful marker of transitions in South Africa's biopolitical landscape: over a decade after the trial first started in 2001, ARVs were no longer the scarce resource they were when people like Miriam, Thobani, Bongiwe and Nondumiso first started taking these medicines. It is perhaps for this reason that, as my own research unfolded across time (starting in 2003) and across epidemics (most recently with COVID-19), I have observed a shift in the embodied accounts of the intra-action of HIV and ARVs in people's lives. I refer to embodied accounts here, as it was through hanging out and in verbal and visual narratives (in the body maps) that the people I worked with over the last decade communicated how they embodied these actants in their lives, across time. This chapter traced these fluid accounts across time, and in relation to two groups of people with whom I worked most closely during my fieldwork: the BWG and the core group of women. It is therefore with the understanding that I worked with this particular group of people, who had engaged as activists in the historical context of the struggle for HIV medicine in South Africa (as described in Chapter 1), that I situate the following observations.

I suggest that if we really are going to move beyond the 'nature/culture' dichotomy that separates biology (the embodied dimension of this book) from socialities (the political dimension), we need to explore how the world 'outside' the body permeates and shapes life 'inside' the body. This requires a shift away from privileging 'biology' as that which exists inside the body to recognizing, through the lens of biopolitical precarity, how the body is porously networked into an assemblage that brings the 'outside' 'inside'. To this end, this chapter juxtaposed interiority with ethnology: it looked between the world 'inside' and the world 'outside' the body. The first section explored how HIV and ARVs, as actants, move into relationships with each other within the body; and it illustrated how these actants are also brought into the body through socialities that take place between multiple actors outside the body, in relationships between the people I worked with, TAC, MSF and the government. The socialities that were formed among the people with whom I worked around their HIV status was a strong feature of my fieldwork as I observed and took part in the networks of connection that brought friends and colleagues together.

Anthropologists like Marsland (2012), Prince (2012), Chapman (2021), Copeland (2021) and Kalofonos (2021), who have also researched HIV treatment programmes in the decade following the initial struggle for ARVs, have suggested a reframing of the historical approach to governmentality, biosociality and biopolitics (see Robins, 2006; Nguyen, 2010). In a special issue on medical anthropology and biomedicine, anthropologists like Marsland (2012) and Prince (2012) reflect on their research and probe the limits of biopolitics as a 'one size fits all' conceptual approach. In response to the assertion that 'biosociality does not look inward to the body, but outward to human relationships' (Marsland, 2012: 473), I suggest that perhaps there is a way of thinking about biosociality that does not ask us to look either into the body, or outward to socialities, but across them.

In conceptualizing HIV and ARVs as actants, this book draws the social dimension of their lives into relief; further, the dual character of the new generation struggles brings the biological dimension of social, political and economic relationships into focus. For HIV not only enters women's lives through human relationships, as we saw in the previous chapter, but as an actant, HIV itself becomes alive and has, in Appadurai's (1988) terms, a 'social life' in the body. Once in the body, the virus learns to intra-act with the body's immune system – its CD4 cells – and, over time, manages to con these cells into mimicking the body's basic biological identity – its DNA. ARVs, like HIV, also call attention to the social, economic and political relationships that women navigated as activists in order to mobilize the government to bring these medicines into South Africa's public health system. However, once in the body, ARVs also take on a social life. They each interact with each other as they are technologically honed – as a triple therapy – to block HIV in its attempts to con the CD4 cells.

Where my research perhaps connects to, but also moves from, these medical anthropological approaches to biosociality is that, as actants, the social lives of ARVs are not solely embodied in positive terms (described by Nguyen, 2005, 2010 and Robins, 2006), nor do they highlight the limitations of biomedical programmes in places where people can sometimes simply not afford to take medicines that make them even more hungry and even less able to work (described by Marsland and Prince, 2012 and Kalofonos, 2021 for example). Thinking about ARVs as actants, things with a social life, highlights another form of sociality as they become felt by the people I worked with, and visible to other people, through their manifestation in side effects, like lipodystrophy. What is held in the body becomes social.

These actants intra-act and move into the social space of people's relationships with each other as they become visible as facets of sociality: through activist networks that mobilize around HIV medicines; around ARVs as they become embodied in people's physiological health and parallel side effects; through the kinds of sexual relationships that women can and cannot negotiate with their partners; through the economic resources they are able to secure by foregrounding one particular subjectivity – HIV – over the multitude of others; and through the emerging citizen claims that draw these women back into a biopolitical relationship with the state to access newer medical technologies that will have fewer negative effects on their bodies and that will be better able to combat HIV as it learns to outwit the older generation medicines.

The second character of the new generation struggles discussed in this chapter relates to the socio-economic contours of these women's everyday lives. We see, in this strand of the new generation struggles, how HIV can and has been used performatively to secure, albeit precariously, resources through which women have been able to navigate the tightly stretched economic landscape in which they live. The previous chapter describes and critiques the construction of women as vulnerable 'victims', biologically and socio-economically more susceptible to HIV infection than men. This chapter considers, too, how women work with this dyad to secure resources through an NGO that was specifically set up to 'empower' women.

The new generation struggles articulated in this chapter offer two perspectives on the way that HIV and ARVs draw attention to the world inside the body as well as the socio-economic contexts in which people live their lives in the world. First, the accounts of complex struggles with HIV medicines, like side effects and viral resistance, confirm the value of moving away from the 'problem/solution' framing of HIV and ARVs. This chapter shows that although HIV can be a form of embodied precarity, as explored in the previous chapter, it can also be a resource. The second related finding, then, is that HIV – as an actant within the body – can also be performatively mobilized 'outside' through economic relationships to manage precarity. In this regard, the women were able to strategically secure critical economic resources in a development milieu that perpetuates the 'gender/HIV' dyad. The women navigated this dyad in quite complex ways that shifted across time: at a time of heightened precarity in a context of profound inequality and unemployment, many of the women I worked with strategically mobilized their HIV status to secure vital resources. While feeling that their embodied precarity – their HIV – was a source of income, they also expressed deep resentment about the NGOs and activist organizations that were exploiting their labour and their HIV status.

Given the dual character of these new generation struggles, the findings in this chapter emphasize the importance of asking 'empirical questions' of the politics of life literature, and particularly the field of biosociality. While recognizing the importance of sociality, this chapter also suggests that we might approach biology itself slightly differently from the way Rose characterized 'our century of biology' (2013). Historically, Rabinow (1996) considered biology with respect to genetics, and Rose (2009, 2013) extended this approach to consider 'bio' with respect to biomedical technologies that could diagnose and treat genetic or other illnesses. Based on the findings in this chapter, and as I go on to discuss in the next chapter, I suggest that biosociality around HIV has shifted as the biology of the virus, too, has intra-acted with ARVs; this shift in the shape of HIV and its socialities has run alongside an emerging acknowledgement that ARVs, like HIV, also hold risk and are embodied as side effects alongside resumed health. The new generation struggles discussed in this chapter are perhaps more difficult to address in public health programmes and less amenable to pre-existing approaches to medicines as 'technologies of life' because they call attention to the complexity of medicines as they intra-act with HIV in individual bodies in highly complex socio-economic contexts. They are further complicated, as I go on to explore in the following chapter, through shifting perceptions of and engagements with the post-apartheid state to secure vital resources, like health care, education and sanitation.

Health Citizenship

While waiting in the very long queue snaking out from the three pharmacy counters to the general waiting area of Miriam's clinic in Khayelitsha, we spent most of our time chatting to the large number of "comrades", as Miriam referred to them, who came up to greet her.[1] The stream of people passing in and out of the clinic, and who joined us as we waited in the queue, created an ever-shifting node of playful, often proud, chatter among friends. This little node of friends cycled in size, growing and shrinking as we waited in an otherwise linear queue where solitude rather than sociality seemed to be the norm. When I commented on Miriam's active social life in the clinic, and particularly in the pharmacy queue, she smiled and said, "Sana, it's because we fought [for antiretrovirals (ARVs)] together." I take this queue as an entry point for this chapter because it points to the way that space and sociality are produced over time, through memory, and because it indicates shifts in citizenship practices as they are embodied and as they coalesce around shifting biopolitical concerns. This chapter considers how the embodied new generation struggles discussed in the previous chapter relate to emergent forms of 'everyday citizenship' and explores how the dual character of these embodied new generation struggles has precipitated a corresponding set of citizen practices around, first, the intra-activity of HIV and ARVs, and second, the socio-economic spaces in which people's lives are lived.

Standing with Miriam, it appeared to me that the conversations in the queue took place between the "comrades" – the generation of Treatment Action Campaign (TAC) activists that the women with whom I worked belonged to – and not necessarily between most of the people who stood in front of or behind us while we waited. Instead, there seemed to be an implicit acknowledgement that although the queue to this particular counter indicated a shared illness, this need not translate into a social relationship. These dynamics may suggest more broadly that this historical context of activism played a role in compelling activists, like the women I worked with, to assert HIV as a central aspect of their identity. In doing so, the space of the clinic became a place where these historical relationships were reinforced. This chapter explores the implications of these shifting socialities among this group of women and also among a larger group of people who may or may not have been standing quietly in front of or behind us in queue. I reflect on the different ways that both groups – former 'comrades' who had fought together, and those who had not been activists in the struggle for ARVs – see and speak to the state in order to develop a fuller understanding of how people conceive the biopolitical relationship between their own vitality and that of the state.

Although I reflect on medical anthropological conceptions of governmentality and citizenship, particularly therapeutic citizenship (Nguyen, 2005; King et al, 2018; Zhou, 2019) and biological citizenship (Petryna, 2004; Bosire et al, 2018; Young et al, 2019), my fieldwork emphasized the importance of understanding 'everyday citizenship' (Nedlund, 2019; Lemanski, 2020) as it is lived and embodied. Recently, scholars in psychology, behavioural economics, sociology, political science and anthropology have similarly argued that studies around state–citizen interactions need to be dislocated from abstract political theory and located in people's everyday lives (Berenschot and Van Klinken, 2018; Tshishonga, 2019; Lemanski, 2020; Mize, 2020; Dziuban and Sekuler, 2021; Rosengarten et al, 2021). Through their empirical research, these scholars find that quotidian engagements with the state move into people's bodies, psyches, relationships, sexual expression, economic wellbeing and illness experiences. As Andreouli observes: 'Citizenship in our current times is very much a lived practice: citizenship rights are not just the rights that are enshrined in law but 'living rights' that have relevance for people's everyday realities and, as such, they are mobilised, claimed, and enacted in everyday life (2019: 5). In their discussion of citizenship in Indonesia, Berenschot and Van Klinken (2018) argue that people's experience of citizenship in postcolonial states is not only dependent on the formulation and implementation of formal laws and regulations but strongly shaped by the strength of their social relationships. They call for a rethinking of normative theories of citizenship and foreground scholarship from the Global South that details how, in postcolonial contexts like India, Indonesia and South Africa, informal networks enable citizens to navigate interactions with state institutions (Cornwall et al, 2011; Dumbrava, 2017; Bosire et al, 2018; Andreouli, 2019; Drerup, 2020; Lemanski, 2020). Reflecting this scholarship that calls for a more nuanced understanding of particular contexts, or states, of citizenship as they unfold across time and in very different spaces, this chapter engages with the visual methods of my fieldwork to explore people's imaginaries of the state as they 'saw' and 'spoke to' the state through the lens of their cameras.

Cornwall et al (2011) articulate two pertinent imaginaries – how citizens see the state (Corbridge, 2005) and how states see citizens (Scott, 1999) – that generate the 'mutually constitutive nature of the citizen–state relationship, and the extent to which different kinds of states make different kinds of citizenship possible' (2011: 8). Building on recent ethnographies that explore these imaginaries through the lens of health, illness and medicine (Young et al, 2019; Lees and Enria, 2020; Costa and Gonçalves, 2021; Dziuban and Sekuler, 2021), this chapter draws on visual anthropological methods like photography and film to explore how women perceive and interact with the state in their everyday lives. In the fieldwork I conducted after ARVs became available in the public health system, it was apparent that women's political engagement with the state through their citizen practices was fundamentally connected to the embodied ramifications of HIV medicines in their lives. Moreover, I found that, with the provision of ARVs, the landscape of citizen action had fanned out from a set of therapeutic claims that linked access to medicine with the right to life to include conditions that made life possible in contexts of intransigent socio-economic inequalities.

These emergent citizenships relate to the new generation struggles that were salient in my fieldwork. Chapter 4 considers the dual character of these struggles as they flowed between the 'inside' and 'outside' of the body; looking into the body, we saw how women embodied precarity linked to the dynamic intra-activity of HIV and ARVs as they were felt in side effects, treatment fatigue and viral resistance. The first section of this chapter outlines the emergent political concerns that relate to these embodied accounts of precarity with(in) the body. The second characteristic of the new generation struggles centred on the socio-economic context in which women navigated their everyday lives. Following this structure, the second section of this chapter considers the political dimension of these embodied concerns with respect to 'life as it is lived' beyond the historical activist construction of ARVs as 'technologies of life'. This section traces these emergent struggles around the contingencies of life, now with ARVs, that remain biopolitically linked to the state's responsibility to ensure a broader set of rights around gender, sexuality, education, housing and sanitation. It suggests that historic socialities built around HIV as a shared predicament have diffracted from this singular focus to include these plural struggles that, too, are embodied as biopolitical precarity.

This chapter explores how 'everyday citizenships' were articulated through multiple forms of citizen action across the continuum between private and public spaces, and as they surfaced in people's visual and narrative accounts of where they saw and spoke to the state. Together, these imaginaries point to the intimate and intricate relationship between the state and people's everyday lives. I therefore show how the two facets of my research focus – the embodied and political dimensions of access to HIV medicines – come together in this chapter. Across the two sections of this chapter, I suggest that it is through the body that people experience the extent to which they are networked into a biopolitical assemblage, and that, because biopolitical precarity is embodied, it is also through the body that people experience and practise dynamic forms of citizenship in relation to similarly dynamic forms of governance.

Sustaining life on ARVs: between rights and responsibility

Most of the people I hung out with during my fieldwork in Khayelitsha from 2010 had joined TAC between 1999 and 2001. This period in South Africa's history, as Steven Robins (2010) has observed through his research with activists in Khayelitsha, was marked by a cadre of therapeutic citizens who testified to the transformative effects of ARVs in their lives; at this time, many of the public 'testifying' activists, like Nondumiso, received ARVs through the Médecins Sans Frontières (MSF) trial. Robins describes how biosociality was forged with this particular group of activists through a set of practices, like wearing the iconic HIV-positive T-shirt, attending marches and testifying to the power of ARVs; these practices cohered around a set of discourses that asserted the positive effects of ARVs as life-giving in order to compel the government to provide these medicines through the public health sector (Robins, 2006). In making a set of biopolitical claims on the state at this time in South Africa's history, before ARVs were publicly available, HIV activists asserted an almost 'democratic body' in which all HIV-positive people's bodies were cast as equally vulnerable to the effects of the virus, and therefore equally in need of ARVs.

Biosociality persisted in my own research in Khayelitsha, but in a less cohesive structure to the early form it took among HIV activists, a group described by Rose and Novas (2005: 449) as the 'main example of biosociality'. Returning to Rabinow's (1996) assertion that the social cannot be separated from the biological, if we think about HIV and ARVs as actants, as 'things' with a social life, and as things that move into the permeable body through social, economic and political relationships, then perhaps it is possible to start thinking about intersections of biosociality: as the effects of these actants are individually embodied but socially visible and as they are collectively articulated through forms of 'everyday citizenship' as people saw and spoke to the state.

"I voted for my treatment": health, rights and citizenship

In May, a week after the municipal elections, Thandeka and I were walking down Queen Victoria Street in central Cape Town; not only did the name of the street speak to the colonial legacy of South Africa but the memorialized 'Slegs Blankes' – 'Whites Only' – bench that we passed outside the High

Court was a reminder of South Africa's more recent history. At this point in the road, Thandeka stopped me and pointed – not at the bench, but across the road to the parliament buildings. Thandeka was speaking about a much more recent history – one that she had actively shaped through her affidavit and testimony in the court case TAC brought against the government to compel them to provide prevention of mother-to-child transmission (PMTCT) treatment. When we met earlier that day, the first thing she did was to show me the indelible black stain on her thumbnail – a sign she had voted. I asked her why she had chosen to vote. She replied, "I voted for my treatment."

We were on our way to TAC's national office, just two blocks down the road from parliament, walking slowly and talking even more slowly. Our conversation moved across time as our bodies, too, moved through spaces that had been politically potent in apartheid South Africa's struggle for democracy and, later, in post-apartheid South Africa's struggle for ARVs. Moving back in time as we moved through these city spaces, I asked Thandeka about her recollections of the 2004 national elections. At that time, she had been working with TAC for a number of years and had been particularly instrumental in TAC's early struggle against the pharmaceutical companies in 2001, and then against the South African government to access PMTCT treatment. Her response was striking for me because, for the time ARVs were not available in the public sector, it appeared that Thandeka had attributed this to specific members of the African National Congress (ANC), whereas she believed that the government as a whole would eventually come to fulfil its obligations to HIV-positive citizens. Speaking about this period in South Africa's history, she said, "I put my eggs next to government. To give the people the treatment because the people, they infect the children. So they must access the AZT azidothymidine and nevirapine."

Thandeka pointed at parliament, its white buildings barely visible over the green trees of the bordering Company Gardens that ran along Queen Victoria Street, and said: "I was here in Parliament; I was talking about the treatment." We walked in silence past the bench; our conversations had more silences than words. When Thandeka spoke, it was very softly, and I needed to lean in to really hear her. Thandeka's voice has been particularly powerful for TAC's activism; her activism, like Lilian's, was born from her anger with the government for failing to provide PMTCT treatment to stop HIV from travelling along vertical pathways into her daughter's body. She explained her work in TAC to me as we walked:

'I was pressuring the government, saying, 'You must give us the treatment because the people are dying.' The government – [former Health Minister] Manto Tshabalala-Msimang – was not giving us the treatment. They were telling us that if we had HIV, we must take the veg. They didn't tell us about the treatment; they didn't want to tell us what was the right thing to us. They ignored the virus.'

"When did they start taking things seriously?" I asked. "As I give them pressure!" she replied as we turned right on to Wale Street and walked to the bottom of the stairs of the St George's Anglican Cathedral. The cathedral is situated next to the parliament buildings, in the Company Gardens, and has been used historically by apartheid and post-apartheid activists alike as a site of resistance and a place of mourning. It was, in fact, the same place where TAC had first assembled in 1998. The gardens, which move out from the cathedral, mark an important politico-juridical intersection with the High Court on the right and parliament on the left. It was through these two spaces of the state spanning policy development and juridical implementation that Thandeka worked with TAC to challenge the pharmaceutical companies, and later the government, to provide HIV medicines to stop HIV from travelling along vertical and horizontal pathways into people's bodies.

Looking up at the cathedral's towering façade, Thandeka said, "I know this church. I was here for the funeral service for Nkosi Johnson. My daughter came to light the lamp in the service." We were silent for a time before she said, "You know Nkosi [Johnson] died of HIV?" Nkosi Johnson, like Thandeka's daughter, contracted HIV at birth; he was 12 years old when he died on 1 June 2001. As a young HIV activist, he worked with his mother, Gail Johnson, to challenge the government's failure to provide PMTCT treatment and called for access to education for all young children (Rwafa and Rafapa, 2014). At the time of his funeral, Thandeka's daughter was three years old and extremely frail. Both Thandeka and her daughter had just started ARVs through the MSF trial in 2001. The fragility of life and the possibility of death was, in biopolitical terms, underpinned by the rapid rate at which Thandeka's colleagues in TAC were dying because, unlike Thandeka, they did not live in the catchment area to qualify for the MSF trial, and they could not afford to pay for private health care. We stood outside the cathedral, our necks straining. I commented that Nkosi had, like Thandeka, also spoken to former President Mbeki. "TAC's a very good organization. They opened my eyes to see what is the wrong way, and what is the right way. Because HIV is killing everyone. It's not just killing the Black people. So Mbeki was wrong." This quote highlights TAC's pivotal role in reshaping government policy in order to really 'democratize' health because, as Thandeka notes, the virus did not discriminate; this comment also speaks to Mbeki's assertion that HIV was being discursively mobilized by racists to perpetuate the myth that Black people are more likely to be sexually active and therefore more likely to be HIV-positive (see Van der Vliet, 2004; Fassin, 2007; Gevisser, 2008).

Like Thandeka, Yvonne worked with TAC in the early 2000s to compel the government to provide ARVs. She spoke with vehemence, saying, "I was angry then as I am still angry now. I was angry at that time because I knew that the government we were trying to approach is the government we voted for. And they kept denying our needs as a citizen in society." During our work together, Yvonne took many photographs in which she spoke to the state and directed her criticisms towards poor housing and education and the escalation of rape. Yvonne also took photographs of her medicines, but in this case, her photographs spoke to the work she had done as a TAC activist to challenge the government, as health citizens, to provide HIV medicines through the public health system. She had voted in the municipal election, but as she said, "I vote to vote." She had, however, opted to abstain from voting in the 2004 national election because

'I hated the government at that time, even during the voting times, I preferred not to vote, I thought what is the use of voting? I thought that soon I'd die and what's the use of voting for people who don't care about me. In order to vote I need to vote for someone who is taking care of me, of my needs, ARVs is the first need I knew I needed … They kept playing with words, saying that HIV doesn't cause AIDS, although you knew that if you're living with HIV you know at some point you'd have AIDS. They were politicizing everything, they were playing with our minds … ANC members would follow whatever statement Manto [Tshabalala-Msimang] or [former President] Mbeki said because they are our leaders … We need healthy food and healthy diet, but we need ARVs. They must work together.'

Although Yvonne expressed discontent with the conditions of life, particularly linked to service delivery and safety, she acknowledged that, with the rollout of ARVs, the government had made significant advances towards fulfilling its obligations to HIV-positive citizens by providing AIDS therapies: "Now, I don't lie. They are trying a lot: from the changing the ARV protocols, to convincing people to test, doing more campaigns on HIV, and also taking a lead … That's what people need, to see their leaders take a stand on HIV." With the changes in health care provision that Yvonne describes, I wondered if Thandeka, too, felt that the government had started to 'care' about citizens' health now. Her decision to 'put her eggs next to the government' seemed prescient: she explained to me that "t's better now, because if you go to the clinic, to get treatment, you see the changes … They're monitoring the people, who're taking the treatment all the time. Now it's easy to go to ARVs; we see that people are healthy on the treatment." As I came to know Thandeka and learnt more about her history as an anti-apartheid activist and then later as a HIV activist, I realized that it was important for her – and many others, including Yvonne's mother, for example – to distinguish between challenging the government (as she had during the struggle for democracy) and challenging the government's HIV treatment policy (as she had during the struggle for ARVs). TAC's founder, Zackie Achmat, also asserted this distinction, saying that he did not question the government's leadership but rather the leadership of then President Mbeki and Health Minister Tshabalala-Msimang who were advocating pseudo-scientific approaches that questioned the link between HIV and AIDS and challenged the efficacy of ARVs (Geffen, 2010).

Thandeka and I spent about six months searching for a photograph that had been taken of her and her daughter. Our search took us through the Company Gardens, past parliament and down into the basement of the adjacent South African National Gallery. The outcome of this search was unanticipated, and I describe it here because it encapsulates the journey that, in part, brought activists like Thandeka and Yvonne to believe that the government has come closer to fulfilling its constitutional obligation to ensure citizens' rights to life and health by providing HIV medicines in the public sector.

We did not find Thandeka's photograph among the hundreds of images we went through in the National Gallery; nor did we have any record of the name of the photographer in order to track the photograph down in this way. It happened that one day, in July, I asked to use the adjacent office to the one I worked in at TAC's national office to conduct an interview. I walked in and saw Thandeka and her daughter's face looking out defiantly from the photograph on the wall. Inside the frame and next to the photograph was Thandeka's affidavit in which she called on 39 pharmaceutical companies to drop their case against South Africa (because the government had used the 1997 Medicines Act to accord power to the Health Minister to override patent laws in health emergences). TAC worked with the government to win the case (the 39 pharmaceutical companies backed out) and, as described in Chapter 3 (and as I discuss further in Chapter 7), went on to sue the government in 2001 for going back on its agreement to provide nevirapine (NVP) to prevent vertical transmission. Thandeka gave an affidavit in support of TAC's claim against the pharmaceutical companies in 2000. She also testified in the subsequent trial against the Health Minister in 2001. The salient points in Thandeka's affidavit, which ran alongside a photograph of her and her daughter in their home in Khayelitsha, said:

'It is very painful for me to see my child suffering from the same illness like mine and I think that if the MTCT prevention programme had been implemented, my baby wouldn't be HIV positive. I would be very happy if we (me and my baby) could have access to treatment to help us live longer and healthier lives. It pains me to see people suffering and some die because they can't afford treatments. Because of their prices. I would be very happy if pharmaceutical companies would give us treatment at cheaper prices. Most people who are now living with AIDS are unemployed and we can't even buy something to eat, so how can we pay for expensive treatments?'

On a crisp winter's morning in July, Thandeka and I met outside the train station in central Cape Town and walked together to TAC's national office, climbing the stairs that spiralled up past Sonke Gender Justice's expanding offices. We were going to look at the photograph. After first looking at it and telling my colleagues working in TAC about the journey she had taken as an activist with TAC many years previously, we went upstairs to say hello to the people Thandeka knew in TAC's administration. We went back to look at the photograph one more time before leaving. I had thought that perhaps Thandeka would mind that her photograph was in this office and not in her home or that, at a minimum, she would mind that it was being sold for a large amount of money online by the photographer and that she had not received any payment herself. However, when I asked her, she smiled and said, "Look at me now Beth! If you saw that woman and child from the photograph then, all those years back, you would not believe they would still be alive today. But here I am. I am fit; I am me." The only other times I had seen Thandeka smile like that was when she was with her daughter. I realized that my concerns were not hers, and that finding the photograph was not a journey to reclaim the image but one to acknowledge the distance she and her daughter had travelled over the past decade as they navigated their will to live.

The changes in the governance of HIV over time in South Africa indicate the power of large-scale forms of activism led by organizations like TAC and the former AIDS Law Project. But they also came down to the individual acts of people like the women I worked with as they argued for their rights, as citizens, with a government that they voted for, a government that, as Thandeka said, people "Put their eggs next to" in the hope they would, eventually, fulfil some − if not all − of their responsibilities. In this sense, Fassin's comment on the continuities across apartheid and democracy is pertinent: 'Despite facile academic use of the prefix post-, this can indeed be called the postapartheid period. No other term expresses so well the dialectic of a social world that has survived its own disappearance' (2007: xvi). Anti-apartheid activists had fought to give life to a democratic government, led by the ANC, with the belief that their own vitality would become less precarious than it had been under apartheid. However, as we see here, and with Yvonne's mother's perplexed relationship with the government she too had fought for, the possibility of life for HIV-positive people was powerfully constrained by the post-apartheid state's refusal to provide medicines.

Until it finally did. Then, as my ethnography shows, a new range of struggles became prominent in people's bodies and in their social, political and economic relationships; specifically, the coherent set of biosocial discourses that positioned ARVs as a 'solution' to the shared predicament of HIV started to diffract. The provision of HIV medicines, and their role in sustaining people's lives, was perceived as absolutely critical, but this appeared to be enmeshed with more complex sets of narratives including: an emergent ambivalence towards ARVs linked to the side effects, viral resistance and adherence and an expansion of the biopolitical relationship with the state – formerly tightly articulated around HIV medicines – as HIV-positive citizens called for the provision of a broader set of resources that were necessary to support life in addition to ARVs. In the following sections, I look at how responsibilities for 'life' draw in adjurations by activists to be 'disciplined' and care for the self, in Foucault's (1998) terms; and I also show how these imaginaries of the state connect to diffracted biosocialities as people articulated, through everyday citizenships, their perception of the state's responsibility to sustain their vitality beyond the provision of ARVs.

"[The government] is … managing our health": rights and responsibilities in the era of ARVs

Me: Why do you think it's the government's responsibility to provide ARVs?

Zama: Because he's the one who's got money.

Me: But why does that mean it's the government's responsibility?

Zama: Well, whose responsibility should it be?

Me: Well, to play the devil's advocate: why should we not pay for the ARVs ourselves?

Zama: Because we don't have money. Other people are not working. Some people are working, but their salaries are very low and the medicines are expensive.

Me: I know I'm starting to drive you crazy. But …

Zama: But …

Me: Ok, so what if the American government offers to provide all the ARVs in South Africa; should our government still pay for the ARVs?

Zama: Ya, to show responsibility, mos. Because we see the government as the person who is managing our country. He is part of managing our health, employment, other areas, poverty. Most of the areas in our life. I think that is why we feel the government should be taking the responsibility.

Me: Because it's managing all these areas, it should be managing our bodies?

Zama: Well, not managing our bodies in that way … Hm … Well, sometimes it's ok.

Me: Do you feel it's ok for the government to manage your body?

Zama: In some contexts, yes. Sometimes people, they don't listen. You tell them this, then they do things the other way. They know that HIV can kill you; that condoms must be used. We know that ARVs can save you. We know that we must be honest with our partner. We know we must go for a test earlier to prevent illness and other infections. But people don't do that. It's scary … So now. We must test those people. By force. Nicely [laughing]. So that they know, man.

Although anthropologists like Nguyen (2011, 2019) and Petryna (2013) explore systems of claims that arise from biopolitical techniques that govern populations, they foreground distinct subjectivities that collectives lay claim to through citizen practices. The emergence of a new range of struggles discussed previously, after the public provision of ARVs, points to the importance of understanding the dynamic ways in which ARVs and HIV, as actants, intra-act with(in) people's bodies. This confounds prevalent conceptions of citizenship linked to health or illness, like biological and therapeutic citizenship: although people still conceptualize their relationship with the state in biopolitical terms, as Zama does here – "[the government] is part of managing our health" – their embodied experience of precarity is subjective and shifting, held in individual bodies and not necessarily shared by a collective citizenry. I introduce these diffracted biosocialities in relation to the new generation struggles in the previous chapter. In this section, I explore how, despite these shifting subjectivities, there was a consistent view among the people I worked with that the state was still implicated in their embodied precarity, and that it continued to be responsible for ensuring a set of rights linked to a broader set of concerns beyond access to HIV medicines.

The people who coalesced around Miriam in the 'ARV queue' had been part of the biosociality that emerges from shared activist practices, and in my fieldwork there were two overarching approaches to managing these struggles. On the one hand, as discussed in Chapter 4, the people I worked with asserted the importance of self-care practices. These 'self-care practices' resonate with Robin's (2006) notion of 'responsibilised health citizenship' and, more recently, research by Luca Marelli and colleagues (2022) on 'techno-solutionism' where responsibility for providing medical therapies lies with the state, but the responsibility for adhering to the medicines and 'living responsibly' lies with the individual. On the other hand, the people I worked with said that although self-care practices were important, it was also the government's responsibility to ensure that people were supported to manage the new generation struggles linked to side effects, viral resistance and adherence.

Some of the activists I came to know berated people for failing to adhere because they were "not managing their health" and argued that an individual's failure to adhere to treatment warranted 'punishment'. This took many forms: in some cases, it was simply a matter of asserting the right of doctors and nurses to scold HIV-positive people for failing to strictly adhere to their treatment regimens. In other cases, as with Thandiswa's sister, it entailed a refusal on the part of her sister's doctor to move her sister on to a better but more expensive ARV with fewer side effects:

Thandiswa: My sister, this one, she likes freaky! She drinks and likes parties; they're careless ... She's on ARVs. But she didn't take ARVs now ... because she likes to spend time with the drinking and the dancing.

Me: So she forgets to take her ARVs?

Thandiswa: You see! ... This new treatment, they give if people have a serious problem. But they want to know if you are responsible to take it all the time. If you don't, like my sister as they do now, they didn't give to her because they tell us this treatment is very *very* expensive.

Thandiswa's account speaks to a broader field of ethnographic research in which relationships in health centres are viewed through the lens of governmentality and biopower (Hörbst and Wolf, 2014; Harris et al, 2016; Larsson, 2018). For example, through her ethnography of life in Kisumu, Prince (2012) critiques a straightforward application of the 'politics of life' framework on large-scale antiretroviral therapy (ART) interventions:

ART programs have a circumscribed objective: to ensure what Arendt (1958) calls 'sheer survival' ... through providing the basic necessity – medication. At the same time, they present successful survival on ART as a matter of 'positive living', of orienting one's life to the goal of health. ART programs both encourage people to think of themselves in terms of their biology, and triage survival, as they produce new forms of inclusion and exclusion. (2012: 537)

In a comprehensive five-year study of access and barriers to HIV treatment, tuberculosis (TB) and maternal health delivery services in South Africa, Harris and colleagues (2016) analyse the conduct of health care providers and the nature of their work in the context of a public health system that is rooted in colonial and apartheid injustice. Just as the findings in this section of the chapter reflect discourses around living 'responsibly', so too do the findings of Harris and colleagues' research reflect ways in which people living with HIV reproduce discourses of being a responsible patient. Conversely, they found that if patients were viewed by providers as 'irresponsible', they were strongly chastised by people working in health facilities. For instance, in a labour ward, the researchers made the following observations as the cleaners shouted at the women who were in labour:

> 'Who has made this mess? Bring the mop and clean up your mess. You are dirty, your husband or boyfriend is going to leave you. How will they love you when you mess like this?' The mothers just keep quiet. The cleaners then bring the mop and clean up being angry … There was a male clerk who also shouted at the women. He shouted at a woman who was bleeding and touched the desk. He shouted at everyone, 'How dirty they all are, these mothers they need to be taught. You are dirty and careless.' (Harris et al, 2016: 580)

These punishing behaviours are, as the authors argue, part of a much larger picture in which the government seeks to operationalize ambitious health policies with very limited financial and human resources. Government ambition without significant fiscal and infrastructural changes to a historically under-resourced health system means that health providers and clients operate in cramped and often cold buildings with severe staff and medical shortages and very high patient volumes (Harris et al, 2016).

The creation of 'responsibilized health citizens' through punitive discourses that admonish people for non-adherence can perhaps then be read as a strategic response to shifting responsibility from the state – as it functions through a frail, fractured health system – to the individual. Harris and colleagues (2016) observe that the 'responsibilization' is experienced and reproduced by both health care providers and health care users. They argue that existing biopolitical analyses of South Africa's health system tend to focus on the clients. Understanding the legacy of the country's colonial and apartheid history calls attention to how health care providers are also powerfully impacted by punitive practices of governmentality that function through a highly hierarchical and under-resourced health system.

In my fieldwork with *Luvuyolwethu*, a home-based care organization in Nyanga, Cape Town, in 2003 and 2004, I observed a similar dynamic, where the responsibility for health was actively shifted on to informal care providers as well as people living with HIV in highly under-resourced areas. In 1994, the ANC created the National Health System (NHS) policy which strongly invoked democratic principles like 'empowerment', 'local innovation' and 'accountability' to rationalize the proliferation of home-based care organizations that were stepping in to provide palliative care to people who were dying of AIDS and could not access HIV treatment that would sustain their lives. In this foundational Act, the government proposed a 'continuum of care' across the different levels of the health system; importantly, it extended these levels to include informal health care provision through home-based care organizations and justified this approach on the basis that it would enable them to reach people who had been discriminated against under the apartheid government and lived in areas with limited formal health care services. In my research with *Luvuyolwethu*, however, I found a tension between the democratic discourse of the foundational NHS policy that sought to shift responsibility for providing care on to unpaid care workers in home-based care organizations and the government's tacit acknowledgement that it required the (largely unpaid) labour of home-based carers because it simply did not have the resources within the formal health system to meet the health care needs of people living with HIV.

I spent time with Thandiswa a decade after conducting research with *Luvuyolwethu*, and by then South Africa's treatment policy had shifted dramatically: the government no longer equivocated on the efficacy of HIV treatment and was implementing the largest ARV rollout in the world. However, the theme of shifting responsibility from the state on to individuals persisted. Thandiswa's account indicates an interpolation of the 'right kind' of patient that ARV programmes produce through the discourse of positive living, in which 'liking freaky', drinking and staying up are not considered 'responsible' behaviours. However, her account also takes the 'politics of life' critique further as it points to economic rationalities (and fears) of the state's limited capacity to provide ARVs; and it links these deep concerns about sustaining life on ARVs in the future with discourses that are, perhaps, less about moral forms of exclusion and more about wishing that her sister would lift some of the weight of responsibility in the strained household they shared. Her account also speaks to an awareness of the costs the government was 'carrying' in providing HIV medicines through the public sector.

While Thandiswa concurred with the way her sister, Yoliswa, was punished by the nurses in the clinic for failing to adhere to treatment, she also asserted an economic rationality for this punishment: "this treatment is very *very* expensive". In his research on the Brazilian government's response to AIDS in its early years of democracy, Biehl (2005, 2012) describes a set of economic value systems that draw pharmaceutical commerce into public health care; Thandiswa, here, points out this value system, where 'discipline' should correct aberrant behaviour that undermines adherence to expensive medicines and therefore 'costs' the government money. An unspoken concern, perhaps, was that if the government was 'wasting money' by treating people who did not adhere to their drugs, then it would also be less able to afford to provide newer and more effective medicines to those who did. This, too, fuelled the logic of governmentality in which biopower, operationalized by health practitioners through adherence checks for example, conditions people's bodies by 'rewarding' those who conform to disciplinary practices.

Another aspect of Thandiswa's account here, and of the relationship I observed with her sister over the course of my fieldwork, was an abiding frustration that her sister's social behaviour placed an additional responsibility on Thandiswa to care for her sister's children. Yoliswa lived with her two children in a small shack in the back garden of Thandiswa's Reconstruction and Development Programme home. One child, the same age as Thandiswa's daughter, was also born with HIV and had become severely disabled in the 'window period' in the late 1990s before the government provided PMTCT treatment or any HIV medicines for babies with HIV. Often, when extremely drunk, Yoliswa did not come home in the evening and implicitly relied on Thandiswa to feed and bath her children and help them finish their homework. This, on top of struggling with her own son's drug addiction and daughter's precarious health, was extremely taxing for Thandiswa. If Yoliswa was 'successfully' disciplined by the state to amend her behaviour to qualify for better medicines, then it was conceivable that these changed behaviours – like abstaining from alcohol – would relieve some of the burden of responsibility that Thandiswa felt in caring for Yoliswa's children. There is a further dimension, then, to Yoliswa's economic rationalization underpinning 'good adherence behaviour'. Mandisa Mbali (2016, 2018) and Shauna Mottiar and Vuyiseka Dubula (2020) have described this process as one in which people, particularly women like Thandiswa who were linked to TAC and MSF, articulate their relationship with the state as 'responsibilized citizens'.

In the course of his fieldwork with HIV-positive activists in Khayelitsha, Robins observed how people's illness narratives and treatment testimonies produced 'radical transformations in subjectivity and identity that go well beyond conventional liberal democratic conceptions of "rights" and "citizenship"' (2010: 128). I also observed this among the group of people I worked with who had not necessarily been activists but who were also on ARVs: almost everyone said they had changed their lives radically after learning they were HIV-positive. These changes included abstinence from alcohol, increased condom use and a reduction in the number of concurrent partners with whom they were having sex. It seems, though, that when people like Yoliswa do not adhere to the set of behaviours expected from 'responsibilized citizens', that they are not only punished by the health system but also by their peers. Here, too, this may relate to the economic rationalization that I discuss earlier: 'good people's' ability to access drugs is conditional on the government's ability to pay for them (which, as I discuss in the next two chapters, links them into a global assemblage). This, in turn, is conditional on people agreeing to be responsible not only for their own lives but for the lives of others by adhering to these life-giving and costly medicines.

Citizens like Thandiswa therefore actively enter a biopolitical relationship with the state in which they agree to 'behave' in particular ways in order to access the biomedicines on which their vitality hinges. This dialectic of punishment and reward has direct and embodied implications. As I discuss in Chapter 4, many of the women I worked with struggled with issues around adherence, but they were reluctant to discuss these struggles because of the stigma attached to being an 'irresponsible citizen'.

By placing the responsibility on individuals to 'behave' and punishing them if they do not, I suggest that this form of governmentality creates a value system linked to what Biehl (2021: 309) describes as the 'pharmaceuticalization of health', which can then crystallize new inequalities. In this respect, these inequalities are embodied as people are 'permitted' to access newer and better medicines if they 'behave', and they emerge in social relationships as those people who struggle to adhere, for a complex range of reasons, are deemed 'irresponsible' and less 'deserving' of expensive medicines.

In my ethnography, this form of governmentality, held in a contract of vitality where ARVs are 'given' to 'responsible' individuals, was mobilized around multiple notions of responsibility: as individuals are told to be 'responsible for their own health'; and as the government was described as 'responsible for managing our health' by providing ARVs to its citizens. As ARVs were made increasingly available in South Africa, and as people were on the medicines for a substantial period (more than a decade, for many of the women I worked with), this contract of vitality drew a broader set of concerns around medicines into focus.

In a conversation with Miriam and Yandisa, they told me that not only should the government be working harder to bring more advanced medicines, including long-acting injectable treatments like lenacapavir, into South Africa but that it should be working to eradicate HIV from their bodies altogether. In talking about why she believed the government was responsible for these newer biomedical technologies, Miriam echoed the economic argument that both Zama and Thandiswa had explained to me:

'The private companies are doing this for profit – they can't give us the medicines for free, so the government is responsible. They make promises to do everything for us. Firstly, they must supply work. It's difficult to be employed these days. Medicines are expensive and we don't have money. The only thing we want is health. We've got children to live for. And there are these children who are HIV-positive now, they didn't go out and find HIV, we infected them with HIV. At least he must find a cure so that our children must be healthy and live their own lives.'

For many women in the core group, their sense of precarity was not linked to whether or not they could access medicines at all, but whether or not they would be able to access more advanced and effective HIV treatment in the future when their current ARVs were no longer successfully intra-acting with HIV to stop it from replicating.

For Yvonne, the possibility of developing resistance was not only an abstract concern but a 'new generation struggle' that she had already experienced. As discussed in Chapter 4, she had found that AZT had made her anaemic and that NVP was damaging her liver. Yvonne was then put on to a different treatment but struggled with lipodystrophy. Yvonne echoed Zama and Thandiswa in saying that the government needs to work harder to support people with these emerging struggles around HIV treatment. One such route, she suggested, was by reinstating support groups for people not only as they start their ARVs but as they manage the longer-term struggles that surface in people's bodies and lives over time.

Sibongile, Zama, Yvonne, Miriam, Lilian and Brenda had all been members of support groups when they started their ARVs. This may perhaps account for their concern that, with fewer support groups available to those living with HIV, people were less likely to discuss concerns around side effects with member of their group and then with medical staff and therefore more likely to default from their treatment:

> 'Sometimes people get bored because it's a life-long treatment because people say, 'All these years I've been on treatment, and now I'm tired.' Also side effects … I tell myself that if the doctor does not want to change me, I'll stop taking ARVs … [Now] I think their main focus now should be, yes, ARVs are here and how do we keep people on them.'

The historic recognition that ARVs are an essential part of managing HIV was not questioned in my fieldwork; but an emerging and embodied ambivalence about these medicines became salient, diffracting the coherence of earlier forms of biosociality based on the construction of ARVs as the solution to HIV, with implications for the broader set of claims made by HIV-positive citizens on the state. Yvonne points to the importance of taking time into account when thinking about ARVs. In this and the previous chapters, we see how HIV medicines came to be embodied in ambiguous ways over time: in addition to playing an important role in sustaining life, they were also embodied as side effects. Some older medicines like stavudine, for example, surfaced visibly in the body as lipodystrophy, and as we see in the next chapter, some of the effects of ARVs do not simply recede into the body with time when people move on to different drugs. Similarly, the effects of HIV, too, can remain visible as we see in the embodied memory of the virus held in Nondumiso's skin, as she depicted on her body map. Further, embodied precarity is not only related to the lives of HIV and ARVs individually, as actants in the body, but also to their intra-action with each other; this is evident, for example, in viral resistance as new strains of the virus become better able to combat the effects of older HIV medicines.

These new generation struggles are linked: daily adherence to medicines that sustained life but also generated side effects became a fraught personal battle for the women I worked with. With erratic adherence (to minimize side effects), and also with unprotected sex with another HIV-positive person, the virus becomes adept at mutating, and therefore resisting ARVs, weakening the body and making it more susceptible to opportunistic infections. In Chapter 3, Miriam's and Brenda's accounts of having unprotected sex with their partners suggest the social and economic dimensions entailed in their 'self-care': they may be 'living positively' in respect to their adherence, but their ability to practise safe sex is relational. It is also reflective of entrenched socio-economic inequalities where, for instance, Miriam's education was halted by her uncle so that she could be 'a good girl' and care for her dying mother. Lilian's and Yvonne's experiences of lipodystrophy and liver dysfunction, also discussed in Chapter 4, point to the social dimensions of their encounters with biomedical health practitioners who did not, initially, take their concerns about side effects seriously.

Therefore, although the virus mutates inside the individual body, it is able to do so because of the intersecting pathways of precarity that foreground sociality. This includes horizontal pathways and women's constrained ability to negotiate the frequency of sex, and the use of condoms, with their partners. Further, although women experience the side effects of older and less effective ARVs in their body, their struggles around adherence and viral resistance point to a broader set of social relationships with their medical doctors and political relationships with the state and its capacity (or will) to provide more effective HIV medicines to minimize these effects.

Diffracted biosocialities emerged as women started to articulate their embodied struggles with what had historically been cast as the solution to managing HIV. The articulations of their struggle – not only with HIV but now also with HIV medicines – traversed roads that had been well worn in the earlier struggle for ARVs, including: their relationships with biomedical health care practitioners, an array of national and transnational activist organizations and local, provincial and national government officials. As I go on to discuss, these social, political and economic relationships are not distinct but networked into each other; they are also indicative of diffracted biosocialities as women negotiate their relationship with the actants they embody and with the broader intersecting inequalities and opportunities they navigate in their daily lives and within a network of actors that co-construct their embodied precarity and their vitality.

The injunctions entailed in 'positive living' have been strongly critiqued by other anthropologists in their ethnographies of ARV programmes for placing responsibility on the individual while failing to account for the complex realities of their lives; realities that, as shown in Kalofonos's (2021) ethnographic research in Mozambique for example, may mean that ARVs make it even more difficult to live because living entails having enough money to buy food in order to manage taking ARVs. Research from across Sub-Saharan Africa that explores the economic contexts in which ARV programmes are implemented shows that context matters (Marsland, 2012; Decoteau, 2013; Cousins, 2016; Shubber et al, 2016; Adeniyi et al, 2018; Kagee et al, 2019). In research from Kenya, Ruth Prince (2012, 2017) shows how ARVs can exacerbate hunger pangs, creating an almost impossible cycle: because ARVs can make people quite dizzy, it becomes even more difficult for them to work the long hours necessary to earn the money they need to buy food for themselves and their household. Being HIV-positive has been historically considered in light of its biosocial potential to connect people to resources – problematized in Chapter 4 with respect to *uYaphi's* income-generation programme. However, when these resources dwindle, the biopolitics of life beyond biomedicine become more keenly apparent, as I observed in the range of claims that people made when 'seeing' and 'speaking to' the state.

Sustaining life beyond ARVs: seeing and speaking to the state

In addition to calling on the government to respond to emerging struggles linked to the intra-action of HIV and ARVs, this group of women spoke about the linked struggles they encountered as they navigated the longer life that was, in part, made possible through HIV medicines. This second strand of emergent citizenship forms the focus of this section as people articulated spaces in which they saw the state and practices through which they spoke to the state in order to make it listen to their concerns.

Over the course of my fieldwork, the women in the core group and I would reflect on our relationship with the state in the different spaces of our lives. We started quite generally, by playing with photographs and films, capturing the most important moments and people that had surfaced in the time between seeing each other. Over time, our conversations moved into reflecting on where we had felt disappointed by the government: in my frustration at South Africa's performance at the UN and its vote on the removal of sexual orientation from extrajudicial killings (in a photograph of the march outside parliament); or in Miriam's anger at the police who had arrested her brother for selling alcohol illegally (in a photograph of the locked up shebeen). These visual accounts became a layered conversation that looped across time. For example, I took a photograph of an image of a blindfolded woman holding the scales of justice one evening, when I was walking home past the parliamentary buildings. When I showed Thandiswa this photograph, she told me about her frustration with the ANC's Women's League, who, she felt, were blind to the very intimate forms of violence that were being perpetrated against their much less privileged comrades. Thandiswa would, after this conversation, take a series of photographs of derelict open toilets in the field next to her home: one of her neighbours had been raped using this toilet in the middle of the night. She had taken these photographs because she saw the state in its failure to provide safe housing and sanitation and wanted to speak to the government – to the women in the ANC Women's League – and express her and other women's sense of embodied precarity in Khayelitsha.

Through an ethnographic montage of photographs, films and participant observation in public protests, pickets and marches, I came to see that the state was imagined and engaged with in myriad ways that span public and private spaces of citizen action; and that these imaginaries corresponded with a sense that the state, in failing to uphold a set of rights around gender, sexuality, education and housing, continued to engender embodied precarity for its citizens despite the provision of ARVs. The photographs and films in which women 'saw the state' took me into the more private spaces of their everyday lives, whereas the public marches, pickets, court cases, moved me through more public spaces where people of all genders brought their bodies to bear witness to the issues they wanted the state to see. The first part of this section engages with the way the women in the core group 'saw the state'. The second part moves out in scale to explore the implications of these broader concerns on the forms of activism and activist organizations that were most visible in my ethnography as I observed how people 'spoke to the state'.

"It was … amazing, the president passing by my house": seeing the state

Walking through Nkanani one day, Yandisa pointed to the sandals on my feet and told me to wear tougher shoes. By way of explanation, she pointed down to the ground we were standing on. It took me a bit of time before I saw the cables: they were camouflaged by sand and snaked along the gravel road. In some places, the flex had been worn down by car tyres, the sun or people's shoes, and tiny wires bundled out into the sand. Over time, my eyes adjusted to reading the sand, and I learnt to discern the character of the cables quickly enough to miss walking over the live wires. I also started wearing thick rubber-soled shoes. I was privileged to be able to purchase this degree of safety. Miriam, who lived two-minutes' walk from Yandisa's home, told me about the neighbour who lived in the house between them. Her child had gone out in the middle of a thunderstorm to collect water from the tap shared by all of Nkanini's residents. On the way to the tap, the child had stepped on one of these worn-down cables, screaming in shock; when the mother ran out to pull him away, she was electrocuted. The neighbours rushed out to try and help her, but she really needed emergency medical attention, and by the time the sluggish ambulance had arrived, she had died. The government refused to sufficiently subsidize electricity costs through its national company, Eskom, and these accounts spoke to the cost of the state's absence in the presence of these wires: electricity was too expensive for most people in Khayelitsha to afford, and so some residents chose to pay people to siphon illegal electricity lines away from the neighbouring wealthier suburb (Somerset West) into their homes. Illegal electricity, however, came at a cost that was experienced by everyone who was connected – often not by choice – along the winding routes that these lines followed across their roofs, along their roads and sometimes under their feet.

There were also many photographs in which people 'saw the state' in large piles of rubbish that collected in the roads and siphoned around people's homes. Sibongile had, for example, taken a series of photographs in which she had 'seen the state' in the open field just over the road from her home. Through these photographs, she told me about President Zuma's visit to her neighbourhood as part of the ANC's election campaign.

Over the course of many photographs, I watched an unfolding picture in which two different imaginaries of the state ran alongside each other. The first imaginary of seeing the state was, quite literally, of seeing President Zuma arriving to speak to a group of supporters at the rally. In these photographs, I saw, first, the supporters waiting for his arrival; this is followed by a set of photographs of bodyguards surrounding President Zuma as he walked to the stage to, eventually, address the assembled supporters. Sibongile watched this visit unfold from a distance with her two children, and she recorded it on her camera. She said: "These are the pictures I took when Zuma came. My street actually. He passed by my house. I was standing by the gate. It was kind of like amazing, the president passing by my house. I couldn't capture a full picture of him, you know everyone coming to see the president."

Her photographs captured another powerful picture of the state, however, as she pointed to the large open rubbish dump that featured in the foreground of the photographs that she had taken documenting President Zuma's visit. She explained to me that the municipality had stopped collecting rubbish from her neighbourhood, and so she and her neighbours had started piling their rubbish on this site during the week. Each Saturday, they would burn the rubbish in the morning, but on this particular Saturday they had postponed the fire until President Zuma left because the smoke would have sullied the slick preparations. Sibongile was excited about President Zuma's visit but also angry that the government had not done more to address the economic and racial inequalities she still felt. She pointed to the rubbish heap in these photographs and said, "You see, this is how they expect us to live. What's that? That's not right. It's not good for our children's health to have all this rubbish right on the doorstep like this, every day, every week."

I asked Sibongile if she was going to vote in the elections, and she said, quite strongly, "Yes, my grandmother fought hard for the ANC; I will only ever vote for them myself. But I don't think they will do anything to make my life better." Seeing these different forms of the state in Sibongile's photographs suggested to me that people's concern with issues like sanitation ran alongside an imaginary in which the state was understood to be transitory – to come "to my street", to speak, and then to leave – and ultimately divorced from citizens' everyday struggles. This was most striking in the final photograph, where Sibongile's children are seen sitting on their doorstep, watching the rubbish burn after President Zuma and his supporters had left the open field.

Sibongile's concern with sanitation was reflected in the many photographs of various kinds of public toilets – sometimes broken or locked – that were scattered around Khayelitsha. Yvonne, for example, took a photo of a group of toilets near her home. In the photo, each toilet had a lock on it. Even where public toilets had been constructed, therefore, many people were unable to use them if they had not negotiated with their neighbours to claim – with a lock – a particular cubicle. The women I worked with were particularly concerned about their safety at night because of the numerous accounts of women who were raped when using the toilets. An interim measure, one that was still not acceptable but that was preferable to public toilets, were small portable toilets that had a detachable waste-carrier. Yandisa and Miriam each had one of these toilets in their homes. Yandisa said, showing me a photograph of her portable toilet, that they were an indication that "[t]his government does not want dignity for us". Her sentiment was echoed by thousands of other residents in Khayelitsha during my fieldwork and, as discussed subsequently, has become a significant point of activism by the Social Justice Coalition (SJC).

On Freedom Day – 27 April, the day commemorating South Africa's first democratic election – the SJC organized a march in Khayelitsha to demand safe and dignified sanitation. More than 2,500 people marched on this day, explicitly pointing to the link between the struggle for democracy and the continued struggle for the rights held in the constitution of this new democracy. As we saw earlier, the SJC's call for 'dignified sanitation' was echoed by the people with whom I worked and the photographs they took to speak to the state. The way in which people saw the state, most often in its absence, connected, too, with how people then spoke to the state through various forms of citizen action.

"Every generation has its struggle": speaking to the state

In this sub-section, I explore the relationship between the broader set of concerns, discussed earlier in relation to new generation struggles, and the emergence of a network of activist organizations through which citizens 'spoke to the state'. The new generation struggles that were salient in my fieldwork point to the diffraction of concerns that had previously centred closely on HIV and access to ARVs. Now, with ARVs, these concerns relate to the dual struggles around the embodiment of actants (ARVs' side effects and HIV's viral mutations) and the broader socio-economic context in which people lived their lives on ARVs. I explore the associated forms of citizenship around these new generation struggles in the paragraphs that follow. I suggest that the legacy of citizen action that emerged with the anti-apartheid movement features strongly in the diffracted biosocialities linked to these emerging struggles. I propose that despite these legacies of action and shifts in salient concerns, there is continuity in the way that people embody precarity across these generations of struggle and, further, that HIV-positive citizens continue to hold the state accountable for the extent to which they live precarious lives in post-apartheid South Africa.

"My vote must speak for me": having voice

Thandeka's stained thumb pointed to a set of beliefs held by all of the women with whom I worked in the core group. On the whole, they conceived voting as part of an array of citizen practices, like marches and civil disobedience campaigns, that were necessary to make the government listen. Throughout my fieldwork, when people – including those who had not been HIV activists – spoke about why they were going to vote, the word most often used in their explanation was 'voice'. For example, in an interview with Witness, a fifty-nine year old man living in Khayelitsha, he said: "It is said that your vote is your voice." Bongiwe, similarly, said: "I vote so that I have the right to speak out; the right to voice out my opinion … My vote must speak for me."

Khayelitsha's streets offered a slightly different story. These stories, spray painted on walls or scrawled over posters, reflected a disdain towards the electoral system and towards the leading party. The messages encouraged people to boycott the elections and were on the walls of clinics, streets, taxi ranks and bus shelters. The following two figures (see Figures 5.1 and 5.2) speak to the conjunction of past and present, with their messages written along a wall bordering a street named after one of South Africa's most prominent anti-apartheid activists, and the founder of the Black Consciousness movement, Steve Biko. Further down the road, near the

Figure 5.1: Don't vote, graffiti

Source: Author's own

Figure 5.2: Fuck all politics, graffiti

Source: Author's own

Magistrates' Court – also iconic of a hard-won and, as I discuss subsequently, flawed democratic juridical system – someone had written, "Fuck all politics." The disdain expressed in the public spaces of Khayelitsha reflected the deep disillusionment in the government expressed by the people I worked with, particularly around the conditions of life as discussed in the following section.

The use of graffiti to express political discontent has a long history in South Africa. Scholars have traced this form of political protest back to the Sharpeville Massacre of 21 March 1960, when the apartheid government killed 69 Black protesters who were demonstrating against the racist legal system that governed Black people's right to move freely in the country (Bodunrin, 2014; Thomas, 2023). In the 1980s, Cape Town became well known for the proliferation of subversive art and commentary throughout its public spaces. As Bodunrin (2014: 2) writes, '[graffiti] became a radical and an alternative medium that challenged the status quo in the absence of the government-controlled mainstream media'. As my research, and the research of numerous other scholars (Coombes, 2003; McAuliffe, 2012; Smith, 2017; Lee, 2019), shows, graffiti continues to hold significant value as a form of expression and resistance in post-apartheid South Africa.

Public artist collectives have emerged across the country to memorialize protesters who have been killed in police violence in post-apartheid South Africa (Makhubu, 2013, 2017; Thomas, 2023). For instance, in a street art festival in Langa in 2014, an impoverished township near Khayelitsha, the Tokolos Stencils Collective created a large-scale work with the words 'Remember Marikana' repeated in a pattern that created an image of an eye (Makhubu, 2017). By creating this art, the Tokolos Stencils Collective were calling on South Africans to 'remember' the Marikana Massacre that had taken place just a year earlier, where the police killed 34 protesters who were among thousands of miners calling on the British-owned Lonmin platinum mine to pay its workers the same wages that workers were paid at its mines in Australia (R12,500 or $700/day) (Chinguno, 2013). This art was painted over just a day after it had been created on the wall (Thomas, 2018).

Walls can become sites for thinking through control and containment on the one hand and for offering a space for resisting this control and challenging attempts at containment on the other. In Johannesburg, Tom Penfold (2017) explores how the street art created by the Westdene Graffiti Project reveals contemporary tensions around the city's boundaries, the construction of belonging and the nature of political control and dissidence. Looking across multiple 'global cities', including Johannesburg, Cairo and the West Bank, Davies (2017) argues that graffiti reveals the precarity of state power held in walls that, too often, are constructed to police the movement of people through city spaces. Engaging with Wendy Brown's (2010) writing on the 'walling' or 'territorialization' of nation-states, Davies suggests that, '[g]raffiti seizes on this precarity as it manifests in the law/wall infrastructure, turning it into a canvas that levers open the oppressive violence ingrained within its physical materiality' (2017: 8).

In my fieldwork, the political discontent expressed in the graffiti on the walls in Khayelitsha spoke to a significant socio-spatial intersection: the history of the struggle for democracy was signified by Biko and intersected with the presence of a faulty but democratically-grounded judicial system, represented by the Magistrates' Court. This juncture of past and present speaks to a fundamental dissonance that surfaced across my fieldwork in which the rights contained in South Africa's highly respected and sophisticated constitution are constrained by a faulty overburdened socio-economic infrastructure. Like Khayelitsha's streets, and indeed the kinds of lives that people continue to live as they walk them, this infrastructure is inherited from apartheid and falters under the weight of the post-apartheid state's obligations to its citizens.

Among the people who lived in Khayelitsha, but who had not necessarily been HIV activists, many believed that voting would not generate positive change. Instead, voting was a matter of principle, an assertion of a hard-won right that extended beyond the struggle for ARVs to the struggle for democracy. For example, Nozuko said: "I vote because it is free to vote; before Black people never got the chance to vote. They were just decided for. For me it's good to make a contribution by voting." Also looking towards a history in which voting was limited to the White population, Nomphuthumo said: "I am a South African citizen. Before [under apartheid] things were hard ... Now where we stand, things are better." Zakhele, a 60-year-old man, also spoke about his vote as his voice in South Africa's democracy. He recalled how, during apartheid, his movement around the country had been limited by the Pass Laws and said: "[I am] voting to have a say and not be limited in where I want to go. If I want to go somewhere I can be able to go."

These accounts reflect a broader set of views among the larger group of people who did not necessarily have a history of HIV activism. These views also did not differ across the age or genders of the people in this larger group and suggest that the presence of South Africa's oppressive history under apartheid continues to compel people to assert their right to vote as a condition of democracy. Voting, for people in this group, it seemed, was less about a way of shaping particular kinds of governance in the future and more about a historically driven assertion of democratic governance in general. Thobani, as you may recall from Chapter 4, reflected on voting in his second body map; he spoke about this bifurcation where voting is a means to assert one's right in a democracy but that it does not lead to the fulfilment of obligations by the government. He says, "You see I'm told to vote to obtain my rights ... but that's just what I've not obtained yet." Sindiswa, a friend of Thobani's who I interviewed and who had worked with Thobani to set up one of TAC's branches in her home district in the Eastern Cape, similarly reflects a cynicism in the government's capacity to fulfil its responsibilities, saying, "I vote to keep my country, my government ... But I feel that my party does not meet my needs." Like Thobani and Sindiswa, many of the people I worked with believed that voting was an acknowledgement of South Africa's historical legacy and its transition to democracy, but the elections were not viewed by the people I worked with as a way to make the government listen. This sense of 'looking back' and asserting a democratic right when voting differed from other forms of citizen action I observed: these more direct forms of engagement with the state seemed to 'look forward' with the aim of speaking so loudly that the government would be compelled to listen.

When we spoke about specific articulations of 'voice' that were necessary to make the government listen, it was collective public action, including strikes and marches, that were described as the key mechanisms for 'showing a fist' to the government. Ntombentsha, a 30-year-old woman living with HIV, echoed the majority of participants' assertions on how to make the government listen when she said: "People strike, burn tyres, or go to parliament with posters ... When people *toyi toyi*, the government ends up responding to them." *Toyi toyi*, as way to express discontent in public spaces, echoes activist strategies under apartheid: when challenged by the apartheid police, the activists would argue they were simply singing and dancing. Because the songs were predominantly sung in local languages and not in English, the apartheid police did not understand the political content and were unable to justify intervention. *Toyi toying* and amended protest songs were also characteristic of the marches that TAC organized to challenge the post-apartheid government, especially during the height of the government's AIDS denialism. *Toyi toyi* as a form of collective action, and a way to speak to the state, sustained its anti-apartheid legacy in the marches I participated in during my fieldwork. As Noncedo, a 47-year-old HIV-positive woman who also worked at *uYaphi*, notes: "In this time it's like those old days ... where people were burning tyres. You see, we are going back to the past because every time we want the government to listen we have to do action instead of just talking. You need to show a fist!"

"You need to show a fist": between having voice and being heard

"It's strike season", said *Equal Treatment*'s (ET) editor, as the sound of the protesters on Adderley Street filtered up the five flights of stairs to our open-plan and – in March's summer heat – open-windowed workspace in TAC's national office in Cape Town. This was not an acerbic dismissal but an accurate observation that spoke to the timing and nature of collective action through which citizens spoke to the state. Hearing the sounds of the protest filtering up to our office, I looked out of the window and saw a sea of red umbrellas – an international signifier of sex worker rights. I flew down the flights of stairs to join the marchers as they rounded the corner of Adderley Street, just below parliament, and started walking up Wale Street to the provincial government's offices. The protesters were marching to deliver a memorandum calling on the government to address police brutality against sex workers.

In South Africa, sex work continues to be criminalized, and sex workers, particularly those working in public spaces like streets, are exposed to violence by the state. In this case, the protesters were challenging the Provincial Government to address brutality exerted through its mechanisms of control, as police 'disciplined' sex workers' bodies with arbitrary arrests, physical violence and rape. It was striking to see how, as the marchers delivered their memorandum to the Provincial Government, the building was flanked by policemen. The entrance to this physical space of the state was guarded by the same 'arms' of the state that had brutally violated the spaces of citizen's bodies. This is an example of biopolitical precarity as the state not only failed to protect groups differentially exposed to violence but actively perpetrated violence through these forms of 'punishment'. The policemen stood at the top of the stairs, legs apart, arms crossed, sniggering at the marchers as we stood below them.

The protesters may have been precariously positioned on the street, without much possibility of speaking directly to key officials in the provincial government, but they refused to be silenced. *Toyi toying* with placards that said, "My body, my rights" and "Legalise sex work now", about 200 protesters sang, "My mother was a kitchen girl / my father was a garden boy / that's why I'm a feminist." In the course of my life and fieldwork in South Africa, I had heard many different endings to that chant including "that's why I'm a freedom fighter; that's why I'm a communist; that's why I'm an AIDS activist". The mutable final line brings South Africa's history of apartheid into the present: it links the range of contemporary struggles to the legacy of structural violence exerted by the apartheid government through its legislative infrastructure in which Black South African men and women were denigrated, stripped of rights, referred to as children – garden boys and kitchen girls. This refrain, and indeed the marches I participated in, indicates a fluidity that draws past modes of activism into the present: we see in the refrain and in the ways that citizens performatively 'show a fist' to the post-apartheid government that anti-apartheid resistance tactics have been reconstituted and re-performed. Indeed, TAC's success in mobilizing the democratic government to provide HIV medicines can be attributed to its 'organizational memory', with many of its activists bringing their knowledge of resistance from decades of engaged activism in the anti-apartheid struggle and the LGBTQIA+ liberation movement (Jungar and Oinas, 2010).

A broad coalition of activist organizations were represented among the protesters at the sex worker march and included Sonke Gender Justice, the Sex Workers Education and Advocacy Taskforce, the Triangle Project, TAC and the SJC. I had come to recognize the same network of organizations at most of the marches and protests I attended across time, starting in the early 2000s when TAC mobilized thousands of people to bring entire cities to a halt. A month before the sex worker march, in January, I had joined many of these same organizations outside parliament calling on the government to make South Africa safer for women, and just two weeks prior to this march, many of us had been in Khayelitsha's Magistrates' Court to attend a trial of nine men accused of killing Zoliswa Nkonyana because she was a lesbian. It was noteworthy that a consistent network of activists and activist organizations participated in a wide-ranging set of citizen actions, and although almost all the marches were strongly supported by TAC activists, none of the marches were about HIV or access to treatment.

With the political commitment evinced by the government, under the then-President Zuma, to rapidly scale up the provision of ARVs, there was a corresponding change in the activist landscape as TAC's primary role in the struggle for ARVs shifted. What could be described as 'TAC's success' also created what was described to me by members of TAC at the time as "an identity crisis". The plurality of activist struggles that emerged in the wake of TAC's activism is perhaps also an indication of TAC's success. Similarly, it was evident to me, working with TAC on the ET magazine, that there had been an internal reorientation in TAC's advocacy agenda away from the primary goal of ensuring access to ARVs. In my fieldwork, I observed how TAC's advocacy also started to engage with some of the emerging struggles that I describe earlier, as we realized through our conversation with members of TAC's branches across the country that TAC's members were increasingly struggling with side effects, treatment fatigue, poor sanitation, inadequate housing and unemployment.

Although TAC continues to work alongside civil society organizations to 'raise a fist' and call on the government to address structural inequality – through, for example, the call, in 2022, for the government to fulfil the 'political freedom and bread' development agenda discussed in Chapter 4 – TAC also continues to advocate for health equality and access to essential medicines. Over the last few years, for example, TAC has worked – with some success – through a coalition of 40 local and international civil society organizations under the 'Fix the Patent Laws Campaign' (FPLC). As I discuss in Chapter 7, the FPLC is closely aligned with MSF's international 'Access Campaign' and calls on the South African government to change its outdated patent laws in order to better navigate international patent legislation and access better, more affordable medicines.

Conclusion

A hinge-pin linking the first two ethnographic chapters on South Africa with the following two chapters on activist coalitions in Brazil and international patent legislation linking Brazil, South Africa and India, the accounts in this chapter speak to the intersection of embodied struggles on ARVs with the political context in which these struggles are situated. This chapter articulates two key facets of 'everyday citizenship' that connect the embodied and political dimensions of my fieldwork together and speak to the call, articulated by scholars of Southern Theory like Pallavi Banerjee and Raewyn Connell (2018), to situate people's experiences in the Global South at the heart of any robust theoretical engagement, particularly around gender.

The first facet relates to how women embody and make sense of the government in relation to their lives and bodies. In this respect, this chapter explores the myriad ways that the state's presence was felt very directly in people's lives: in emerging struggles around older HIV medicines that caused visible side effects and were photographed on bedside tables or next to the television; in the bruised bodies of sex workers who had been violated by the police; in the physically unbearable accumulation of waste in portable toilets when the municipal truck failed to arrive on the much anticipated Tuesday morning to collect and replace the containers.

The second facet is linked to the first, as people found ways to 'act up' and on the state through a range of citizen practices in order to 'raise a fist' and compel the government to listen to their concerns around these new generation struggles linked to newer medicines, physical safety and improved sanitation. In this respect, as HIV medicines became more available, activist struggles shifted to encompass the contextual conditions in which people live. I describe these emergent responses to the dual character of the new generation struggles as diffracted biosocialities. I suggest subsequently and in the following chapters that this concept highlights the limits of agency in historical readings of biopolitics as the state and its citizens are porously networked into an assemblage they are both only partially able to navigate.

By moving away from a governmentality approach that considers how the state exerts control in and through people's and population's bodies, it can become possible to explore how people themselves conceptualize and strategically navigate their relationship with the state. In working to understand how people make sense of the state through various methods like participatory photography, I was trying to understand biopolitics from a different angle. Reflecting on fieldwork in Bihar, Jharkhand and West Bengal, Corbridge (2005, 2010, 2018) has similarly sought to integrate visuality in order to understand how different actors came to see the state and the different pathways they followed when engaging with the state, writing that '[w]e are used to the idea of the state seeing its population or citizenry. Visuality is at the heart of many theories of power and governmentality' (2005: 15). Just as the activists with whom I engaged in my fieldwork formed and solidified social networks that then enabled them to access a range of social and economic resources (although not without discontent, as we see in Chapter 4 and the women's sense that their "HIV was being exploited") to mitigate against their precarity, so too did the women in Eastern India draw on non-state networks to access resources to secure their livelihoods. Reflecting on the everyday state in India, Corbridge (2005, 2018) describes how the state conditions the mechanisms through which governmentality operates in citizens' lives and suggests that even when viewed slightly less directly as the state, these mechanisms – the health system, for example – still function to discipline and control the vitality of bodies.

I found resonance with these reflections in my research, as people's visual and narrative accounts revealed how they experienced the state in a range of direct and indirect ways. For example, some of the less direct ways of experiencing the state include the punishments meted against so-called 'defaulters' for failing to adhere to their ARVs. However, Corbridge (2005) does not look, in the way that I did in my research, at how vitality is not only managed through these mechanisms but also rendered precarious, as Butler (2012) and others have articulated (Fineman and Grear, 2016; Han, 2018), when certain populations are differentially exposed to violence from the state, and in some cases, from non-state actors without protection from the state. Through my research, I found that it was predominantly Black, HIV-positive women who experienced a heightened sense of precarity in their everyday lives, as they navigated locked toilets at night, worried about developing resistance to their HIV treatment or – as I have discussed in the previous two chapters – negotiated profound gender and sexual violence without any protection from the state.

Building on postcolonial critiques of citizenship studies that call for greater attention to be paid to the ways that the state's formal rules and regulations move into people's everyday lives (Chatterjee, 2018; Finn, 2021), my ethnography found that everyday citizenship is embodied in the quieter and more private spaces of individuals' lives alongside the public, and more frequently theorized, spaces of collective citizen action performed through pickets, protests and marches. I found that 'seeing the state' is a layered sensory process in which people bring their bodies, their voices, their sight, into their relationship with a porous state in very different ways through performance, across a trajectory of political engagement spanning the apartheid and post-apartheid eras. Further, I found that states of citizenship are forged through shifting imaginaries of the state as individuals' embodied precarity changed over time. I discussed some of these shifting dynamics in relation to a series of new generation struggles in the previous chapter and biosocial diffraction in the post-apartheid era in this chapter.

I suggest that not only does the state make different kinds of citizenship possible but that different kinds of citizenship, as they are embodied and performed, act on different kinds of states. To this end, I found that biopolitics cannot be understood as functioning through a unidirectional and linear relationship between the state and citizen, but that people's embodied precarity is forged through a complex relationship that is shaped by a much broader range of actors beyond the state–citizen dyad. As the following two chapters go on to discuss, these actors are assembled in a network that includes actants (like HIV and ARVs) and regional and global actors (like Brazil, India and the World Trade Organization [WTO]). I argue that not only is the biopolitical reach of the state constrained by this network but the women with whom I worked underlined the myriad ways in which they, too, acted in and through this network to compel the state to provide ARVs and other essential resources to sustain their lives.

There is an underlying political logic to the argument I make for bringing the political and embodied facets of my research together in this and the following two chapters through the concept of biopolitical precarity. The relationship between people's lives and the state is evident in democratic systems because here the vitality of the state is clearly tied to that of the population it governs. As we see in the United Kingdom with the introduction of alarming legislation that limits political action and extends police powers in the Police, Crime, Sentencing and Courts Act (the Policing Act 2022) or with South Africa's nationwide strike in August 2022 demanding the government address skyrocketing inflation (Diseko, 2022), democracy is not an endpoint in the struggle for rights. This was most pertinently captured for me in my fieldwork by Yvonne's mother. She had fought for democracy and lost her husband in the course of this struggle. Yet, when she learnt she was HIV-positive, her biopolitical relationship with the post-apartheid government was called into focus as she realized that here, again, she would need to fight for her right to life.

In their work as activists, the women I worked with brought their bodies into public spaces. They made their embodied precarity visible to the government through their intimate affidavits bearing witness to their children's deaths and their own precarious lives; through their permission to have their lives, and their embodied poverty, photographed and exhibited globally; through their powerful body maps; through their testimonies of grief in TAC's court cases to compel global pharmaceutical companies to reduce the cost of essential HIV medicines. To this end, women were fundamentally networked into a global assemblage of actors through their actions as citizens, in multiple public fora, and for shifting biopolitical struggles including the struggle for democracy during apartheid and the struggle for HIV medicine in the post-apartheid era.

However, and herein lies the first of the two underlying political arguments I wish to make: the women with whom I worked were not entirely able to control how their voices, their stories, their images, were used in this assemblage. This is most evident in the case of Thandeka's photograph, a visual icon of a poor Black woman's struggle to access medicines that would, for future generations, prevent what she had herself experienced: vertical transmission of HIV through to her child, because she could not access PMTCT. I met Thandeka and her daughter through this image years before I met her in person, before I saw Thandeka's face and could see the pride with which she looked at the face of her younger self and child in this image. Women's socialities forged through this history of activism were perhaps not only a very powerful indicator of their agency as they acted up on the networks of actors that governed access to medicines that would save their lives. Their accounts, their lives and relationships, also came to take on a disembodied life as actors in this network. Given the nature of my fieldwork with TAC, and with women who had worked in TAC, this was most evident as activist organizations like TAC and its partners mobilized these women's stories in the name of the post-apartheid nation's right to life. I observed this too, for instance, in earlier research on the mobilization of women's narratives for national healing in the Truth and Reconciliation Commission (Gobodo-Madikizela et al, 2005) and learnt of the extent to which it risked distorting women's accounts to foreground their sexual precarity over their political agency (Ross, 2003; DeLaet and Mills, 2018).

The second argument builds on the first: women's ability to mediate the networks into which their lives are woven points to the discursive distance that is promulgated by actors in this network in order to distance themselves from the very real and embodied implications of their policies. In this chapter and over the next two chapters, I explore how citizenship practices have diffracted and expanded beyond the initial assertions of biological and therapeutic citizenship at the height of HIV activism in South Africa. I suggest that there is a space between historical conceptions of biopolitics that 'acts down' and the 'active citizen' that 'acts up'. This is evident in the diffracted forms of biosociality that reflect the broader set of claims that include calls for access to HIV medicines that are easier to adhere to and have fewer side effects but, importantly, also extend beyond the focus on HIV medicines to include concerns around housing, sanitation and security. I suggest, however, that the government's capacity to respond to these claims is, in part, shaped by the extent to which it is networked into regional economic blocs (like BRICS [Brazil, Russia, India, China and South Africa]) and global actors (like the WTO and EU–India trade agreements). Thus, the extent to which citizens can act on the state, and to which the state can intervene in the vitality of its citizens, is constrained by the fact that not only is the state porous in relation to citizens but also in relation to other regional and international actors. I turn, therefore, to the final two substantive chapters in which I trace the state and these women's capacity to secure their vitality within this assemblage and indicate how these global actors are, in turn, implicated in women's embodied precarity.

6

Therapeutic Governance

The street outside Hospital Universitário Oswaldo Cruz in Boa Vista, Recife, was lined with buses bearing number plates from towns in Sertão, the semi-arid interior in the western-most part of Pernambuco, a province in Brazil that, in 2023, was home to over 9 million people (CEIC, 2023). Many people, my friend Rafaela explained to me, travelled between one and two days to come in from the interior to access the hospital's tertiary health services. Renato Athias, an anthropologist I met in Recife, echoed Rafaela's observation. Having worked with indigenous groups (most notably with the Pankararu Indigenous people) in the Amazon region of Pernambuco's interior, he noted the absence of secondary and tertiary health care – provided by Brazil's Unified Health Care System, Sistema Único de Saúde (SUS) – outside Pernambuco's urban hubs (Oliveira et al, 2017; Viana et al, 2019). In addition to the limited reach of tertiary health care in the province, HIV activists in Recife were concerned about the encroaching privatization of the city's public hospitals (see Ortega and Orsini, 2020). The walls of this particular hospital bore witness to some of the more visible implications of public–private partnerships. The municipal government had incrementally withdrawn funding from the hospital's maintenance budget with the intention of compelling private health insurance companies to start investing more directly in the hospital's running costs. Recife's humidity had crept into the old building and slowly peeled the red paint off its walls, leaving a peach-stained concrete memory of its former façade. A small, newer-looking building, with bare brick walls, ran behind the hospital's main entrance. It was here that people living with HIV were cared for by a team of social workers, nurses, specialist doctors and, at times, complementary therapists like acupuncturists.

In Khayelitsha, I had come to know the clinics and their long queues viscerally: my body, like those of the women I worked with, ached at the end of the days we spent in the clinic moving from one long queue to another, often standing but sometimes sitting on wooden benches, in the monthly ritual to get these hard-to-swallow but hard-won medicines. In this specialist clinic in Recife, about 20 comfortably spaced chairs lined the small reception area and only half of them were used by patients at any one time; even the architecture of the clinic spoke to the difference between South Africa's and Brazil's HIV epidemics. The clinic was located outside the main hospital, providing dedicated care to people living with HIV in a very much smaller building than any of the community health centres or clinics that provided integrated care to all of Khayelitsha's residents.

Epidemiologists in 1988 would have been surprised to see each country's dramatically different HIV profile in 2024. In 1988, Brazil had the second highest number of reported HIV cases in the world (after the United States) compared to South Africa, which had an HIV prevalence of just under 1 per cent (Simelela et al, 2015; Socal et al, 2020). Now, Brazil's HIV prevalence is 0.4 per cent compared to South Africa's HIV prevalence of 12.7 per cent (Montenegro et al, 2020; UNAIDS, 2022d; HSRC, 2023; Johnson and Dorrington, 2023). This chapter is concerned with understanding some of the factors that may account for the very different trajectories that HIV prevalence took in Brazil and South Africa.

As outlined in the first chapter, the two states have an important regional relationship and historical dynamic. This relationship, and dynamic, can be traced across three significant phases. In the first phase, the two countries faced each other as they moved, together, into a new democracy in the 1980s and early 1990s with a hopeful constitution that, in both countries, was actively worded to redress the inequalities wrought through their former governments. In the second phase, relatively soon after their transitions to democracy, the two countries turned away from each other as Brazil followed a route of actively working to ensure the rights of HIV-positive citizens to life by providing antiretrovirals (ARVs). This route contrasted vividly with South Africa's early approach to the HIV epidemic, as the government obstructed citizens' access to ARVs. Looking out from South Africa, I was aware of the construction – by activists – of Brazil as the 'activist state'. I therefore undertook research in Brazil to understand the evolution of the state's response to HIV-positive citizens. However, I was challenged, again, to reconfigure my initial assumptions about Brazil as an 'activist state'. This reconfiguration necessitated an analytical shift in focus that moved out in scale to locate Brazil and South Africa within a global assemblage that governed the production and distribution of affordable HIV medicines. In this third phase, Brazil and South Africa worked with each other through regional coalitions like BRICS (Brazil, Russia, India, China and South Africa) to place pressure on global actors like the World Trade Organization (WTO) to reconfigure international trade law governing access to affordable medicines. In this chapter, I focus on the first two phases, and I explore the third phase in the following chapter.

In the sections that follow, I first look 'into' Brazil and then 'across' Brazil and South Africa to explore the dynamics of their relationship, as discussed earlier, alongside some of the historical and emerging challenges around access to HIV medicines in both countries. In the first section, I focus on Brazil and trace the tension between neoliberal reforms and redistributive politics that I observed in my fieldwork in Recife, Pernambuco. The remaining two sections explore the implications of these reforms and politics on people's experience of Brazil's democracy and their own embodied experiences of health and illness. The first of these two sections challenges the construction of Brazil as an 'activist state' by exploring how activists worked with the newly democratic government to co-construct the juridical infrastructure governing access to HIV medicines. Thereafter, I move out to bring South Africa into focus and contrast the new generation struggles linked to HIV medicines I found in Brazil with those I observed in South Africa. Historical and current challenges around access to newer and more affordable HIV medicines are articulated across the three sections in this chapter, and the implications for navigating these challenges, at a national, transnational and global level, are explored in the following chapter with a focus on international patent legislation and Brazil, India and South Africa's role in challenging the governance of essential medicines.

Brazil's rising power and the tide of neoliberal reform

The politics of Brazil's publicly funded, universal, rights-based health system needs to be contextualized against the backdrop of Brazil's emergence as an economic power. SUS came to life in Brazil through its 'citizens' constitution' at a time when international neoliberal reforms spurred the marketization of health, particularly in Latin America (Ortega and Orsini, 2020; Socal et al, 2020). Access to health care through SUS reflected a broader national commitment to social welfare in Brazil. Here too, however, there is a tension between neoliberal reform and socio-economic equity. Committed to addressing the structural dynamics of poverty, the administrations of Fernando Henrique Cardoso (1995–2003) and Luiz Inácio Lula da Silva, known mononymously as Lula (2003–2011 and again from 2023), introduced a raft of social welfare policies that expanded Brazil's conditional cash transfer (CCT) programmes (Hall, 2006, 2008). Under the more recent authoritarian leadership of Bolsonaro, elected in 2018, the exemplar of CCT programmes – *Bolsa Família* – has undergone substantial changes to its structure (Waisbich et al, 2022). For the purpose of the discussion in this chapter, I refer to *Bolsa Família* as it existed at the time of my fieldwork in Brazil under Presidents Lula and Dilma Rousseff (2011-2016) in the following section, and I reflect on more recent discussions around Brazil's rise and fall as 'policy exporter' (Waisbich et al, 2022) in the second section that critiques the notion of Brazil as the 'activist state'.

Bolsa Família formed part of the *Fome Zero* federal assistance programme and was the principal source of support for Gabriela, a HIV-positive woman I first met in 2009 and whom I came to know over the course of my subsequent fieldwork during the following few years. She moved from Floresta, a small city in Pernambuco's interior, to Recife in 1997 and had two children, eight and 12 years old. Gabriela had been able to send her children to school in Recife because of the education stipend she received through the *Bolsa Família* programme. At that time, in 2011, *Bolsa Família* had four sub-programmes (with stipends for school attendance, maternal nutrition, food supplements and a domestic gas subsidy). Under President Lula Brazil's social welfare policies became recognized internationally as an indication of the country's commitment to equality and its citizens' wellbeing. This was not unlike the characterization of Brazil's response to HIV in the late 1990s and early 2000s (Biehl, 2004). These factors may account for why, in March 2013, the World Bank Group and United Nations announced that they would adopt Brazil's *Bolsa Família* programme as an international model for social inclusion. World Bank President Jim Yong Kim said:

> This agreement ... recognizes Brazil as a global leader in reducing poverty and inequality. Progress made during the last decade has been remarkable and the world can learn a lot from the Brazilian experience. In Brazil, the percentage of the population living under extreme poverty has fallen from about 20 percent in the early 1990s to about 7 percent in recent years ... Boosting shared prosperity and equality go hand in hand. Brazil has demonstrated that solid economic policies coupled with social responsibility are not only possible but desirable. And that growing while at the same time reducing inequality is an attainable goal. (2013: np)

With this rationale, the World Bank went on to support the implementation of CCT systems in 60 countries around the world, including China and South Africa. In South Africa, the initiative focused on delivering health services in under-resourced areas like Khayelitsha. Although this programme is a flagship for CCT programs in other parts of the world, its implementation was strongly critiqued among the people with whom I worked in Brazil.

These critiques were also borne out through my fieldwork as I saw the extent of inequality that people embodied in their homes and lives in Recife. Like Cape Town, historically entrenched socio-economic inequality was etched into Recife's cityscape; but unlike Cape Town, where race and class inequalities are layered into and also separated through space, Recife's poverty was defiantly visible. People had, for example, made their homes in some of the abandoned buildings that stood next to glittering skyscrapers along the long stretches of beach in the wealthier sections of the city like Boa Vista.

More often, though, people built their homes in the small wrinkles of land between high-rise buildings or lived in large favelas that were located, like Khayelitsha, on the periphery of Recife's historic centre. Sometimes even solid ground was difficult to find. On my bus journey across Bacia Portuaria, I learnt to mark the rise and fall of the tide according to the length of exposed wooden legs holding up the small homes that had been built on the side of the estuary. The sense that the state was receding from people's lives, becoming less accountable to its citizens and more entrammelled in international neoliberal networks, surfaced frequently in my conversations with medical professionals, social workers and activists.

"I belong to another generation", said Dr Inês Mendes, a paediatric doctor working at a renowned maternity hospital that also provides specialized care for HIV-positive parents and children in Recife. Pointing to the specialist HIV unit, she said: "There are three doctors here and we need to attend to 1,200 people [per month]; it's just too much for us. The government doesn't value our work anymore … It's not like the old days." Mariana Rossi, a social worker and professor in social development, similarly pointed out the government's failure to provide the necessary resources to address social inequality in Recife. Describing the role of social workers as the "interface between medical systems and social justice and human rights", Mariana recounted her memories of Brazil's transition to democracy in the 1980s and the hope she felt for Brazil's future as the democratically elected government came into power. Brazil's political transition, she explained, took place alongside an epistemological transition in the field of social work. Prompted by the politics of the centre-left *Partido dos Trabalhadores* (Workers' Party), the clinical social work paradigm shifted from conceptualizing the individual as the problem to a Marxist paradigm that engages the structures in which individuals are located. However, echoing Dr Mendes's observation, Rossi said that in its third decade of democracy, Brazil's government no longer had the interests of its citizens at the heart of its policies. She explained that rather than addressing structural inequality, the state had adopted a neoliberal logic in which wellbeing was constructed as an individual's responsibility. This, she said, was a legacy of the Lula administration: "Lula let people down: he compromised to accommodate the interests of the other political parties … I am the government. I pay taxes, I want to benefit. But not only me – all Brazilians."

Rafaela, a prominent feminist activist and educator, also spoke about the tension between the Marxist principles of President Lula's Workers' Party and the neoliberal agenda that had emerged through 'compromises' with centre and centre-right parties in Brazil's government, most recently represented under the leadership of former President Bolsonaro. In contrast with the World Bank leader's statement quoted earlier, the people with whom I worked in Brazil under Presidents Lula and Dilma (both of the Workers' Party) did not believe that it was possible to reconcile "solid [neoliberal] economic policies" with economic equality. They felt there was an inherent trade-off in the quality of public services as they became tied into economic reforms that, for example, encouraged the proliferation of public–private partnerships in the health sector. Rafaela explained that the social assistance programmes, although founded on the principle of economic redistribution to flatten stark economic hierarchies, have become co-opted by capitalist logic:

'Brazil is among the ten most unequal countries [in the world]. Compensatory policies, such as quotas and policies of income redistribution like *Bolsa Família*, have undoubtedly changed and is changing the lives of millions of Brazilians who were refused these basic rights. No doubt it is a profound change, but also the neoliberal capitalist logic follows a deepening of its relations and business interests. It is difficult to have full access to justice and social rights amid the capitalist rules.'

Just as we saw in Khayelitsha in the previous chapter (and as has been observed around the world), graffiti in the public spaces of Recife bore witness to its residents' political discontent. This discontent was expressed in shorter phrases than Rafaela's quote but with a similar bottom line: Marxist principles have been replaced by a capitalist logic, and Brazilians are bearing the brunt. One day, when walking back from lunch with Rafaela, Rossi, Gabriela and a number of other people who were participating in a conference on HIV in South Africa and Brazil, I asked about the messages that had been scrawled on the electricity hubs on each building. Rafaela explained that there had been a call by unions across the country – including those linked to universities – to boycott the general election that had taken place five months earlier. The messages said 'Tudo para todos totalmente' (Everything to everybody in totality) and echoed those written across bridges, construction sites and other public spaces throughout the city, saying: 'Lute pelo socialismo' (Fight for socialism); 'Votar nao! Rebelar – se e justo' (Don't vote! Rebel – it is fair); and 'Elećao não há transformacão. Boicote!' (Elections don't bring transformation. Boycott!).

This sentiment of discontent ran alongside another prevailing concern among health activists in particular that, from my perspective as a South African, seemed to complicate the narrative that Brazil's government was 'abandoning' its citizens in order to follow a neoliberal logic that benefitted a few at the expense of many. This parallel concern related to, what I perceived to be, the long-term challenges emerging from the country's long history of providing HIV medicines to its citizens. In Brazil, these challenges speak to the emerging struggles I perceived through my fieldwork in South Africa, discussed in Chapter 4.

In contrast with South Africa, these struggles were not new in Brazil. They were, as I learnt from activists in *Saúde Para Todos* (SPT), an established and serious issue for people living with HIV and receiving ARVs through Brazil's public health sector. SPT has, since the early 1990s, advocated for the rights of HIV-positive people to access HIV treatment in Brazil. The following section traces the history of activist engagement with the government to access these essential medicines and brings this history into the present by exploring some of the struggles people experienced as they embodied AIDS therapies in my own and many others' ethnographic engagements in Brazil over the 2010s.

Looking into Brazil: beyond the 'activist state'

Over the course of numerous conversations across almost three years, João Agustín, a prominent HIV activist and academic, painted a layered picture of Brazil beyond its narrow narrative as an 'activist state'. Through these conversations, and through his own life story, I learnt about a network of activists who had come together to support and shape the government's response to HIV through its public health system. I trace these stories here, in relation to João's own life, to highlight a set of actors within and beyond Brazil's boundaries that assembled to bring HIV medicines into João's body.

João recounted how activists from the LGBTQIA+, sex worker, feminist and health reform movements formed a broad coalition in the late 1980s and early 1990s to promote equitable access to prevention and treatment services. Numerous NGOs emerged from this coalition that, using innovative media tactics, kick-started a high-visibility media campaign that promoted HIV awareness and prevention across Brazil, but particularly in the south and south-east regions where HIV prevalence was highest in the late 1990s and early 2000s (Valle, 2015). Nunn and colleagues note the institutional ties between activists and the government over this time and the role of World Bank loans in formalizing these links:

> The AIDS movement's ongoing informal partnerships with policy-makers were formalised in the early 1990s, when HIV activists were asked ... to help draft World Bank loan proposals for AIDS assistance. Brazil's AIDS programme was a well-functioning bureaucracy by the mid-1990s, and the World Bank loans helped institutionalise formal partnerships between civil society and the state. (2012: 5)

Rafaela and João, however, said that although the World Bank loans – particularly the first loan, in 1992, of US$160 million – funded important HIV awareness activities in NGOs, it also meant that the government did not invest enough of its national budget in HIV in the early 1990s. "The loans changed activities by NGOs and the public sector", he said, and went on to clarify that the government initially did not want to invest funding in treatment activities and instead focused on prevention. NGOs, in turn, were caught between wanting to source funding through the World Bank by collaborating with the government on its prevention programmes while seeing the emerging availability of medical treatments on an international scale and making the national government similarly see the imperative of sourcing these extremely expensive but life-sustaining medicines. For the people I worked with in Brazil, as in South Africa, these imperatives had direct implications for their ability, or not, to live, and on their likelihood of transmitting HIV along vertical and horizontal pathways. João reflected, for example, on the difficulties he encountered when trying to access HIV medicines through São Paulo's state programme after he was diagnosed with HIV in 1989, and his despair as he witnessed his friends, colleagues and lovers die of AIDS in the late 1980s and early 1990s.

The tension between the government's economic reforms and its constitutional commitment to its citizens emerged as a strong theme in my fieldwork. Writing about Brazil and the relationship between biopolitics, democracy and neoliberalism, Biehl (2021) articulates two paradoxical and parallel trends that shaped the country's health care system in the late 1990s. He suggests that on the one hand citizens and state bureaucrats alike shared a vision of the role of the newly elected government as one that would fulfil the social rights of its citizens. To this end, the federal government became responsible for health care funding, and the regional and municipal governments became responsible for assessing health care needs and managing funds to deliver appropriate care. Although this approach may have made sense on paper, in practice it was implemented without adequate training and capacity-building to ensure funding compliance or effective and responsible implementation of the funds. As Biehl (2021: 312) writes: 'In practice, administrators were not able to effectively manage a complex health care system under increasing technological, infrastructural, and economic demands from the public and private sectors, which themselves were becoming increasingly indistinguishable.' The move to decentralize state functions, like the provision of health care, speaks to the second trend that Biehl (2021) observed and reflects the shift to neoliberal governance that was a strong feature of Brazil's economic policies. Given the tension between the push for equitable access to health resources alongside the pull of neoliberal reform both within and beyond Brazil, activists like João and Rafaela became powerfully adept at crafting techniques to maximize equity, particularly linked to accessing HIV therapies.

The judicialization of the right to health

The breakthrough in HIV treatment, in 1987, was marked by the US government's approval of azidothymidine (AZT), the first drug that was found to successfully inhibit the replication of HIV in patients. This breakthrough fuelled the fervour with which João had been mobilizing the government through *Grupo Pela Vidda* (GPV) to invest in treatment alongside prevention. Set up in 1989, GPV was the first activist organization founded by individuals living with HIV in Brazil, and it remains one of Brazil's most prominent activist organizations today. Like the Treatment Action Campaign (TAC), GPV framed their activism around the citizenship ideals of the larger health care movement, using the concept of solidarity to broaden the reach of the movement by highlighting that all people in Brazil – regardless of their HIV status – were vulnerable should the state fail to provide a range of essential medicines for chronic and acute illnesses (Cajado and Monteiro, 2018).

São Paulo, João's home in 1987, was the first state in Brazil (and the first programme in Latin America) to provide AZT, and in 1991 the government committed to making the drug available to all Brazilians. The next major medical breakthrough, according to João, took place five years later when he attended the 11th International Conference on AIDS in Vancouver, in 1996. It was here that triple therapy was first declared an effective treatment capable of transforming HIV into a chronic and manageable condition. João returned to Brazil where he met with the Ministry of Health to discuss the value and viability of providing ARVs to all Brazilians. He recalled how, when he asked whether the cost of providing treatment would be a constraint, he was told, "No, I want your expert knowledge; we will take care of the bill."

Thus began, as he described it, "the hurricane of triple therapy." The legislative machinery still, however, had to catch up with these therapeutic advances and government mandates. João, for example, needed to engage multiple legal processes (up to 1,250 per month in July/August that year). The courts met each action favourably because, as he said, "[t]he rights of a person could be hurt irreparably [if the state did not provide ARVs]". He describes this legal process as a personal victory, because it had such direct implications on his ability to live: "I won! One week later I had my therapy. Justice that came late would not be useful. You had to get it quickly, or you would die."

Biehl, working in Brazil as the government started to provide HIV medicines in the late 1990s and early 2000s, has observed a broader trend in the use of courts by citizens – like João – to access treatment. He writes:

Since the early part of the first decade of the 2000s (in the wake of a successful universal AIDS treatment policy that put Brazil in the international spotlight), a growing number of citizens have been seeking, and sometimes realizing, access to treatment through the courts, a phenomenon that has been termed 'the judicialization of the right to health'. (2021: 312)

Biehl argues that contrary to claims by the media and government officials, the 'judicialization of the right to health' is not driven by private interests and the urban elite but that 'it is in fact a widespread practice, accessible even to the very poor' (2021: 312). João's account tessellates with Biehl's discussion of the judicialization of the right to health, and it also speaks to the range of national and international actors that came together to enable him to support him to pursue the 'the hurricane of triple therapy' through the courts. João spoke of his ability to live, his vitality, as an outcome of his engagement with activist networks (including the *Associação Brasileira Interdisciplinar de AIDS* [ABIA] and GPV) and, in turn, their engagement with the judicial system, particularly its judges, and the various levels of state and federal government. He described this engagement as relentless, an engagement that "did not sleep" in the faith that the government would stay awake to the shifting international medical and legislative landscape. Activist networks like GPV and ABIA therefore used the judicial system strategically to compel the Brazilian government to generate and implement HIV policies at a pace that would keep up with rapid developments in new medical technologies and – as I discuss in the next chapter – in shifting international legislation that governed access to these technologies (Valle, 2015). These accounts from long-standing activists like João and Rafaela emphasize the value of moving beyond the label of Brazil as the 'activist state' towards conceptualizing Brazil's actions to manage the early HIV epidemic as compelled by mechanisms like the judiciary and enabled through a complex configuration of activist organizations and networks.

In the following section, I look across Brazil and South Africa to explore some of the historical and current challenges linked to HIV medicines, with a focus on adherence, treatment fatigue and viral resistance. In South Africa, I had come to know about the 'treatment gap' as a quantitative assessment of the number of people needing ARVs against the number of people receiving ARVs. In Brazil, the 'treatment gap' meant an entirely different thing among the people with whom I conducted fieldwork and perhaps speaks to each country's very different history with regard to AIDS therapies. As I go on to discuss, when Brazilians referred to a 'treatment gap' they meant that they were stopping their medicines for a period in order to have a 'break' from the responsibilities entailed in adherence and from the side effects that some people experienced from the intra-action of ARVs with their bodies.

Looking across Brazil and South Africa: evolving challenges

Taking me into an examination room in the HIV specialist unit, Dr Mendes opened the door of a floor to ceiling cupboard and gestured at the metal shelves holding hundreds of little cardboard boxes of medicine. They were half-used packs of first- and second-line ARVs that her patients had returned to the clinic when they decided to terminate their treatment. Dr Mendes explained to me that "[s]ometimes patients stop ARVs because of personal prejudice. There are side effects, sure. But also, people who can read the side effects [on the insert] will have all the side effects."

In contrast with South Africa, a 'treatment gap' in Brazil did not necessarily refer to gaps in ARV coverage based on population-level data. Instead, it was another term for an 'ARV holiday' where people stop taking their ARVs for a few weeks, or months. Lucas, for example, recounted to me some of the serious side effects he had experienced from ARVs since starting them in 1997. He had travelled down from his home in Fortaleza, capital of the north-eastern province of Ceará, to attend a conference on HIV vaccines. We had both given presentations that morning and were – at this point – having lunch on the broad steps that led out on to the large garden of this conference centre in Olinda, Recife's much smaller and extremely beautiful neighbour. The previous night, we had been out in Olinda's cobbled streets together, watching a procession of giant paper puppets, marching bands and dancing troupes in celebration of Olinda's formal recognition as a town (on 12 March 1537). It had been a late night of music and dancing, and one that gave me a sense of the kinds of celebrations that took place around Olinda's legendary 'Carnival of Participation'.

The principle of participation is the same reason that, according to Rafaela and João, the health movement had so successfully mobilized the government to institute SUS through its 'citizens' constitution' of 1988 (Cornwall and Shankland, 2008; Montenegro et al, 2020) and to provide ARVs in 1996 through the constitution. In 2018, almost 9 million people were living with HIV in Brazil, and of this number, 66 per cent were on HIV treatment (UNAIDS, 2022f). Lucas is one of the people who make up these official numbers, and yet, unofficially, when we met each other at this conference on HIV vaccines, he was on an 'ARV holiday'.

Sitting outside while people milled around during the lunch break, we picked up the conversation we had started the previous night. I spoke about how TAC had been concerned about stock-outs of some HIV medicines like tenofovir (TDF) in clinics in rural parts of the country.

These stock-outs had followed an update to South Africa's ARV treatment guidelines in which TDF replaced stavudine (d4T), a drug that caused long-term irreversible side effects for many of the women I had worked with in South Africa but that had been more affordable than its alternatives. The issue of access to newer HIV medicines in Brazil – particularly more advanced medicines that would be able to suppress resistant strains of HIV – had been raised that morning by a number of Lucas's colleagues. Our presentations, too, had underlined some of the issues I had been finding in my fieldwork and that he had found through the HIV rights organization he worked with, and that was a partner to SPT, in Fortaleza. We had spoken about the importance of introducing new medical technologies into the public health sector and the historic role that each of our governments played in negotiating the domestic production and international procurement of these medicines.

Now, sitting in the sun, away from the formal space of presentations and discussions, our conversation moved in halting English but flowed easily with a quieter non-verbal exchange, as we took turns getting up to get each other refills of the black coffee that stung our hands through the thin plastic cups. Putting down his coffee cup and holding my eye, Lucas swivelled his body to face mine and with both of his hands he traced the sharp line of his cheekbones. Then, almost as if he was stroking his face, he made a scooping motion to emphasize his hollowed-out cheeks. I got up, nodding my head and, in this non-verbal exchange about lipodystrophy, ran my hands down my legs, shrinking them down in size and making similar scooping motions to flatten my breasts and buttocks. He stood up, nodding, pointing to his body and showing me where, on his body, he still bore the effects of d4T's lipodystrophy, pointing to his cheeks again, and also to his round stomach and thin legs. The intra-action of this medicine with his body had, he said, saved his life when he first started ARVs but had also marked him as HIV-positive to those around him who were able to read the 'marks' of ARVs on people's bodies. He had subsequently moved off d4T but was concerned about the general damage that ARVs may be quietly wreaking on his body, without him being able to 'see'. Lucas explained that he believed ARVs 'worked' because he was alive, but that they also put his body under strain. He said that he took a break from ARVs "[n]ot because they don't work. But to give my body a break now and then." Unlike the newer HIV medicines, the life of d4T – as an actant – remained visible on the outside of his body, borne through these kinds of side effects. The quieter lives of newer ARVs, and their possible long-term side effects, were harder to identify. This concern was underlined at the conference the next day when a member of the Brazilian Ministry of Health said: "[N]ot only would a therapeutic vaccine reduce the need for ARVs, it could go further towards eradicating side effects: in our country we have increased rates of cancer, psychological effects, lipodystrophy."

Gabriela, whom I introduced earlier, is also an active member of the HIV community with a long history of working to compel the government to provide better health services and newer HIV medicines to HIV-positive people. Unlike Lucas, Gabriela had not spoken openly about stopping her treatment but had told Rafaela in a fit of exasperation at the pressure she felt to "represent" the movement while also just wanting to "[g]et on with living". Gabriela had just a few days earlier told me about her relationship with Rafaela as we were travelling across Recife after spending the day in meetings with municipal health officials. After initially working with a larger HIV organization in Recife, Gabriela had opted to leave and form a smaller organization that would be run for and, importantly, by HIV-positive people. Rafaela, at this point, moved from her work with a feminist organization in Recife to direct her energies, with Gabriela and this team of people, to form an organization based on the principles of equality and citizenship.

The network of people and organizations I engaged with in my fieldwork were, as far as I could tell, connected through splices of shared politics and fundamentally through their shared relationship with Rafaela, prominent feminist, educator and health activist. The two organizations I came to know best were SOS Corpo and SPT. Rafaela worked in SOS Corpo for over two decades following Brazil's democratic transition with the intention of harnessing the opportunities for integrating feminist politics into federal and provincial policy spaces. Rafaela explained how her vision of the world was shaped, in part, through her work with activists like Gabriela and with organizations like SPT:

'Working for 20 years in the feminist movement gave me the basis for my political and conceptual understanding of the world through the perspective of equality and difference. And education was an important principle of feminism that made me realize the meaning of socialism that I adopt in my political positions. But mostly it was the people who were living with AIDS in Brazil that allowed me to connect my political activism with feminist education. It was the people who were living with AIDS that particularly touched my heart with their struggles and their resistance that gave energy to the movement in Brazil.'

Gabriela said that it was through working with Rafaela that she had first learnt about her rights as a citizen in Brazil, and that it was with Rafaela that she had started to claim her rights as a HIV-positive citizen in the political spaces of HIV and health care policy.

It was striking, therefore, that Gabriela's 'holiday' from HIV medicines coincided with her assertive declaration to another member of the Brazilian Ministry of Health, also at this conference, that "[w]e can live with HIV, but we need medicine and support to be active citizens". As I discuss in Chapter 4 with respect to the 'new generation' struggles experienced by activists in South Africa, this was not a form of cognitive dissonance in which the private self, struggling with HIV medicines, becomes split from the public self as an active citizen, advocating for HIV medicines. Instead, it points to the complexities of HIV medicines as they come to be embodied by individuals who have, historically, formed part of a larger biosocial coalition based on a shared illness and who have made a set of claims, as therapeutic citizens (Nguyen, 2008; Nguyen, 2011; Zhou, 2019), around corresponding treatments. Gabriela's and Lucas's accounts resonate with those in Chapter 4 as they indicate an ambivalence created by the, at times precarious, intra-action of HIV therapies with bodies.

On the one hand, as Lucas said, these medicines prevented HIV from replicating in his body, thus "saving his life"; on the other hand, his body held the memory of d4T's toxicity, visible, still, in his hollow cheeks. It is, perhaps, because Nondumiso's body holds the memory of HIV – and not HIV medicines – in the 'brown map' on her skin, that 'ARV holidays' were not really considered an option by most of the women I worked with in South Africa. The 'previous generation's' struggle for HIV medicines remains visible on Nondumiso's skin as a form of embodied history, a history that is also reflected in her second body map. Perhaps, then, the presence of this embodied history of precarity accounts for Nondumiso's insistence on adhering to her medicines, whereas the more recent new generation struggles that Lucas describes may account for his decision to have a 'treatment gap'.

These new generation struggles, and attendant 'treatment gaps', reflect the importance of shifting away from narrow conceptions of both biosociality and citizenship. As Gabriela asserted in her address to a member of the Brazilian Ministry of Health, access to medicines was not only an outcome of health citizenship that centred on the fight for ARVs but ARVs themselves were fundamental in enabling HIV-positive people's capacity to be 'active citizens'. Through my fieldwork, as discussed earlier and in Chapters 4 and 5, I found that people living with HIV in Brazil and in South Africa were asserting a wider range of rights – including rights to education, housing, toilets, safe water and electricity – alongside their right to medicine. Biosocialities therefore were not simply built around sharing the same health condition, but they draw attention to the socio-economic contexts in which these health conditions are navigated and around which HIV-positive people mobilized as 'active citizens'. The diffraction of biosociality alongside the shift in narrow framings of health citizenship reflects Andreouli and colleagues' conception of 'everyday citizenship' as a lived practice that is 'mobilised, claimed, and enacted in everyday life' (2019: np). Building on research on quotidian forms of citizenship in postcolonial contexts around the world (Cornwall et al, 2011; Dumbrava, 2017; Bosire et al, 2018; Andreouli, 2019; Drerup, 2020; Lemanski, 2020), these acts of resistance and compliance around HIV medicines reflect the complex ways that individuals and activist networks are acting up and on the state in quite different contexts, in Recife and in Khayelitsha.

Conclusion

Although South Africa has scaled up treatment services to reach 90 per cent of those who know their status in 2023 (Johnson and Dorrington, 2023), its historical 'treatment gap' is still, as discussed in the earlier chapters, held in people's embodied memory of the precarity of their and others' lives prior to the public provision of ARVs. While 90 per cent coverage is laudable, in reality it represents only 73.2 per cent of all those in need of treatment (factoring in those people who are not aware that they are HIV-positive), with a gap of 26.8 per cent remaining in the provision of treatment to all those who need it in South Africa (Johnson and Dorrington, 2023). In Brazil, the provision of HIV treatment has been severely constrained by the Bolsonaro-administration and its systematic stripping away of funding for SUS and for public health campaigns (Montenegro et al, 2020; Iamamoto et al, 2021). As a result of former President Bolsonaro's highly conservative agenda, the very people who are already most marginalized in Brazil have been even further alienated from health services. This includes, importantly, Black, Indigenous and queer people. Resources for transgender women, for example, have been almost entirely removed from Brazil's social care system, leading to significant reductions in access and adherence to HIV treatment (Montenegro et al, 2020; Rocha et al, 2020; Sabino et al, 2021). At a general population level, only 66 per cent of the HIV-positive population received HIV treatment in 2018 (UNAIDS, 2022b).

The structural barriers preventing marginalized groups of people from accessing HIV treatment have led scholars working in Brazil like João Biehl (2004, 2012, 2021), Laura Murray (2019), Mariana Socal (2020) and Simone Gomes and Talita Tanscheit (2022) and many others to problematize the international conceptualization of Brazil as an 'activist state' simply because the government was the first in the Global South to make AIDS therapies available to the 'registered AIDS cases'. This terminology is important because as Biehl (2008) observes in his own ethnographic work, it reflects how the government's AIDS response, including 'registering AIDS cases', dovetailed with former President Cardoso's efforts to internationalize Brazil's economy. These efforts, argues Biehl (2004, 2008), created 'zones of abandonment' where socio-economically marginalized groups, like transgender people, sex workers and intravenous drug users, were less able to access these public health services than wealthier sections of the population deemed more 'legitimate' and who were more able to access HIV tests and become 'registered cases'.

Now, in 2024, the very people who have been most structurally marginalized under Bolsonaro's homophobic, sexist and transphobic policies of exclusion experience the highest rates of HIV prevalence in the country (Beckham et al, 2024): currently, transgender people are estimated to have a HIV prevalence of 30 per cent, gay men and men who have sex with men have a HIV prevalence of 18.3 per cent, people who inject drugs have a prevalence of 5.9 per cent and prisoners 4.5 per cent. These figures contrast strongly with 0.4 per cent prevalence among the general population (Montenegro et al, 2020; Iamamoto et al, 2021; UNAIDS, 2022f; Waisbich et al, 2022). The gap in the provision of treatment combined with the higher prevalence rates among these highly marginalized groups speaks to the importance of understanding the limits of Brazil's historical claim to be an 'activist state'. While Brazil has been described as an important 'Southern Hub' in the circulation of global policy over this time, Waisbach and colleagues (2022) suggest that although the country's active promotion of progressive development-related policies under the Workers' Party might have led to this framing of the country as working to secure the health rights of its citizens, this framing has shifted radically over the last decade and particularly under the leadership of President Bolsonaro (2018–22).

In my fieldwork, I was struck that South Africa's struggle for ARVs was well known among the people and organizations I engaged with in Brazil. This was partly because TAC had been so widely covered in international media and also because TAC and the AIDS Law Project had worked closely with Brazil's activist networks (Mauchline, 2008). The activists I came to know in Brazil used South Africa as an example of the power of activist coalitions, spanning countries around the world, to effect national and global change. Just as I was cautioned against constructing Brazil as the 'activist state', I found in my research that South Africa's capacity to meet the needs of its citizens was contingent on these activist coalitions as well as the state's ability to act on international health policy and organizations (like the WTO) through transnational networks (like BRICS).

My fieldwork in both countries also found a set of emerging challenges, among people living with HIV, that included access to newer and more effective HIV treatments. By looking across Brazil and South Africa, rather than holding them in contrast with one another, it becomes more possible to situate them within a global assemblage that includes regional and global actors (like BRICS and the WTO) that govern access to essential medicines in the Global South. As I go on to discuss in the next chapter, access to effective HIV treatments is governed at an international level through intellectual property rights legislation. By moving out in scale to focus on these global dynamics in the next chapter, this book concludes by foregrounding both the constraints faced by countries in the Global South, and it speaks to networks of solidarity, resistance and connection between activists, governments and global health organizations that work together to resist and reshape these constraints.

7

Global Health Governance

Various movements are afoot in the field of global health: from the collective control of epidemics to the personalization of disease; from trial and error to the standardization of evidence and policy; from health as a public good to the pharmaceuticalization of health care; from governmental detachment to the industrialization of the nongovernmental sector and a privatized politics of survival. Alongside them, critical questions abound: has the biopolitical morphed into a multilevel turf war of private versus public stakeholders battling over the utility of government? (Biehl and Petryna, 2013: 243)

In July 2022, sitting near a heater in a coffee shop on a cold winter's day in Cape Town, Nondumiso and I caught up on how our children were doing as they navigated nursery and primary school, and on how we were finding life after a series of gruelling COVID-19 lockdowns in South Africa and the United Kingdom respectively. Our conversation moved fluidly as we compared the different ways both countries had responded to the COVID-19 pandemic over the previous few years. Earlier in the week, I had met with Nandisa, a 38-year-old woman who, like Nondumiso, lived in Khayelitsha; I was struck by Nandisa's sense that government officials were financially invested in rolling out the COVID-19 vaccine and that the government did not have the best interests of its people at heart. In another interview, also in July 2022, community worker Sibusiso also shared her sense that the government was benefitting financially from the vaccine programme, saying, "I don't believe that anything worked well because I believe that government took advantage of this COVID thing just to make their pockets warm because our country did receive funds to fight this thing but what did they do they put it in their pockets."

A year later, in 2023, I met with Sibusiso in Bertha House, a building that seeks to offer 'radical hospitality' and is set up specifically for activists on Mowbray's main road in Cape Town. Sibusiso explained that she believed that COVID-19 had functioned as a "permission slip" for the government to shut the country down through successive lockdowns; the impact of these lockdowns on increased rates of domestic violence and skyrocketing unemployment has been well documented (Casale and Posel, 2020; Khambule, 2020; Burger and Calitz, 2021; Campbell et al, 2022). The government's actions, Sibusiso explained, were not simply to "protect" people from COVID but were a way to stop people from connecting with each other and mobilizing against the state's failure to provide effective health care for the thousands of people dying of the virus and living with long-COVID. This sense of distrust in the government may have also supported wariness about the medical management of COVID-19, as scholars have recently found in research across South Africa on the escalation of conspiracy theories and scepticism linked to COVID-19 vaccines (Katoto et al, 2022; Mutanga and Abayomi, 2022; Sipeyiye, 2022; Mishi et al, 2023; Steenberg et al, 2023).

Nondumiso, too, had observed a wariness about the COVID-19 vaccine programme among her friends and family but emphasized that, in her view, it was the best tool available to the government to contain the pandemic. Our conversation in July 2022 had turned to reflecting on the difference between the South African government's failure to provide life-saving treatment in the first decade of the HIV pandemic and its quick actions to limit the COVID-19 pandemic a decade after it had started to make antiretrovirals (ARVs) universally available. In fact, just nine months prior to these conversations, South Africa along with India had tabled a proposal to members of the World Trade Organization (WTO) to waive restrictive patents on COVID-19 therapeutics and diagnostics (Usher, 2020; Vawda et al, 2021). With reference to Biehl and Petryna's (2013) remarks quoted at the start of this chapter and speaking to the relative utility of governments like India and South Africa in this international forum, the proposal was vehemently challenged by European countries. After months of debate, a watered-down proposal was passed that made minor concessions around COVID-19 diagnostics but still limited access to vital therapies like vaccines.

It was around the time of my conversation with Nondumiso, in July 2022, that a ground-breaking new HIV treatment was announced by Gilead: called Sunlenca (or lenacapavir), this long-acting HIV treatment would only need to be taken twice a year (Dvory-Sobol et al, 2022). The potential for lenacapavir not only to treat HIV but also prevent or cure it entirely is currently being researched through a clinical trial in Masiphumelele, an under-resourced township also in Cape Town (Bekker, 2022). The development of lenacapavir as a long-lasting HIV treatment follows the earlier development of cabotegravir (CAB-LA), a drug that has been shown to reduce HIV infection by up to 88 per cent among women who took part in these trials in Botswana, Kenya, Malawi, South Africa, Eswatini, Uganda and Zimbabwe (Phillips et al, 2021). These cutting-edge medicines offer radical hope for safe, effective and long-acting HIV treatment and prevention. Yet, the very people who have supported the testing and development of these medical technologies in Sub-Saharan Africa are not yet able to access them through their government's national public health system.[1]

This chapter reveals how national, regional and international actors assemble around a rapidly changing set of international agreements on intellectual property (IP) that govern the development and distribution of these cutting edge medical technologies. I suggest that restrictive patent legislation, globally governed by the Trade-Related Aspects of Intellectual Property Rights (TRIPS) Agreement, raises the question of the utility of national governments, and I show how this legislation presents a fundamental challenge to the ability of countries in the Global South to address public health emergencies, like HIV and COVID-19. I argue that what is needed is a robust reconfiguration of global and national patent legislation that can make medicines more affordable and ensure that they move from pharmaceutical laboratories and factories, across and within the borders of countries, through government-funded public health systems into clinics and into people's bodies.

In the sections that follow, I consider a set of patent-related challenges around access to affordable treatment for low- and middle-income countries (LMICs), like India, South Africa and Brazil, and I outline the biopolitical implications of these global challenges for HIV-positive people whose vitality is precariously networked into this assemblage. The previous chapters explored how citizens act up and into this assemblage through activist organizations and everyday forms of citizen practices. This chapter extends this analysis and explores how regional actors like BRICS, as well as activist networks and global health organizations, have sought to resist and reconfigure harmful IP legislation.

Even when governments are aligned with activist organizations to provide life-saving treatment through their public health systems, a set of barriers remain that constrain access to and provision of essential medicines. These barriers function across scale. At the level of the individual and their community, access to HIV treatment is impacted by social barriers including concerns around the side effects of medicines, experiences of stigma and discrimination and a lack of privacy and confidentiality. At a national level, organizational barriers can limit access to medicines, and these barriers include supply chain disruptions, lack of trained health care workers and long distances to treatment centres. Even without social and organizational barriers, access to essential medicines is impacted by a third barrier: the cost of the treatments themselves. These costs – and therefore access to these medicines – are governed by a complex legal and policy infrastructure built around intellectual property rights (IPRs). This chapter focuses on the actors that have shaped this infrastructure first across time and then across scale. To this end, the first section traces the evolution of the global governance of medicines with a focus on IPRs and the political and economic regimes that hold prohibitive restrictions in place. The second and third sections explore how actors have worked across scale – at a global, transnational and national level – to resist and reconfigure restrictive mechanisms that govern IPRs and impinge on global health.

This chapter also marks a shift in tone away from ethnographic accounts, as it analyses debates and policies linked to IPRs. It is a drier, more technical chapter. However, I use examples where appropriate to demonstrate how these often rather abstract concepts, debates and policies have very real implications for the embodied vitality of people living with HIV. These examples show how countries like South Africa, Brazil and India are not simply 'acted on' by global actors like the WTO but also show how coalitions linking national governments and civil society organizations can work to 'act up' on these global actors to reconfigure international and national law and advance equitable access to essential medicines.

IPRs and the global governance of health

In July 2022, I met with a team of prominent health activists working in South Africa. This time, instead of meeting in person in Cape Town where I was based at the time, we were meeting online. My screen slowly filled up with little squares holding the names of the members of the team. We were meeting online because, at that time, most of the team were in India at conference with international activist organizations to discuss avenues to challenge the global dominance of pharmaceutical companies, who were, as one member said, "[m]aking so much profit from misery and poverty". Through this conversation I heard how, as HIV treatment improved, there was a need to focus on ensuring access to essential medicines that could treat other HIV-related illnesses, including tuberculosis (TB) and COVID-19. However, as the activists explained to me, one of the key barriers to accessing these treatments in South Africa related to the global IPR infrastructure and to South Africa's own outdated IPR laws. In this section, I focus on the global governance of essential medicines, and I turn to the discussion of national laws in the subsequent sections.

The global governance of essential medicines through IP legislation can be traced back to the creation of the WTO in 1995 and the subsequent formation of TRIPS. This section summarizes this history and then details five key limitations to TRIPS along with some of the legislative tools – or flexibilities – that have been created to enable LMICs to access affordable medicines. The final part of this section looks at the ways LMICs are disciplined within this global infrastructure through sanctions and trade agreements that make it more difficult for these countries to produce or access affordable medicines.

The WTO, patents and the governance of medicine

Currently, the WTO represents 164 member states and more than 98 per cent of global trade (WTO, 2023). WTO agreements are negotiated and agreed upon by its members, and these international agreements are then ratified (or contested) in each country's parliament. Prior to the establishment of the WTO, and the subsequent TRIPS Agreement, IP laws differed from country to country. LMICs, for instance, either restricted or did not allow patents on medicines or other health technologies, and where patents were in force, these countries restricted their enforcement in order to prioritize the health of their citizens (Abbott, 2018). The introduction of TRIPS in 1989 at the Uruguay Round of the General Agreement on Tariffs and Trade marked a significant departure from preceding agreements on IPRs. Unlike these other agreements, TRIPS is enforced through a powerful dispute settlement mechanism that works to enhance the harmonization of IP norms by WTO member states (De Beer et al, 2018). As I go on to discuss in this chapter, the WTO's introduction of TRIPS, along with the enforcement mechanisms that accompany the agreement, severely constrain the ability of LMICs to devise their own IP systems and meet the health needs of their populations (Horner, 2014; Malhotra, 2008; Pigoni, 2020; Plahe and McArthur, 2021).

The TRIPS Agreement, which came into effect in January 1995, includes a set of IPR standards that member states are required to uphold in their law. Under this legislation, all member states agreed to observe patent protection (on process and composition) for a period of 20 years. This applied to all new patents, and any other patents that had been filed after January 1995. Unless ARV-producing countries like India, Brazil and South Africa make use of TRIPS flexibilities, they are unable to import or export these medicines at a reasonable price. Although patents are not specifically defined in the TRIPS Agreement, Taubman and colleagues (2020: 95) offer the following definition: 'A patent, which is granted by the authorities in a specified jurisdiction, gives its owner an exclusive right to prevent others from exploiting the patented invention in that jurisdiction for a limited period of time without his or her authorization, subject to a number of exceptions.' Patents, particularly those that apply to pharmaceuticals, function within a broader intellectual property system and are framed as a tool for stimulating creativity and protecting innovations that result from investment in research and development (R&D) (Taubman et al, 2020). In practice, however, patents on pharmaceuticals tend to make them more expensive and less available by preventing competition from companies who would be able to manufacture cheaper generics during the patent term, and the economic rationale for patents has been thoroughly debunked given that much of the R&D investment in pharmaceuticals is publicly funded by taxpayers. For example, the US-based Treatment Action Group found that in 2018 over 40 per cent of R&D on pharmaceuticals was funded by governments and non-profit organizations (ITPC, 2022). The commodification of this intellectual work, by pharmaceutical companies in the case of the US, is highly problematic for a range of reasons, not least because taxpayers tend to pay higher prices for patented medicines, and these higher prices include both government-collected taxes that fund R&D and the premium charged by pharmaceutical companies for developing the medicines (Pigoni, 2020).

A decade after TRIPS was agreed, and just as HIV was escalating in South Africa and Brazil, it became clear that LMICs were unable to balance their public health obligations with their obligations to protect patent holders under the TRIPS Agreement. In 2001, in a radical act of resistance to the TRIPS Agreement, South Africa amended its national law to enable the government to import generic HIV medicines (Sun, 2004; Sun et al, 2014). The government was swiftly sued by 39 pharmaceutical companies. This prompted global outrage and led the WTO members to adopt the Doha Declaration on TRIPS and Public Health in 2001 (WTO, 2001; Sun, 2004). In the Doha Declaration, the WTO acknowledges the impact of TRIPS on global public health, stating, in Article 3: 'We recognize that intellectual property protection is important for the development of new medicines. We also recognize the concerns about its effects on prices' (WTO, 2001). The Doha Agreement goes on to state, in Article 4, that 'the TRIPS Agreement does not and should not prevent members from taking measures to protect public health' (WTO, 2001). Article 5 introduces a set of flexibilities that can be applied by national governments in contexts of 'national emergency' or 'circumstances of extreme urgency', stating that public health crises are understood to relate to HIV/AIDS, TB, malaria and other epidemics (WTO, 2001).

As a result of South Africa's political resistance to the WTO in 2001 and the subsequent adoption of the Doha Agreement, the price of HIV medicines has seen a dramatic decline: in the late 1990s, ARVs cost over US$10,000 per person per year, and by 2022 this had reduced to around US$95 per person per year in many LMICs (Mattur and Habiyambere, 2022). UNAIDS (2016: 2) notes that the drop in the price of ARVs 'was the result of sustained advocacy on the part of countries and communities affected by HIV to increase the availability of quality-assured generic antiretroviral medicines, in part by addressing intellectual property rights (IPR) issues'. These flexibilities are discussed in detail subsequently, along with case studies demonstrating how numerous LMICs—and Brazil and India, in particular—have used the flexibilities to varying degrees of success to access and distribute essential HIV medicines.

While TRIPS flexibilities can be understood as safeguards in the TRIPS Agreement, LMICs remain constrained by multilateral and bilateral trade agreements that build in more stringent TRIPS measures. These measures, known as TRIPS-plus, are typically built into free trade agreements (FTAs) with countries and blocs that originally lobbied for the creation and strict implementation of TRIPS including Japan, South Korea, the United States and the European Union (WHO, 2010; Palmedo, 2015; ITPC, 2022). TRIPS-plus measures require protection of IPRs far in excess of TRIPS requirements and can include, for example, patent term extension beyond the 20 years required under TRIPS (WHO, 2010).

TRIPS-plus measures result in significantly higher costs of medicines for countries that have relatively weak economic bargaining power compared to the country or region that insists on TRIPS-plus measures in FTAs. For example, a 2015 study found that 'the negotiated prices of branded antiretrovirals are, on average, 57% higher in countries with FTAs than they are in other countries' (Palmedo, 2015: np). Speaking to the value of utilizing TRIPS flexibilities, and the dangers of entering into FTAs that include TRIPS-plus measures, UNAIDS have explicitly noted the danger of wealthier countries prioritizing their profit over the public health of LMICs, recommending that 'to retain the benefits of TRIPS Agreement flexibilities, countries, at minimum should avoid entering into FTAs that contain TRIPS-plus obligations that can impact on pharmaceuticals price or availability' (UNAIDS, 2022c: np). As I go on to discuss in the next section, despite TRIPS flexibilities, the TRIPS Agreement and TRIPS-plus measures in FTAs significantly impact the capacity of LMICs to reach the 95–95–95 targets set by UNAIDS to eliminate diseases like HIV, viral hepatitis and sexually transmitted diseases.

Global health and the problem with patents

The ambitious 95–95–95 targets set by UNAIDS seeks to ensure that, by 2025, 95 per cent of all people living with HIV are diagnosed, 95 per cent of all HIV-positive people receive HIV treatment and 95 per cent of all people living with HIV and receiving treatment have suppressed viral loads. This goal can only be reached by ensuring that affordable HIV treatments reach people living in LMICs. Further, as noted in the previous chapters, even when HIV treatments are available through the public health system in countries like Brazil and South Africa, they may be older and therefore more affordable medicines. Older medicines tend to generate more side effects than newer medicines, prompting some people to respond to these embodied ramifications by taking an 'ARV holiday' to manage the strain these medicines place on their bodies.

As I discuss subsequently, TRIPS-plus measures constrain the ability of countries like Brazil and South Africa to access affordable medicines and therefore meet the targets set by UNAIDS. Looking at the constraints imposed by TRIPS-plus measures, Pigoni argues that 'these provisions, limiting the possibility of using the flexibilities allowed under the TRIPS agreement, tend to maximise the profit of wealthier countries over developing countries' public health by limiting the competition between generic drugs and patented ones' (2020: np). There are many complex issues with the TRIPS agreement, but for the sake of brevity I summarize five main issues as articulated by the International Treatment Preparedness Coalition (ITPC, 2022), a global organization fighting for universal access to HIV treatment and life-saving medicines.

First, patents create profound pricing disparities. For example, the World Health Organization (WHO) (2017) found that the same first-line HIV treatments could be procured for as little as US$115 per person per year in China, Cuba and Ecuador but for as much as US$1,000 in countries like Brazil, Kazakhstan and Russia. The higher prices were a result of purchasing treatments from companies where all or part of the treatment regime was under patent. Looking more closely at Ukraine as an example, the All-Ukrainian Network of People Living with HIV found that in 2018 the Ukrainian government spent US$19 million to purchase the HIV medicine lopinavir from the pharmaceutical company AbbVie. If the patents on lopinavir were invalidated, the government would have been able to buy the medicine at a price that was three times lower (US$5 million) a year, extending treatment to another 138,000 people living with HIV in the country (MMA, 2019; ITPC, 2022).

Second, evergreening enables pharmaceutical companies to extend their exclusivity by applying for multiple, overlapping patents on a single medicine (ITPC, 2022). Also described as 'thickets', these multiple patents interlock to prevent or delay generic competition. For example, lopinavir is sold as Kaletra by Abbott, and in theory it should be off patent in most countries. However, this second-line HIV medicine remains highly priced in middle-income countries because of evergreening practices. One study found 108 patents for lopinavir which could delay generic competition until at least 2028, which is over 12 years after the patents on the drug's compounds expired and 39 years after the first patents were filed (Amin and Kesselheim, 2012; see also Sinha, 2021).

Third, high levels of resistance to first-line HIV medicines, particularly in resource-limited settings, increase the need for more effective second-line treatments, many of which remain locked into patents and therefore unaffordable for most LMICs (Gupta et al, 2016; ITPC, 2022). Currently most LMICs pay triple the price for second-line HIV treatment compared to first-line treatment. In 2020, it was estimated that LMICs spent US$4.7

billion dollars on HIV treatment, which accounted for a quarter of all HIV spending globally (Mattur and Habiyambere, 2022). This speaks to the need to challenge patents on second-line treatment to make them more affordable and therefore more accessible given the risks of treatment failure on first-line medicines. For example, in a 2018 study of people living with HIV in Africa, Asia, South America and the Caribbean, researchers found significantly high levels of treatment failure on first-line HIV medicines (Grinsztejn et al, 2019; Wallis et al, 2019). This finding is consistent with research conducted by the WHO (2021) which found high levels (over 10 per cent) of resistance to two of the most commonly used first-line HIV medicines (efavirenz and nevirapine) in LMICs. The urgency of addressing patents and avoiding TRIPS-plus provisions in new trade agreements was recently highlighted by UNAIDS (2023), which estimates that by 2025, 3.5 million people living with HIV are likely to need second-line treatment.

Fourth, global funding for HIV has contracted significantly over the 2010s and early 2020s, and this affects the ability of countries to purchase HIV medicines, particularly medicines that remain locked into patents (for the reasons discussed earlier) and therefore too expensive for most LMICs to access and provide through their public health systems (ITPC, 2022). In 2018, for example, UNAIDS reported a decrease of US$900 million over the preceding year in global funding to manage HIV. Prior to this acknowledgement in 2018, UNAIDS had been strongly criticized for its optimistic reporting on the HIV epidemic, with many activists and scholars arguing that this messaging had influenced donor priorities, therefore leading to significant reductions in funding for managing HIV, including funding for HIV medicines (Medlock et al, 2017; Burki, 2018; De Lay et al, 2021; Lancet, 2022). More recently, in July 2022, UNAIDS (2022e) published its global report entitled 'In danger: UNAIDS global HIV update' in which it paints a sobering picture of the global HIV crisis that speaks to the fragility of international funding to support LMICs to access essential medicines. In this report, UNAIDS calculates that LMICs will need US$29.3 billion by 2025 to achieve the 95–95–95 targets in HIV prevention, testing and treatment. This represents a shortfall of US$8 billion, given current funding commitments. In the report, UNAIDS argues that it would be short-sighted not to commit to this level of funding given the increasing rates of HIV incidence and HIV death that can already be seen in Central Asia, Eastern Europe, Latin America, the Middle East and North Africa (UNAIDS 2022e; ITPC, 2022).

An article published by *The Lancet*, in September 2022, calls on global donors to reaffirm their commitment to meeting the UNAIDS targets by replenishing the Global Fund to Fight AIDS, Tuberculosis and Malaria when they meet later in 2022 to discuss the seventh replenishment to cover the period 2023–27 (Lancet, 2022). In the UNAIDS Global HIV Update (2022e), affordability of HIV prevention and treatment is highlighted as a significant barrier for managing HIV in countries around the world. Referring specifically to cabotegravir (CAB-LA), which I discussed earlier in this chapter, UNAIDS notes the immense potential of this long-acting injectable for reducing the risk of HIV acquisition. They argue that a year's supply of CAB-LA (US$22,000) was prohibitive and that this 'current pricing drastically limits the potential public health impact of this prevention option' (2022e: 111). The combination of prohibitively expensive medicines that are priced out of reach for most countries around the world, along with the reduction in global funding, results in LMICs having severely constrained national capacity to procure medicines that can effectively treat HIV.

Finally, the 'graduation' of countries to 'middle-income status' (per the World Bank's classification) results in LMICs – particularly those facing rising levels of HIV infection – no longer qualifying for donor funding or meeting eligibility criteria to use TRIPS flexibilities (ITPC, 2022). For example, the Global Fund's eligibility policy stipulates that middle-income and upper-middle-income countries would have to have a 'high' burden of disease to qualify for funding. But the change in a country's income status rarely corresponds with on-the-ground reality: for example, Venezuela was reclassified as upper-middle income in 2020 (for financial year 2020–21). The World Bank used Venezuela's official GDP to inform its ranking. However, in practice, the gap between the official and unofficial GDP is tenfold (Maldonado and Olivo, 2022), and the country is reeling from the worst social, political and economic crisis in its history. The reclassification of Venezuela as an 'upper-middle income' country using incorrect data, during this crisis, contributed to the rapid deterioration of the country's health system alongside a systematic withdrawal of global health funding (Caraballo-Arias et al, 2018; WHO, 2019; Maldonado and Olivo, 2022). Venezuela was unclassified by the World Bank a year later due to lack of available data.

The combination of funding cuts and trade restrictions means that many countries are increasingly unable to provide effective HIV medicines. As discussed earlier in this book, dolutegravir (DTG) is a gold-standard first-line HIV treatment. The WHO recommended that all countries included DTG in their first-line treatment regimens because it has fewer side effects, results in faster viral suppression and has a stronger genetic barrier to resistance compared to older first-line treatments. The pharmaceutical company that developed DTG, ViiV Healthcare, has issued multiple evergreening patents on DTG that restrict generic production or procurement until at least 2031. Although ViiV has signed separate voluntary licences with the United Nation's-backed Medicines Patent Pool to ensure that some generic producers can manufacture adult DTG for LMICs, 49 countries are excluded from this licence and must pay extortionate costs. For example, Bulgaria pays US$9,656 for DTG (per person per year), whereas countries that are able to use voluntary licences only pay US$365 for the same medicine (ITPC, 2022). There are a range of options for countries to ensure access to affordable HIV treatment through mechanisms like voluntary licences, as I go on to discuss, but these are frequently only available to certain countries that are able and prepared to make use of TRIPS flexibilities.

These five key 'problems with patents' (ITPC, 2022) draw into focus a range of global actors that play a role in the ability of national governments to provide affordable treatment through their public health systems. These actors include UNAIDS and its impact on donor priorities based on its evaluation of the severity of the global HIV crisis; the World Bank and the role it plays in classifying which countries can access which types of aid or qualify for TRIPS flexibilities; and, fundamentally, the WTO, which governs the creation and implementation of TRIPS across its 164 members.

Trips flexibilities: mechanisms for ensuring access to essential medicines

The plethora of knotty challenges linked to the WTO's TRIPS Agreement speaks to the considerable constraints under which national governments operate within a global assemblage that governs access to affordable HIV medicines. However, as discussed previously and in more detail later, TRIPS flexibilities can be used by national governments to 'act up' on this global assemblage in order to produce, import or export affordable HIV treatments.

The preamble to the Doha Agreement introduces the term 'flexibility' to indicate that 'least-developed countries' (LDCs) have scope for non-compliance with the TRIPS Agreement. While not a legal term per se, 'TRIPS flexibilities' have been widely referenced in a number of resolutions by UN agencies, including the Human Rights Council, the WHO and the UN General Assembly (Correa, 2022). The Sustainable Development Goals also refer to TRIPS flexibilities in goal 3 (under target 3.b):

> Support the research and development of vaccines and medicines for the communicable and noncommunicable diseases that primarily affect developing countries, provide access to affordable essential medicines and vaccines, in accordance with the Doha Declaration on the TRIPS Agreement and Public Health, which affirms the right of developing countries to use to the full the provisions in the Agreement on Trade-Related Aspects of Intellectual Property Rights regarding flexibilities to protect public health, and, in particular, provide access to medicines for all. (UN, 2015: np)

There are numerous TRIPS flexibilities, and I outline them here as they relate to public health before returning to elaborate on them in detail in the following section where I work through a series of case studies to explore how national and transnational activist organizations and countries like India, South Africa and Brazil have mobilized around these flexibilities.

First, pre-grant flexibilities allow countries a degree of flexibility on their interpretation of 'patentability'. The TRIPS Agreement stipulates that patents must be granted if a process or product, like a medicine, is new, inventive or capable of industrial application, but, importantly, it does not define these terms. Instead, this aspect of the agreement is subject to interpretation. For instance, India has adopted strict patentability standards to prevent unnecessary patenting or evergreening (ITPC, 2022).

Second, post-TRIPS flexibilities offer a range of options for countries to bypass existing patents. There are three main post-TRIPS flexibilities: Bolar provisions (allowing generic manufacturers to undertake any necessary research to prepare for regulatory approval of the medicine before the patent expires, enabling generic medicines to enter the market as soon as the patent barrier is removed); parallel imports (enabling countries to import a patented product from another country where it is sold at a lower price by the patent holder or under a compulsory licence); compulsory and government-use licences (compared to voluntary licences, these licences are issued by a government or court to allow the production, supply, import or export of generic versions of patented products before the patents expires) (ITPC, 2022). The last of these post-TRIPS flexibilities, compulsory licences, can be issued by countries in cases of extreme emergency or for public non-commercial use, and they do not require prior negotiations with the patent holder. This contrasts with voluntary licences which are issued by the patent holder themselves, rather than a government, and usually entail a range of geographic and economic restrictions as illustrated with reference to ViiV's voluntary licence for DTG in the previous section (Hyland, 2020; Garagancea, 2021).

Third, LDCs have two transition periods: prior to 2021, these countries were not required to comply with TRIPS, and until 2033 they are not required to grant or enforce patents and data protection for pharmaceuticals (ITPC, 2022). The fourth flexibility concerns enforcement: all of these flexibilities rely on non-enforceability of patent legislation as a key criterion, and this is built into the Doha Agreement. The TRIPS Agreement does not require criminal enforcement of patent infringement, and it allows for personal imports or small consignments of generic versions of patented medicines. Finally, patent oppositions enable third parties, like civil society groups or generic competitors, to challenge patent applications (ITPC, 2022; Le, 2022b).

Given that these flexibilities, or safeguards, exist within TRIPS, one could ask why national governments would consider not asserting them through their own national legislatures. There are a range of economic and political reasons, and I discuss some of them briefly in the following section as they relate to trade agreements. Thereafter, in the final two sections of this chapter, I consider how governments and global health and civil society organizations have worked together to challenge powerful actors that are invested in maintaining restrictive IPRs that limit access to affordable HIV medicines.

The maximalist agenda and mechanisms for restricting access to essential medicines

While the Doha Agreement asserts the importance of TRIPS flexibilities, a maximalist trend in IPR among high-income countries is evident in recent bilateral, regional and multilateral trade agreements. This trend is described as 'maximalist' because it seeks to 'maximize' the protection of IP, increase international harmonization and limit or remove TRIPS flexibilities (Menezes, 2018). The maximalist agenda has emerged from a biased perception within private (and some government) organizations that TRIPS flexibilities have led to poorly enforced IPRs which, in turn, had damaged economies and the welfare of citizens (Krizic and Serrano, 2017). As a result, countries like the US, Japan and South Korea and regional blocs like the European Union started to introduce more stringent criteria around IP protection within preferential and multilateral trade agreements. This maximalist trend has effectively established an additional regulatory framework outside of the WTO and, as I discuss subsequently, has had significant implications for undermining global public health and fragmenting multilateralism in the Global South.

One of the first articulations of the 'maximalist agenda' can be traced back to October 2007 when the United States Trade Representative (USTR), Susan Schwab, asserted that the US would open negotiations with a swathe of countries to establish a new international regulatory framework on IPR, and that this framework would be independent of any existing international institution (like the WTO) (Menezes, 2018). These negotiations started in 2008 and were finalized in 2011 through the Anti-Counterfeiting Trade Agreement (ACTA). Signatories included the US, the EU, Japan, Canada, Switzerland, Australia, South Korea, Mexico, Morocco and New Zealand. The EU parliament rejected this agreement in 2012 but has pursued its own approach to IP 'strengthening' through, for instance, its FTAs. The text proposed by the European Commission in several FTA negotiations includes compelling countries in the Global South to conform to longer patent terms, data exclusivity and more stringent TRIPS-plus enforcement. FTAs form one of at least three main sets of trade agreements that have worked to bolster IP protections and undermine TRIPS flexibilities. In addition to FTAs, the Trans-Pacific Partnership Agreement includes some of the most aggressive TRIPS-plus measures seen in any trade negotiations (Gleeson et al, 2018); these negotiations are currently stalled. Currently, a third type of restrictive trade agreement – the Regional Comprehensive Economic Partnership (RCEP) – is under negotiation with 16 countries in the Asia-Pacific region (Yu, 2022). The RCEP is significant because it includes countries like China, India and Thailand that produce significant quantities of essential medicines. Very recently, Japan and South Korea have introduced TRIPS-plus measures into the RCEP negotiations (Huang, 2022; ITPC, 2022; Tae Yoo and Chong-Han Wu, 2022).

These existing and unfolding trade agreements all seek to introduce TRIPS-plus regulations that far exceed the minimum global standards on IP and often eliminate recourse to TRIPS flexibilities. The asymmetry of power is clear: high-income countries like the US and Japan, and regions like the European Union, introduce IP rules in trade agreements with less-wealthy countries, undermining the ability of these countries to use TRIPS flexibilities to produce or access affordable medicines. TRIPS-plus regulations also work in the interest of pharmaceutical companies by enabling them to extend patent terms beyond the statutory 20 years, expand patentability, extend data exclusivity and limit the provision of compulsory licences (Tenni et al, 2022).

The types of IP agreements that were negotiated after TRIPS speak to two interconnected dynamics. On the one hand, as noted earlier, these agreements form part of a larger strategy for negotiating TRIPS-plus agreements in multilateral fora with a consequence of limiting national governments' policy space and capacity for developing appropriate frameworks to secure affordable essential medicines. In a nutshell, TRIPS-plus agreements jeopardize any meaningful capacity for countries to use TRIPS flexibilities. Given that TRIPS flexibilities were established to strike a balance between protecting the private sector and promoting public welfare, TRIPS-plus measures shift this balance firmly towards protecting the private sector (Menezes, 2018). A second and connected dynamic of TRIPS-plus agreements is the fragmentation of multilateralism, particularly between countries in the Global South. If national governments in the Global South have their capacity to utilize TRIPS flexibilities curtailed by trade agreements that stipulate TRIPS-plus conditions, then their ability to engage multilaterally with other countries to provide or access affordable treatments is similarly limited.

A range of additional mechanisms – beyond restrictive trade agreements – have been used to compel governments to resist using TRIPS flexibilities. These mechanisms include legal pressure and costly litigation by pharmaceutical companies against countries that use TRIPS flexibilities. For instance, in 2006, Novartis, a Swiss pharmaceutical giant, entered a seven-year battle with the Indian government and Indian generic companies that produced a critical cancer drug called Glivec (Gabble and Kohler, 2014). In 2013, the Indian Supreme Court ruled against Novartis and upheld the strict interpretation of India's patent law on evergreening; this also meant that Glivec could be produced and exported to countries in order to treat chronic myeloid leukaemia at an affordable price (Gabble and Kohler,

2014). Currently, Brazil and Argentina are facing litigation by multiple pharmaceutical companies because of these countries' strict patent criteria that push back against restrictive international IP regulations (Vieira and Di Giano, 2018; Le, 2022a; 2022b). In addition to legal pressures from pharmaceutical companies, LMICs face bilateral pressure from high-income countries like the US. The US, for example, pressures countries that it believes are not adequately protecting US IP by placing them on a 'Watch List' or 'Priority Watch List' and threatening sanctions and investigations.

While the US and EU have used trade agreements in a bid to strengthen IP regulations, there has also been a long-standing and concerted resistance to these regulations at a national, regional and transnational level. For instance, the African Group, along with China, India, South Africa and Brazil, strongly criticized the maximalist agenda at the 2010 TRIPs Council meeting (Sun et al, 2014). They argued that the maximalist agenda threatened both the content and governance of TRIPS by the WTO (Ruschman, 2020). In a subsequent event in 2014 entitled 'Access to medicines: challenges and opportunities for developing countries', the BRICS countries (Brazil, Russia, India, China and South Africa) convened a discussion to explore two key issues: first, the need for BRICS countries to ensure that affordable medicines were made available to more countries in the Global South; and second, to lobby for an international IP protection regime that supports the use of TRIPS flexibilities including local production, compulsory licences, parallel imports and other mechanisms that make medicines more affordable (Sun et al, 2014; Hopewell, 2017; Duggan et al, 2022). Two years later, in the Goa Declaration following the 2016 BRICS Summit, the member countries again emphasized the dangers of TRIPS-plus regulations and concurred with Brazil's stance that ACTA could surpass the WTO and become the main international organization that would enforce IP rights, which would have a serious and negative impact on economic multilateralism (Hopewell, 2017). These meetings and subsequent statements speak to an awareness of the need for multilateral cooperation to resist the power asymmetries that limit the use of TRIPS flexibilities and that have been increasingly entrenched through trade agreements with high-income countries.

As I go on to discuss, India, Brazil and South Africa have worked together through BRICS to raise substantive issues with the proliferation of TRIPS-plus agreements, and this collaboration extends back to their cooperation through the India, Brazil and South Africa Dialogue Forum in 2004. Over almost two decades, these three countries have consistently argued against the pursuit of the maximalist agenda by high-income countries like the US, suggesting that extension of TRIPS-plus measures through trade agreements and other multilateral tools would lead to the weakening of basic civil rights. In a comparative analysis of the BRICS countries' efforts to secure affordable HIV treatment, Sun and colleagues (2014) suggest that while each country has followed quite different paths to securing affordable treatment, they have all actively utilized TRIPS flexibilities, often in defiance of powerful global actors like the WTO, the US and the EU.

In the following two sections, I trace a set of actors that have worked to resist harmful IP regulations at a national and transnational level within the global assemblage that governs access to affordable medicines. The first section considers the role of governments as actors in using national legislation and transnational coalitions to push back against powerful global actors like the EU, US and WTO. The final section of this chapter explores some of the broader actions taken by national and transnational civil society actors to compel national governments to use TRIPS flexibilities, and it moves out in scale to consider the role of global health development agencies in supporting national governments and civil society to advance the rights of individuals and countries to access essential HIV medicines.

IPRs and resistance: BRICS and the case of Brazil, India and South Africa

BRICS has a chequered history, with many analysts arguing that the actions taken by the bloc have been inconsequential at best. These analysts have focused on the impotency of the bloc since it was first formalized and the folly of bringing together five countries that have very different political and economic profiles (Beausang, 2012; Vandemoortele et al, 2013; Bishop, 2016; Hopewell, 2017). As Hopewell notes:

> Much of the discussion to date has accordingly been dominated by what could be called the Goldman Sachs view of the BRICS – as primarily an economic phenomenon, centred on rapid economic growth in these countries and resulting opportunities for investment. Consequently, now that growth has slowed in most of the BRICS – with China's annual rate falling from double digits to less than 7 per cent, and Brazil and Russia currently in recession – the frenzy surrounding the rise of the BRICS has been replaced by equally fervent declarations of their demise. (2017: 1377)

While declarations that the BRICS are 'broken' may be valid in some respects (see Bishop, 2016; Gómez and Harris, 2016), there is a substantial body of research that challenges binary-thinking about BRICS as either a success or failure (Vandemoortele et al, 2013; Zhao, 2015; Bishop, 2016; Duggan et al, 2022). Several scholars have found examples of relative success that can be attributed to knowledge sharing and international mobilization by splinter-groups within BRICS (Zhao, 2015; Menezes, 2018; Adeyemo et al, 2020). One of the most striking areas of relative success has been the ability of some of the BRICS countries to challenge international institutions, like the WTO, and international agreements, like TRIPS, that impact access to affordable treatment and therefore public health, particularly in the Global South (Sun et al, 2014; Gómez and Harris, 2016; Hopewell, 2017). In this section, I explore three national actors – Brazil, South Africa and India – as they are networked into regional and international alliances through BRICS and with the European Union.

As noted earlier, over the last decade BRICS summits and meetings of BRICS health ministers have generated a series of position statements on IPRs that reflect agreement, at least in theory, among the member countries. At the first meeting of BRICS health ministers in 2011, for example, the UNAIDS Executive Director, Michel Sidibé, affirmed the 'intimately connected' relationship between people's embodied precarity and the role of BRICS in the global AIDS response and argued that universal access to essential medicines will not be possible without the leadership of BRICS member states:

> BRICS are faced with unique opportunities to accelerate access to medicines. It is clear that if generic medicines are, for any reason, made unavailable, millions of people will die. The world is looking to the BRICS, who are spearheading a shift in norms, leading the world to accept that access to affordable medicines is a moral obligation – but more than that, a fundamental element of the right to health. It is the BRICS that hold the political and economic clout to defend health against influences that restrict access to generic medicines. (Sidibé, 2011: np)

At this formative meeting, the BRICS ministers of health identified four principal challenges to accessing affordable generic medicines in the Global South. The first challenge centres on the threat posed by regional and international actors on the ability of individual countries to use TRIPS flexibilities. I discuss, in particular, the potential implications of the EU–India FTA on access to affordable ARVs in the following paragraphs. The second, third and fourth challenges relate to the maximalist agenda discussed earlier and the pressure placed on national countries to amend the legislative infrastructure governing the development, distribution and procurement of medical technologies. This includes the push, through trade agreements for example, to compel countries to amend their IPR legislation to include TRIPS-plus provisions, like patent term extensions and data exclusivity.

The commitment by BRICS countries to address these four main challenges was highlighted again at the June 2022 BRICS Summit held in Beijing, China, just months after India and South Africa had tabled a proposal at the WTO to introduce TRIPS flexibilities around COVID-19 diagnostics and therapeutics. In the fourteenth BRICS Summit Beijing Declaration, the countries call for 'affordable and equitable access to global public goods for all' and specify that '[w]e recognize the importance of the discussions in the WTO on relevant IP waiver proposals, as well as capacity building and strengthening local production of vaccines and other health tools, especially in developing countries' (BRICS, 2022: np). These declarations are powerful indicators of a shared position among BRICS countries, and, as I go on to discuss, they also speak to actions taken by emerging powers in this coalition to actively challenge the WTO's trade regime.

Both India and Brazil have made use of TRIPS flexibilities in order to produce ARVs but at different points in relation to South Africa's history. Brazil signed on to TRIPS in 1996, almost a decade before India. Like India (although on a smaller scale) and South Africa, Brazil has a robust domestic pharmaceutical industry and in 2000 threatened to use compulsory licensing if international pharmaceutical companies did not reduce the cost of HIV medicines. At the 2000 International AIDS Conference in Durban, Paulo Teixeira, then Director of Brazil's National AIDS Programme, spoke out publicly against the US government for undermining Brazil's ability to provide HIV treatment to its citizens and openly discussed the value of compulsory licensing for producing several patented HIV medicines (Nunn et al, 2009a; Montenegro et al, 2020; Le, 2022a). This prompted a WTO trade dispute with the US in 2001, just as South Africa amended its national law to enable the government to import generic HIV medicines. Together, the actions taken by the Brazilian and South African governments in 2000 and 2001 prompted a global outcry against the restrictive nature of the TRIPS agreement and led to the Doha Agreement and the formalization of TRIPS flexibilities (Nunn et al, 2009a).

Brazil has continued to strongly criticize global actors like the US and the WTO for limiting the ability of countries in the Global South to produce and access affordable medicines (Le, 2022a). Despite adopting some stricter rules than the TRIPS minimum standards, Brazil has also introduced some important legislative changes to enable it to circumnavigate the maximalist trend in international IP law. In addition to threatening – and, in 2007, using – compulsory licences to produce and access essential medicines, Brazil's Intellectual Property Law includes the Bolar exemption which allows for experimental use of patented inventions (Urias, 2019).

The Brazilian government challenged criticisms of its use of TRIPS flexibilities by business experts and pharmaceutical companies by asserting their decision as one grounded in its democratic constitution, thus legitimizing its decision to foreground the lives of HIV-positive citizens over the profits of pharmaceutical companies (Biehl, 2004; Chaves et al, 2008; Nunn et al, 2009a; Vieira and Di Giano, 2018). For example, a publicity poster jointly issued by the Ministry of Health and civil society organizations stated 'Local manufacturing of many of the drugs used in the anti-AIDS cocktail permits Brazil to continue to control the spread of AIDS. The drugs industry sees this as an act of war. We see it as an act of life' (Celentano and Beyrer, 2008: 142). While this biopolitical discourse positively and directly positions the vitality of citizens as a function of the 'activist state', it may also strategically obscure other equally radical and less life-affirming biopolitical dynamics. It is worth noting, briefly, that the choice of language in this poster, and in government leaders' description of Brazil's response to HIV, eclipses more complex dynamics, as Biehl observes in his ethnographic research (Biehl, 2004b, 2021; Biehl et al, 2012), and as I discuss in the previous chapter.

In a bid to fulfil the Brazilian government's initial conceptualization of HIV treatment as a fundamental element of its citizens' right to health, the government mobilized its domestic pharmaceutical industry, and particularly the state-owned laboratory Farmanguinhos, to produce ARVs in 1997 (Nunn et al, 2009a). Between 1997 and 2002, Farmanguinhos became the main supplier of generic ARVs to Brazil's Unified Health Care System (Sistema Único de Saúde), increasing production sevenfold (Urias, 2019). Brazil's early threat of compulsory licences has also led the way for many other countries in the Global South to similarly threaten, or use, this particular TRIPS flexibility to reduce the cost of HIV medicines (Hyland, 2020; Le, 2022a). In a systematic review of country studies, Tenni and colleagues (2022) found that compulsory licences were the most frequently invoked TRIPS flexibility used to secure affordable HIV medicines.

Although the Brazilian government demonstrated its commitment to using TRIPS flexibilities to access and produce affordable medicines, the country's pharmaceutical industry did not have the capacity to produce raw materials like active pharmaceutical ingredients (APIs) at an industrial level. As it started to scale up its ARV production in the early 2000s, Brazil relied on India and China's ability to produce and export APIs for eight of the 12 ARVs that it was manufacturing domestically (Urias, 2019). Over time and through sharing scientific expertise with India on processes involved in reverse engineering APIs (Hyland, 2020), Brazil's pharmaceutical industry was able to develop the capacity to produce APIs, and it now manufactures most of the country's HIV medicines (Biehl, 2021; Pereira, 2021; Le, 2022a). Developing the knowledge and capabilities to produce APIs at an industrial level was central to Brazil's ability to negotiate the prices of HIV medicines with pharmaceutical companies in the subsequent decades. Further, by developing a global trading system of active ingredients and, later, of knowledge and capabilities around reverse engineering, Brazil and India worked in concert to challenge the dominance of the US, and with backing from other countries like China, they were able to substantively reconfigure the WTO's IP regime. As Hopewell argues: 'Far from being merely a mirage or passing fad, Brazil, India and China collectively emerged as a major political and economic force at the WTO and have had a significant impact on global trade governance' (2017: 1378).

As noted in the preceding sections, and in Chapter 1, India's technological capacity to identify and reverse engineer APIs is a result of the government's commitment, from the 1960s, to protect its domestic pharmaceutical market. At a national level this protection was achieved through the 1970 Patents Act (Banerjee, 2017). This legislation enabled Indian scientists and pharmaceutical companies to develop an expertise in reverse engineering (Kamiike, 2020). This pharmaceutical expertise, backed by India's Patent Act, has been relatively successful in deterring international companies from competing with the country's domestic and international pharmaceutical market. India currently has the third largest pharmaceutical industry in the world (in terms of volume), and it is the largest provider of generic medicines, accounting for 20 per cent of global exports (Guerin, Singh-Phulgenda and Strub-Wourgaf, 2020; Bjerke, 2022). In 2018–19, it exported US$19 billion worth of pharmaceuticals to over 200 countries (Cherian et al, 2021). Indian firms account for over 90 per cent of donor-funded ARV procurement in LMICs (Orsi et al, 2018) and over two thirds of all medicines used by global health organizations like Médecins Sans Frontières (MSF) to treat HIV, TB and malaria are sourced from India (MSF, 2016; Guerin et al, 2020).

Like Brazil, India reformed its patent laws to make use of TRIPS flexibilities and to meet national and international demand for affordable medicines. One of the most important changes to India's patent laws, when they changed to become TRIPS-compliant in 2005, was the introduction of higher patentability requirements. This meant that in order to qualify as 'patentable', inventions needed to possess prominent and differentiating characteristics that would distinguish them from any prior inventions (Menezes, 2018). It is perhaps because of these in-built legislative protections, like higher patentability requirements, that the Indian Patent Act is currently under threat.

The multinational pharmaceutical industry, with backing from the US, EU member states and other countries, is placing enormous pressure on India to reform its IP law in order to grant monopoly power to pharmaceutical companies that are producing expensive patented medicines – the same medicines that India is producing but for a much cheaper price as a generic formulation (Löfgren, 2017; Hyland, 2020; Cherian et al, 2021; Plahe and McArthur, 2021). One of the clearest threats to India's ability to continue providing affordable medicine is the EU–India FTA.

The EU–India FTA has been under negotiation since 2007 and it has stalled, in part, because of the strong push by the EU for India to change its Patents Act. Leaked text on the EU–India FTA found that the EU was demanding extensive TRIPS-plus measures including new exclusive rights on medicines and longer patent terms (MSF, 2018b; Köhler-Suzuki, 2021; ITPC, 2022; MSF, 2023). Further, enforcement measures in the proposed EU–India FTA could increase the risk of generics being blocked and seized at international borders. This precedent was heralded in 2008, when generic medicines from India were seized as they passed through Europe's border because European pharmaceutical companies had claimed that they infringed upon their patents (Waning et al, 2010). As argued earlier, the extent to which global and regional actors become networked with national governments highlights the limits of Foucault's (1978) historic conception of biopower in which the vitality of the state is drawn into a relationship with the vitality of populations and individuals. This web of relations governing vitality is significantly shaped by the nature of the free market and is evident as pharmaceutical companies slip out of countries and into transnational space between them. The India–EU FTA could, for example, include an investment chapter that would make provision for companies to sue governments; these companies could conduct proceedings out of the public's view (in national courts) through secretive forums (MSF, 2018b; Köhler-Suzuki, 2021).

The negotiations on the EU–India FTA have been stalled or reshaped by global and national activist networks that have strongly advocated against the FTA given the implications it would have for global access to HIV medicines (MSF, 2018b). In 2017, for instance, networks of people living with HIV staged sit-in protests and marches outside the EU offices in Delhi to highlight their concerns about the impact of the FTA on the lives of people living with HIV in India and globally (ITPC, 2022). This coordinated and vocal opposition from activists around the world and organizations like MSF has been shown to have had some success in stalling the EU–India negotiations; they have also led to a commitment from the EU to remove some of the TRIPS-plus measures, speaking to the role of activist coalitions in acting 'up' and through global assemblages that govern access to vital medicines. In 2018, for example, MSF received an expressed written commitment from the European Commission to remove patent term extensions and data exclusivity from the draft EU–India agreement (MSF, 2018b). However, in the draft EU-India FTA text published in July 2022, the EU reintroduced harmful provisions (including data exclusivity) that, if accepted in the upcoming negotiations in 2024, will delay the registration of generic medicines even where there is no longer a patent on the medicine. MSF (2023) argues that this will block the entry of generic competition on newer treatments by several years.

South Africa's capacity and will to negotiate with the international actors that influence the development and distribution of new AIDS therapies has been significantly different from India's and Brazil's approaches. This is not, as we see with countries like Brazil and India, simply a matter of South Africa being forced to capitulate to oppressive trade agreements, capital-driven pharmaceutical companies or the WTO's neoliberal agenda, for example. I suggest instead that, at this point in South Africa's political life, it is predominantly a consequence of South Africa's failure to adequately amend its patent legislation. I discuss this legislation briefly in the following paragraphs and contrast it with other regional actors in BRICS as they negotiate the global assemblage governing AIDS therapies in significantly different ways.

In 1997, the newly democratic South African government indicated its commitment to providing medicines to citizens by introducing amendments, including TRIPS flexibilities, to the Medicines and Related Substances Control Amendment Act. The amendments in this Act allowed the state to substitute brand-name medicines with generics once a patent had expired. This move by the government, one that actively sought to make provisions for providing critical medicines to citizens, was viewed as a threat by the international pharmaceutical community, and in 1998 the Pharmaceutical Manufacturers Association (PMA), including 37 multinational drug companies, initiated legal action against the South African government. Although this period of time was predominantly characterised by opposition rather than collaboration between TAC and the government, TAC joined the government to challenge the PMA and in April 2001 the PMA dropped the case (TAC, 2010). As discussed in Chapter 1, this victory had global implications not only because it compelled pharmaceutical companies to revise the way ARVs were priced (in order to remain competitive with cheaper generic medicines) but also because it built momentum for positive changes to TRIPS legislation at an international level. As discussed earlier in this chapter, the Doha Declaration on the TRIPS Agreement and Public Health (the Doha Declaration) was signed by members of the WTO in November 2001, affirming countries' rights to enact TRIPS flexibilities and protect their citizens' health. The Declaration marked a significant turn in the global governance of essential medicines like HIV treatment (WTO, 2001; Sun, 2004; Correa, 2022).

Over the course of my fieldwork, another barrier to accessing ARVs emerged as the major focus of the activists with whom I worked from 2011 onwards. This struggle related to a much older law: the Patents Act (No. 57), passed in 1978. South Africa's sluggish response to changing this law and to incorporating the flexibilities provided through TRIPS has implications for the amount of money spent on HIV medicines in South Africa and therefore on the *kinds* of medicines that are offered through the public sector to HIV-positive people. For this reason, South Africa's patent legislation was the focus of an *Equal Treatment* publication (issue 41) that I worked on with TAC. The title, 'Fix the laws – save our lives', calls attention to the relationship between South Africa's juridical infrastructure and people's lives, again highlighting the biopolitical relationship between the government and its citizens.

I wrote an article with Nondumiso Hlwele and Nobuhle Qabazi in this issue, and in it we discussed the implications of international regulations for access to new medicines on HIV-positive people's embodied experiences of side effects from older but more affordable medicines (highlighting the value of new HIV therapies and the importance of compulsory licences and generic production). Just as TAC had used the constitution, particularly Section 27, to support its cases against the government prior to the ARV rollout, TAC and a broad coalition of activist organizations under the 'Fix the Patent Laws Campaign' (FPLC), again referred to this section of the constitution to support its calls for juridical reform. The second paragraph of Section 27 stipulates that '[t]he state must take reasonable legislative and other measures, within its available resources, to achieve the progressive realisation of each of these rights'. For example, MSF found that from 2003 to 2008, Brazil only granted 273 patents on medicines compared to South Africa, which granted 2,442 patents in 2008 alone (MSF, 2018c).

Under the current law, South Africa has a 'Depository Patent' system that automatically grants patents for new uses and formulations of existing medicines; this is not required by international law and is an effect of the national government's failure to update its patent legislation (Hill, 2014). As a result, South Africa's patent laws currently block access to affordable medicines for cancer, diabetes, epilepsy, mental health, HIV and TB (Tomlinson et al, 2019). In 2020, as the COVID-19 pandemic was escalating, the Executive Director of Section 27 (the organisation that replaced the AIDS Law Project), and founding member of the FPLC, Umunyana Rugege wrote:

> Exciting new research means we may soon have an HIV prevention injection, which, if accessible, will be a major breakthrough for women in South Africa. Affordability is key, however, and that means that we must ensure that the legal environment can respond to public health needs. The same issues will arise with other new HIV treatments that are found to be safe and effective, whether it is other forms of long-acting antiretroviral treatment, potential antibody treatments, or if things go really well, a vaccine or a cure. As new drugs for HIV and TB are developed and health technologies for COVID-19 become available, we must ensure that we meet the challenge in line with the constitutional right to access health care services. When it comes down

to it, we cannot allow people to die while treatments that may save their lives remain out of reach because of legal obstacles. (2020: np)

Over the last decade, starting in 2011, activist organizations like TAC and Section 27 have worked as a coalition through the FPLC to argue that the one of the most important issues facing the sustainable provision of essential medicines in the public health system concerns the South African government's failure to update its patent laws (Baker, 2015; MSF, 2018c; t'Hoen et al, 2018; Tomlinson et al, 2019).

MSF and the FPLC have articulated a number of key concerns with South Africa's current patent laws (MSF, 2018c; MSF, 2023). First, these laws require patent applications to be examined to check that they meet patentability criteria. This in turn keeps prices artificially high and unaffordable. Second, weak patent standards in South Africa's current patent laws enable pharmaceutical companies to make minor modifications to existing medicines to receive multiple patents (described in the previous section as 'evergreening'). For example, although South Africa has the highest rate of TB and drug-resistant TB (DR-TB), the government has not been able to access several key TB medicines because they have been priced out of reach for the government through its own patent laws. Two new medicines for treating DR-TB, bedaquiline and delamanid, have been patented multiple times in South Africa, extending beyond the TRIPS-mandated 20 years. Looking specifically at Johnson and Johnson's (J&J) bedaquiline, this DR-TB treatment has been placed under extended patent monopoly through evergreening practices which means that J&J will hold a monopoly in South Africa until 2027. Currently South Africa is paying US$900 for a six-month course of bedaquiline. If South Africa had stronger patent standards, like India, it would have been able to access generic versions of this medicine for just US$48–$102. In contrast to South Africa, the Indian Patent Office rejected J&J's attempt to extend its monopoly in 2019, and in July 2023 the patent for bedaquiline expired, enabling India to produce and provide generic versions of this medicine. A recent agreement between the Stop TB Partnership/Global Drug Facility and J&J means that the GDF can now provide generic versions of bedaquiline to LMICs. However, because of South Africa's outdated patent laws, J&J still holds the monopoly for benaquiline and, further, because of its procurement laws the country cannot benefit from the new J&J/GDF partnership (MSF, 2023).

MSF and the FPLC have highlighted two further concerns around the limited use of TRIPS flexibilities under South Africa's current patent law. First, at a domestic level, South Africa's overly complicated and outdated patent laws constrains meaningful research and development of newer, more effective therapies (Baker, 2015; Tomlinson et al, 2019; Rugege,

2020). Second, although compulsory licences have been one of the most effective ways to access affordable medicines, South Africa has not pursued this TRIPS flexibility because the country's patent laws have made this process extraordinarily burdensome. This means that to date South Africa has not issued a single compulsory licence on a medicine. South Africa has also failed to use parallel importation, a key TRIPS flexibility, to bring in patented medicines from countries – like India – where they are sold at a lower price. For example, lenalidomide is a highly effective treatment for multiple myeloma, an incurable and highly treatable blood cancer of the plasma cells in bone marrow. Lenalidomide currently costs R729, 372 (US$38,536) for a year's course of treatment. In India, a year's course of the generic version costs just R28, 476 (US$1,504), or less than 4 per cent of the South African price. Described by the WHO (2018) as a 'cash cow', the cost of lenalidomide increased 1000-fold in 2016 when Bristol Myers Squibb (BMS) registered it under the brand, Revlimid. Prior to this registration, it had been possible for patients and their clinicians to import lenalidomide into the country using a Section 21 authorisation; this is a legal avenue for importing unregistered medicines. However, after its registration, the medicines regulator halted the importation of lenalidomide. The new cost of the treatment took it out of reach of South Africans unless they were able to pay privately for it. After a protracted legal battle with the South African regulator, Section 21 authorisations were reinstated but only for patients who had accessed lenalidomide prior to BMS's registration of Revlimid. Now, for those seeking this treatment, some people are resorting to buying the medicine in India and bringing it surreptitiously into South Africa. It was only after BMS became aware of the local and global advocacy to access affordable myeloma treatment that it committed to not undertake legal action that would block the use of lenalidomide generics in South Africa (Tomlinson, 2023).

Given the ramifications of South Africa's outdated patent laws on people's ability to access life-saving medicines through the country's public health system, activists that have coalesced under the FPLC have called on the government to move away from the existing 'Depository Patent' system and towards a more substantive 'Search and Examination' system where patentability criteria can be checked prior to granting 20-year monopoly patents (Baker, 2015; Section 27, 2022). The 'Search and Examination' system would follow some of the provisions held in India's Patent Law to prevent patent evergreening, encourage the use of compulsory licences and create a more open medicines market that would enable more generics to compete in the market, lowering their prices and extending their accessibility (T'Hoen et al, 2018; Tomlinson et al, 2019). In May 2022, the Minister of Trade, Industry and Competition, Ebrahim Patel, announced that a draft Patents Amendment Bill would be sent to cabinet by October 2022. At the time of finalizing this book, in 2023, the Draft Patents Amendment Bill had not yet been approved by cabinet (MSF, 2023; Sabinet, 2023).

Towards the sustainable governance of medicines: civil society organizations and global health agencies

Even where countries might have appropriate patent laws in place, they may still not be willing to use TRIPS flexibilities given the economic, legal and political ramifications they might encounter from countries like the US. However, for countries that do use TRIPS flexibilities there is frequently a domino effect: for instance, when Brazil threatened to use compulsory licences in the early 2000s, this drove down the price of ARVs not only for Brazil but for other LMICs. Similarly, pharmaceutical companies that are compelled to issue voluntary licences for one country may then go on to extend these licences to cover other previously excluded countries. Civil society organizations have played a vital role in compelling national governments to utilize TRIPS flexibilities, often working at a national and transnational level. In this section, I outline five key areas where civil society organizations have worked to reconfigure the global governance of medicines, sometimes but not always in concert with national governments.

First, civil society organizations have been successful at compelling national governments, like India, the Philippines and Argentina, to introduce stricter patentability criteria in their national laws to prevent evergreening patent applications (ITPC, 2022). In India, for example, networks of people living with HIV have successfully lobbied the government to introduce provisions in the national legislature to challenge evergreening patent applications. Seeing the success of India's civil society organizations has prompted organizations in countries like China, Russia, Ukraine and Thailand to compel their own governments to file applications to prevent pharmaceutical companies from evergreening patents (Nunn et al, 2012; Anderson, 2018; Duggan et al, 2022; ITPC, 2022).

Second, civil society organizations have created 'buyers clubs' using the 'personal use exception' within the TRIPS Agreement to move small consignments of patented medicines across borders (ITPC, 2022). Buyers clubs first emerged in the US at the start of the HIV epidemic when locally produced medicines were priced out of reach of most people living in the US, and so civil society organizations worked through these clubs to bring in more affordable generic medicines from countries like India or Thailand. For example, in the early 2000s TAC purchased a generic HIV medicine, fluconazole, from Thailand and flew boxes of this medicine into South Africa using this TRIPS flexibility. Activists displayed the medicines prominently at the airport when they landed, raising awareness about Pfizer's excessive profiteering and daring the pharmaceutical company to sue them. At the time, fluconazole cost the South African government R28 (US$1.40) for a 200 mg capsule compared to the generic version that was available in Thailand for only R1.78(US$0.09) per 200 mg capsule. As a result of TAC's defiance in bringing generic versions of fluconazole into the country from Thailand, Pfizer laid a charge against TAC; this was met with a global outcry against the company, and not only did it withdraw the charge but within weeks it agreed to provide fluconazole free of charge to South African hospitals and clinics (ACTUP, 2000). More recently, civil society organizations in LMICs like Indonesia have been working through buyers clubs to purchase APIs from countries like India and asking local pharmaceutical manufacturers to produce these medicines at a more affordable price than if the country had imported the patented medicine as a complete product (Son and Lee, 2018; ITPC, 2022).

Third, civil society organizations have advocated for national governments to use compulsory licences in their legislature in order to access and distribute affordable medicines (ITPC, 2022). In the previous section, I discuss Brazil's threat of using compulsory licences and the power that this had on compelling pharmaceutical companies to reduce the cost of HIV medicines that they sold to the Brazilian government. India has also used numerous TRIPS flexibilities, the most notable example has been the use of compulsory licences to enable Cipla, an Indian pharmaceutical company, to start producing generic versions of HIV medicines and thus rapidly reducing the cost of first-line treatment from US$10,000 per person per year in 2000 to around US$95 per person per year in 2022 (Bekker, 2022; ITPC, 2022).

Fourth, and as discussed in the previous section, civil society organizations have also worked in concert with one another at a national level to compel their government to amend its legislation in order to make better use of TRIPS flexibilities (ITPC, 2022). This is evident in the coalition of over 40 activist organizations in South Africa, which, through the FPLC, have drawn attention to the country's outdated patent laws and the cost of failing to utilize important TRIPS flexibilities in order to purchase and provide more effective and affordable treatments for HIV, TB and cancer.

Finally, as noted earlier in the discussion of the EU–India FTA, civil society organizations have worked to discourage national governments from entering agreements that would introduce more stringent TRIPS-plus measures (ITPC, 2022). In India, for example, networks of people living with HIV have worked enormously hard for over a decade to discourage the government from capitulating to the EU's insistence on TRIPS-plus measures. These measures would have serious negative consequences for India's domestic provision of essential HIV medicines, and it would have catastrophic implications for countries in the Global South that purchase up to 90 per cent of HIV medicines from India at an affordable price (Löfgren, 2017; Köhler-Suzuki, 2021; Plahe and McArthur, 2021).

In addition to the work of civil society organizations, global health agencies have played a role in supporting national governments to fully utilize TRIPS flexibilities by providing guidance, funding and technical assistance. The role these agencies have played has shifted over the last twenty years, and it also varies from agency to agency. Most global health agencies have articulated a commitment to TRIPS flexibilities through their agency's mandates or constitutions (ITPC, 2022). For example, UNAIDS have a long-standing commitment to foregrounding the impact of large pharmaceutical companies on the prices of HIV medicines and have attempted to address this issue, in part, by setting up the Drug Access Initiative. The WHO, too, has raised concerns around the impact of the maximalist agenda set by countries like the US and has issued numerous resolutions, including the resolution on the Revised Drug Strategy, to report on the impact of the WTO on the cost of essential medicines and national drug policies (ITPC, 2022). The Global Fund to Fight AIDS, Tuberculosis and Malaria has integrated a number of resolutions to encourage donor recipients to apply TRIPS flexibilities as fully as possible in order to achieve the lowest prices for all purchased medicines. Importantly, it has more recently offered to provide funds to contract the necessary expertise for countries that do not have the capacity to evaluate and challenge international IPR law or make suitable amendments to its own national legislation. These global health institutions regularly publish documents and policy briefs to support countries to use TRIPS flexibilities and participate in high-level panels and meetings to discuss avenues for resisting the maximalist agenda that has been pursued through trade agreements and other measures discussed earlier in this chapter (WHO, 2010; De Beer et al, 2018; Islam et al, 2019).

Despite these global health organizations' expressed commitment to TRIPS flexibilities, they have also come under strong criticism for failing to invest in concrete measures to support national governments to effectively use TRIPS flexibilities. Instead, some agencies have promoted (and funded) countries to use alternative strategies including negotiating donations or reduced prices from pharmaceutical companies rather than using TRIPS flexibilities. Currently, with the exception of UNITAID, very few donors fund work related to TRIPS flexibilities at a global level with almost no funding reaching civil society organizations to lobby for TRIPS flexibilities at a national level (ITPC, 2022). Where global health agencies have focused on promoting TRIPS flexibilities, many have come under enormous pressure from high-income countries and large pharmaceutical companies. For example, in 2016 the US strongly criticized the UN Secretary General's High-Level Panel on Access to Medicine, stating that that it was 'regrettable that the Panel worked under the presumption of 'policy incoherence' between intellectual property rights, international trade liberalization, and human rights' (US, 2016: np). More recently, in 2023, the Pharmaceutical Research and Manufacturers of America (PhRMA) (representing the country's largest biopharmaceutical research companies) included a submission to the US Special 301 Report (a congressionally mandated annual review of the global state of IPRs) that targeted a number of global health agencies for promoting the use of TRIPS flexibilities (particularly around COVID-19 vaccines) (PhRMA, 2023). This reflects a longer history where PhRMA has acted strongly, through statements to the Office of the U.S. Trade Representatives, to challenge the use of TRIPS flexibilities by health agencies including the WHO, United Nations Development Programme, United Nations Conference on Trade and Development and UNITAID (Baker, 2021; ITPC, 2022).

Conclusion

As the world strives to make progress towards the 2030 goals, it is crucial to remember that without tackling the issue of patents and high prices of medicines, the goal of healthy lives and well-being for all will remain out of reach. (ITPC, 2022: np)

Not only is the HIV epidemic far from being on track to ending but, as argued in a powerful *Lancet* report, the prevailing discourse on HIV has bred a dangerous complacency among global and national actors that has contributed to a weakened global resolve to combat HIV (Bekker et al, 2018). This chapter traces a set of national and global actors that play a role in shaping – and re-shaping – IPRs that govern access to affordable medicines in countries most affected by HIV. It is noteworthy that this *Lancet* report was co-published by eminent scholars like Prof Linda-Gail Bekker, who have, most recently, been working in South Africa on clinical trials of long-acting HIV medicines like lenacapavir. Without substantial changes to South Africa's patent laws, and without meaningful changes to the global maximalist IP regime, important new technologies like lenacapavir may remain out of reach for most people living in the Global South.

This chapter has explored the relationship between the governance of medicine (by global and national actors) and the technologies of governance (through legislation) across a network of actors, affecting the movement of technologies over borders and into bodies. By exploring this relationship of actors across a global assemblage, it highlighted the porosity of bodies, of individuals but also of regional and international coalitions. I propose that there are two aspects of the biopolitical assemblage that governs biomedical technology: the first relates to substance, the second to actors. The national and international legislative infrastructure governing the development and trade of medicines is extremely complex, and it is not the focus of this book. In this chapter, I focused on one substantive aspect of this infrastructure – patent laws governing the development and distribution of HIV medicines – because it was, of all aspects of the global governance of medicines, the most salient concern among the people I worked with. Laws concerning patents and generics all centre back on the active ingredient: when the patent for an active ingredient expires, or when a compulsory licence is issued, it is possible to create generic forms of this active ingredient and to sell the medicine for a much cheaper price than their patented counterpart.

The ability of countries in the Global South to produce and access affordable medicines has direct, embodied, ramifications on the lives of people living with HIV in these countries. For, returning to Miriam in the first chapter, we see that the horizon of her life is conditional on her body's ability to work with ARVs in order to continue to outwit HIV's mutations. Her body's ability to 'tame' HIV, as discussed with relation to the new generation struggles, is not only Miriam's individual responsibility but also relates to her ability to negotiate the use of condoms in her sexual relationship with Samkelo. Part of the reason Miriam is able to negotiate the conditions of her sexual relationship is because she maintains an independent household and works to secure her own income in extremely difficult working conditions in *uYaphi*. These broader socio-economic conditions are biopolitical, as they draw the state into focus in its historic abuse of power, through apartheid, in creating deeply oppressive structures of governance that systematically disenfranchised the majority of South Africa's population. These factors intersect and create conditions of precarity for Miriam: Miriam was threatened by her brother because he was unable to secure his own income and, in a drunken state, said he would demolish her home if she did not give him money. In order to protect herself and her child, she was compelled to move into Samkelo's home; and here, she felt unable to insist on using a condom, thus risking the possibility of contracting new viral strains and developing resistance to her ARVs. If South Africa does not change its patent legislation, and if the EU succeeds in forcing India to adhere to the TRIPS-plus regulations, Miriam will have very limited options for securing her life on ARVs when she develops resistance to her second- or third-line medicines.

The second point relates to the actors in this assemblage. ARVs, as an actant, draw in a network of actors that spans South Africa, Brazil and India's legislative infrastructures, and their relationship with regional bodies including BRICS and the European Union, and with international bodies like the WTO. I engaged with this set of actors because they were most salient in my fieldwork, and they were perceived to most significantly impinge on people's embodied experience of particular kinds of medicines. Like Miriam, most of the women with whom I worked in South Africa are either on first- or second-line ARVs, and for the moment, these actants are effectively intra-acting with HIV to stop the virus from multiplying in their bodies. However, the emergence of new generation struggles linked to HIV medicines prompts a fresh appraisal of the biopolitical relationship between citizens and the state: as viruses continue to move along pathways of precarity, they become – over time and through contact with different viral strains – adept at mutating to resist older HIV medicines. This new horizon of biopolitical precarity will, over time, become more salient as people develop side effects or resistance to current treatments available in the public sector. Therefore, just as the historic struggle for ARVs in South Africa drew in a transnational network of actors to enable, and then compel, the government to provide these essential medicines, this chapter demonstrated how this new horizon of biopolitical precarity similarly draws attention to the value of understanding how this global assemblage governs access to affordable medicines and has direct implications for people's embodied vitality.

However, as I have argued across this book and as I conclude in the following chapter, the extent to which life is contingent on international actors runs alongside another narrative: people do not simply embody precarity because they are acted 'on' by actants, like HIV, and actors, like national governments or international organizations that regulate a country, and therefore a citizen's, access to life-sustaining medicines. As the accounts in this chapter illustrate, and as I have explored throughout this book, people have actively engaged with this global assemblage, often through activist organizations like SPT, Grupo Pela Vidda, TAC and MSF, to bring ARVs out of laboratories and factories in places like US and India into their country, into their public health systems and into their bodies.

8

Conclusion

With Table Mountain etched against the horizon, my plane landed in Cape Town on a cold winter's morning in June 2023. Walking through the partially lit terminal building, the semi-darkness imposed through a national system of rolling electricity blackouts, I joined throngs of jetlagged people as I navigated my body and luggage trolley out of the airport and to the car. With Khayelitsha behind me and Table Mountain in front of me, I drove past the green mosque that marked the turn-off to Nyanga – Khayelitsha's neighbouring township and my field site in 2003 and 2004. In the course of my ethnography with *Luvuyolwethu*, an HIV home-based care organization, I came to know Nyanga's streets as I walked from one home to another with the carers during their 'rounds'. This is how I met Peggy. She lived with her 22-year-old son, Zithulele, and her 25-year-old daughter, Patricia. When I started my fieldwork, Patricia was still able to sit up in the bed that *Luvuyolwethu* had set up in the sitting area of Peggy's home. Without antiretrovirals (ARVs), HIV had become AIDS, and Patricia had become immobile. We did not realize – or perhaps articulate – that when we moved Patricia from her bed to lie down in the back seat of my car, eventually to lie down in Groote Schuur Hospital, that she would not come back home. We went to visit Patricia a few days later: on the cusp of death, she had been heavily sedated with morphine. After driving in silence most of the way back home, Peggy pulled her jersey more tightly around her body and said, "I fought in the streets for this government. Now the holes in my roof are just bigger and they are not giving me medicine for my daughter." Patricia died three days later, just a month before the government was forced by cabinet to initiate the ARV rollout.

Peggy's dismay that the government she had fought to give life to had not fought harder to give life to her daughter was echoed by a large, loud public surge of anger across the country. As the Treatment Action Campaign (TAC) launched a civil disobedience campaign demanding a public sector ARV programme, academics and activists alike looked to countries like Brazil as a model for delivering ARVs to people, like Patricia, whose lives were precariously woven into the life of South Africa's decade-old government. By navigating complex international intellectual property regulations on pharmaceutical production and procurement in order to provide ARVs in its public health system, Brazil had highlighted the South African government's capacity and constitutional responsibility to deliver these medicines (Biehl, 2004b, 2021; Gomes and Tanscheit, 2022; Le, 2022a; Waisbich et al, 2022). At that time and place, in 2003 in Nyanga, the presence of the post-apartheid state in people's lives was felt through its absence, embodied in death, evident in the blossoming of wooden crosses on graves carefully dug to run as closely as possible alongside each other. In the course of my fieldwork that year, the graves had pushed out and against the feeble fence that lined N1 – the main road that ran like Nyanga's spine between this space of death and homes of *Luvuyolwethu*'s clients as they navigated their precarious lives. On a bitterly cold winter's day in July 2003, Peggy's family and I clustered around the parcel of earth that had been designated for Patricia's grave as her minister led the funeral. When we returned to Peggy's home after the ceremony, we all washed our hands in one of the three buckets that had been placed on the street outside her front yard. Peggy explained to me that by washing our hands after Patricia's burial, we signified to the ancestors that we had distanced ourselves from death and looked, instead, towards life.

In this pre-ARV era, HIV became AIDS became death so rapidly that the forward slash between HIV/AIDS made sense. In 2024, it no longer does. HIV medicines have pried open the space between HIV and AIDS, making HIV a chronic, manageable health condition. Now, as I have argued across this book and conclude in this chapter, this opening out of life brings to light a set of complex challenges around the biopolitics of HIV medicines and the socio-economic conditions in which everyday life is lived. These emergent struggles call into focus an assemblage of actants and actors that, together, are networked into women's embodied precarity. This book has shown that while a longer life with HIV is possible through 'technologies of life' like HIV medicines, for the women I have worked with it is still a precarious life that, every day, pushes out and against the possibility of premature death.

The first section of this chapter returns to the starting point of this book; while it is not an ethnography that starts from the point of bare minimalisms, it is also not an ethnography of hope. It lies somewhere in between, and the first section explores the ethical implications of this location through the notion of the right to a nonprojected future. The section traces the key findings and contributions of the book, before moving to the conclusion in the final section.

The right to a nonprojected future

In 1971, Albert Hirschman challenged social scientists to disrupt their assumptions about the world, to relinquish their attempts to fit complex social, economic and political transformations into paradigms that had become so familiar they stopped being analytically helpful. Instead, looking particularly to South American countries, he challenged us to engage the unexpected. The ethical implication of this challenge is captured by Biehl and Petryna's description of the right to a nonprojected future, where thinking beyond what we perceive to be possible is not only intellectually important but ethically critical: 'At stake is the development of institutional capacities that go beyond the repetition of history and help to defend, in Hirschman's words "the right to a nonprojected future as one of the truly inalienable rights of every person and nation"' (2013: 14). In his reflections on Hirschman's call with respect to his pathbreaking ethnography of precarious life and access to HIV medicines in Brazil, Biehl (2005) explains that engaging the unexpected is not simply an abstract academic principle but that it is an ethical task. By thinking beyond the limits of what is perceived to be possible, Biehl argues that we call into focus the biomedical horizon of HIV-positive people's future. In a nonprojected future, life opens up to unexpected potential; it does not, as it did for Peggy's daughter, close down towards premature and imminent death without access to essential medicines.

When Zama spoke of the skies that fight in Chapter 3, she reminded us of this ethical task and complicated its application. Her account of these skies took us to the Eastern Cape, and the moment in her life when lightning struck and HIV entered her body. At this time, too, HIV medicines were not available in the public sector, and the hope for living a long life with HIV was not yet a reality. Zama's account of her rapidly weakening body, at first glance, perhaps offers up a figure of *homo sacer* (Agamben, 1998) and may resonate with Thin's description of ethnography that starts from the point of 'sheer minimalism' (2008: 149). For, a reading of the skies that fight may cast Zama as a HIV-positive citizen whose life, and death, is almost wholly tied into the state's failure to provide life-saving medicines. However, the chapter moved from Zama's description of the skies that fight, the dystopic starting point in her own political struggle for life linked to medicines, to a time ten years later. At this time, South Africa had the largest ARV rollout in the world, and activists like Zama were looking to a precarious future that, with ARVs, also held hope.

The hip-hop and poetry event that Zama and I attended at the City Hall also looked to South Africa's history in acknowledging the work of James Matthews, an anti-apartheid poet; but it brought the country's history into the present with a mash-up of hip-hop dancing and beat poetry that spoke to contemporary challenges facing South Africans, like unemployment and gang violence. It was in response to a question by Matthews' grandson that Zama explained that her dreamt future as a much younger woman – from a time before the fighting skies – had become a present reality. She said, "I am an artist. I am my dream."

Zama's account of dreamt hope as reality was entwined with another set of quieter narratives that I learnt to hear more clearly over time. I discussed these layered narratives in relation to the pathways of precarity that brought HIV into the bodies and lives of the women with whom I worked. It was only once I had recognized the importance of looking towards a future of hope, and once I had acknowledged the presence of this future in Zama's life, that – after almost a decade of knowing each other – we began to have conversations that moved into the space between the 'sheer minimalisms' of structural violence that 'acted down' and the 'hope' offered by HIV medicines and activism that 'acted on' these structures. This book – like my relationship with Zama – has shifted across time and is rooted in a more subtle middle ground between the hope that lies in imagining future possibility and the dystopic violence and threat of death that call into focus the present precarity of people's everyday lives in South Africa.

While the ethical task for this ethnography was to look to the horizon of possibility, of a long life where Zama raises her son into adulthood and continues 'being her dream', I found that this is not enough. In addition to looking out to the horizon, towards the hope of a nonprojected future, I have argued in this book that we need to recognize that biopolitical precarity is embodied in the present, and that it is a discursive outcome of an assemblage of actants and actors that coalesce around the governance of medicine. Because this ethnography is situated in this complex middle ground, I propose an ethics of accountability in which we hold actors at the greatest distance from us in the global arena accountable for the extent to which they are implicated in shaping the very lives of the smallest nonhuman actants, like HIV and HIV medicines, in the most intimate space of our bodies. Further, I propose an ethics of accountability in which we recognize the fraught terrain of agency in this middle ground: while calling actors to account for their implications in women's embodied precarity, this ethnography has shown that it is critical to gauge calibrations (rather than absolute assertions) of agency in the space between structures that 'act down' and agents that 'act up'. By focusing only on agency and hope, or only on structures and bare life, we risk eliding the everyday ways that people navigate a vitality that is both precious and precarious.

Between hope and dystopia: findings and contributions

Technology is not neutral. We're inside of what we make, and it's inside of us. We're living in a world of connections – and it matters which ones get made and unmade. (Haraway, 2006: 149)

One of the ways that we can engage the unexpected, according to Latour (1993), is to move away from analytical approaches that ask us to compartmentalize complex networks into 'only science, only economy, only social phenomena, only local news, only sentiment, only sex' (1993: 2). Like Haraway (1991) before him, Latour (1993) calls us to think more carefully about the world of connections in which we live. As far back as 1991, when Latour wrote *We Have Never Been Modern*, HIV had already become a powerful exemplar of the value in tracing the 'delicate network' that mixes up 'heaven and earth, the global stage and the local scene, the human and the nonhuman' (1993: 2). HIV is indisputably powerful as an actant in its capacity to shift the coordinates in which we think and act. Together with the similarly shape-shifting lives of HIV medicines, these actants call for theoretical agility. In developing the concept of biopolitical precarity, and by exploring the politics of medicine through the lens of actants like HIV and its medicines, this book articulated the nature, function and implications of a global assemblage as it is woven into people's lives and their embodied precarity. Further, it considered how actants and actors are not only 'acted on' but how they act up and through this assemblage to navigate their vitality.

In the years after first working with *Luvuyolwethu* in 2003, I witnessed the increasing availability of HIV medicines in South Africa alongside the shift in HIV activism towards a fuller collaboration with the government; this shift prompted me, in my fieldwork in the decade after 2010, to understand the challenges that emerged in the wake of the visible struggle for life linked to HIV medicines. These challenges, which I discuss as new generation struggles in Chapter 4, had a dual character: first, they related to accessing newer medical technologies that had fewer side effects, and third- or fourth-line treatments that would enable people to continue living when HIV started to resist the medicines currently available through the public health system. Second, they related to the socio-economic dimensions of precarity, including chronic unemployment and economic insecurity, that women embody as they navigate their lives in Khayelitsha. Therefore, while my research has over time explored these shifting biomedical and political landscapes, I have also come to recognize their intersection more fully since first starting my fieldwork in 2003. This book, completed two decades later, emerges from and articulates an integrated biopolitical landscape in which the vitality of citizens and the state is porously networked into an assemblage of actors and actants that coalesce around the global governance of HIV medicines. The five chapters detailed this assemblage across scale, starting under the skin as HIV and HIV medicines became animate in women's bodies and lives, and moving out to the national space as women saw and spoke to the state, and to the global arena where national and international legislation governs the extent to which these women are able to access the hope of a long life on affordable, effective HIV treatment.

Chapters 3 and 4 introduced HIV and ARVs as nonhuman actants in the assemblage. Together, these chapters engaged with the dimension of my research focus that concerned women's embodied experience of HIV medicines. Looking back in time to the 'skies that fight', Chapter 3 traced the vertical, horizontal and diagonal pathways of precarity that the virus travelled to enter the lives and bodies of the women I worked with. In doing so, I argued that these pathways complicate social science readings of the 'gender–HIV' dyad in which poor Black women are constructed as socio-economically and biologically vulnerable. While these three pathways connect to a larger background of studies on socio-economic inequality and HIV transmission in South Africa, we see a further two dynamics that muddy this reading when analysed through the lens of biopolitical precarity. First, this chapter not only explored how HIV entered women's bodies but also demonstrated that women actively 'acted on' the implications of HIV in their lives through engaging politically as activists within TAC to bring HIV medicines into the country and into their bodies. It also demonstrated the myriad, and often fraught, tactics women employed in their sexual relationships to balance their desire for intimacy with their awareness of the embodied risks and sometimes the material benefits of unprotected sex with their partners. Second, in considering these pathways through a biopolitical lens, this chapter proposed that by analytically focusing in on women as vulnerable victims and men as active perpetrators, we place the state on the periphery of our vision and therefore do not hold it accountable for addressing the structures (primarily linked to health, education and employment) that engender biopolitical precarity for both men and women.

When HIV travels along these biopolitical pathways, it enters a new phase of life within the body: here it learns to mimic the DNA structure held in the CD4 (cluster of differentiation) cells – the very cells of the body that would have otherwise been responsible for blocking HIV from replicating and enabling a syndrome of illnesses to plague the body. HIV medicines were originally developed in order to block the life of HIV inside the body; now they are developed, too, to intra-act with particular strains of the virus as it mutates and changes shape in the body over time in this shifting biopolitical landscape. Since conducting fieldwork with *Luvuyolwethu* in 2003 and during the time I had worked with the Deputy Minister of Health and a coalition of activists and academics to develop the 2007–11 HIV/AIDS National Strategic Plan, I had witnessed a decade-long struggle to bring these critical medicines into South Africa's public health system, and into the frail bodies of people like Patricia who would die because they could not afford to buy a longer life in the private health system. However, in my subsequent research following the more effective ARV rollout in 2009, I found that access to ARVs was no longer the primary problem for people living with HIV in areas like Khayelitsha. Instead, as discussed in Chapter 4, I observed a set of new struggles that related to the intra-action of HIV and HIV medicines with and in the body and to the socio-economic context in which people navigated their lives on these medicines.

By drawing HIV medicines into focus as nonhuman actants, Chapter 4 introduced the argument that women's embodied experiences of precarity are not only related to HIV (as a problem) or medicines (as a solution to HIV) but to the complex intra-action of these actants within the body; further, it argued that women's everyday struggles to navigate their bodies and their lives in a context of intransigent socio-economic inequality is fundamentally embodied. The dual character of these new generation struggles speaks to recent ethnographies from Mozambique (Chapman, 2021; Kalofonos, 2021), Kenya (Bosire et al, 2018; Copeland, 2018; Musyoki et al, 2021) and South Africa (Le Marcis, 2012; Pienaar, 2016b) that similarly call attention to the limits of the 'politics of life' literature as it does not pay sufficient attention to contexts in which people live and the forms of inequality that shape their lives and even affect their ability to sustain life on ARVs.

In Chapters 3 and 4, I traced the pathways that brought HIV and ARVs 'to life' in people's lives. By integrating an analysis of these pathways with the concept of biopolitical precarity, I proposed a reading of the body as permeable. I considered the political implications of this argument in Chapters 5, 6 and 7 and, across all five chapters, proposed that there is value in thinking across the boundaries that separate what happens 'inside' the body from what happens 'outside', also described as the context in which people live. Looking 'inside' the body, this ethnography found that HIV medicines are embodied in many different ways, and that this embodiment was not uniformly positive. Sindiswa, for instance, described how older biomedicines like stavudine became visible as lipodystrophy, whereas Yvonne found that nevirapine had placed strain on her liver. The accounts of side effects, viral resistance and treatment fatigue are not a totalizing view of the effect of ARVs on the bodies and lives of the people I worked with; but they were an important finding of my ethnography as these narratives surfaced frequently as complaints during clinic visits, or in conversations with friends while standing in the queue for ARVs. I saw, too, that for people like Nondumiso, the embodiment of HIV was not uniformly negative; she explained that HIV had been a resource that had enabled her to travel to countries like Canada, and to engage with international artists who, like her, acknowledged that they lived with a chronic illness but refused to be identified by their illness. As Nondumiso explained, "I live with X, where X could mean anything."

A tension emerged: by acknowledging that HIV was a present reality in her life, Nondumiso and the other women I worked with had managed to secure a stable income through their social ties into a network of HIV activist organizations and academic programmes in Cape Town. However, their employment was also tied into a global terrain of AIDS funding and into the Global Fund in particular. Chapter 4 detailed the implications of being networked into these organizations and precarious funding structures, as Lilian, Yvonne, Zama and Sindiswa had all lost their secure income as the government shifted towards a more collaborative proactive stance in the early 2010s. This brings us to the second character of the new generation struggles, which related to the persistent precarity that women experienced 'outside' their bodies in their homes, in Khayelitsha's streets, in uncertain employment as they navigated entrenched socio-economic inequalities and pushed back against the ever-present threat of poverty. The tension around wanting to avoid categorizations like 'HIV-positive' while accessing resources through their HIV status persisted as the women I worked with struggled with organizations that offered a meagre but vital wage for work that was built and sold around assumptions of poor, Black, HIV-positive women as 'deserving subjects'. Here too, as discussed in Chapter 4, women resisted these categories through everyday tactics – like talking in isiXhosa about the income-generation manager in his presence and frustrating him because he knew that they were discussing him but was powerless to challenge them. This is very much in line with de Certeau's (1984) description of 'making do' in everyday life through these tactics of resistance.

Therefore, as 'things' with social lives (Appadurai, 1988), HIV and ARVs intra-acted with each other and with(in) individual bodies in complex ways that disrupt the binary that positions ARVs as the 'technofix' to the problem of HIV. Further, we see that these actants themselves are not uniform: specific forms of older HIV medicines were identified as causing side effects, whereas newer medicines were perceived as more desirable for managing both HIV and possible side effects from ARVs. HIV, too, is not a fixed virus but has many hundreds of thousands of strains that require scientists to constantly work at generating newer medicines that can outwit the ever-changing virus. Further, HIV was not only embodied as a problem; it was also strategically mobilized by the women's subversive performance of precarity in order to access economic resources directed to them as the 'deserving poor'. However, this performance, itself, was precarious as the wave of AIDS-specific funding receded, and as organizations appropriated these labels, thus "exploiting my HIV", in order to propel gross profits through national and international sales of paper mâché bowls made by 'poor, HIV-positive, Black women'.

As stated earlier, when starting fieldwork with *Luvuyolwethu* in 2003, activists and activist organizations like TAC and Médecins Sans Frontières (MSF) called for epistemological solidarity that unequivocally foregrounded the efficacy of ARVs. This activist discourse had social and political implications as it worked to draw people together around their sense of precarity linked to the absence of ARVs in the public health system, and therefore created strong social ties between people based on their shared HIV status. Since ARVs were first introduced in the public sector in the late 2000s, South Africa has moved into a muddier middle ground, as the government and activist organizations like TAC entered a collaborative rather than combative relationship. This political shift in the national governance of HIV and its treatment ran alongside two other dynamics that I observed in my fieldwork over this time and that bridge the embodied and political dimensions of my research. First, at an individual level, HIV and ARVs intra-act with each other and with(in) the body in complex ways, across time, that ask us to look more closely at these actants and their social lives. HIV is not a uniform virus: it has many different forms, and when it meets another form of the virus, through unprotected sex, it is able to mutate within the body, and through this process, it can learn to resist older forms of ARVs. ARVs too, are not uniform but unique technologies that have different properties and are also under constant scientific development to more effectively block the life of HIV.

This takes us out to the second dynamic: the global development and distribution of HIV medicines. While the first three chapters consider the ways women conceptualized the biopolitical role of the state in their lives and bodies through the lens of HIV medicines, Chapters 5, 6 and 7 point to the porosity of the state and the limited capacity of both individuals and governments to negotiate access to these medicines within a global assemblage. I argued, through these chapters, that although historical readings of biopolitics (see Agamben, 1970, 1998) position citizens and their vitality as a function of the state, HIV medicines confound this reading. Instead, they point to the value of thinking about networked governance that extends beyond the citizen–state dyad to include a range of global actors that permeate the boundaries of this dyad. Because India has asserted, through its own national patent legislation, its right to produce and sell generic medicines, countries like South Africa and Brazil have been in a position to afford to purchase these medicines at a scale that reaches most of its citizens through their public health systems. Chapter 6 explored some of the historic judicial challenges that Brazilian activists engaged in, in order to compel the state to provide newer and more effective HIV medicines; and it also explored some of the emerging challenges that Brazil's health system and citizens were encountering with the shift towards neoliberalism in the 2010s and early 2020s. Moving out in scale, Chapter 7 traced the connections that weave women's embodied precarity into an assemblage that includes these national governments (South Africa, Brazil and India), regional coalitions (like BRICS [Brazil, Russia, India, China and South Africa] and the EU) and global actors (like the World Trade Organization). In Chapter 7, I argued that, together, these national, regional and global actors govern the development and distribution of more effective medical technologies that have fewer side effects, like dolutegravir, and cutting-edge new medicines, like lenacapavir, that offer hope for a longer life when HIV develops resistance to older treatments.

When we acknowledge that HIV and HIV medicines are differentially embodied, and that the context in which people live is embodied as biopolitical precarity, what happens to the historical social ties built around HIV as a shared illness, and what are the implications of these diffracted socialities for biopolitics and citizenship?

I offer two responses to this question. First, the women's accounts of their differentiated experiences of both HIV and ARVs inside their body – historically read as the 'bio' in 'biosociality' theory – indicate that the nature of biosocialities in South Africa has shifted away from a single focus on HIV: now, they have diffracted out to include an emergent set of struggles and corresponding social and political responses to the embodiment of HIV and ARVs over time. As outlined earlier, the dynamic intra-action of HIV with ARVs has resulted in a set of emergent concerns around viral resistance, side effects and treatment fatigue. The conversations I observed were no longer about the risk of dying without access to HIV medicines and the resultant political actions through which women asserted their right to life in court rooms and public marches. Instead, these quieter conversations within this network of activists, who had now become friends, were around side effects of older biomedicines and the importance of sustained social support, through support groups, to manage these side effects. By articulating the ambivalent embodiments of biomedicines with each other and in the ways they 'saw' and 'spoke to' the state in their photographs and films, the women with whom I worked called on the government to provide newer medical technologies, including newer medical treatments, and to invest in finding a cure to eradicate HIV altogether. These socialities, forged through the longitudinal concerns raised by both HIV and ARVs, have also precipitated a series of political actions. TAC, for instance, has joined a coalition of broad-based social movements under the Fix the Patent Law Campaign to call on the government to amend its patent laws in order to better utilize the Trade-Related Aspects of Intellectual Property Rights (TRIPS) flexibilities and secure more affordable, and more effective, HIV medicines.

Second, in addition to the embodied struggles linked to these shifting actants within the body, Chapter 5 described the multiple forms of embodied precarity that bring the 'outside' context in which people live 'inside' their bodies; these emergent claims were communicated as people saw the state each time they left their home in the middle of the night to use the single, often locked and poorly lit, public toilet in their neighbourhood. They were communicated, too, through photographs of live electricity lines that ran through the sand, under their feet, or over the heads of their children as they played in the garden. By exploring how socio-economic inequalities are embodied, this book integrates the political and embodied research dimensions and argues that inequalities that are conceptualized as existing 'outside' the body – in electricity lines and darkly lit public toilets – are, like HIV and ARVs, embodied 'inside' as forms of biopolitical precarity. Not only are these multiple forms of biopolitical precarity embodied, but like HIV and ARVs in the era prior to the ARV rollout, they have created new social and political ties. Activist organizations, like TAC, and individuals who had historically called on the state to provide HIV medicines, had, with time, started to support – and even start – a plethora of social justice organizations that lobbied the government for better sanitation, an end to sexual and gender-based violence, and equitable education. I propose, then, that 'contextual' inequalities are fundamentally embodied; and because these inequalities are perpetuated by the state in its failure to address issues of sanitation, housing and safety, they, too, are a form of biopolitical precarity.

By working with the concept of biopolitical precarity, I propose that we cannot separate the embodiment of medicine from the politics that govern its development and distribution. In doing so, this book draws together the sets of literature that have historically concerned either the state of the body (and medical anthropological literature on embodiment and biosociality) or the body of the state (and political anthropological literature on networked governance, imaginaries of the state and citizenship). By drawing on this combined literature, in conjunction with actor networks and assemblages, the concept of biopolitical precarity more accurately denotes the intra-action of actants and actors in an assemblage that is networked into people's embodied precarity. In this respect, it connects to and reflects a long trajectory in the field of feminist new materialism and medical anthropology that emphasizes the fluidity of boundaries between medical technologies and bodies (Whyte, 2009; Lock, 2012; Hörbst and Wolf, 2014; Kloos, 2020; Chapman, 2021). Thus, in contrast with historical conceptions of the bounded body as a slate for inscription (see Douglas, 2003) and the bounded state that is autonomous (Weber, 1984) and that 'acts on' these bounded bodies, this book has articulated a reading of the body as permeable, and of boundaries separating states/citizens, technologies/bodies, culture/nature as porous.

In addition to the forms of biopolitical precarity that draw the state into people's bodies, the accounts in this book emphasize, too, the importance of understanding biopolitical precarity beyond the reading of the state–citizen dyad historically proposed by Foucault (1978) and later politicized by Agamben (1998, 2005). To this end, and by using actor networks (Latour, 2005) and assemblages (Ong and Collier, 2008; Collier, 2009; Buchanan, 2017; Prince, 2017) as conceptual tools, the chapters in this book traced the threads further out from the body to show how the biopolitical actions of the state are affected by decisions made at a regional and global level. It suggested that although South Africa and Brazil may be committed to providing HIV medicines to its HIV-positive citizens, the capacity of the state to import or produce affordable generic medicines is tied into a dynamic global arena where international trade agreements, such as the EU–India Free Trade Agreement, bring TRIPS flexibilities under negotiation and threaten the development of generic ARVs in India, the largest producer of these medicines in the world. Further, the book also traced the threads into the body and showed that the boundaries of actants themselves – HIV and ARVs – are porous and co-constructed with the body through their intra-action, even becoming the body, as Thobani's description of his body map attests.

Looking back across this book, and summarizing the preceding discussion, I propose that the following five main conclusions can be drawn from this ethnography. First, by tracing the connections of actants out of and into the permeable body, this book moved away from linear arguments that position global and national actors as active perpetrators of structural violence enacted on individuals as passive subjects and developed, instead, a composite narrative through the notion of biopolitical precarity. Second, by illustrating the network of human and nonhuman actants within the body, this book demonstrated the overlapping complicity of these actants in the embodiment of biopolitical precarity. Third, in arguing that biopolitical precarity is networked into the permeable body, this book challenged the discursive construction of distance in which policy spaces are conceptualized as distinct and hierarchical, cascading down from global coalitions to national, provincial and local levels of governance. This construction of distance facilitates the distancing of culpability from global coalitions, which include national governments, and reflects, I propose, a discourse of collateral damage in which lives are reduced to numbers, and deaths become side effects of global economic crises. Fourth, the dual character of the new generation struggles drew in these actants and actors across scale and highlighted the value of paying attention to the shifting biopolitical landscape in South Africa following the height of HIV activism, when the light turns and the less-visible struggles to navigate life sift to the surface. By considering HIV and ARVs as actants, this book looks to their intra-active complicity in generating both risk (viral resistance and side effects) and hope (of a long life) within the body. Further, by considering how people, too, are actors through their social and political relationships in this assemblage, this book argued for a calibrated reading of their agency through the notion of diffracted biosocialities. Finally, building on the previous arguments, the book challenged the construction of women as passive subjects. In addition to outlining women's historic role in calling on global and national actors to make HIV medicines available to all South Africans, this book has demonstrated how women also subvert hegemonic development subjectivities in order to strategically anchor their lives along the knife-edge of precarity.

Conclusion

The possibility of death ran across the years of my fieldwork like a quiet underground water source that very rarely came to the surface. When it did surface, it was always unexpected. I started this book with a vignette of Miriam's life and the threads that link her vitality into the pills in the tubs on her dressing table, outside and into the muddy street with the single tap that provided water to her home, across the city and into MSF's offices where I learnt, with her, that she might not have access to more advanced HIV medicines when and if she developed resistance to her current treatment regimen.

A few years after we first met, Miriam gave birth to Alizwa. She told me over the phone's crackling static that Alizwa meant "God has given me another girl." You may recall that she has a daughter, Nena, who was born in the 'window period' before the government provided medicines to block HIV from moving along vertical pathways from Miriam's body into her daughter's body. However, Miriam's activism to bring prevention of mother-to-child transmission treatment into South Africa has meant that when she went into labour with Alizwa, she was able to access nevirapine to protect her second daughter from contracting HIV. I saw Miriam just before she had her baby; she was about eight months pregnant and had such swollen feet that it was very difficult to walk. Sitting on the beach after lunch, the quiet rippling thread of threat rose to the surface of our conversation. She started speaking without words, squeezing my hand. I turned to her. She said, "Beth. What if." I pretended I did not understand, and said, "What if what, Miriam?" She laughed at me, letting me know that she could see that I knew what she was talking about. "What if these stupid pills stop working? What happens then?" Just as I had no words for her when we spoke after my meeting with MSF all those years previously, this time on the beach, we sat without words and looked out at the horizon over the sea together. Later, in the car on the way home, we took a bet on when her baby would be born, and Miriam said, "Ya, but you won't be here then, will you? ... Anyway, when you come back, you will meet her. And me. You will see me too; I'm not going anywhere sana." With that, we said goodbye.

Notes

Chapter 1

[1]   Shebeen is a name for (legal and illegal) pubs in South Africa.

[2]   An isiXhosa word meaning 'dear'.

[3]   Professor of molecular and cell biology at the University of California, Berkley, he claimed that HIV does not cause AIDS.

[4]   The use of racial terms is problematic as it assigns essentialist categories of difference to people based on their skin colour. In South Africa, these categorizations have been used to exert social, economic and political power in deeply oppressive regimes. I therefore use the capitalized term 'Black', in line with the Black Consciousness Movement (BCM), to indicate my awareness of the political dimension of race in South Africa and to denote (as the BCM does) the range of 'racial groups' that were systematically marginalized through pseudo-scientific constructions of racial difference under colonial and apartheid rule.

Chapter 3

[1]   This chapter is derived in part from an article published in *Reproductive Health Matters* in May 2016, and in *Critical Public Health* in January 2017 © Taylor & Francis Ltd, and reprinted by permission of Taylor & Francis Ltd. Available online: https://www.tandfonline.com/10.1080/09581596.2017.1282153; https://www.tandfonline.com/doi/full/10.1016/j.rhm.2016.04.006.

[2]   *Imphepho*, or *Helichrysum*, is known to have powerful healing properties and is frequently used by *sangomas*, who are traditional healers, in South Africa.

Chapter 4

[1]   This chapter draws on fieldwork that is included in a chapter in an edited volume, published by Bristol University Press: Mills, E. (2023). 'Ambivalent embodiment and HIV treatment in South Africa', in T. Sikka (ed). *Genetic Science and New Digital Technologies: Science and Technology Studies and Health Praxis*, Bristol: Bristol University Press.

[2]   I use the term 'intra-action', coined by Karen Barad (2008), in place of interaction to reflect the agency of actants like HIV and ARVs as well the porosity of boundaries between them.

[3]   The series is structured around a support group of HIV-positive people, and each week they discuss a different issue related to HIV, including gender-based violence, stigma and women's reproductive health rights, for example.

Chapter 5

[1]   Sections from this chapter were originally published by the Institute of Development Studies (IDS). You can access it at: 'You have to raise a fist!': seeing and speaking to the state in South Africa', *IDS Bulletin*, 41(1): 69–81, Brighton: Institute of Development Studies.

Chapter 7

[1] ViiV, the company that has produced cabotegravir, initially refused to grant voluntary licences that would make this medicine far more affordable, and it was only after vigorous campaigning by organizations like the community treatment network, AfroCAB, that the company shifted its stance. Currently, cabotegravir is priced at US$22,000 per person per year, but the Clinton Health Access Initiative has estimated that it could be produced for less than US$16 per person per year. Although ViiV has entered an agreement with the Medicines Patent Pool to enable low- and lower-middle-income countries access to generic formulations, this agreement still requires confirmation of a bridging price to enable companies to start producing generic versions of this life-saving medicine.

References

Abadía-Barrero, C.E. (2022) 'Medicine: colonial, postcolonial, or decolonial?', in M. Singer, P.I. Erickson and C.E. Abadía-Barrero (eds) *A Companion to Medical Anthropology*, Hoboken: John Wiley & Sons, pp 373–87.

Abbott, F.M. (2018) 'The WTO TRIPS agreement and global economic development', in J. Kelsey (ed) *International Economic Regulation*, London: Routledge, pp 305–326.

Actup (2000) 'Defiance campaign against patent abuse and aids profiteering by drug companies defy trade laws that place profits before health' [online], Available from: https://actupny.org/treatment/tac2000.html [Accessed 05 November 2022].

Adeniyi, O.V., Ajayi, A.I., Ter Goon, D., Owolabi, E.O., Eboh, A. and Lambert, J. (2018) 'Factors affecting adherence to antiretroviral therapy among pregnant women in the Eastern Cape, South Africa', *BMC Infectious Diseases*, 18: 1–11.

Adeyemo, K.S., Sing, N. and Adewusi, A.G. (2020) 'Education and training policies in South Africa and the BRICS countries: successes and failures', in K.S. Adeyemo (ed) *The Education Systems of Africa*, Cham: Springer, pp 1–15.

Agamben, G. (1970) *L'uomo senza contenuto*, Milan: Rizzoli.

Agamben, G. (1998) *Homo sacer: Sovereign Power and Bare Life*, Stanford: Stanford University Press.

Agamben, G. (2005) *State of Exception*, Chicago: University of Chicago Press.

Ahooja-Patel, K. (2007) *Development Has a Woman's Face: Insights from within the UN*, New Delhi: APH Publishing.

Akobirshoev, I., Valentine, A., Zandam, H., Nandakumar, A., Jewkes, R., Blecher, M. et al (2022) 'Disparities in intimate partner violence among women at the intersection of disability and HIV status in South Africa: a cross-sectional study', *BMJ Open*, 12: e054782.

Allen, Q. (2012) 'Photographs and stories: ethics, benefits and dilemmas of using participant photography with Black middle-class male youth', *Qualitative Research*, 12: 443–58.

Amin, T. and Kesselheim, A.S. (2012) 'Secondary patenting of branded pharmaceuticals: a case study of how patents on two HIV drugs could be extended for decades', *Health Affairs*, 31: 2286–94.

Anderson, J.L. (2018) 'Global humanitarian organizations and African goals: the case of Médecins Sans Frontières in South Africa', in J. Warner and T.M. Shaw (eds) *African Foreign Policies in International Institutions*, New York: Springer, pp 229–244.

Andreouli, E. (2019) 'Social psychology and citizenship: a critical perspective', *Social and Personality Psychology Compass*, 13: e12432.

Appadurai, A. (1988) *The Social Lives of Things: Commodities in Cultural Perspective*, Cambridge: Cambridge University Press.

Arendt, H. (1958) 'What was authority?', *NOMOS: Am. Soc'y Pol. Legal Phil.*, 1: 81–111.

Ashforth, A. and Nattrass, N. (2006) 'Ambiguities of "culture" and antiretroviral rollout in South Africa', CSSR Working Paper Series.

Ashman, R., Radcliffe, L., Patterson, A. and Gatrell, C. (2022) 'Re-ordering motherhood and employment: mobilizing "mums everywhere" during COVID-19', *British Journal of Management*, 33: 1125–43.

Astawesegn, F.H., Stulz, V., Conroy, E. and Mannan, H. (2022) 'Trends and effects of antiretroviral therapy coverage during pregnancy on mother-to-child transmission of HIV in Sub-Saharan Africa: evidence from panel data analysis', *BMC Infectious Diseases*, 22: 1–13.

Babatunde, A.O., Akin-Ajani, O.D., Abdullateef, R.O., Togunwa, T.O. and Isah, H.O. (2023) 'Review of antiretroviral therapy coverage in 10 highest burden HIV countries in Africa: 2015–2020', *Journal of Medical Virology*, 95: e28320.

Baker, B.K. (2015) 'International collaboration on IP/access to medicines: birth of South Africa's Fix the Patent Law campaign', *NYLS Law Review*, 60: 297–332.

Baker, B.K. (2021) 'Access to medicines activism: collaboration, conflicts, and complementarities', in S. Ragavan and A. Vanni (eds) *Intellectual Property Law and Access to Medicines*, London: Routledge, pp 295–326.

Baleta, A. (2007) 'Boost for South African AIDS programme while health minister is off sick', *The Lancet Infectious Diseases*, 7: 15.

Banerjee, A. (2017) 'Background note: Standard essential patents, innovation and competition: challenges in India', *IP Theory*, 7: 1.

Banerjee, P. and Connell, R. (2018) 'Gender theory as southern theory', in B.J. Risman, C.M. Froyum and W.J. Scarborough (eds) *Handbook of the Sociology of Gender*, Cham: Springer, pp 57–68.

Barad, K. (2003) 'Posthumanist performativity: toward an understanding of how matter comes to matter', *Signs*, 28: 801–31.

Barad, K. (2008) 'Living in a posthumanist material world: lessons from Schrodinger's Cat', in A. Smelik and N. Lykke (eds) *Bits of Life: Feminism at the Intersections of Media, Bioscience, and Technology*, Seattle: University of Washington Press, pp 165–76.

Barad, K. (2020) 'After the end of the world: entangled nuclear colonialisms, matters of force, and the material force of justice', *Estetyka i Krytyka*, 58: 85–113.

Barad, K. (2022) 'Agential realism: a relation ontology interpretation of quantum physics', in O. Freire (ed) *The Oxford Handbook of the History of Quantum Interpretations*, Oxford: Oxford University Press, pp 1031–54.

Barad, K. and Gandorfer, D. (2021) 'Political desirings: yearnings for mattering (,) differently', *Theory & Event*, 24: 14–66.

Bateman, C. (2007) 'Unity on joint AIDS plan: now the real work begins', *South African Medical Journal*, 97: 482.

Beausang, F. (2012) *Globalization and the BRICs: Why the BRICs Will Not Rule the World for Long*, Hampshire: Palgrave MacMillan.

Beckham, S.W., Glick, J., Malone, J., Rich, A.J., Wirtz, A. and Baral, S. (2024) 'HIV/AIDS among sexual and gender minority communities globally' in *Global LGBTQ Health: Research Policy, Practice and Pathways*, Cham: Springer International Publishing, pp 183–220.

Bedelu, M., Ford, N., Hilderbrand, K. and Reuter, H. (2007) 'Implementing antiretroviral therapy in rural communities: the Lusikisiki model of decentralized HIV/AIDS care', *Journal of Infectious Diseases*, 196: S464–S468.

Bekker, L.-G. (2022) 'Long-acting agents for HIV treatment and prevention', *Nature Medicine*, 28: 1542–3.

Bekker, L.-G., Alleyne, G., Baral, S., Cepeda, J., Daskalakis, D., Dowdy, D. et al (2018) 'Advancing global health and strengthening the HIV response in the era of the Sustainable Development Goals: the International AIDS Society – Lancet Commission', *The Lancet*, 392: 312–58.

Béné, C. and Merten, S. (2008) 'Women and fish-for-sex: transactional sex, HIV/AIDS and gender in African fisheries', *World Development*, 36: 875–99.

Benton, A., Sangaramoorthy, T. and Kalofonos, I. (2017) 'Temporality and positive living in the age of HIV/AIDS: a multisited ethnography', *Current Anthropology*, 58: 454–76.

Benzaken, A.S., Pereira, G.F., Costa, L., Tanuri, A., Santos, A.F. and Soares, M.A. (2019) 'Antiretroviral treatment, government policy and economy of HIV/AIDS in Brazil: is it time for HIV cure in the country?', *AIDS Research and Therapy*, 16: 1–7.

Berenschot, W. and Van Klinken, G. (2018) 'Informality and citizenship: the everyday state in Indonesia', *Citizenship Studies*, 22: 95–111.

Bernard, H.R. (2011) *Research Methods in Anthropology: Qualitative and Quantitative Approaches*, Lanham: AltaMira Press.

Bharadwaj, A. (2013) 'Subaltern biology? Local biologies, Indian odysseys, and the pursuit of human embryonic stem cell therapies', *Medical Anthropology*, 32: 359–73.

Bhattacharya, S. (2019) 'The transgender nation and its margins: the many lives of the law', *South Asia Multidisciplinary Academic Journal*, 20: 1–19.

Biehl, J.G. (2004) 'The activist state: global pharmaceuticals, AIDS, and citizenship in Brazil', *Social Text*, 22: 105–32.

Biehl, J. (2005) *Vita: Life in a Zone of Social Abandonment*, Berkeley: University of California Press.

Biehl, J. (2007) *Will to Live: AIDS Therapies and the Politics of Survival*, Princeton: Princeton University Press.

Biehl, J. (2008) 'Drugs for all: the future of global AIDS treatment', *Medical Anthropology*, 27: 99–105.

Biehl, J. (2021) 'The pharmaceuticalization and judicialization of health: on the interface of medical capitalism and magical legalism in Brazil', *Osiris*, 36: 309–27.

Biehl, J. and Petryna, A. (2013) *When People Come First: Critical Studies in Global Health*, Princeton: Princeton University Press.

Biehl, J. and Locke, P. (2017) *Unfinished: The Anthropology of Becoming*, Durham: Duke University Press.

Biehl, J., Amon, J.J., Socal, M.P. and Petryna, A. (2012) 'Between the court and the clinic: lawsuits for medicines and the right to health in Brazil', *Health and Human Rights*, 14: E36–52.,

Bishop, M.L. (2016) 'Rethinking the political economy of development beyond "the rise of the BRICS"', SPERI Paper No 30.

Bjerke, L. (2022) 'Antibiotic geographies and access to medicines: Tracing the role of India's pharmaceutical industry in global trade', *Social Science & Medicine*, 312: 1–15.

Blanco, I., Lowndes, V. and Pratchett, L. (2011) 'Policy networks and governance networks: towards greater conceptual clarity', *Political Studies Review*, 9: 297–308.

Bodunrin, I. (2014) 'Rap, graffiti and social media in South Africa today', *Media Development*, 4: 10–15.

Bor, J. (2007) 'The political economy of AIDS leadership in developing countries: an exploratory analysis', *Social Science and Medicine*, 64: 1585–99.

Bosire, E., Mendenhall, E., Omondi, G.B. and Ndetei, D. (2018) 'When diabetes confronts HIV: biological sub-citizenship at a public hospital in Nairobi, Kenya', *Medical Anthropology Quarterly*, 32: 574–92.

Bourdieu, P. (2001) 'Structure, habitus, practice', in P. Erickson and I. Murphy (eds) *Readings for a History of Anthropological Theory*, Ontario: Broadview Press, pp 101–27.

Boyce, P. and Dasgupta, R.K. (2019) 'Alternating sexualities: sociology and queer critiques in India', in S. Srivastava, Y. Arif and J. Abraham (eds) *Critical Themes in Indian Sociology*, New Delhi: Sage, pp 330–45.

Bradley, B. (2021) 'From biosociality to biosolidarity: the looping effects of finding and forming social networks for body-focused repetitive behaviours', *Anthropology & Medicine*, 28: 543–57.

Brasil (2018) *Boletim Epidemiológico HIV/AIDS 2018*, Departamento de Vigilância, Prevenção e Controle das IST, do HIV/Aids e das Hepatites Virais, Brasília: Ministério da Saúde. Available at: https://antigo.aids.gov.br/pt-br/pub/2018/boletim-epidemiologico-hivaids-2018 [Accessed 12 June 2022].

BRICS (2022) 'XIV BRICS Summit Beijing Declaration' [online], Available from: http://brics2022.mfa.gov.cn/eng/hywj/ODS/202207/t20220705_1 0715631.html#:~:text=We%20welcome%20the%20BRICS%20Joint,Natio nal%20Security%2C%20held%20on%2015 [Accessed 07 November 2022].

Brotherton, P.S. and Nguyen, V.-K. (2013) 'Revisiting local biology in the era ofglobal health', *Medical Anthropology*, 32: 287–290.

Brown, B.B. (1987) 'Facing the "Black peril": the politics of population control in South Africa', *Journal of Southern African Studies*, 13: 256–73.

Brown, C.A., Siegler, A.J., Zahn, R.J., Valencia, R.K., Sanchez, T., Kramer, M.R. et al (2023) 'Assessing the association of stigma and HIV service and prevention uptake among men who have sex with men and transgender women in South Africa', *AIDS Care*, 35: 1497–1507.

Brown, T., Craddock, S. and Ingram, A. (2012) 'Critical interventions in global health: governmentality, risk, and assemblage', *Annals of the Association of American Geographers*, 102: 1182–9.

Brown, W. (2010) *Walled States, Waning Sovereignty*, Princeton: Princeton University Press.

Buchanan, I. (2017) 'Assemblage theory, or, the future of an illusion', *Deleuze Studies*, 11: 457–74.

Burger, P. and Calitz, E. (2021) 'COVID-19, economic growth and South African fiscal policy', *South African Journal of Economics*, 89: 3–24.

Burki, T. (2018) 'AIDS, Africa, and high ambition', *The Lancet Infectious Diseases*, 18: 606.

Burton, R., Giddy, J. and Stinson, K. (2015) 'Prevention of mother-to-child transmission in South Africa: an ever-changing landscape', *Obstetric Medicine*, 8: 5–12.

Butler, J. (2009) 'Performativity, precarity and sexual politics', Antropólogos Iberoamericanos en Red (AIBR). Available from: https://genderandsecur ity.org/sites/default/files/Butler_-_Performativity_Precarity_Sexual_Pol. pdf [Accessed12 July 2021].

Butler, J. (2012) 'Precarious life, vulnerability, and the ethics of cohabitation', *Journal of Speculative Philosophy*, 26: 134–51.

Cajado, L.C.D.S. and Monteiro, S. (2018) 'Social movement of women with HIV/AIDS: an experience between posithive citizen from Rio de Janeiro, Brazil', *Ciência & Saúde Coletiva*, 23: 3223–32.

Campbell, C.K. (2021) 'Structural and intersectional biographical disruption: the case of HIV disclosure among a sample of Black gay and bisexual men', *Social Science & Medicine*, 280: 114046.

Campbell, L.S., Masquillier, C., Knight, L., Delport, A., Sematlane, N., Dube, L.T. et al (2022) 'Stay-at-home: the impact of the COVID-19 lockdown on household functioning and ART adherence for people living with HIV in three sub-districts of Cape Town, South Africa', *AIDS and Behavior*, 26: 1905–22.

Cancelliere, F. (2020) 'The politics of adherence to antiretroviral therapy: between ancestral conflicts and drug resistance', *DADA Rivista di Antropologia post-globale*, 2: 13–41.

Candea, M. (2016) 'Arbitrary locations: in defence of the bounded field-site', in M.-A. Falzon (ed) *Multi-Sited Ethnography*, London: Routledge, pp 25–46.

Caraballo-Arias, Y., Madrid, J. and Barrios, M.C. (2018) 'Working in Venezuela: how the crisis has affected the labor conditions', *Annals of Global Health*, 84: 512–522.

Carvalho, S.R., Andrade, H.S.D., Marçon, L., Costa, F.D.D. and Yasui, S. (2020) 'Our psychiatric future and the (bio) politics of mental health: dialogues with Nikolas Rose', *Interface: Comunicação, Saúde, Educação*, 24: 24:e190732. Available from: https://www.scielosp.org/article/icse/2020.v24/e190732 [Accessed 18 April 2022].

Casale, D. and Posel, D. (2020) 'Gender and the early effects of the COVID-19 crisis in the paid and unpaid economies in South Africa', *National Income Dynamics (NIDS): Coronavirus Rapid Mobile Survey (CRAM) Wave*, 1: 1–25.

Cassier, M. and Correa, M. (2008) 'Scaling up and reverse engineering: acquisition of industrial knowledge by copying drugs in Brazil', in B. Coriat (ed) *The Political Economy of HIV/AIDS in Developing Countries: TRIPS, Public Health Systems, and Free Access*, Cheltenham: Edward Elgar, pp 130–49.

Cataldo, F. (2008) 'New forms of citizenship and socio-political inclusion: accessing antiretroviral therapy in a Rio de Janeiro', *Sociology of Health and Illness*, 30: 900–12.

CEIC (2023) 'Brazil population: northeast; Pernambuco' [online], Brazilian Institute of Geography and Statistics: CEIC, Available from: https://www.ceicdata.com/en/brazil/population/population-northeast-pernambuco [Accessed 07 September 2023].

Celentano, D.D. and Beyrer, C. (eds) (2008) *Public Health Aspects of HIV/AIDS in Low and Middle Income Countries: Epidemiology, Prevention and Care*, New York: Springer.

Cesarino, L.M.C.D.N. (2012) 'Brazilian postcolonialism and emerging South–South relations: a view from anthropology', *Portuguese Cultural Studies*, 4(1): article 8.

Chapman, R.R. (2021) 'Therapeutic borderlands: austerity, maternal HIV treatment, and the elusive end of AIDS in Mozambique', *Medical Anthropology Quarterly*, 35: 226–45.

Chatterjee, P. (2018) 'Governmentality in the east', in S. Legg and D. Heath (eds) *South Asian Governmentalities: Michel Foucault and the Question of Postcolonial Orderings*, Cambridge: Cambridge University Press, pp 37–57.

Chaves, G.C., Vieira, M.F. and Reis, R. (2008) 'Access to medicines and intellectual property in Brazil: reflections and strategies of civil society', *SUR: International Journal on Human Rights*, 5: 163–89.

Cherian, J.J., Rahi, M., Singh, S., Reddy, S.E., Gupta, Y.K., Katoch, V.M. et al (2021) 'India's road to independence in manufacturing active pharmaceutical ingredients: focus on essential medicines', *Economies*, 9: 71.

Chigwedere, P. and Essex, M. (2010) 'AIDS denialism and public health practice', *AIDS and Behavior*, 14: 237–47.

Chigwedere, P., Seage 3rd, G.R., Gruskin, S., Lee, T.H. and Essex, M. (2008) 'Estimating the lost benefits of antiretroviral drug use in South Africa', *Journal of Acquired Immune Deficiency Syndrome*, 49: 410–15.

Chinguno, C. (2013) 'Marikana massacre and strike violence post-apartheid', *Global Labour Journal*, 4: 160–66.

Chong, J. and Kvasny, L. (2007) 'A disease that "has a woman's face": the social construction of gender and sexuality in HIV/AIDS discourses', *Intercultural Communication Studies*, 16(3): 53–65.

Clifford, J. (1997) 'Spatial practices: fieldwork, travel, and the disciplining of anthropology', in A. Gupta and J. Ferguson (eds) *Anthropological Locations: Boundaries and Grounds of a Field Science*, Berkeley: University of California Press, pp 185–222.

Cloete, A., Mabaso, M., Savva, H., van der Merwe, L.L.-A., Naidoo, D., Petersen, Z. et al (2023) 'The HIV care continuum for sexually active transgender women in three metropolitan municipalities in South Africa: findings from a biobehavioural survey 2018–19', *The Lancet HIV*, 10: e375–84.

Coetzee, C. and Nattrass, N. (2004) *Living on AIDS Treatment: A Socio-economic Profile of Africans Receiving Antiretroviral Therapy in Khayelitsha, Cape Town*, Cape Town: Centre for Social Science Research, University of Cape Town.

Coetzee, A. and du Toit, L. (2018) 'Facing the sexual demon of colonial power: decolonising sexual violence in South Africa', *European Journal of Women's Studies*, 25: 214–27.

Cole, A.L. and Knowles, J.G. (2001) *Lives in Context: The Art of Life History Research*, Lanham: AltaMira Press.

Collier, S.J. (2009) 'Topologies of power: Foucault's analysis of political government beyond "governmentality"', *Theory, Culture & Society*, 26: 78–108.

Connell, R. (2020) *Southern Theory: The Global Dynamics of Knowledge in Social Science*, London: Routledge.

Coombes, A.E. (2003) *History after Apartheid: Visual Culture and Public Memory in a Democratic South Africa*, Durham: Duke University Press.

Copeland, T. (2018) 'To keep this disease from killing you: cultural competence, consonance, and health among HIV-positive women in Kenya', *Medical Anthropology Quarterly*, 32: 272–92.

Corbridge, S. (2005) *Seeing the State: Governance and Governmentality in India*, Cambridge: Cambridge University Press.

Corbridge, S. (2010) 'The political economy of development in India since independence', in P. Brass (ed) *Routledge Handbook of South Asian Politics*, London: Routledge, pp 305–20.

Corbridge, S. (2018) 'Economic growth and poverty reduction in contemporary India', in G.L. Clark, M. Feldman, M.S. Gertler and D. Wójcik (eds) *The New Oxford Handbook of Economic Geography*, Oxford: Oxford University Press, pp 97–112.

Cornwall, A. (1997) 'Men, masculinity and "gender in development"', *Gender and Development*, 5: 8–13.

Cornwall, A. (2002) 'Body mapping: bridging the gap between biomedical messages, popular knowledge and lived experience', in A. Cornwall and A. Welbourne (eds) *Realizing Rights: Transforming Approaches to Sexual and Reproductive Well-being*, London: Zed Books, pp 219–31.

Cornwall, A. (2020) 'Decolonizing development studies: pedagogic reflections', in D. Bendix, F. Müller and A. Ziai (eds) *Beyond the Master's Tools: Decolonizing Knowledge Orders, Research Methods and Teaching*, Lanham: Rowman & Littlefield, pp 191–204.

Cornwall, A. and Lindisfarne, N. (2004) *Dislocating Masculinity: Comparative Ethnographies*, London: Routledge.

Cornwall, A. and Shankland, A. (2008) 'Engaging citizens: lessons from building Brazil's national health system', *Social Science & Medicine*, 66: 2173–84.

Cornwall, A., Harrison, E. and Whitehead, A. (2007) 'Gender myths and feminist fables: the struggle for interpretive power in gender and development', *Development and Change*, 38: 1–20.

Cornwall, A., Robins, S. and von Lieres, B. (2011) 'States of citizenship: contexts and cultures of public engagement and citizen action', IDS Working Papers, 1–32.

Correa, C.M. (2022) 'Interpreting the flexibilities under the TRIPS agreement', in C.M. Correa and R.M. Hilty (eds) *Access to Medicines and Vaccines*, Cham: Springer, pp 1–30.

Costa, A.B., Fontanari, A.M.V., Catelan, R.F., Schwarz, K., Stucky, J.L., Da Rosa Filho, H.T. et al (2018) 'HIV-related healthcare needs and access barriers for Brazilian transgender and gender diverse people', *AIDS and Behavior*, 22: 2534–42.

Costa, A.H.C. and Gonçalves, T.R. (2021) 'Pharmaceutical globalization and biological citizenship: notes on the implementation of post-exposure prophylaxis in the State of Rio Grande do Sul, Brazil', *Cadernos de Saúde Pública*, 37(1): 1–11.

Cousins, T. (2016) 'Antiretroviral therapy and nutrition in Southern Africa: citizenship and the grammar of hunger', *Medical Anthropology*, 35: 433–46.

Crenshaw, K. (1993) 'Beyond racism and misogyny: Black feminism and 2 Live Crew', in D.T. Meyers (ed) *Feminist Social Thought: A Reader*, New York: Routledge, pp 245–63.

Crenshaw, K. (1997) 'Mapping the margins: intersectionality, identity politics, and violence against women of color', in K. Maschke (ed) *The Legal Response to Violence against Women 5*, New York: Routledge, pp 1241–299.

Crenshaw, K. (2017) *On Intersectionality: Essential Writings*, New York: New Press.

Crewe, M. (2000) 'South Africa: touched by the vengeance of AIDS 1; responses to the South African epidemic', *South African Journal of International Affairs*, 7: 23–37.

Davies, D. (2017) ' "Walls of freedom": street art and structural violence in the global city', *Rupkatha Journal on Interdisciplinary Studies in Humanities*, 9: 6–18.

De Beer, J., Baarbé, J. and Ncube, C. (2018) 'International law, Africa, intellectual property (IP), treaty ratification, development, data visualisation, WIPO, WTO, trade, harmonisation', *The African Journal of Information and Communication*, 2: 53–82.

De Certeau, M. (1984) *The Practice of Everyday Life*, Berkeley: University of California Press.

De Lay, P.R., Benzaken, A., Karim, Q.A., Aliyu, S., Amole, C., Ayala, G. et al (2021) 'Ending AIDS as a public health threat by 2030: time to reset targets for 2025', *PLoS Medicine*, 18: 1–5.

De Paoli, M.M., Grønningsæter, A.B. and Mills, E. (2010) 'HIV/AIDS, the disability grant and ARV adherence', Summary report FAFO, Oslo.

De Paoli, M.M., Mills, E.A. and Grønningsæter, A.B. (2012) 'The ARV roll out and the disability grant: a South African dilemma?', *Journal of the International AIDS Society*, 15: 1–10.

Decoteau, C. (2013) *Ancestors and Antiretrovirals: The Biopolitics of HIV/AIDS in South Africa*, Chicago: University of Chicago Press.

Delaet, D.L. and Mills, E. (2018) 'Discursive silence as a global response to sexual violence: from Title IX to truth commissions', *Global Society*, 32: 496–519.

Defend our Democracy (2022) 'Declaration of the Conference for Democratic Renewal and Change'. Available from: https://defendourde mocracy.co.za/wp-content/uploads/2022/07/Final-declaration-DODCon ference-for-Democratic-Renewal-and-Change.docx.pdf [Accessed 05 July 2022].

Devisch, R. and Nyamnjoh, F.B. (2011) *The Postcolonial Turn*, Leiden: African Books Collective.

Diggins, J. (2013) 'Plantain Island sirens: love and fish in coastal Sierra Leone', PhD dissertation, University of Sussex, Brighton.

Diggins, J. (2018) *Coastal Sierra Leone: Materiality and the Unseen in Maritime West Africa*, Cambridge: Cambridge University Press.

Diseko, L. (2022) 'South Africans in nationwide strike in protest against cost of living', BBC, 24 August. Available from: https://www.bbc.co.uk/news/world-africa-62659893 [Accessed 11 November 2022].

Donohue, D. and Bornman, J. (2014) 'The challenges of realising inclusive education in South Africa', *South African Journal of Education*, 34: 1–14.

Dorrington, R., Johnson, L., Bradshaw, D. and Daniel, T. (2006) 'The demographic impact of HIV/AIDS in South Africa: national and provincial indicators for 2006', Cape Town: Centre for Actuarial Research, South African Medical Research Council. Available from: http://media.witht ank.com/d9a6c65e76/demographic_impact_hiv_indicators.pdf [Accessed 07 June 2012].

Douglas, M. (2003) *Purity and Danger: An Analysis of Concepts of Pollution and Taboo*, London: Routledge.

Drerup, J. (2020) 'Global citizenship education, global educational injustice and the postcolonial critique', *Global Justice: Theory Practice Rhetoric*, 12: 27–54.

Duby, Z., Nkosi, B., Scheibe, A., Brown, B. and Bekker, L.-G. (2018) ' "Scared of going to the clinic": contextualising healthcare access for men who have sex with men, female sex workers and people who use drugs in two South African cities', *Southern African Journal of HIV Medicine*, 19: 1–8.

Duggan, N., Hooijmaaijers, B., Rewizorski, M. and Arapova, E. (2022) 'Introduction: the BRICS, global governance, and challenges for South–South cooperation in a post-Western world', *International Political Science Review*, 43: 469–80.

Dumbrava, C. (2017) 'Citizenship and technology', in A. Shachar, R. Bauböck, I. Bloemraad and M.P. Vink (eds) *The Oxford Handbook of Citizenship*, New York: Oxford University Press, pp 767–88.

Dunkle, K.L., Jewkes, R., Nduna, M., Jama, N., Levin, J., Sikweyiya, Y. et al (2007) 'Transactional sex with casual and main partners among young South African men in the rural Eastern Cape: prevalence, predictors, and associations with gender-based violence', *Social Science & Medicine*, 65: 1235–48.

Dvory-Sobol, H., Shaik, N., Callebaut, C. and Rhee, M.S. (2022) 'Lenacapavir: a first-in-class HIV-1 capsid inhibitor', *Current Opinion in HIV and AIDS*, 17: 15–21.

Dzingirai, V., Mutopo, P. and Landau, L.B. (2014) 'Confirmations, coffins and corn: kinship, social networks and remittances from South Africa to Zimbabwe'. Migrating out of Poverty Research Consortium. Working Paper 18. Available from: http://www.migratingoutofpoverty.org/files/file.php?name=wp18-dzingerai--mutopo-landau-2014-confirmations-coff ins--corn-final.pdf&site=354 [Accessed 18 August 2021].

Dziuban, A. and Sekuler, T. (2021) 'The temporal regimes of HIV/AIDS activism in Europe: chrono-citizenship, biomedicine and its others', *Critical Public Health*, 31: 5–16.

Edwards, C. and Fernández, E. (2017) 'Analysing health and health policy: introducing the governmentality turn', in C. Edwards and E. Fernandez (eds) *Reframing Health and Health Policy in Ireland*, Manchester: Manchester University Press, pp 1–22.

Eimer, T. and Lütz, S. (2010) 'Developmental states, civil society, and public health: patent regulation for HIV/AIDS pharmaceuticals in India and Brazil', *Regulation & Governance*, 4: 135–53.

Epstein, D. and Morrell, R. (2012) 'Approaching Southern theory: explorations of gender in South African education', *Gender and Education*, 24: 469–82.

Epstein, S. (1996) *Impure Science: AIDS, Activism and the Politics of Knowledge*, Berkeley: University of California Press.

Erlenbusch-Anderson, V. (2020) 'The beginning of a study of biopower: Foucault's 1978 lectures at the Collège de France', *Foucault Studies Lectures*, 3(1): 5–26.

Falzon, M.-A. (ed) (2016) *Multi-sited Ethnography: Theory, Praxis and Locality in Contemporary Research*, Abingdon: Routledge.

Farmer, P. (2005) *Pathologies of Power: Health, Human Rights, and the New War on the Poor*, Berkeley: University of California Press.

Fassin, D. (2007) *When Bodies Remember: Experiences and Politics of AIDS in South Africa*, Los Angeles: University of California Press.

Fassin, D. (2009) 'Another politics of life is possible', *Theory, Culture & Society*, 26: 44–60.

Fassin, D. (2013) 'A case for critical ethnography: rethinking the early years of the AIDS epidemic in South Africa', *Social Science & Medicine*, 99: 119–26.

Fassin, D. (2020) 'Epilogue: in search of global health', in J.-P. Gaudillière, C. Beaudevin, C. Gradmann, A.M. Lovell and L. Pordié (eds) *Global Health and the New World Order*, Manchester: Manchester University Press, pp 230–46.

Fassin, D. and Schneider, H. (2003) 'The politics of AIDS in South Africa: beyond the controversies', *BMJ*, 326: 495–7.

Ferguson, J. (2002) 'Spatializing states: toward an ethnography of neoliberal governmentality', *American Ethnologist*, 29: 981–1002.

Ferlie, E., Mcgivern, G. and FitzGerald, L. (2012) 'A new mode of organizing in health care? Governmentality and managed networks in cancer services in England', *Social Science and Medicine*, 74: 340–7.

Figueiredo Catelan, R., Azevedo, F.M.D., Sbicigo, J.B., Vilanova, F., Da Silva, L.P., Zanella, G.I. et al (2022) 'Anticipated HIV stigma and delays in HIV testing among Brazilian heterosexual male soldiers', *Psychology & Sexuality*, 13: 317–30.

Fineman, M.A. and Grear, A. (2016) 'Equality, autonomy, and the vulnerable subject in law and politics', in M. Fineman and A. Grear (eds) *Vulnerability: Reflections on a New Ethical Foundation for Law and Politics*, London: Routledge, pp 13–27.

Finn, B.M. (2021) 'The popular sovereignty continuum: civil and political society in contemporary South Africa', *Environment and Planning C: Politics and Space*, 39: 152–67.

Fischer, C. and Dolezal, L. (2018) *New Feminist Perspectives on Embodiment*, Cham: Springer.

Flämig, K., Decroo, T., van den Borne, B. and van de Pas, R. (2019) 'ART adherence clubs in the Western Cape of South Africa: what does the sustainability framework tell us? A scoping literature review', *Journal of the International AIDS Society*, 22: e25235.

Flint, A., Günsche, M. and Burns, M. (2023) 'We are still here: living with HIV in the UK', *Medical Anthropology*, 42(1): 35–47.

Foks, F. (2018) 'Bronislaw Malinowski, "indirect rule," and the colonial politics of functionalist anthropology, ca. 1925–1940', *Comparative Studies in Society and History*, 60: 35–57.

Fomunyam, K.G. and Teferra, D. (2017) 'Curriculum responsiveness within the context of decolonisation in South African higher education', *Perspectives in Education*, 35(2): 196–207.

Foucault, M. (1978) *The History of Sexuality, Vol. 1*, New York: Pantheon.

Foucault, M. (1991) 'Governmentality', in G. Burchell, C. Gordon and P. Miller (eds) *The Foucault Effect: Studies in Governmentality*, Chicago: University of Chicago Press, pp 87–104.

Foucault, M. (1998) 'Technologies of the self', in L. Martin (ed) *Technologies of the Self*, Amherst: University of Massachusetts Press, pp 16–49.

Foucault, M. (2008) *The Birth of Biopolitics: Lectures at the Collège de France 1978–1979*, New York: Palgrave Macmillan.

Fox, N.J. and Alldred, P. (2020a) 'Climate change, economics and the policy-assemblage: four policies and a materialist synthesis', *Globalizations*, 18: 1248–58.

Fox, N.J. and Alldred, P. (2020b) 'Re-assembling climate change policy: materialism, posthumanism, and the policy assemblage', *The British Journal of Sociology*, 71: 269–83.

Fullagar, S. and Pavlidis, A. (2021) 'Thinking through the disruptive effects and affects of the coronavirus with feminist new materialism', *Leisure Sciences*, 43: 152–9.

Fúnez-Flores, J.I. (2022) 'Decolonial and ontological challenges in social and anthropological theory', *Theory, Culture & Society*, 39(6): 21–41.

Gabble, R. and Kohler, J.C. (2014) 'To patent or not to patent? The case of Novartis' cancer drug Glivec in India', *Globalization and Health*, 10: 1–6.

Gaitho, W. (2021) 'Curing corrective rape: socio-legal perspectives on sexual violence against Black lesbians in South Africa', *William & Mary Journal of Race, Gender and Social Justice*, 28: 329–62.

Galvao, J. (2005) 'Brazil and access to HIV/AIDS drugs: a question of human rights and public health', *American Journal of Public Health*, 7: 1110–16.

Garagancea, L. (2021) 'Access to medicines: the interplay between parallel imports, compulsory licensing, and voluntary licensing', *European Pharmaceutical Law Review*, 5: 37–56.

Garcia, A. (2010) *The Pastoral Clinic: Addiction and Dispossession along the Rio Grande*, Berkeley: University of California Press.

Geertz, C. (2001) *Available Light: Anthropological Reflections on Philosophical Topics*, Princeton: Princeton University Press.

Geffen, N. (2005) 'Echoes of Lysenko: state-sponsored pseudo-science in South Africa', *Social Dynamics*, 31: 182–210.

Geffen, N. (2010) *Debunking Delusions: The Inside Story of the Treatment Action Campaign*, Auckland Park: Jacana Media.

Gevisser, M. (2008) *Thabo Mbeki: The Dream Deferred*, Cape Town: Jonathan Ball Publishers.

Giddens, A. (1990) *The Consequences of Modernity*, Cambridge: Cambridge University Press.

Gittings, L., Colvin, C.J. and Hodes, R. (2022) 'Blood and blood: anti-retroviral therapy, masculinity, and redemption among adolescent boys in the Eastern Cape Province of South Africa', *Medical Anthropology Quarterly*, 36: 367–90.

Gleeson, D., Lexchin, J., Lopert, R. and Kilic, B. (2018) 'The Trans Pacific Partnership Agreement, intellectual property and medicines: differential outcomes for developed and developing countries', *Global Social Policy*, 18: 7–27.

Gobodo-Madikizela, P. with Ross, F. and Mills, E. (2005) Women's Contributions to South Africa's Truth and Reconciliation Commission. Women Waging Peace Policy Commission. Available at https://inclsvescurity.wpenginepowered.com/wp-content/uploads/2012/08/11_women_s_contributions_to_south_africa_s_truth_and_reconcilliation_commission.pdf [Accessed 17 September 2020].

Gomes, S.D.S.R. and Tanscheit, T.S.T. (2022) 'Authoritarian neoliberalism and gender based violence: notes on the COVID-19 pandemic in Brazil', *Interdisciplinary Perspectives on Equality and Diversity*, 7: 122–40.

Gómez, E.J. and Harris, J. (2016) 'Political repression, civil society and the politics of responding to AIDS in the BRICS nations', *Health Policy and Planning*, 31: 56–66.

Grimshaw, A., Owen, E. and Ravetz, A. (2021) 'Making do: the materials of art and anthropology', in A. Schneider and C. Wright (eds) *Between Art and Anthropology: Contemporary Ethnographic Practice*, London: Routledge, pp 147–62.

Grinsztejn, B., Hughes, M.D., Ritz, J., Salata, R., Mugyenyi, P., Hogg et al (2019) 'Third-line antiretroviral therapy in low-income and middle-income countries (ACTG A5288): a prospective strategy study', *The Lancet HIV*, 6: e588–e600.

Groes-Green, C. (2014) 'Journeys of patronage: moral economies of transactional sex, kinship, and female migration from Mozambique to Europe', *Journal of the Royal Anthropological Institute*, 20: 237–55.

Grugel, J. and Uhlin, A. (2012) 'Renewing global governance: demanding rights and justice in the Global South', *Third World Quarterly*, 33: 1703–18.

Gubrium, A. and Harper, K. (2016) *Participatory Visual and Digital Methods*, London: Routledge.

Guerin, P.J., Singh-Phulgenda, S. and Strub-Wourgaft, N. (2020) 'The consequence of COVID-19 on the global supply of medical products: Why Indian generics matter for the world?', *F1000Research*, 9: 1–11.

Gupta, A., Juneja, S., Vitoria, M., Habiyambere, V., Nguimfack, B.D., Doherty, M. et al (2016) 'Projected uptake of new antiretroviral (ARV) medicines in adults in low- and middle-income countries: a forecast analysis 2015–2025', *PLoS One*, 11: e0164619.

Hacking, I. (1990) *The Taming of Chance*, Cambridge: Cambridge University Press.

Hall, A. (2006) 'From Fome Zero to Bolsa Família: social policies and poverty alleviation under Lula', *Journal of Latin American Studies*, 38: 689–709.

Hall, A. (2008) 'Brazil's Bolsa Família: a double-edged sword?', *Development and Change*, 39: 799–822.

Hamers, R.L., De Wit, T.F.R. and Holmes, C.B. (2018) 'HIV drug resistance in low-income and middle-income countries', *The Lancet HIV*, 5: e588–e596.

Han, C. (2018) 'Precarity, precariousness, and vulnerability', *Annual Review of Anthropology*, 47: 331–43.

Hankivsky, O., Grace, D., Hunting, G., Giesbrecht, M., Fridkin, A., Rudrum, S. et al (2014) 'An intersectionality-based policy analysis framework: critical reflections on a methodology for advancing equity', *International Journal for Equity in Health*, 13: 1–16.

Haraway, D. (1991) 'Situated knowledges: The science question in feminism and the privilege of partial knowledge' in J. Agnew, D.N. Livingstone and A. Rodgers (eds) *Human Geography: An Essential Anthology*. Maldon: Blackwell, pp 108–28.

Haraway, D. (2006) 'A cyborg manifesto: science, technology, and socialist-feminism in the late 20th century', in J. Weiss, J. Nolan, J. Hunsinger and P. Trifonas (eds) *The International Handbook of Virtual Learning Environments*, Dordrecht: Springer, pp 117–58.

Haraway, D. (2013) *When Species Meet*, Minneapolis: University of Minnesota Press.

Harker, R., Mahar, C. and Wilkes, C. (eds) (2016) *An Introduction to the Work of Pierre Bourdieu: The Practice of Theory*, London: Palgrave MacMillan.

Harris, B., Eyles, J. and Goudge, J. (2016) 'Ways of doing: restorative practices, governmentality, and provider conduct in post-apartheid health care', *Medical Anthropology*, 35: 572–87.

Harrison, A., Colvin, C.J., Kuo, C., Swartz, A. and Lurie, M. (2015) 'Sustained high HIV incidence in young women in Southern Africa: social, behavioral, and structural factors and emerging intervention approaches', *Current HIV/AIDS Reports*, 12: 207–15.

Hassim, S. (2014) 'Violent modernity: gender, race and bodies in contemporary South African politics', *Politikon*, 41: 167–82.

Hawari, Y., Plonski, S. and Weizman, E. (2019) 'Seeing Israel through Palestine: knowledge production as anti-colonial praxis', *Settler Colonial Studies*, 9: 155–75.

Herzfeld, M. (2010) 'Purity and power: anthropology from colonialism to the global hierarchy of value', *Reviews in Anthropology*, 39: 288–312.

Heywood, M. (2003) 'Preventing mother-to-child HIV transmission in South Africa: background strategies and outcomes of the Treatment Action Campaign case against the Minister of Health', *South African Journal on Human Rights*, 19: 278–315.

Heywood, M. and Cornell, M. (1998) 'Human rights and AIDS in South Africa: from right margin to left margin', *Health and Human Rights*, 2(4): 60–82.

Hill, J.E. (2014) 'Changes to intellectual property policy in South Africa: putting a stop to evergreening?', *Expert Opinion on Therapeutic Patents*, 24(8): 839–43.

Hinton, P. (2014) ' "Situated knowledges" and new materialism(s): rethinking a politics of location', *Women: A Cultural Review*, 25: 99–113.

Hjorth, L., Horst, H., Galloway, A. and Bell, G. (eds) (2017) *The Routledge Companion to Digital Ethnography*, New York: Routledge.

Hodes, R. (2007) 'HIV/AIDS in South African documentary film, c. 1990–2000', *Journal of Southern African Studies*, 33: 153–71.

Hodes, R. (2018) 'HIV/AIDS in South Africa', *Oxford Research Encyclopedia of African History*. Available from: https://doi.org/10.1093/acrefore/978019 0277734.013.299 [Accessed 25 October 2020].

Hopewell, K. (2017) 'The BRICS: merely a fable? Emerging power alliances in global trade governance', *International Affairs*, 93: 1377–96.

Hörbst, V. and Wolf, A. (2014) 'ARVs and ARTs: medicoscapes and the unequal place-making for biomedical treatments in sub-Saharan Africa', *Medical Anthropology Quarterly*, 28: 182–202.

Horner, R. (2014) 'The impact of patents on innovation, technology transfer and health: a pre-and post-TRIPs analysis of India's pharmaceutical industry', *New Political Economy*, 19: 384–406.

Horst, C. (2016) 'Expanding sites: the question of "depth" explored', in M.-A. Falzon (ed) *Multi-sited Ethnography*, London: Routledge, pp 119–33.

Horst, C. (2018) 'Making a difference in Mogadishu? Experiences of multi-sited embeddedness among diaspora youth', *Journal of Ethnic and Migration Studies*, 44: 1341–56.

Howard-Merrill, L., Wamoyi, J., Nyato, D., Kyegombe, N., Heise, L. and Buller, A.M. (2022) ' "I trap her with a CD, then tomorrow find her with a big old man who bought her a smart phone": constructions of masculinities and transactional sex; a qualitative study from north-western Tanzania', *Culture, Health & Sexuality*, 24: 254–67.

HSRC (2023) *New HIV Survey Highlights Progress and Ongoing Disparities in South Africa's HIV Epidemic*. Press Briefing, Human Sciences Research Council. Available at https://hsrc.ac.za/press-releases/sabssm/new-hiv-survey-highlights-progress-and-ongoing-disparities-in-south-africas-hiv-epidemic/#:~:text=SABSSM%20VI%20found%20that%20the,in%20 2017to%2012.7%25%20in%202022 [Accessed 8 December 2023].

Huang, Z. (2022) 'Overview of "WTO-extra Rules and WTO-plus Rules" ', *Frontiers in Business, Economics and Management*, 4(2): 16–18.

Hyland, M. (2020) 'Compulsory licensing for patented medicines: a comparative legal analysis of India, Brazil and Thailand', *Manchester Journal of International Economic Law*, 17: 252–73.

Iamamoto, S.A., Mano, M.K. and Summa, R. (2021) 'Brazilian far-right neoliberal nationalism: family, anti-communism and the myth of racial democracy', *Globalizations*, 20: 782–98.

Ibrahim, A. (2022) *Historical Imagination and Cultural Responses to Colonialism and Nationalism*, Petaling Jaya: Strategic Information and Research Development Centre.

India (2021) 'India HIV estimates 2021', in New Delhi: NACO.

Ingle, K. and Mlatsheni, C. (2017) 'The extent of churn in the South African youth labour market: evidence from NIDS 2008–2015'. Cape Town: SALDRU, UCT. (SALDRU Working Paper Number 201/ NIDS Discussion Paper 2016/17). Available from: https://opensaldru.uct.ac.za/ handle/11090/884?show=full [Accessed 12 November 2021].

Iqbal, J.M. (2009) 'AIDS and the state: a comparison of Brazil, India and South Africa', *South Asian Survey*, 16: 119–35.

Islam, M., Kaplan, W.A., Trachtenberg, D., Thrasher, R., Gallagher, K.P. and Wirtz, V.J. (2019) 'Impacts of intellectual property provisions in trade treaties on access to medicine in low and middle income countries: a systematic review', *Globalization and Health*, 15: 1–14.

Issar, S. (2021) 'Theorising "racial/colonial primitive accumulation": settler colonialism, slavery and racial capitalism', *Race & Class*, 63: 23–50.

Itano, N. (2007) *No Place Left to Bury the Dead: Denial, Despair and Hope in the African AIDS Pandemic*, New York: Atria Books.

ITPC (2022) 'The problem with patents: access to affordable HIV treatment in middle-income countries', Brighton: Frontline AIDS.

Jacques-Aviñó, C., Garcia de Olalla, P., Gonzalez Antelo, A., Fernandez Quevedo, M., Romaní, O. and Caylà, J.A. (2019) 'The theory of masculinity in studies on HIV: a systematic review', *Global Public Health*, 14: 601–20.

Jamar, A. (2022) 'Accounting for which violent past? Transitional justice, epistemic violence, and colonial durabilities in Burundi', *Critical African Studies*, 14: 73–95.

Jasanoff, S. (2005) *Designs on Nature: Science and Democracy in Europe and United States*, Princeton: Princeton University Press.

Jasanoff, S. (2019) 'Future-making as a mode of governance', Public Lecture at the Max Planck Institute for the Study of Societies, 2019.

Jayaraman, K. (2013) 'India flouts patent for blockbuster biologic', *Nature Biotechnology*, 31(9), Available from: https://doi.org/10.1038/nbt0113-9 [Accessed 25 August 2021].

Jennings, L., Kellermann, T., Spinelli, M., Nkantsu, Z., Cogill, D., van Schalkwyk, M. et al (2022) 'Drug resistance, rather than low tenofovir levels in blood or urine, is associated with tenofovir, emtricitabine, and efavirenz failure in resource-limited settings', *AIDS Research and Human Retroviruses*, 38: 455–62.

Jewkes, R.K., Sikweyiya, Y., Morrell, R. and Dunkle, K. (2009) 'Understanding men's health and use of violence: interface of rape and HIV in South Africa', MRC Policy Brief. Accessible from: https://www.samrc.ac.za/policy-briefs/understanding-mens-health-and-use-violence-interface-rape-and-hiv-south-africa [Accessed 07 July 2010].

Jobson, R.C. (2020) 'The case for letting anthropology burn: sociocultural anthropology in 2019', *American Anthropologist*, 122: 259–71.

Johnson, L.F. (2012) 'Access to antiretroviral treatment in South Africa, 2004–2011', *Southern African Journal of HIV Medicine*, 13: 19–26.

Johnson, L.F. and Dorrington, R.E. (2023) 'Modelling the impact of HIV in South Africa's provinces: 2023 update', Centre for Infectious Disease Epidemiology and Research working paper, Cape Town: Centre for Infectious Disease Epidemiology and Research.

Johnson, L.F., Mossong, J., Dorrington, R.E., Schomaker, M., Hoffmann, C.J., Keiser, O. et al (2013) 'Life expectancies of South African adults starting antiretroviral treatment: collaborative analysis of cohort studies', *PLoS Medicine*, 10: e1001418.

Joshi, D.K. (2021) 'Neo-authoritarianism in India under Narendra Modi: growing force or critical discourse?', in S. Widmalm (ed) *Routledge Handbook of Autocratization in South Asia*, London: Routledge, pp 23–44.

Jungar, K. and Oinas, E. (2010) 'A feminist struggle? South African HIV activism as feminist politics', *Journal of International Women's Studies*, 11: 177–91.

Kagee, A., Coetzee, B., Toit, S.D. and Loades, M. (2019) 'Psychosocial predictors of quality of life among South Africa adolescents receiving antiretroviral therapy', *Quality of Life Research*, 28: 57–65.

Kalichman, S.C. and El-Krab, R. (2021) 'Social and behavioral impacts of COVID-19 on people living with HIV: review of the first year of research', *Current HIV/AIDS Reports*, 19: 54–75.

Kalichman, S., Mathews, C., El-Krab, R., Banas, E. and Kalichman, M. (2021) 'Forgoing antiretroviral therapy to evade stigma among people living with HIV, Cape Town, South Africa', *Journal of Behavioral Medicine*, 44: 653–61.

Kalofonos, I. (2008) '"All I eat is ARVs": living with HIV/AIDS at the dawn of the treatment era in central Mozambique', PhD dissertation, University of California – San Francisco.

Kalofonos, I. (2021) *All I Eat Is Medicine: Going Hungry in Mozambique's AIDS Economy*, Berkeley: University of California Press.

Kalra, A. and Siddiqui, Z. (2015) 'Funding crisis puts India's AIDS programme and lives at risk', Reuters, 24 July.

Kapp, C. (2006) 'South Africans hope for a new era in HIV/AIDS policies', *The Lancet*, 368: 1759–60.

Kamiike, A. (2020) 'The TRIPS agreement and the pharmaceutical industry in India', *Journal of Interdisciplinary Economics*, 32(1): 95–113.

Katoto, P.D., Parker, S., Coulson, N., Pillay, N., Cooper, S., Jaca, A. et al (2022) 'Predictors of COVID-19 vaccine hesitancy in South African local communities: the VaxScenes study', *Vaccines*, 10 (353): 1–23.

Kavanagh, M.M., Cohn, J., Mabote, L., Meier, B.M., Williams, B., Russell, A. et al (2015) 'Evolving human rights and the science of antiretroviral medicine', *Health and Human Rights Journal*, 17: 76–90.

Kerr, L., Kendall, C., Guimarães, M.D.C., Mota, R.S., Veras, M.A., Dourado, I. et al (2018) 'HIV prevalence among men who have sex with men in Brazil: results of the 2nd national survey using respondent-driven sampling', *Medicine*, 97: S9–S15.

Khambule, I. (2020) 'The effects of COVID-19 on the South African informal economy: limits and pitfalls of government's response', *Loyola Journal of Social Sciences*, 34: 95–109.

Kim, J.C. and Watts, C.H. (2005) 'Gaining a foothold: tackling poverty, gender inequality, and HIV in Africa', *BMJ*, 331: 769–72.

Kim, J.Y. (2013) 'Statement on a memorandum of understanding signing on knowledge and innovation initiative in Brazil', in the World Bank. Accessible from: https://documents1.worldbank.org/curated/en/569 291467991975584/101862-WP-Box393267B-PUBLIC-2013-03-05-JK-Statement-on-a-Memorandum-of-Understanding-Signing-on-Knowledge-and-Innovation-Initiative-in-Brazil.docx [Accessed 08 July 2021].

King, B., Burka, M. and Winchester, M.S. (2018) 'HIV citizenship in uneven landscapes', *Annals of the American Association of Geographers*, 108: 1685–99.

Klazinga, L., Artz, L. and Müller, A. (2020) 'Sexual and gender-based violence and HIV in South Africa: an HIV facility-based study', *South African Medical Journal*, 110: 377–81.

Kloos, S. (2020) 'Humanitarianism from below: Sowa Rigpa, the traditional pharmaceutical industry, and global health', *Medical Anthropology*, 39: 167–81.

Köhler-Suzuki, N. (2021) 'Determinants and impediments of the EU–India Bilateral Trade and Investment Agreement: the proof of this old pudding is in the eating', in P. Gieg, T. Lowinger, M. Pietzko, A. Zürn, U.S. Bava and G. Müller-Brandeck-Bocquet (eds) *EU–India Relations*, Cham: Springer, pp 151–84.

Konadu, K. (2008) 'Medicine and anthropology in twentieth century Africa: Akan medicine and encounters with (medical) anthropology', *African Studies Quarterly*, 10: 45–69.

Krizic, I. and Serrano, O. (2017) 'Exporting intellectual property rights to emerging countries: EU and US approaches compared', *European Foreign Affairs Review*, 22: 57–75.

Kruger-Swanepoel, G.E., Lubbe, M.S., Rakumakoe, D.M. and Vorster, M. (2022) 'Adherence and clinical outcomes of HIV patients switching to a fixed-dose combination regimen', *Southern African Journal of Infectious Diseases*, 37: 1– 9.

Kwenda, P., Benhura, M. and Mudiriza, G. (2020) 'Former homeland areas and unemployment in South Africa: a decomposition approach', IZA Discussion Papers. Bonn, Institute of Labor Economics (IZA). Accessible from: https://www.econstor.eu/handle/10419/215337 [Accessed 21 June 2021].

Lallemant, M., Jourdain, G., Le Coeur, S., Mary, J.Y., Ngo-Giang-Huong, N., Koetsawang, S. et al (2004) 'Single-dose perinatal nevirapine plus standard zidovudine to prevent mother-to-child transmission of HIV-1 in Thailand', *New England Journal of Medicine*, 351: 217–28.

Lambert, H. and McDonald, M. (2009) 'Introduction', in H. Lambert and M. McDonald (eds) *Social Bodies*, New York: Berghahn Books, pp 1–16.

Lancet (2022) 'Funding the future of the HIV response', *The Lancet Journal*, 9(9): E595.

Larsson, M. (2018) 'Constructions of safe sex: between desire and governmentality', in E. Björklund and M. Larsson (eds) *A Visual History of HIV/AIDS*, London: Routledge, pp 150–64.

Latour, B. (1988) *The Pasteurization of France*, Cambridge, MA: Harvard University Press.

Latour, B. (1993) *We Have Never Been Modern*, Cambridge, MA: Harvard University Press.

Latour, B. (2005) *Reassembling the Social: An Introduction to Actor-Network-Theory*, Oxford: Oxford University Press.

Law, J. (2009) 'Actor network theory and material semiotics', in B.S. Turner (ed) *The New Blackwell Companion to Social Theory*, Oxford: Blackwell, pp 141–58.

Le Marcis, F. (2012) 'Struggling with AIDS in South Africa: the space of the everyday as a field of recognition', *Medical Anthropology Quarterly*, 26: 486–502.

Le, V.A. (2022a) 'The Brazilian case study of compulsory licensing', in V.A. Lee, *Compulsory Patent Licensing and Access to Medicines: A Silver Bullet Approach to Public Health?*, Cham: Springer, pp 113–43.

Le, V.A. (2022b) 'International patent law and the pharmaceutical industry', in V.A. Lee, *Compulsory Patent Licensing and Access to Medicines: A Silver Bullet Approach to Public Health?*, Cham: Springer, pp 15–5.

Leach, M., Scoones, I. and Wynne, B. (2005) 'Introduction: science, citizenship and globalisation', in M. Leach, I. Scoones and B. Wynne (eds) *Science and Citizens: Globalisation and the Challenge of Engagements*, London: Zed Books, pp 3–14.

Leach, M., Bloom, G., Ely, A., Nightingale, P., Scoones, I., Shah, E. et al (2007) 'Understanding governance: pathways to sustainability', STEPS Working Paper 2. Accessible from: https://steps-centre.org/wp-content/uploads/final_steps_governance.pdf [Accessed 7 July 2010].

Leclerc-Madlala, S. (2003) 'Transactional sex and the pursuit of modernity', *Social Dynamics*, 29: 213–33.

Lee, R. (2019) 'Art, activism and the academy: productive tensions and the next generation of HIV/AIDS research in South Africa', *Journal of Southern African Studies*, 45: 113–19.

Leeds, T. (2020) 'The state schema: seeing politics through morality and capacity', *Qualitative Sociology*, 43: 543–64.

Lees, S. and Enria, L. (2020) 'Comparative ethnographies of medical research: materiality, social relations, citizenship and hope in Tanzania and Sierra Leone', *International Health*, 12: 575–83.

Lefebvre, H. (1991) *The Production of Space*, Oxford: Blackwell.

Lemanski, C. (2020) 'Infrastructural citizenship: the everyday citizenships of adapting and/or destroying public infrastructure in Cape Town, South Africa', *Transactions of the Institute of British Geographers*, 45: 589–605.

Levenson, Z. (2021) 'Becoming a population: seeing the state, being seen by the state, and the politics of eviction in Cape Town', *Qualitative Sociology*, 44(1): 1–17.

Levinas, E. (1979) 'Ethics and the face', in E. Levinas, *Totality and Infinity*, Dordrecht: Springer, pp 194–216.

Lewis, D. (1973) 'Anthropology and colonialism', *Current Anthropology*, 14: 581–602.

Lewis, L., Kharsany, A.B., Humphries, H., Maughan-Brown, B., Beckett, S., Govender, K. et al (2022) 'HIV incidence and associated risk factors in adolescent girls and young women in South Africa: a population-based cohort study', *PLoS One*, 17: e0279289.

Li, J.Z., Stella, N., Choudhary, M.C., Javed, A., Rodriguez, K., Ribaudo, H. et al (2021) 'Impact of pre-existing drug resistance on risk of virological failure in South Africa', *Journal of Antimicrobial Chemotherapy*, 76: 1558–63.

Lock, M. (1993) 'Cultivating the body: anthropology and epistemologies of bodily practice and knowledge', *Annual Review of Anthropology*, 22: 133–55.

Lock, M. (2012) 'The epigenome and nature/nurture reunification: a challenge for anthropology', *Medical Anthropology*, 32: 291–308.

Lock, M. and Nguyen, V.-K. (2018) *An Anthropology of Biomedicine*, Oxford: Wiley-Blackwell.

Löfgren, H. (2017) *The Politics of the Pharmaceutical Industry and Access to Medicines: World Pharmacy and India*, Abingdon: Routledge.

Lupton, D. (2019) 'Toward a more-than-human analysis of digital health: inspirations from feminist new materialism', *Qualitative Health Research*, 29: 1998–2009.

Mabaso, M., Sokhela, Z., Mohlabane, N., Chibi, B., Zuma, K. and Simbayi, L. (2018) 'Determinants of HIV infection among adolescent girls and young women aged 15–24 years in South Africa: a 2012 population-based national household survey', *BMC Public Health*, 18: 1–7.

Mabaso, M., Makola, L., Naidoo, I., Mlangeni, L., Jooste, S. and Simbayi, L. (2019) 'HIV prevalence in South Africa through gender and racial lenses: results from the 2012 population-based national household survey', *International Journal for Equity in Health*, 18: 1–11.

MacGregor, H. (2009) 'Mapping the body: tracing the personal and the political dimensions of HIV/AIDS in Khayelitsha, South Africa', *Anthropology and Medicine*, 16: 85–95.

Mackworth-Young, C.R.S., Bond, V. and Wringe, A. (2020) 'Secrets and silence: agency of young women managing HIV disclosure', *Medical Anthropology*, 39: 720–34.

Macleod, A., Cameron, P., Ajjawi, R., Kits, O. and Tummons, J. (2019) 'Actor-network theory and ethnography: sociomaterial approaches to researching medical education', *Perspectives on Medical Education*, 8: 177–86.

Madiba, S. and Ngwenya, N. (2017) 'Cultural practices, gender inequality and inconsistent condom use increase vulnerability to HIV infection: narratives from married and cohabiting women in rural communities in Mpumalanga province, South Africa', *Global Health Action*, 10: 55–62.

Madlala-Routledge, N. and the Treatment Action Campaign, (2007) 'The unjustifiable firing of Nozizwe Madlala-Routledge', *Lancet*, 369: 815–16.

Maldonado, L. and Olivo, V. (2022) 'Is Venezuela still an upper-middle-income country? estimating the GNI per capita for 2015–2021', *Inter-American Development Bank*. December 2022, pp 1–28.

Mahadea, D. and Kaseeram, I. (2018) 'Impact of unemployment and income on entrepreneurship in post-apartheid South Africa: 1994–2015', *The Southern African Journal of Entrepreneurship and Small Business Management*, 10: 1–9.

Maingi, M., Stark, A.H. and Iron-Segev, S. (2022) 'The impact of option B+ on mother to child transmission of HIV in Africa: a systematic review', *Tropical Medicine and International Health*, 27(6): 553–63.

Makama, R., Helman, R., Titi, N. and Day, S. (2019) 'The danger of a single feminist narrative: African-centred decolonial feminism for Black men', *Agenda*, 33: 61–9.

Makhubu, N. (2013) 'Open debate: ephemeral democracies; interrogating commonality in South Africa', *Third Text*, 27: 415–18.

Makhubu, N. (2017) 'Changing the city after our heart's desire: creative protest in Cape Town', *Journal of Postcolonial Writing*, 53: 686–99.

Makino, K. and Shigetomi, S. (2009) 'Institutional conditions for social movements to engage in formal politics: the case of AIDS activism in post-apartheid South Africa', in S. Shigetomi and K. Makino (eds) *Protests and Social Movements in the Developing World*, Cheltenham: Edward Elgar, pp 110–27.

Malhotra, P. (2008) 'The impact of TRIPS on innovation and exports: a case study of the pharmaceutical industry in India', *Indian Journal of Medical Ethics*, 5: 61–5.

Mampane, J.N. (2018) 'Exploring the "blesser and blessee" phenomenon: young women, transactional sex, and HIV in rural South Africa', *Sage Open*, 8: 1–9.

Marcus, G.E. (2012) 'Multi-sited ethnography', in S. Coleman and P. von Hellermann (eds) *Multi-sited Ethnography: Problems and Possibilities in the Translocation of Research Methods*, New York: Routledge, pp 16–32.

Marcus, G.E. (2021) 'Affinities: fieldwork in anthropology today and the ethnographic in artwork', in A. Schneider and C. Wright (eds) *Between Art and Anthropology*, London: Routledge, pp 83–94.

Marelli, L., Kieslich, K. and Geiger, S. (2022) 'COVID-19 and techno-solutionism: responsibilization without contextualization?', *Critical Public Health*, 1: 1–14.

Marino, E.K. and Faas, A. (2020) 'Is vulnerability an outdated concept? After subjects and spaces', *Annals of Anthropological Practice*, 44: 33–46.

Marino, S. (2020) 'Multi-sited ethnography and digital migration research: methods and challenges', in K. Schuster and S. Dunn (eds) *Routledge International Handbook of Research Methods in Digital Humanities*, London: Routledge, pp 76–90.

Marsland, R. (2012) '(Bio)sociality and HIV in Tanzania: finding a living to support a life', *Medical Anthropology Quarterly*, 26: 470–85.

Marsland, R. and Prince, R. (2012) 'What is life worth? Exploring biomedical interventions, survival, and the politics of life', *Medical Anthropology Quarterly*, 26: 453–69.

Martin, E. (1991) 'The egg and the sperm: how science has constructed a romance based on stereotypical male-female roles', *Signs: Journal of Women in Culture and Society*, 16: 485–501.

Martin, E. (1992) 'The end of the body?', *American Ethnologist*, 19: 121–40.

Martin, E. (1995) *Flexible Bodies*, Boston: Beacon Press.

Maskew, M., Jamieson, L., Mohomi, G., Long, L., Mongwenyana, C., Nyoni, C. et al (2018) 'Implementation of option B and a fixed-dose combination antiretroviral regimen for prevention of mother-to-child transmission of HIV in South Africa: a model of uptake and adherence to care', *PLoS One*, 13: e0201955.

Massey, D.B. (2005) *For Space*, London: SAGE.

Mattur, D. and Habiyambere, V. (2022) 'Variation in average unit prices (2020) of antiretroviral drugs in generic accessible low-and middle-income countries', *Journal of the International AIDS Society*, 2022(25): 50–2.

Mauchline, K. (2008) 'Official government justifications and public ARV provision: a comparison of Brazil, Thailand and South Africa', CSSR Working Paper Series.

Mauss, M. (2002) *The Gift: The Form and Reason for Exchange in Archaic Societies*. Oxford: Routledge.

Mbali, M. (2016) 'AIDS activism and the state in post-apartheid South Africa at twenty', in A. Pallotti and U. Engel (eds) *South Africa after Apartheid*, Leiden: Brill, pp 47–67.

Mbali, M. (2018) 'South African AIDS activism: lessons for high-impact global health advocacy', in R. Parker and J. García (eds) *Routledge Handbook on the Politics of Global Health*, London: Routledge, pp 33–43.

McAlister, M. (2021) 'Analyzing actants', *Diplomatic History*, 45: 532–7.

McAuliffe, C. (2012) 'Graffiti or street art? Negotiating the moral geographies of the creative city', *Journal of Urban Affairs*, 34: 189–206.

McKinnon, S., Gorman-Murray, A. and Dominey-Howes, D. (2017) 'Remembering an epidemic during a disaster: memories of HIV/AIDS, gay male identities and the experience of recent disasters in Australia and New Zealand', *Gender, Place & Culture*, 24: 52–63.

Medlock, J., Pandey, A., Parpia, A.S., Tang, A., Skrip, L.A. and Galvani, A.P. (2017) 'Effectiveness of UNAIDS targets and HIV vaccination across 127 countries', *Proceedings of the National Academy of Sciences*, 114: 4017–22.

Menezes, H.Z.D. (2018) 'South–South collaboration for an intellectual property rights flexibilities agenda', *Contexto Internacional*, 40: 117–38.

Merten, S., Kenter, E., Mckenzie, O., Musheke, M., Ntalasha, H. and Martin-Hilber, A. (2010) 'Patient-reported barriers and drivers of adherence to antiretrovirals in sub-Saharan Africa: a meta-ethnography', *Tropical Medicine & International Health*, 15: 16–33.

Michael, M. and Rosengarten, M. (2012) 'HIV, globalization and topology: of prepositions and propositions', *Theory, Culture & Society*, 29: 93–115.

Mignolo, W.D. (2011) 'Geopolitics of sensing and knowing: on (de) coloniality, border thinking and epistemic disobedience', *Postcolonial Studies*, 14: 273–83.

Mills, E. (2005) 'HIV illness meanings and collaborative healing strategies', *Social Dynamics*, 31: 126–60.

Mills, E. (2006) 'From the physical self to the social body: expression and effect of HIV-related stigma in South Africa', *Journal of Community and Applied Social Psychology*, 16: 498–503.

Mills, E. (2008) 'Swimming in confusion: a qualitative study of factors affecting uptake and adherence to antiretroviral treatment in South Africa', Centre for Social Science Research Working Paper, University of Cape Town.

Mills, E. (2016) ' "You have to raise a fist!": seeing and speaking to the state in South Africa', *IDS Bulletin*, 41(1): 69–81.

Mills, E. (2017) 'Biopolitical precarity in the permeable body: the social lives of people, viruses and their medicines', *Critical Public Health*, 27: 350–61.

Mills, E. (2018) 'At a crossroads: health and vulnerability in the era of HIV', in B.J. Steele and E. Heinze (eds) *Routledge Handbook of Ethics and International Relations*, London: Routledge, pp 37855–62391.

Mills, E. (2019) 'Art, vulnerability and HIV in post-apartheid South Africa', *Journal of Southern African Studies*, 45: 175–95.

Mishi, S., Anakpo, G., Matekenya, W. and Tshabalala, N. (2023) 'COVID-19 vaccine hesitancy and implications for economic recovery: evidence from Nelson Mandela Bay municipality in South Africa', *Vaccines*, 11(1339): 1–16.

Mize, M. (2020) 'Congratulations, you're having twins! But only one is a US citizen: how constitutional avoidance should be used to avoid discrimination against same-sex couples through the denial of birthright citizenship', *George Washington Law Review*, 88: 1014–41.

Mkhwanazi, N. (2016) 'Medical anthropology in Africa: the trouble with a single story', *Medical Anthropology*, 35: 193–202.

MMA (2019) 'Action against AbbVie: Money that could treat HIV patients "goes up in smoke" in Kiev' [online], Kyiv, Ukraine, Available from: https://makemedicinesaffordable.org/action-against-abbvie-money-that-could-treat-hiv-patients-goes-up-in-smoke-in-kiev [Accessed 17 October 2022].

Mojola, S.A., Angotti, N., Denardo, D., Schatz, E. and Xavier Gómez Olivé, F. (2020) 'The end of AIDS? HIV and the new landscape of illness in rural South Africa', *Global Public Health*, 17: 13–25.

Montenegro, L., Velasque, L., Legrand, S., Whetten, K., Rafael, R.D.M.R. and Malta, M. (2020) 'Public health, HIV care and prevention, human rights and democracy at a crossroad in Brazil', *AIDS and Behavior*, 24: 1–4.

Montgomery, C.M. (2015) ' "HIV has a woman's face": vaginal microbicides and a case of ambiguous failure', *Anthropology & Medicine*, 22: 250–62.

Morrell, R. (2016) 'Making southern theory? Gender researchers in South Africa', *Feminist Theory*, 17: 191–209.

Mottiar, S. and Dubula, V. (2020) 'Shifting consciousness and challenging power: women activists and the provision of HIV/AIDS services', *Law, Democracy and Development*, 24: 158–76.

Moyer, E. (2015) 'The anthropology of life after AIDS: epistemological continuities in the age of antiretroviral treatment', *Annual Review of Anthropology*, 44: 259–75.

MSF (2015) 'At EU-India Summit, India must defend its "pharmacy of the developing world"'. Press Release, 2016. Available at https://www.msf.org/eu-india-summit-india-must-defend-its-%E2%80%98pharmacy-developing-world%E2%80%99 [Accessed 16 January 2024].

MSF (2018a) 'Country takes landmark step for access to medicines' [online], Available from: https://www.msf.org/south-africa-country-takes-landmark-step-access-medicines [Accessed 01 November 2022].

MSF (2018b) 'Open letter to European Commissioner on EU India Free Trade Agreement and its impact on access to medicines' [online], Available from: https://msfaccess.org/open-letter-european-commissioner-eu-india-free-trade-agreement-and-its-impact-access-medicines [Accessed 01 November 2022].

MSF (2018c) 'Why we need to fix the patent laws in South Africa' [online], Available from: https://www.cansa.org.za/files/2015/06/Fix-Patent-Laws-Briefer.pdf [Accessed 01 November 2022].

MSF (2023) South Africa's patent system encourages profits over lives. Available from: https://www.msf.org.za/news-and-resources/press-release/south-africas-patent-system-encourages-profits-over-lives [Accessed 12 December 2023].

Msila, V. (2020) 'Basic education and decolonisation in South Africa: preparing schools for new challenges', in V. Msila (ed) *Developing Teaching and Learning in Africa: Decolonising Perspectives*, Stellenbosch: African Sun Media, pp 1–16.

Muchena, K.C. and Kalenga, R. (2021) 'Adherence to anti-retroviral therapy during COVID-19 pandemic among adolescents born HIV-positive', *HIV & AIDS Review: International Journal of HIV-Related Problems*, 20: 166–72.

Murray, L.R., Kerrigan, D. and Paiva, V.S. (2019) 'Rites of resistance: sex workers' fight to maintain rights and pleasure in the centre of the response to HIV in Brazil', *Global Public Health*, 14: 939–53.

Mushonga, R.H. and Dzingirai, V. (2022) '"Becoming a somebody": mobility, patronage and reconfiguration of transactional sexual relationships in postcolonial Africa', *Anthropology Southern Africa*, 45: 1–15.

Musyoki, H., Bhattacharjee, P., Sabin, K., Ngoksin, E., Wheeler, T. and Dallabetta, G. (2021) 'A decade and beyond: learnings from HIV programming with underserved and marginalized key populations in Kenya', *Journal of the International AIDS Society*, 24: 53–58.

Mutanga, M.B. and Abayomi, A. (2022) 'Tweeting on COVID-19 pandemic in South Africa: LDA-based topic modelling approach', *African Journal of Science, Technology, Innovation and Development*, 14: 163–72.

Myburgh, H., Meehan, S., Wademan, D., Osman, M., Hesseling, A. and Hoddinott, G. (2023) 'TB programme stakeholder views on lessons from the COVID-19 response in South Africa', *Public Health Action*, 13: 97–103.

Nadesan, M.H. (2010) *Governmentality, Biopower and Everyday Life*, New York: Routledge.

Naseemullah, A. (2023) 'The political economy of national development: A research agenda after neoliberal reform?', *World Development*, 168: 1–15.

Nattrass, N. (2004) *The Moral Economy of AIDS in South Africa*, Cambridge: Cambridge University Press.

Nattrass, N. (2007) *Mortal Combat: AIDS Denialism and the Struggle for Antiretrovirals in South Africa*, Scottsville: University of KwaZulu-Natal Press.

Nattrass, N. (2008) 'AIDS and the scientific governance of medicine in post-apartheid South Africa', *African Affairs*, 107: 157–76.

Nattrass, N. (2012) *AIDS Conspiracy: Science Fights Back*, New York: Columbia University Press.

Nedlund, A.-C. (2019) *Everyday Citizenship and People with Dementia*, Edinburgh: Dunedin Academic Press.

Nel, J., Wattrus, C., Osih, R., Meintjes, G. (2023) 'Southern African HIV clinicians society adult antiretroviral therapy guidelines: what's new?', *S Afr J HIV Med*, 24: 1–3.

Nguyen, V.-K. (2005) 'Antiretroviral globalism, biopolitics and therapeutic citizenship', in A. Ong and S.J. Collier (ed) *Global Assemblages: Technology, Politics and Ethics as Anthropological Problems*, Malden: Blackwell Publishing, pp 124–44.

Nguyen, V.-K. (2008) 'Antiretroviral globalism, biopolitics and therapeutic citizenship', in A. Ong and S.J. Collier (ed) *Global Assemblages: Technology, Politics and Ethics as Anthropological Problems*, Malden: Blackwell Publishing, pp 124–44.

Nguyen, V.-K. (2010) *The Republic of Therapy: Triage and Sovereignty in West Africa's Time of AIDS*, Durham: Duke University Press.

Nguyen, V.-K. (2011) 'Trial communities: HIV and therapeutic citizenship in West Africa', in W. Geissler and C. Molyneux (eds), *Evidence, Ethos and Experiment: The Anthropology and History of Medical Research in Africa*, New York: Berghahn Books, pp 429–44.

Nguyen, V.-K. (2019) 'Of what are epidemics the symptom? Speed, interlinkage, and infrastructure in molecular anthropology', in A.H. Kelly, F. Keck and C. Lynteris (eds) *The Anthropology of Epidemics*, London: Routledge, pp 154–77.

Nhemachena, A., Mlambo, N. and Kaundjua, M. (2016) 'The notion of the "field" and the practices of researching and writing Africa: towards decolonial praxis', *Africology: The Journal of Pan African Studies*, 9: 15–36.

Nonyana, J.Z. and Njuho, P.M. (2018) 'Modelling the length of time spent in an unemployment state in South Africa', *South African Journal of Science*, 114: 1–7.

Nunn, A., da Fonseca, E.M. and Gruskin, S. (2009a) 'Changing global essential medicines norms to improve access to AIDS treatment: lessons from Brazil', *Global Public Health*, 4: 131–49.

Nunn, A., da Fonseca, E.M., Bastos, F.I. and Gruskin, S. (2009b) 'AIDS treatment in Brazil: impacts and challenges', *Health Affairs*, 28: 1103–13.

Nunn, A., Dickman, S., Nattrass, N., Cornwall, A. and Gruskin, S. (2012) 'The impacts of AIDS movements on the policy responses to HIV/AIDS in Brazil and South Africa: a comparative analysis', *Global Public Health*, 7: 1031–44.

Nyamjoh, F. (2007) 'From bounded to flexible citizenship: lessons from Africa', *Citizenship Studies*, 11: 73–82.

Okie, S. (2006) 'Fighting HIV: lessons from Brazil', *The New England Journal of Medicine*, 354(19): 1977–81.

Okyere-Manu, B.D., Ssebunya, M. and Chirongoma, S. (2022) 'When survival precedes faith: decolonial perspectives on the ethical dilemma confronting female Christian sex workers in Africa', in L. McGrow (ed) *Religious Responses to Sex Work and Sex Trafficking*, London: Routledge, pp 155–73.

Oliveira, C.M.D., Bonfim, C.V.D., Guimarães, M.J.B., Frias, P.G., Antonino, V.C.S. and Medeiros, Z.M. (2017) 'Infant mortality surveillance in Recife, Pernambuco, Brazil: operationalization, strengths and limitations', *Epidemiologia e Serviços de Saúde*, 26: 413–19.

Ong, A. (2005) '(Re)articulations of citizenship', *PS: Political Science and Politics*, 38: 697–9.

Ong, A. and Collier, S.J. (eds) (2008) *Global Assemblages: Technology, Politics, and Ethics as Anthropological Problems*, Chichester: John Wiley & Sons.

Orsi, F., Singh, S. and Sagaon-Teyssier, L. (2018) 'The creation and evolution of the donor funded market for antimalarials and the growing role of southern firms', *Science, Technology and Society*, 23: 349–70.

Ortega, F. and Orsini, M. (2020) 'Governing COVID-19 without government in Brazil: ignorance, neoliberal authoritarianism, and the collapse of public health leadership', *Global Public Health*, 15: 1257–77.

Ourabah, M. (2020) *The Social Life of a Herstory Textbook: Bridging Institutionalism and Actor-Network Theory*, Singapore: Springer.

Oyedemi, T.D. (2021) 'Postcolonial casualties: "born-frees" and decolonisation in South Africa', *Journal of Contemporary African Studies*, 39: 214–29.

Paiva, C.H.A. and Teixeira, L.A. (2014) 'Health reform and the creation of the Sistema Único de Saúde: notes on contexts and authors', *História, Ciências, Saúde-Manguinhos*, 21: 15–36.

Palanee-Phillips, T., Rees, H.V., Heller, K.B., Ahmed, K., Batting, J., Beesham, I. et al (2022) 'High HIV incidence among young women in South Africa: data from a large prospective study', *PLoS One*, 17: 1–12.

Palmedo, M. (2015) 'A comparison of negotiated antiretroviral prices in countries with, and without, trade agreements with the US' [online], American University, Available from: http://infojustice.org/archives/34679 [Accessed 17 October 2022].

Parker, R. (2007) 'Networked governance or just networks? Local governance of the knowledge economy in Limerick (Ireland) and Karlskrona (Sweden)', *Political Studies*, 55: 113–32.

Patterson, E.J., Becker, A. and Baluran, D.A. (2022) 'Gendered racism on the body: an intersectional approach to maternal mortality in the United States', *Population Research and Policy Review*, 41: 1261–94.

Peck, J., Theodore, N. and Brenner, N. (2010) 'Postneoliberalism and its malcontents', *Antipode*, 41: 94–116.

Peltzer, K., Weiss, S.M., Soni, M., Lee, T.K., Rodriguez, V.J., Cook, R. et al (2017) 'A cluster randomized controlled trial of lay health worker support for prevention of mother to child transmission of HIV (PMTCT) in South Africa', *AIDS Research and Therapy*, 14: 1–12.

Penfold, T. (2017) 'Writing the city from below: graffiti in Johannesburg', *Current Writing: Text and Reception in Southern Africa*, 29: 141–52.

Pereira, G.F.M. (2021) 'Brazil sustains HIV response during the COVID-19 pandemic', *The Lancet HIV*, 8: e65.

Persson, A., Newman, C.E., Mao, L. and De Wit, J. (2016) 'On the margins of pharmaceutical citizenship: not taking HIV medication in the "treatment revolution" era', *Medical Anthropology Quarterly*, 30: 359–77.

Petryna, A. (2004) 'Biological citizenship: the science and politics of Chernobyl-exposed populations', *Osiris: Landscapes of Exposure; Knowledge and Illness in Modern Environments*, 19: 250–65.

Petryna, A. (2010) 'Biological citizenship', in B. Good (ed) *A Reader in Medical Anthropology: Theoretical Trajectories, Emergent Realities*, Chichester: Wiley-Blackwell, pp 199–212.

Petryna, A. (2013) *Life Exposed: Biological Citizens after Chernobyl*, Princeton: Princeton University Press.

PhRMA (2023) 'PhRMA 2023 Special 301 Overview'. Available from: https://phrma.org/-/media/Project/PhRMA/PhRMA-Org/PhRMA-Refresh/Policy-Papers/PhRMA-2023-Special-301-Comments.pdf [Accessed 11 December 2023].

Phillips, A.N., Bansi-Matharu, L., Cambiano, V., Ehrenkranz, P., Serenata, C., Venter, F. et al (2021) 'The potential role of long-acting injectable cabotegravir–rilpivirine in the treatment of HIV in sub-Saharan Africa: a modelling analysis', *The Lancet Global Health*, 9(5): 620–27.

Pienaar, K. (2016a) 'Disease in theory and practice', in K. Pienaar, *Politics in the Making of HIV/AIDS in South Africa*, London: Palgrave Macmillan, pp 20–34.

Pienaar, K. (2016b) *Politics in the Making of HIV/AIDS in South Africa*, London: Palgrave Macmillan.

Pigoni, A. (2020) 'TRIPS-Plus provisions and the access to HIV treatments in developing countries' [online], E-International Relations, Available from: https://www.e-ir.info/2020/04/19/trips-plus-provisions-and-the-access-to-hiv-treatments-in-developing-countries [Accessed 25 October 2022].

Pillay-Van Wyk, V., Msemburi, W., Dorrington, R., Laubscher, R., Groenewald, P. and Bradshaw, D. (2019) 'HIV/AIDS mortality trends pre and post ART for 1997–2012 in South Africa: have we turned the tide?', *South African Medical Journal*, 109: 41–4.

Plagerson, S., Patel, L., Hochfeld, T. and Ulriksen, M.S. (2019) 'Social policy in South Africa: navigating the route to social development', *World Development*, 113: 1–9.

Plahe, J.K. and McArthur, D. (2021) 'After TRIPS: can India remain "the pharmacy of the developing world"?', *South Asia: Journal of South Asian Studies*, 44: 1167–85.

Poletti, A. (2011) 'Coaxing an intimate public: life narrative in digital storytelling', *Continuum*, 25: 73–83.

Portelli, A. (2019) 'Living voices: the oral history interview as dialogue and experience', *The Oral History Review*, 45: 239–48.

Powers, T. (2013) 'Institutions, power and para-state alliances: a critical reassessment of HIV/AIDS politics in South Africa, 1999–2008', *The Journal of Modern African Studies*, 51: 605–26.

Prince, R. (2012) 'HIV and the moral economy of survival in an East African city', *Medical Anthropology Quarterly*, 26: 534–56.

Prince, R. (2017) 'Local or global policy? Thinking about policy mobility with assemblage and topology', *Area*, 49: 335–41.

Probst, C., Parry, C.D. and Rehm, J. (2016) 'Socio-economic differences in HIV/AIDS mortality in South Africa', *Tropical Medicine & International Health*, 21: 846–55.

Psaros, C., Smit, J.A., Mosery, N., Bennett, K., Coleman, J.N., Bangsberg, D.R. et al (2020) 'PMTCT adherence in pregnant South African women: the role of depression, social support, stigma, and structural barriers to care', *Annals of Behavioral Medicine*, 54: 626–36.

Purkayastha, B. (2021) 'Knowledge hierarchies and feminist dilemmas: contexts, assemblages, voices, and silences', in A. Adomako Ampofo and J.A. Beoku-Betts (eds) *Producing Inclusive Feminist Knowledge: Positionalities and Discourses in the Global South*, Bingley: Emerald Publishing, pp 23–41.

Puumala, E. and Maïche, K. (2021) '"Whether you like it or not, this is the future!": everyday negotiations of the community's boundary in urban space', *Citizenship Studies*, 25: 808–24.

Rabinow, P. (1996) *Artificiality and Enlightenment: From Sociobiology to Biosociality*, New York: Zone Books.

Raman, S. and Tutton, R. (2010) 'Life, science, and biopower', *Science, Technology & Human Values*, 35: 711–34.

Ramlagan, S., Peltzer, K., Ruiter, R.A., Barylski, N.A., Weiss, S.M. and Sifunda, S. (2018) 'Prevalence and factors associated with fixed-dose combination antiretroviral drugs adherence among HIV-positive pregnant women on option B treatment in Mpumalanga Province, South Africa', *International Journal of Environmental Research and Public Health*, 15: 1–12.

Rapp, R. (2000) 'Extra chromosomes and blue tulips: medico-familial interpretations', in M. Lock, A. Young and A. Cambrosio (eds) *Cambridge Studies in Medical Anthropology*, Cambridge: Cambridge University Press, pp 184–208.

Rapp, R. (2014a) 'Constructing amniocentesis: maternal and medical discourses', in L. Lamphere, H. Ragoné and P. Zavella (eds) *Situated Lives: Gender and Culture in Everyday Life*, Hoboken: Taylor & Francis, pp 128–41.

Rapp, R. (2014b) 'Moral pioneers', in E. Baruch, A.F. D'Adamo and J. Seager (eds) *Embryos, Ethics, and Women's Rights*, New York: Routledge, pp 101–16.

Rasmussen, L.M. and Richey, L.A. (2012) 'The Lazarus Effect of AIDS treatment: Lessons learned and lives saved', *Journal of Progressive Human Services*, 23(3): 187–207.

Rhodes, T., Egede, S., Grenfell, P., Paparini, S. and Duff, C. (2019) 'The social life of HIV care: on the making of "care beyond the virus"', *BioSocieties*, 14: 321–44.

Riccio, B. (2021) 'Exploring mobility through mobility: some of the methodological challenges of multi-sited ethnography in the study of migration', in V. Matera and A. Biscaldi (eds) *Ethnography: A Theoretically Oriented Practice*, Cham: Springer, pp 293–309.

Robins, S. (2005) 'AIDS, science and citizenship after apartheid', in M. Leach, I. Scoones and B. Wynne (ed) *Science and Citizens: Globalisation and the Challenge of Engagements*, London: Zed Books, pp 113–29.

Robins, S. (2006) 'From "rights" to "ritual": AIDS activism in South Africa', *American Anthropologist*, 108: 312–23.

Robins, S. (2010) *From Revolution to Rights in South Africa: Social Movements, NGOs and Popular Politics after Apartheid*, np: Boydell & Brewer.

Robins, S. and von Lieres, B. (2004) 'Remaking citizenship, unmaking marginalization: the treatment action campaign in post-apartheid South Africa', *Canadian Journal of African Studies*, 38: 575–86.

Robins, S., Cornwall, A. and von Lieres, B. (2008) 'Rethinking "citizenship" in the postcolony', *Third World Quarterly*, 29: 1069–86.

Rocha, A.B.M.D., Barros, C., Generoso, I.P., Bastos, F.I. and Veras, M.A. (2020) 'HIV continuum of care among trans women and travestis living in São Paulo, Brazil', *Revista de Saúde Pública*, 54: 118.

Roomaney, R.A., van Wyk, B., Cois, A. and Pillay-van Wyk, V. (2022) 'Multimorbidity patterns in a national HIV survey of South African youth and adults', *Frontiers in Public Health*, 10: 1–12.

Rose, N. (2009) *The Politics of Life Itself: Biomedicine, Power, and Subjectivity in the Twenty-First Century*, Princeton: Princeton University Press.

Rose, N. (2013) 'The human sciences in a biological age', *Theory, Culture & Society*, 30: 3–34.

Rose, N. (2018) 'The neurochemical self and its anomalies', in A. Doyle and D. Ericson (eds) *Risk and Morality*, Toronto: University of Toronto Press, pp 407–37.

Rose, N. (2019) 'Beyond medicalisation', in J. Oberlander, M. Buchbinder, L.R. Churchill, S.E. Estroff, N.M.P. King, B.F. Saunders et al (eds) *The Social Medicine Reader, Volume II, Third Edition: Differences and Inequalities*, Durham: Duke University Press, pp 700–2.

Rose, N. and Novas, C. (2005) 'Biological citizenship', in A. Ong and S.J. Collier (eds) *Global Assemblages: Technology, Politics and Ethics as Anthropological Problems*, Malden: Blackwell Publishing, pp 439–63.

Rosengarten, M., Sekuler, T., Binder, B., Dziuban, A. and Bänziger, P.-P. (2021) 'Beyond biological citizenship: HIV/AIDS, health, and activism in Europe reconsidered', *Critical Public Health*, 31: 1–4.

Rosevear, E. (2018) 'Social rights interpretation in Brazil and South Africa', *Revista de investigações constitucionais*, 5: 149–83.

Ross, F.C. (2003) *Bearing Witness: Women and the Truth and Reconciliation Commission in South Africa*, London: Pluto Press.

Ross, L.J. (2017) 'Reproductive justice as intersectional feminist activism', *Souls*, 19: 286–314.

Rugege, U. (2020) 'Opinion: why fixing South Africa's patent laws is necessary in the fight against HIV' [online], Spotlight, Available from: https://www.spotlightnsp.co.za/2020/11/27/opinion-why-fixing-south-africas-patent-laws-is-necessary-in-the-fight-against-hiv [Accessed 28 November 2022].

Rutazibwa, O.U. (2018) 'On babies and bathwater: decolonizing international development studies', in S. de Jong, R. Icaza and O.U. Rutazibwa (eds) *Decolonization and Feminisms in Global Teaching and Learning*, Abingdon: Routledge, pp 158–80.

Rutschman, A.S. (2020) 'Steps towards an alignment of intellectual property in South–South exchanges: a return to TRIPS', *Denver Journal of International Law & Policy*, 43: 515–57.

Rwafa, U. and Rafapa, L. (2014) 'Tapestries of hope: film, youths and HIV/AIDs in Zimbabwe and South Africa', *Commonwealth Youth and Development*, 12(1): 47–58.

Sabino, T.E., Avelino-Silva, V.I., Cavalcantte, C., Goulart, S.P., Luiz, O.C., Fonseca, L.A. et al (2021) 'Adherence to antiretroviral treatment and quality of life among transgender women living with HIV/AIDS in São Paulo, Brazil', *AIDS Care*, 33: 31–8.

SAFLI (2002) 'Minister of Health and Others v Treatment Action Campaign and Others (No 2) (CCT8/02) [2002] ZACC 15; 2002 (5) SA 721 (CC); 2002 (10) BCLR 1033 (CC) (5 July 2002)', Southern African Legal Information Institute. Available from: https://www.saflii.org/za/cases/ZACC/2002/15.html [Accessed 11 December 2023].

SAHCS (2022) 'Southern African HIV Clinicians Society (SAHCS) clinical update, May 2022: use of dolutegravir-based regimens for first- and second-line antiretroviral therapy'. Available from: https://sahivsoc.org/Files/SAHCS%20clinical%20statement_TLD%20switching_20220513.pdf [Accessed 10 June 2022].

SANAC (2023) 'South Africa's National Strategic Plan for HIV, TB and STIs 2023–2028', South African National AIDS Council. Available from: https://sanac.org.za/national-strategic-plan-2023-2028/ [Accessed 25 October 2023].

Sandset, T. (2020) 'The ethical and epistemological pitfalls of translating phylogenetic HIV testing: from patient-centered care to surveillance', *Humanities and Social Sciences Communications*, 7: 1–10.

Schäfer, H. (2017) 'Relationality and heterogeneity: transitive methodology in practice theory and actor-network theory', in M. Jonas, B. Littig and A. Wroblewski (eds) *Methodological Reflections on Practice Oriented Theories*, Cham: Springer, pp 35–46.

Scheper-Hughes, N. (2001) 'Bodies for sale: whole or in parts', *Body & Society*, 7: 1–8.

Scheper-Hughes, N. (2002) 'The ends of the body', *SAIS Review (1989–2003)*, 22: 61–80.

Schneider, A. and Wright, C. (2021) 'Between art and anthropology', in A. Schneider and C. Wright (eds) *Between Art and Anthropology*, London: Routledge, pp 1–21.

Scott, J.C. (1999) *Seeing Like a State: How Certain Schemes to Improve the Human Condition Have Failed*, New Haven: Yale University Press.

Seddon, N., Smith, A., Smith, P., Key, I., Chausson, A., Girardin, C. et al (2021) 'Getting the message right on nature-based solutions to climate change', *Global Change Biology*, 27: 1518–46.

Shankar, A. (2019) 'Listening to images, participatory pedagogy, and anthropological (re-)inventions', *American Anthropologist*, 121: 229–42.

Sher, R. (1989) 'HIV infection in South Africa, 1982–1988: a review', *South African Medical Journal = Suid-Afrikaanse tydskrif vir geneeskunde*, 76: 314–8.

Shisana, O., Rehle, T., Simbayi, L., Zuma, K., Jooste, S., Zungu, N. et al (2014) 'South African National HIV Prevalence, Incidence and Behaviour Survey', Human Sciences Research Council. Available from: https://hsrc.ac.za/uploads/pageContent/4565/SABSSM%20IV%20LEO%20final.pdf [Accessed 28 June 2015].

Shore, C. (2012) 'Anthropology and public policy', in R. Fardon, O. Harris, T.H.J. Marchand, C. Shore, V. Strang, R.A. Wilson et al (eds) *The Sage Handbook of Social Anthropology*, Thousand Oaks: Sage, pp 89–104.

Shubber, Z., Mills, E.J., Nachega, J.B., Vreeman, R., Freitas, M., Bock, P., Nsanzimana, S. et al (2016) 'Patient-reported barriers to adherence to antiretroviral therapy: a systematic review and meta-analysis', *PLoS Medicine*, 13: e1002183.

Sidanius, J., Hudson, S.-K.T., Davis, G. and Bergh, R. (2018) 'The theory of gendered prejudice: a social dominance and intersectionalist perspective', in A. Mintz and L.G. Terris (eds) *The Oxford Handbook of Behavioral Political Science*, Oxford: Oxford University Press, pp 1–35.

Sidibe, M. (2011) *BRICS: seizing a leadership role*, UNAIDS. Available from: https://www.unaids.org/sites/default/files/media_asset/20110711_SP_BRICS-health-ministers_en-1_2.pdf [Accessed 28 June 2012].

Simbayi, L., Zuma, K., Zungu, N., Moyo, S., Marinda, E., Jooste, S. et al (2019) 'South African National HIV Prevalence, Incidence, Behaviour and Communication Survey, 2017', Human Sciences Research Council. Available from: https://repository.hsrc.ac.za/bitstream/handle/20.500.11910/15052/11091.pdf?sequence=1&isAllowed=y [Accessed 28 June 2019].

Simbayi, L.C., Moyo, S., van Heerden, A., Zuma, K., Zungu, N., Marinda, E. et al (2021) 'Global HIV efforts need to focus on key populations in LMICs', *The Lancet*, 398: 2213–15.

Simelela, N., Venter, W.F., Pillay, Y. and Barron, P. (2015) 'A political and social history of HIV in South Africa', *Current HIV/AIDS Reports*, 12: 256–61.

Simmel, G. (1978) *The Philosophy of Money*, trans Tom Bottomore and David Frisby, London: Routledge & Kegan Paul.

Sinha, M.S. (2021) 'Costly gadgets: barriers to market entry and price competition for generic drug-device combinations in the United States', *Minnesota Journal of Law, Science & Technology* 23: 296–361.

Sipeyiye, M. (2022) 'Elderly women and COVID-19 vaccination in the indigenous religio-culture of the Ndau of south-eastern Zimbabwe', *HTS Teologiese Studies/Theological Studies*, 78(2): a7768.

Smith, M.R. (2017) 'Telltale signs: unsanctioned graffiti interventions in post-apartheid Johannesburg', in K. Miller and B. Schmahmann (eds) *Public Art in South Africa: Bronze Warriors and Plastic Presidents*, Bloomington: Indiana University Press, pp 284–304.

Snelgrove, C., Dhamoon, R. and Corntassel, J. (2014) 'Unsettling settler colonialism: the discourse and politics of settlers, and solidarity with Indigenous nations', *Decolonization: Indigeneity, Education & Society*, 3: 1–32.

Socal, M.P., Amon, J.J. and Biehl, J. (2020) 'Right-to-medicines litigation and universal health coverage: institutional determinants of the judicialization of health in Brazil', *Health and Human Rights*, 22: 221–35.

Son, K.-B. and Lee, T.-J. (2018) 'Compulsory licensing of pharmaceuticals reconsidered: current situation and implications for access to medicines', *Global Public Health*, 13: 1430–40.

Sontag, S. (1988) *AIDS and Its Metaphors*, London: Penguin Books.

Sørensen, E. and Torfing, J. (2018) 'The democratizing impact of governance networks: from pluralization, via democratic anchorage, to interactive political leadership', *Public Administration*, 96: 302–17.

Squire, C. (2010) 'Being naturalised, being left behind: the HIV citizen in the era of treatment possibility', *Critical Public Health*, 20: 401–27.

StatsSa (2020) 'Quarterly labour force survey: quarter 4; 2019', Pretoria: Statistics South Africa.

Steegen, K., van Zyl, G., Letsoalo, E., Claassen, M., Hans, L. and Carmona, S. (2019) 'Resistance in patients failing integrase strand transfer inhibitors: a call to replace raltegravir with dolutegravir in third-line treatment in South Africa', *Open Forum Infectious Diseases*, 6: ofz377.

Steenberg, B., Sokani, A., Myburgh, N., Mutevedzi, P. and Madhi, S.A. (2023) 'COVID-19 vaccination rollout: aspects of hesitancy in South Africa', *Vaccines*, 11(407): 1–14.

Steinman, E.W. (2016) 'Decolonization not inclusion: indigenous resistance to American settler colonialism', *Sociology of Race and Ethnicity*, 2: 219–36.

Stewart, P., Garvey, B., Torres, M. and Borges De Farias, T. (2021) 'Amazonian destruction, Bolsonaro and COVID-19: neoliberalism unchained', *Capital & Class*, 45: 173–81.

Stiglitz, J. (2003) *Globalization and Its Discontents*, New York: W.W. Norton.

Stones, R. (2017) *Structuration Theory*, London: Bloomsbury.

Strathern, M. (2009) 'Using bodies to communicate', in H. Lambert and M. McDonald (eds) *Social Bodies*, New York: Berghahn Books, pp 148–69.

Subramaniam, B., Foster, L., Harding, S., Roy, D. and Tallbear, K. (2016) 'Feminism, postcolonialism, technoscience', in E.J. Hackett (ed) *The Handbook of Science and Technology Studies*, Cambridge, MA: MIT Press, p 407–33.

Sum, N.-L. (2008) 'Rethinking globalisation: re-articulating the spatial scale and temporal horizons of trans-border spaces', in N. Brenner, B. Jessop, M. Jones and G. MacLeod (eds) *State/Space: A Reader*, Malden: Blackwell Publishing, pp 124–39.

Sun, H. (2004) 'The road to Doha and beyond: some reflections on the TRIPS agreement and public health', *European Journal of International Law*, 15: 123–50.

Sun, J., Boing, A.C., Silveira, M.P., Bertoldi, A.D., Ziganshina, L.E., Khaziakhmetova, V.N. et al (2014) 'Efforts to secure universal access to HIV/AIDS treatment: a comparison of BRICS countries', *Journal of Evidence Based Medicine*, 7: 2–21.

T'Hoen, E.F., Kujinga, T. and Boulet, P. (2018) 'Patent challenges in the procurement and supply of generic new essential medicines and lessons from HIV in the Southern African development community (SADC) region', *Journal of Pharmaceutical Policy and Practice*, 11: 1–8.

TAC (2010) *Fighting for Our Lives: The History of the Treatment Action Campaign*, Cape Town: Treatment Action Campaign.

Tae Yoo, I. and Chong-Han Wu, C. (2022) 'Way of authoritarian regional hegemon? Formation of the RCEP from the perspective of China', *Journal of Asian and African Studies*, 57: 1214–28.

Tait, C.L., Peters, R.P., McIntyre, J.A., Mnyani, C.N., Chersich, M.F., Gray, G. et al (2020) 'Implementation of a PMTCT programme in a high HIV prevalence setting in Johannesburg, South Africa: 2002–2015', *Southern African Journal of HIV Medicine*, 21: 1–7.

Tate, W. (2020) 'Anthropology of policy: tensions, temporalities, possibilities', *Annual Review of Anthropology*, 49: 83–99.

Taubman, A., Wager, H. and Watal, J. (2020) *A Handbook on the WTO TRIPS Agreement*, Cambridge: Cambridge University Press.

Teixeira, P. (2003) 'Universal access to AIDS medicines: the Brazilian experience', *Divulgação em Saúde para Debate*, 27: 84–191.

Tenni, B., Moir, H.V., Townsend, B., Kilic, B., Farrell, A.-M., Keegel, T. et al (2022) 'What is the impact of intellectual property rules on access to medicines? A systematic review', *Globalization and Health*, 18: 1–40.

Thin, N. (2008) ' "Realising the substance of their happiness": How anthropology forgot about Homo gauisus', *Culture and Well-being*: 134–55.

Thomas, K. (2018) ' "Remember Marikana": violence and visual activism in post-apartheid South Africa', *ASAP/Journal*, 3: 401–22.

Thomas, K. (2023) 'Atomized solidarity and new shapes of resistance: visual activism in South Africa after apartheid', in L. Shipley and M.-Y. Moriuchi (eds) *The Routledge Companion to Art and Activism in the Twenty-First Century*, New York: Routledge, pp 255–68.

Tocco, J. (2014) 'Prophetic medicine, antiretrovirals, and the therapeutic economy of HIV in Northern Nigeria', in R. van Dijk, H. Dilger and T. Rasing (eds) *Religion and AIDS Treatment in Africa: Saving Souls, Prolonging Lives*, Farnham: Ashgate Publishing, pp 117–21.

Tomlinson, C. (2023) 'Analysis: Why has the price of this cancer medicine risen and fallen by over a thousand percent since 2016?' In *Spotlight*. Available from: https://www.spotlightnsp.co.za/2023/02/15/analysis-why-has-the-price-of-this-cancer-medicine-risen-and-fallen-by-over-a-thous and-percent-since-2016/ [Accessed 12 December 2023].

Tomlinson, C., Waterhouse, C., Hu, Y., Meyer, S. and Moyo, H. (2019) 'How patent law reform can improve affordability and accessibility of medicines in South Africa: four medicine case studies', *South African Medical Journal*, 109: 387–91.

Tshishonga, N. (2019) 'The legacy of apartheid on democracy and citizenship in post-apartheid South Africa: an inclusionary and exclusionary binary?', *African Journal of Development Studies*, 9: 167–91.

UN (2015) 'Resolution adopted by the General Assembly on 25 September United Nations General Assembly', United Nations. Available from: https://www.eea.europa.eu/policy-documents/resolution-adopted-by-the-general#:~:text=The%20United%20Nations%20General%20Assembly,Development%20on%2025th%20September%202015. [Accessed 17 November 2016].

UNAIDS (2012) 'World AIDS Day report: results 2012', UNAIDS. Available from: https://www.unaids.org/sites/default/files/media_asset/JC2434_WorldAIDSday_results_en_1.pdf. [Accessed 12 July 2014].

UNAIDS (2016) 'Intellectual property and access to health technologies', UNAIDS. Available from: https://www.unaids.org/sites/default/files/media_asset/JC2820_en.pdf. [Accessed 13 July 2021].

UNAIDS (2022a) 'Country factsheets: South Africa' [online], Available from: https://www.unaids.org/en/regionscountries/countries/southafrica [Accessed 08 August 2023].

UNAIDS (2022b) 'Focus on Brazil' [online], Available from: https://www.unaids.org/en/20191011_country_focus_Brazil [Accessed 21 October 2022].

UNAIDS (2022c) 'Global HIV targets' [online], Available from: https://www.beintheknow.org/understanding-hiv-epidemic/context/global-hiv-targets#18c2c8a2-b01f-451b-b3a4-ea65e8ec3162 [Accessed 17 September 2022].

UNAIDS (2022d) 'HIV in South Africa: the biggest HIV epidemic in the world' [online], Available from: https://www.beintheknow.org/understanding-hiv-epidemic/data/glance-hiv-south-africa#36d39c53-c751-4fe0-a543-649966204531 [Accessed 15 September 2022].

UNAIDS (2022e) 'In danger: UNAIDS global AIDS update 2022' UNAIDS. Available from: https://www.unaids.org/sites/default/files/media_asset/2022-global-aids-update-summary_en. pdf [Accessed 17 October 2023.]

UNAIDS (2022f) 'UNAIDS Brazil country profile' [online], Available from: https://www.unaids.org/en/regionscountries/countries/brazil [Accessed 23 October 2022].

UNAIDS (2023) 'Fact sheet 2023: global statistics', UNAIDS. Available from: https://www.unaids.org/en/resources/documents/2023/UNAIDS_FactSheet [Accessed 17 November 2023].

Urias, E. (2019) 'The potential synergies between industrial and health policies for access to medicines: insights from the Brazilian policy of universal access to HIV/AIDS treatment', *Innovation and Development*, 9: 245–60.

US (2016) 'U.S. disappointed over fundamentally flawed report of the UN Secretary-General's High-Level Panel on Access to Medicines' [online], Washington, DC: US Department of State, Available from: https://2009-2017.state.gov/r/pa/prs/ps/2016/09/262034.htm [Accessed 10 November 2022].

Usher, A.D. (2020) 'South Africa and India push for COVID-19 patents ban', *The Lancet*, 396: 1790–1.

Vagiri, R.V., Meyer, J.C., Godman, B. and Gous, A.G.S. (2018) 'Relationship between adherence and health-related quality of life among HIV-patients in South Africa: findings and implications', *Journal of AIDS and HIV Research*, 10: 121–32.

Valle, C.G.D. (2015) 'Biosocial activism, identities and citizenship: making up "people living with HIV and AIDS" in Brazil', *Vibrant: Virtual Brazilian Anthropology*, 12: 27–70.

Van Aardt, I. (2012) 'A review of youth unemployment in South Africa, 2004 to 2011', *South African Journal of Labour Relations*, 36: 54–68.

Van der Merwe, L., Cloete, A., Savva, H., Skinner, D., November, G. and Fisher, Z.-Z. (2023) 'Engaging transgender women in HIV research in South Africa', *BMC Public Health*, 23: 1–9.

Van der Tuin, I. (2011) 'New feminist materialisms', *Women's Studies International Forum*, 34: 271–7.

Van der Vliet, V. (2004) 'South Africa divided against AIDS: a crisis of leadership', in K.D. Kauffman and D.L. Lindauer (eds) *AIDS and South Africa: The Social Expression of a Pandemic*, New York: Palgrave Macmillan, pp 48–96.

Van Esterik, P. (1994) 'Breastfeeding and feminism', *International Journal of Gynecology & Obstetrics*, 47: S41–S54.

Van Esterik, P. (2017) 'The politics of breastfeeding: an advocacy perspective', in P. Stuart-Macadam (ed) *Breastfeeding: Biocultural Perspectives*, New York: Routledge, pp 145–66.

Van Esterik, P. (2020) *Materializing Thailand*, Abingdon: Routledge.

Van Wyk, B.E. and Davids, L.-A.C. (2019) 'Challenges to HIV treatment adherence amongst adolescents in a low socio-economic setting in Cape Town', *Southern African Journal of HIV Medicine*, 20: 1–7.

Vandemoortele, M., Bird, K., du Toit, A., Liu, M., Sen, K. and Veras Soares, F. (2013) 'Building blocks for equitable growth: lessons from the BRICS', Overseas Development Institute. Available from: https://cdn.odi.org/media/documents/8196.pdf [Accessed 25 June 2014].

Vawda, Y., Tomlinson, C., Gray, A., London, L. and Paremoer, L. (2021) 'Intellectual property barriers to access to COVID-19 health products in South Africa', *South African Health Review*, 1: 263–72.

Viana, I.B., Moreira, R.D.S., Martelli, P.J.D.L., Oliveira, A.L.S.D. and Monteiro, ID.S. (2019) 'Evaluation of the quality of oral health care in primary health care in Pernambuco, Brazil, 2014', *Epidemiologia e Serviços de Saúde*, 28(2): 1–11.

Vieira, M.F. and Di Giano, L. (2018) 'Taking on the challenge of implementing public health safeguards on the ground: the experience of Argentina and Brazil from a civil society perspective', in R. Parker and J. García (eds) *Routledge Handbook on the Politics of Global Health*, London: Routledge, pp 332–45.

Vilaca, A. (2009) 'Bodies in perspective: a critique of the embodiment paradigm from the point of view of Amazonian ethnography', in H. Lambert and M. McDonald (eds) *Social Bodies*, New York: Berghahn Books, pp 129–47.

Vokes, R. (2021) '(Re)constructing the field through sound: actor-networks, ethnographic representation and "radio elicitation" in south-western Uganda', in E. Hallam and T. Ingold (eds) *Creativity and Cultural Improvisation*, np: Routledge, pp 285–303.

Von Vacano, M. (2019) 'Reciprocity in research relationships: introduction', in T. Stodulka, S. Dinkelaker and F. Thajib (eds) *Affective Dimensions of Fieldwork and Ethnography*, Cham: Springer, pp 79–86.

Vreeman, R.C., Scanlon, M.L., Tu, W., Slaven, J.E., Mcateer, C.I., Kerr, S.J. et al (2019) 'Validation of a self-report adherence measurement tool among a multinational cohort of children living with HIV in Kenya, South Africa and Thailand', *Journal of the International AIDS Society*, 22: 1–8.

Waisbich, L.T., Luiz, J.R. and de Faria, C.A.P. (2022) 'The rise and fall of Brazil as a "policy exporter": from Lula da Silva to Jair Bolsonaro', in O.P. de Oliveira and G.C. Romano (eds) *Brazil and China in Knowledge and Policy Transfer*, Cham: Springer.

Wakefield, H.I., Yu, D. and Swanepoel, C. (2022) 'Revisiting transitory and chronic unemployment in South Africa', *Development Southern Africa*, 39: 87–107.

Walker, D.M. (2010) 'The location of digital ethnography', *Cosmopolitan Civil Societies: An Interdisciplinary Journal*, 2: 23–39.

Wallis, C.L., Hughes, M.D., Ritz, J., Viana, R., Silva de Jesus, C., Saravanan, S. et al (2019) 'Diverse HIV-1 drug resistance profiles at screening for ACTG A5288: a study of people experiencing virologic failure on second-line ART in resource limited settings', *Clinical Infectious Diseases*, 71(7): e170–e177.

Waning, B., Diedrichsen, E. and Moon, S. (2010) 'A lifeline to treatment: the role of Indian generic manufacturers in supplying antiretroviral medicines to developing countries', *Journal of the International AIDS Society*, 13: 1–9.

Weber, M. (1984) *Legitimacy, Politics and the State*, New York: New York University Press.

Weber-Sinn, K. and Ivanov, P. (2020) ' "Collaborative" provenance research: about the (im)possibility of smashing colonial frameworks', *Museum and Society*, 18: 66–81.

Webster, E. and Francis, D. (2019) 'The paradox of inequality in South Africa: a challenge from the workplace', *Transformation: Critical Perspectives on Southern Africa*, 101: 11–35.

Werleman, C. (2021) 'Rising violence against Muslims in India under Modi and BJP rule', *Insight Turkey*, 23: 39–50.

WHO (2010) 'Public health related TRIPS-plus provisions in bilateral trade agreements: a policy guide for negotiators and implementers in the WHO Eastern Mediterranean Region'. World Health Organisation. Available from: https://applications.emro.who.int/dsaf/dsa1081.pdf. [Accessed 11 March 2011].

WHO (2017) 'Transition to new antiretrovirals in HIV programmes', World Health Organisation. Available from: https://www.who.int/publications/m/item/technical-report-on-pricing-of-cancer-medicines-and-its-impacts. [Accessed 18 November 2022].

WHO /(2018) 'Pricing of cancer medicines and its impacts'. World Health Organisation. Available from: https://www.who.int/publications/m/item/technical-report-on-pricing-of-cancer-medicines-and-its-impacts. [Accessed 21 June 2022].

WHO (2019) 'Trends in maternal mortality 2000 to 2017: estimates by WHO, UNICEF, UNFPA, World Bank Group and the United Nations Population Division', World Health Organization. Available from: https://www.who.int/publications/i/item/9789240068759 [Accessed 17 October 2021].

WHO (2021) 'HIV drug resistance strategy, 2021 update'. World Health Organization. Available from: https://www.who.int/publications/i/item/9789240030565 [Accessed 21 November 2022].

Whyte, S., van der Geest, S. and Hardon, A. (2002) *The Social Lives of Medicines*, Cambridge: University of Cambridge Press.

Whyte, S.R. (2009) 'Health identities and subjectivities', *Medical Anthropology Quarterly*, 23: 6–15.

Wilson, N.J. (2019) ' "Seeing water like a state?": indigenous water governance through Yukon First Nation self-government agreements', *Geoforum*, 104: 101–13.

Woldesenbet, S., Kufa-Chakezha, T., Lombard, C., Manda, S., Cheyip, M., Ayalew, K. et al (2021) 'Recent HIV infection among pregnant women in the 2017 antenatal sentinel cross-sectional survey, South Africa: assay-based incidence measurement', *PLoS One*, 16: e0249953.

Woo, G.L.X. (2011) *Ghost Dancing with Colonialism: Decolonization and Indigenous Rights at the Supreme Court of Canada*, Vancouver: UBC Press.

Wouters, E., van Rensburg, H. and Meulemans, H. (2010) 'The National Strategic Plan of South Africa: what are the prospects of success after the repeated failure of previous AIDS policy?', *Health Policy and Planning*, 25: 171–85.

Wouters, J., Goddeeris, I., Natens, B. and Ciortuz, F. (2013) 'Some critical issues in EU–India Free Trade Agreement negotiations', SSRN. Available from: https://papers.ssrn.com/sol3/papers.cfm?abstract_id=2249788 [Accessed 21 March 2015].

Wright, K. (1986) 'AIDS therapy: first tentative signs of therapeutic promise', *Nature*, 323: 283.

WTO (2001) 'Doha Declaration on the TRIPS agreement and public health', WTO. Available from: https://www.wto.org/english/thewto_e/minist_e/min01_e/mindecl_trips_e.htm [Accessed 14 March 2013].

WTO (2023) 'What is the WTO?' [online], Geneva, Switzerland: World Trade Organization, Available from: https://www.wto.org/english/thewto_e/whatis_e/whatis_e.htm [Accessed 12 September 2023].

Yates-Doerr, E. (2017) 'Counting bodies? On future engagements with science studies in medical anthropology', *Anthropology & Medicine*, 24: 142–58.

Yi, H., Suo, L., Shen, R., Zhang, J., Ramaswami, A. and Feiock, R.C. (2018) 'Regional governance and institutional collective action for environmental sustainability', *Public Administration Review*, 78: 556–66.

Youde, J. (2005) 'The development of a counter-epistemic community: AIDS, South Africa and international regimes', *International Relations*, 19: 421–39.

Young, A. (1982) 'The anthropologies of illness and sickness', *Annual Review of Anthropology*, 11: 257–85.

Young, I., Davis, M., Flowers, P. and McDaid, L.M. (2019) 'Navigating HIV citizenship: identities, risks and biological citizenship in the treatment as prevention era', *Health, Risk & Society*, 21: 1–16.

Youngleson, M.S., Nkurunziza, P., Jennings, K., Arendse, J., Mate, K.S. and Barker, P. (2010) 'Improving a mother to child HIV transmission programme through health system redesign: quality improvement, protocol adjustment and resource addition', *PLoS One*, 5: e13891.

Yu, P.K. (2022) 'Regional Comprehensive Economic Partnership', in P. Torremans, I. Stamatoudi, P.K. Yu and J. Jutte (eds) *Encyclopedia of Intellectual Property Law*, Cheltenham: Edward Elgar Publishing, pp 1–5.

Zhao, Y. (2015) 'The BRICS formation in reshaping global communication: possibilities and challenges', in K. Nordenstreng and D.K. Thussu (eds) *Mapping BRICS Media*, London: Routledge, pp 66–86.

Zhou, A. (2019) 'Therapeutic citizens and clients: diverging healthcare practices in Malawi's prenatal clinics', *Sociology of Health & Illness*, 41: 625–42.

Index